FAVORITE RECIPES FROM QUILTERS

DISTRIBUTED BY
Choice Books
Salunga, PA 17538
We Welcome Your Response

FAVORITE RECIPES FROM QUILTERS

More than 900 Delectable Dishes

Louise Stoltzfus

Good Books

Intercourse, PA 17534

Acknowledgments

I am indebted to Phyllis and Merle Good
and Rachel and Kenny Pellman
for suggesting that a collection of recipes from quilters might actually be possible
and for brainstorming with me as the project developed.
I also thank Dawn J. Ranck for her organizational assistance
and Esther Becker for answering my occasional questions
about obscure ingredients and cooking methods.

Cover design and illustrations by Cheryl Benner
Design by Dawn J. Ranck

FAVORITE RECIPES FROM QUILTERS
Copyright © 1992 by Good Books, Intercourse, Pennsylvania 17534
International Standard Book Number: 1-56148-071-1
Library of Congress Catalog Card Number: 92-31547

Library of Congress Cataloging-in-Publication Data

Favorite recipes from quilters / [compiled] by Louise Stoltzfus.
     p. cm.
  Includes index.
  ISBN: 1-56148-071-1 : $11.95
  1. Cookery. I. Stoltzfus, Louise, 1952-
TX714.F379 1992
641.5—dc2   92-31547
                                                        CIP

Table of Contents

Introduction

Amid the rush and haste of life at the close of the twentieth century, many of us seek rest and quiet in community life. We look for community in churches, in neighborhoods, in places of work and in common goals and activities. Quilters find community in common goals and activities. We talk of needles and thread, fabric and stitches and bedcovers and pieces of art. We gather in homes, in fabric shops, in quilt guilds and in large convention centers to share our ideas and projects.

Many of us are also homemakers. We approach cooking with many shades of intensity. Some of us treat cooking and quilting both as high art forms. Some of us work hard to prepare varied and healthful meals for our busy families and only quilt occasionally. Others experience ongoing disasters because we become engrossed in quilting and forget the carrots or potatoes or beans.

This amazing collection of recipes from a community best known for its gifts with cloth and design includes submissions from Irvine, California to New York's Upper West Side, from Fruitland Park, Florida to Honolulu and from Williams Lake, British Columbia to Florence, South Carolina.

The recipes reflect a diverse group of people whose primary common thread is quilting. It is, in fact, a passion for threads and fabric, for templates and patterns and for sewing machines and quilt frames that draws quilters into community. We know the best fabric stores. We share patterns. We generally piece by machine and quilt by hand. While we attend guild meetings and quilting bees, many of us also spend long hours at home alone stitching. We are first and foremost quilters.

Each of the recipes has been identified with the submitter's name and place of residence. In addition, most submitters also listed the name of the quilt pattern which they were working with at the time they submitted recipes. Those patterns are listed under their names and provide a kaleidoscope of original patterns and homemade names along with many familiar and frequently used pattern names and designs.

To the quilting community I extend warm thanks for your gracious sharing of recipes and stories. I also thank you for your willingness to serve as recipe testers when other pursuits and interests must surely have kept you busy. This book truly belongs to you—the quilting community.

—Louise Stoltzfus

Appetizers

Pickled Shrimp

Jeannette R. Saunders
Albuquerque, NM
Friendship

Makes 10-12 servings

2½ lbs. cooked shrimp,
   peeled and deveined
2 large onions, sliced into
   rings
1½ cups cooking oil
½ cup white vinegar
½ cup lemon juice
2½ tsp. celery seed
⅓ cup sugar
1 Tbsp. capers with juice
4 bay leaves
Several dashes Tabasco
Salt to taste

1. Layer shrimp and onions in glass bowl.
2. Combine all remaining ingredients and pour over shrimp and onions.
3. Refrigerate and marinate at least 24 hours. Drain marinade well and serve shrimp with toothpicks.

Shrimp Appetizers

Elaine A. Halos
Comfrey, MN
Log Cabin & Amish Basket

Makes at least 24 servings

8 ozs. medium cheddar
   cheese, shredded
1 cup mayonnaise
7-oz. can shrimp meat,
   drained
½ tsp. curry powder
3 scallions, chopped
   (optional)
½ tsp. salt *or* less
6 English muffins

1. Mix shredded cheese, mayonnaise, shrimp, curry powder, scallions and salt together.
2. Mound slightly on English Muffins. Cut each muffin into quarters or smaller pieces.
3. Place on broiler sheet or rack and broil until bubbly, about 5 minutes. Serve.

Crab Meat Hors D'oeuvres

Jaclyn Ferrell
Carlisle, PA
Patchwork

Makes 12 servings

8-oz. jar cheddar cheese
   spread
8 Tbsp. butter, melted
Pinch garlic
1 tsp. Worcestershire sauce
8-oz. can crab meat
6 English muffins

1. Combine all ingredients except muffins.
2. Cut muffins in half and spread crab mixture over each muffin. Arrange on flat baking sheet.
3. Bake at 400° for 10 minutes. Quarter and serve immediately.

Crab Mousse

Julie Lynch Arnsberger,
Gaithersburg, MD
Ella Meidinger, Lodi, CA
Rayann Rohrer, Allentown, PA

Makes many appetizer servings

¼ cup cold water
1 pkg. unflavored gelatin
10¾-oz. can cream of
   mushroom soup
8-oz. pkg. cream cheese
1 cup mayonnaise
½ cup finely chopped
   celery
½ cup finely chopped
   onion
2 7-oz. cans crab meat,
   drained

1. Dissolve gelatin in
cold water.
2. Heat soup. Remove
from heat and stir in cream
cheese, mayonnaise, celery,
onion and crab meat. Spoon
mixture into mold and re-
frigerate.
3. Unmold onto plate
and serve with crackers.

Lynne Fritz's Shrimp Dip

Lynne Fritz
Bel Air, MD
My Backyard

Makes 2 cups dip

1 pkg. unflavored gelatin
10¾-oz. can tomato soup
8-oz. pkg. cream cheese,
   softened
1 onion, minced
2 stalks celery, minced
6-oz. can minced shrimp
1 cup mayonnaise
4 drops Tabasco

1. In a saucepan sprinkle
gelatin over tomato soup
and stir well. Heat until dissolved. Remove from heat.
2. Add cream cheese, on-
ion, celery, shrimp, mayonnaise and Tabasco. Mix
well and spoon into a mold.
3. Refrigerate until firm.
Unmold onto a plate and
serve with crackers.

Rose Fitzgerald's Shrimp Dip

Rose Fitzgerald
Delaware, OH
Patience Is a Virtue

Makes 24-30 servings

2 8-oz. pkgs. frozen,
   cooked shrimp
2 8-oz. pkgs. cream cheese,
   softened
8 Tbsp. margarine, melted
1 small onion, finely
   chopped
1¼ tsp. lemon juice
¼ tsp. garlic powder
4 Tbsp. mayonnaise
1 loaf King's Hawaiian
   bread

1. Chop shrimp coarsely.
Add all remaining ingredients except bread and mix
well.
2. Pinch out the center of
bread in chunks. Reserve
chunks until ready to serve.
3. Fill bread shell with
shrimp mixture. Surround
with chunks of bread on a
platter. Serve.

*Note: Substitute your choice of
unsliced gourmet bread for
King's Hawaiian.*

> **Since I've gotten into quilting, my cooking and baking
> have fallen off drastically! Every quilter needs someone
> to cook for him or her.**
>
> —*Jay Conrad, Bedford, TX*

Crab Dip Appetizer

Carol Sucevic
Hopwood, PA
Lady of the East

Makes 36 servings

2 8-oz. pkgs. cream cheese, softened
1 onion, finely chopped
1 green pepper, finely chopped
2 6-oz. cans crab meat
12-oz. bottle cocktail sauce

1. Combine all ingredients except cocktail sauce and shape into a large doughnut on a platter. Cover and refrigerate at least 2 hours.
2. Immediately before serving, fill hole of doughnut with cocktail sauce and arrange crackers around the outside.

Note: This is actually better after several days of refrigeration. Great recipe to make ahead of time.

Cheese Crab Dip

Peggy Smith
Hamlin, KY
Evening View Through the Window

Makes 10-12 servings

12 ozs. cream cheese, softened
2 Tbsp. Worcestershire sauce
1 Tbsp. lemon juice
2 Tbsp. mayonnaise
1 small onion, grated
Dash garlic salt
1 cup chili sauce
6-oz. can crab meat
¼-½ cup chopped, fresh parsley

1. Combine cheese, Worcestershire sauce, lemon juice, mayonnaise, onion and garlic salt. Spread into shallow 8" x 10" baking dish. Top with chili sauce, crab meat and parsley.
2. Cover with plastic wrap and refrigerate overnight.
3. Serve with corn chips.

Maryland Crab Dip

Betty A. Gray
Ellicott City, MD
Miniature Sunbonnet Sue

Makes 10-12 servings

2 8-oz. pkgs. cream cheese
1 cup sour cream
4 tsp. mayonnaise
2 tsp. Worcestershire sauce
1 lb. crab meat
4 ozs. cheddar cheese, shredded

1. Melt cream cheese over low heat. Remove from heat and beat in sour cream, mayonnaise and Worcestershire sauce. Fold in crab meat.
2. Spoon into a baking dish and sprinkle with cheddar cheese.
3. Bake, uncovered, at 350° for 30 minutes. Serve.

A group of quilters between the ages of thirty and seventy meets every Wednesday evening in my basement family room. In spite of our age differences, my husband vows he has never heard a gap in our communication. It is so wonderful to be part of the common thread of quilting.

—*Betty Richards, Rapid City, SD*

Best Crab Ever

Betty K. Fulmer
Quakertown, PA
Garden Windows &
North Carolina Lily

Makes 2 dozen appetizers

2 Tbsp. minced shallots
2½ Tbsp. butter
2 Tbsp. flour
½ cup hot chicken stock
¼ cup light cream
1½ cups flaked, cooked
**   crab**
Dash Tabasco
⅛ tsp. salt
8-oz. pkg. phyllo dough
Butter, melted

1. Sauté shallots in 2½ Tbsp. butter until shallots are translucent.
2. Sprinkle with flour and heat until bubbly, stirring constantly. Slowly add hot chicken stock, stirring constantly until thickened and smooth. Add cream and cook another 5 minutes, stirring constantly. Fold in crab and season with Tabasco and salt. Remove from heat.
3. Cut thawed phyllo dough into 2-inch wide strips. Arrange strips on waxed paper and cover with a damp cloth.
4. Remove 2 strips at a time. Brush each strip with melted butter and lay on top of each other. Spoon 1½ tsp. crab mixture onto short end of strip. Fold 1 corner diagonally over the filling so short edge meets long edge, forming a right angle. Continue folding to end of strip, creating triangular shape.
5. Repeat step 4 with all other strips of phyllo dough. Arrange on baking sheet.
6. Bake at 425° for 15 minutes or until golden brown.

Ken's Terrific Tuna

Maryellen Mross
Bartonsville, PA
Hearts and Flowers

Makes many appetizer servings

7-oz. can white tuna
6 Tbsp. mayonnaise
1 Tbsp. Parmesan cheese
3 Tbsp. sweet pickle relish
⅛ tsp. dried minced onion
¼ tsp. curry powder
1 tsp. dried dill weed
1 Tbsp. dried parsley
**   flakes**
Pinch garlic powder

1. Drain tuna. Flake with fork and mix with mayonnaise.
2. Stir in all remaining ingredients. Spoon into pretty serving dish and chill.
3. Serve with assorted crackers.

Chickpea Spread

Paula Lederkramer
Levittown, NY
Spectrum II & Island in the Sun

Makes 4 servings

1 cup chickpeas, drained
1 Tbsp. olive oil
2 fresh *or* canned tomatoes
1 clove garlic, minced
1 Tbsp. red wine vinegar
Salt and pepper to taste
1 scallion, minced

1. Place chickpeas in a bowl and mash with wooden spoon or potato masher. Add olive oil and mix well.
2. Peel, seed and chop tomatoes. Add tomatoes and all remaining ingredients to chickpea mixture.
3. Serve as an appetizer or as a sandwich filling with pita bread.

Olive Nut Spread

Joyce Shackelford
Green Bay, WI
Sampler
Flossie Sultzaberger
Mechanicsburg, PA
Nine Patch

Makes 2½ cups spread

8-oz. pkg. cream cheese, softened
½ cup mayonnaise
½ cup chopped pecans
1 cup chopped green olives
2 Tbsp. olive juice
Dash pepper

1. Combine all ingredients and mix well until mushy.
2. Refrigerate in a pint jar for 24-48 hours. Serve this rather thick spread with crackers or bread. (It keeps for weeks.)

Chicken and Ginger Spread

Marjorie Mills
Bethesda, MD
Scrap Quilt

Makes 2½ cups spread

2½ cups diced, cooked chicken
¼ cup chopped walnuts

¼ cup chives *or* scallions
3 Tbsp. finely chopped ginger
1½ Tbsp. soy sauce
1 Tbsp. white vinegar
⅓ cup mayonnaise
Salt to taste
Sour cream

1. Combine all ingredients except sour cream. Press into a small bowl, cover with plastic wrap and refrigerate.
2. When ready to serve, unmold onto an attractive plate and cover with sour cream. Serve with crackers or fresh vegetables.

Liver Paté

Carol Weaver
Houston, TX
Cover Up Clowns

Makes 1 small ball

8 ozs. liverwurst
2 Tbsp. soft butter
¼ tsp. Worcestershire sauce
1 Tbsp. diced onion
2 Tbsp. bacon bits
3-oz. pkg. cream cheese, softened

1. Combine all ingredients except cream cheese and turn into a ball.
2. Soften cream cheese by beating it. (Add few drops milk if needed.)

Cover liver ball with cream cheese.
3. Chill and serve with crackers.

Turkey Paté

Alix Botsford
Seminole, OK
Double Wedding Ring

Makes 2 cups paté

2 cups cooked, ground turkey
½ cup diced celery
2 Tbsp. mayonnaise
1 Tbsp. lemon juice
Dash pepper
¼ tsp. salt
3 parsley sprigs, finely snipped

1. Combine all ingredients and mix well.
2. Grease mold with mayonnaise and pack paté into mold.
3. Chill, unmold and serve with crackers.

I have fond memories of learning to quilt as a teenager in our small Amish community. Once a month the church women got together to sew and quilt for the needy. My mother would load the buggy with a quilt frame which stuck out the front and back, a sewing machine tied to the back, a potluck dish for the noon meal and small children and bundles of supplies filling the back seat. Today I watch my grandchildren learning to quilt as our current church group continues to meet once a month.

—*Edna Nisly, Partridge, KS*

❖

Carrot Paté

Ann Foss
Brooklyn, NY

Makes 6-8 servings

1 Tbsp. olive oil
1 small onion, finely
   chopped
3 medium carrots, sliced
¼ cup water
¼ cup orange juice
1 Tbsp. grated orange rind
½ tsp. black pepper
⅛ tsp. salt
⅛ tsp. curry powder
   (optional)
2 Tbsp. mayonnaise
1 tsp. Dijon mustard

1. In medium skillet heat oil over low heat. Add onion; cover and cook until tender but not browned, about 7 minutes.
2. Stir in carrots, water, orange juice, orange rind, pepper, salt and curry. Cover and simmer until carrots are tender, about 6-8 minutes. Uncover and cook on high, stirring occasion-

ally, until liquid evaporates, about 5 minutes. Remove from heat and cool slightly.
3. In food processor or blender process mixture until smooth. Add mayonnaise and mustard and process until combined.
4. Press carrot paté into small bowl or large, hollowed out green pepper. Serve with carrot slices, green pepper slices or crackers.

❖

Baked Artichoke Dip

Ellen Crockett
Springfield, VA
With a Little Help From My Friends

Makes 8 servings

1 cup shredded mozzarella
   cheese
1 cup grated Parmesan
   cheese
1 cup mayonnaise

1 tsp. chopped parsley
1 tsp. minced garlic
1 Tbsp. chopped chives
16-oz. can artichoke hearts
   without marinade,
   chopped

1. Combine all ingredients in a 1½-quart casserole dish.
2. Bake at 325° for 25 minutes until top is golden and cheese is bubbly. Serve with sturdy crackers.

Variation:
Omit parsley, garlic and chives. Substitute 1½ cups Parmesan cheese for 1 cup mozzarella and 1 cup Parmesan.
Mary Saunders
Albuquerque, NM
Trip Around the World

❖

Artichoke Dip

Judi Manos
West Islip, NY
Starry Seas

Makes 1¼ cups dip

6-oz. jar artichoke hearts
8-oz. pkg. cream cheese,
   softened
3 tsp. Dijon mustard
Lettuce leaf
Chives

1. Drain artichoke hearts, reserving marinade. Chop artichoke hearts in food processor.

2. Combine cream cheese with marinade. Add artichoke hearts and mustard and mix well. Chill until ready to serve.

3. Arrange on lettuce leaf. Sprinkle with chives.

4. Serve with crackers or fresh vegetables.

Dill Dip

Nancy Wall
Duncansville, PA
Miniature Trip Around the World

Makes 2 cups dip

1 cup sour cream
1 cup mayonnaise
1 Tbsp. minced onion
1 tsp. Lawry's seasoned salt
1 Tbsp. parsley
2 tsp. dill weed
1/2 tsp. Worcestershire sauce

1. Combine all ingredients and mix well.

2. Serve with crackers or fresh vegetables.

Spinach Dip

Elizabeth Boyton
Gordonville, PA
Irish Chain

Makes 2 1/2 cups dip

1 large loaf pumpernickel bread
1/2 of 10-oz. pkg. frozen, chopped spinach, thawed
1 pint sour cream
1/3 cup mayonnaise
1 pkg. Knorr's vegetable soup mix

1. Cut round opening in top of bread. Remove insides of bread carefully, leaving only a shell. Cut bread pieces into cubes and wrap until ready to serve.

2. Combine all other ingredients and spoon into bread shell.

serve bread cubes with spinach dip.

Vegetable Dip

Judy Steiner Buller
Beatrice, NE
Log Cabin Star Spin

Makes 2 cups dip

1 cup mayonnaise
1 cup sour cream
1 1/2 tsp. dill weed (optional)
1/2 tsp. celery salt

1 1/2 tsp. instant minced onion
1 1/2 tsp. parsley flakes

1. Mix all ingredients and refrigerate several hours or overnight before serving.

2. Serve with a variety of sliced fresh vegetables.

Cheese Dip

Barbara Swartz
Mercer, PA
Sampler

Makes 10-12 appetizer servings

1 cup plain lowfat yogurt
1/2 cup lowfat cottage cheese
2 ozs. shredded lowfat American cheese
2 Tbsp. chopped green onion
2 Tbsp. finely chopped bell pepper
1/4 tsp. garlic powder
1/4 tsp. ground cumin
1/8 tsp. pepper

1. Thoroughly mix all ingredients in a bowl. Cover and chill.

2. Serve with fresh vegetables.

Ranch House Cheese Spread

Bonita Ensenberger
Albuquerque, NM
Jessica's Nine Patch

Makes many appetizer servings

1 lb. sharp cheddar cheese, grated
¼ cup minced onion
3 tsp. prepared horseradish
1 cup mayonnaise

1. Combine all ingredients in mixing bowl and whip well with electric mixer. Chill.
2. Serve with assorted crackers and crisp raw vegetables.

Easy Spicy Dip

Molly Wilson
Gonzales, TX
Marriage Quilt

Makes 8-10 servings

8-oz. pkg. cream cheese
12-oz. jar picante sauce

1. Bring cream cheese to room temperature and blend with picante sauce.
2. Serve with potato chips or refrigerate until needed.

Spinach Balls

Melissa Myers
Indian Head, MD
Bow Tie
Barbara J. Swartz
Mercer, PA
Sampler

Makes 10 dozen tiny balls

2 10-oz. pkgs. frozen chopped spinach
3 cups herb-seasoned stuffing
1 large onion, finely chopped
6 eggs, well beaten
¾ cup butter *or* margarine, melted
½ cup grated Parmesan cheese
1 Tbsp. pepper
1½ tsp. garlic salt
½ tsp. thyme

1. Cook spinach and drain well. Mix spinach and remaining ingredients well. Shape into tiny balls. Place on lightly greased baking sheet.
2. Bake at 350° for 15-20 minutes. Serve.

Note: To freeze balls before baking, place on cookie sheet and freeze until firm. Remove from freezer and store in plastic bags. Thaw slightly and bake at 325° for 20-25 minutes.

Broiled Sauerkraut Balls

F. Elaine Asper
Stroudsburg, PA
Duck and Ducklings

Makes 6 dozen balls

16-oz. can sauerkraut
1 lb. bulk sausage
¼ lb. ground beef
½ cup finely chopped onion
3 Tbsp. snipped parsley
½ tsp. dry mustard
1 tsp. salt
⅛ tsp. pepper
1 tsp. sugar
1 cup bread crumbs
3 eggs
¼ cup milk
1 cup bread crumbs

1. Drain sauerkraut thoroughly and chop into small pieces. In a large skillet combine sauerkraut, sausage, ground beef, onion, parsley, seasonings and sugar. Cook until meat is well browned. Remove from heat and stir in 1 cup bread crumbs.
2. Add 2 slightly beaten eggs and blend well. Form mixture into acorn-sized balls.
3. Beat together 1 egg and milk. Dip each ball into egg mixture and roll it into 1 cup bread crumbs. Arrange on a baking sheet.
4. Broil until golden brown, turning once.

Ham and Cheese Appetizers

Anna Barrow
Hatchville, MA
Sampler

Makes 36 appetizers

2 cups Bisquick
¾ cup finely chopped
  smoked ham
1 cup shredded Swiss *or*
  cheddar cheese
½ cup finely chopped
  onion
½ cup grated Parmesan
  cheese
½ cup sour cream
2 Tbsp. snipped parsley
½ tsp. salt
2 cloves garlic, crushed
⅔ cup milk
1 egg

1. Combine all ingredients and mix well. Spread into greased 9" x 13" baking pan.
2. Bake at 350° until golden brown, 25-30 minutes. Cut into 36 equal rectangles. Serve.

Hot Rye Appetizers

Gail Kozicki
Glen Mills, PA
Untitled

Makes 25-30 servings

5 slices bacon
1 cup grated Swiss cheese
⅔ cup chopped ripe olives,
  drained
¼ cup finely sliced green
  onion
¼ cup mayonnaise
¼ tsp. salt
8-oz. loaf cocktail rye bread

1. Fry, drain and crumble bacon.
2. Combine all ingredients except bread.
3. Spread a rounded teaspoonful of mixture on each slice of bread. Arrange on ungreased baking sheet.
4. Bake at 350° for 10-15 minutes or until cheese melts and browns slightly.

Note: Before baking, freeze for later use. Allow 3-4 minutes longer for baking.

Florentine Party Appetizers

Donna Lantgen
Rapid City, SD
Dresden Plate

Makes 15 servings

4 eggs
10¾-oz. can cream of
  celery soup
8-oz. jar sharp cheddar
  cheese spread
2 10-oz. pkgs. frozen,
  chopped spinach
½ cup water chestnuts
8-oz. pkg. crescent rolls
3 Tbsp. diced pimentos

1. Combine eggs, soup and cheese spread.
2. Thaw and drain spinach, then chop it finely. Add spinach and water chestnuts to cheese mixture.
3. Uncoil crescent rolls, but do not separate. Press into 9" x 13" greased baking pan. Press seams together. Spread spinach mixture over dough. Top with pimentos.
4. Bake at 350° for 1 hour or until knife inserted in center comes out clean.

One day I attended a quilting demonstration at a local craft event. A visitor to the area (or tourists as we call them in Lancaster County) passed by, stopped and commented, "It's so nice to see that all these handicapped ladies have a job." He thought each woman had only one hand! (As we all know, the other hand was under the quilt.)

—*Sarah S. King, Gordonville, PA*

Zucchini Appetizers

Genny Morrow
Lancaster, PA
Irish Chain
Frances D. Bents
Annapolis, MD
Barbara's Bridal Sampler

Makes 20 servings

3 cups grated zucchini
1 cup Bisquick
½ cup finely chopped onion
½ cup grated Parmesan cheese
2 Tbsp. snipped parsley
½ tsp. salt
½ tsp. marjoram *or* oregano
Dash pepper
½ cup cooking oil
4 eggs, lightly beaten

1. Mix all ingredients thoroughly. Spread into greased 9" x 13" baking pan.
2. Bake at 350° until golden brown, about 25 minutes.
3. Cut into 1" x 2" pieces.

Note: This freezes well before baking and may be prepared several days ahead of time.

Appetizer Cheese Ball

F. Elaine Asper
Stroudsburg, PA
Duck & Ducklings

Makes 20 servings

8-oz. pkg. cream cheese, softened
4 ozs. cheddar cheese, shredded
½ tsp. salt
2 tsp. lemon juice
1 Tbsp. milk
2 Tbsp. minced onion
Dash garlic salt
1 cup crushed corn chips

1. Cream softened cream cheese and add cheddar cheese. Add all remaining ingredients except corn chips and refrigerate until firm.
2. Form into a ball and roll cheese ball into crushed corn chips.
3. Serve with crackers.

Party Cheese Ball

Jean Turner
Williams Lake, BC
Trip Around the World
Gerry Fix
Hagerstown, MD
Nine Patch

Makes 1 large or 2 small balls

2 8-oz. pkgs. cream cheese, softened
2 cups shredded sharp cheddar cheese
1 Tbsp. chopped onion
1 Tbsp. chopped pimento
1 Tbsp. chopped green pepper
2 tsp. Worcestershire sauce
1 tsp. lemon juice
⅓ cup finely chopped pecans *or* walnuts

1. Combine cream cheese and cheddar cheese, mixing until well blended. Add all remaining ingredients except nuts and mix well. Chill.
2. Shape into ball and roll into nuts. Store in refrigerator up to two weeks. Serve with crackers.

❖

Cheese Ball

Sue Shelenberger
Conneaut, OH
Ohio Star Challenge

Makes 20 servings

8-oz. pkg. cream cheese,
  softened
¼ cup mustard with
  horseradish
1 Tbsp. ketchup
½ lb. cheddar cheese,
  shredded
1 cup chopped parsley *or*
  nuts

1. Combine cream
cheese, mustard and
ketchup in a bowl and beat
until well blended. Stir in
cheddar cheese. Chill for
several hours.
2. Shape into a ball and
roll into parsley or nuts.
3. Serve with crackers.

❖

Cheese Log

Sharron Higginbotham
Bellville, TX
Baltimore Album

Makes many appetizer servings

10 ozs. sharp cheddar
  cheese, grated
10 ozs. longhorn cheese,
  grated

8-oz. pkg. cream cheese,
  softened
1 clove garlic, minced
½ cup chopped nuts
Chili powder

1. Combine all ingredi-
ents and roll into a log.
Chill.
2. Coat with chili pow-
der and serve with unsalted
crackers.

❖

Special Cheese Fondue

Betty K. Fulmer
Quakertown, PA
*North Carolina Lily & Garden
Window*

Makes 10-12 servings

Fondue:
1 medium onion, diced
6 Tbsp. butter
2 chicken bouillon cubes
2 cups light cream
5 Tbsp. flour
1 tsp. steak sauce
1½ cups grated Swiss cheese
1 cup grated Parmesan
  cheese
½ cup Sauterne *or* apple
  juice

Dunkers:
French bread, cut into
  cubes
Ham cubes
Steamed Shrimp
Raw vegetables, sliced

1. On high heat sauté on-
ion in butter with bouillon
cubes.
2. Mix cream, flour and
steak sauce. Reduce heat on
onions and add cream mix-
ture, stirring constantly until thickened. Add cheeses
gradually and stir until
melted. Add Sauterne or apple juice and mix well.
3. Serve with dunkers as
an appetizer or on your buf-
fet table.

❖

Easy Homemade Cheese

Anita Coker
Bellville, TX
Baby Nine-Patch

Makes many appetizer servings

5-oz. can evaporated milk
8 ozs. Swiss cheese, grated
16 Tbsp. margarine
3 Tbsp. flour
1 Tbsp. caraway seed *or*
  dill weed

1. In a double boiler combine milk, cheese, marga-
rine and flour. Cook until
smooth. Stir in seeds.
2. Store in refrigerator
where it will keep indefi-
nitely. Serve with bread or
crackers.

Homemade Cheese Spread

Iola Joquim
Lodi, CA

Makes 3 pints spread

8 Tbsp. margarine
1 cup evaporated milk
1 tsp. sugar
2 lbs. American cheese,
cubed

1. In top of double boiler melt all ingredients together and blend thoroughly. Pour into glass containers and seal.
2. Serve with crackers.

Hot Bean Dip

Esther Lapp
Sterling, IL
Bear Paw

Makes 12-15 servings

1 lb. ground beef *or* turkey
1 lb. pinto beans
8-oz. can tomato sauce
1 pkg. dry taco seasoning
1 cup sour cream
1-2 cups shredded cheddar
cheese
1-2 cups shredded lettuce
1-2 cups chopped tomatoes
Corn chips

1. Fry the meat and drain off any excess fat.
2. Cook pinto beans according to directions and drain.
3. Combine meat, beans, tomato sauce and taco seasonings and spoon into a 9" x 13" baking pan. Spread mixture with sour cream and 1 cup cheddar cheese.
4. Bake at 350° 25-30 minutes or until heated through.
5. Immediately before serving, top with lettuce, tomatoes and 1 cup cheddar cheese. Serve with corn chips.

Hamburger Bean Dip

Marge Slabaugh
Kalona, IA
Tulip

Makes 12-15 servings

2 lbs. hamburger
½ tsp. onion salt
½ tsp. garlic powder
3 green chilies
1 cup whole tomatoes
1 pkg. dry taco seasoning
mix
16-oz. can refried beans
½ lb. Velveeta cheese,
grated
Tortilla chips

1. Fry hamburger and drain excess fat. Stir in onion salt and garlic powder.
2. Chop green chilies and tomatoes. Stir mixture into hamburger. Add taco seasoning, refried beans and cheese. Heat through, stirring occasionally.
3. Serve warm with tortilla chips.

Walking Chalupa

Sharron Higginbotham
Bellville, TX
Baltimore Album

Makes 12-15 servings

16-oz. can refried beans
8-oz. carton sour cream
1 cup avocado dip
6 green onions, chopped
4-oz. can green chilies,
drained
6-oz. can pitted black
olives, drained
2 tomatoes, chopped
10 ozs. cheddar cheese,
grated
10 ozs. white Monterey
Jack cheese, grated

1. On a large round serving dish layer ingredients in the order given.
2. Surround with tortilla chips and serve.

Tex-Mex Dip

Jul Hoober
New Holland, PA
Roman Stripe
Judy Govotsos
Monrovia, MD
Irish Chain

Makes 15-20 servings

3 medium ripe avocados
2 Tbsp. lemon juice
½ tsp. salt *or* less
¼ tsp. pepper
1 cup sour cream
½ cup mayonnaise
1 pkg. dry taco seasoning
  mix
16-oz. can refried beans
½ cup chopped green
  onions
3 medium tomatoes,
  chopped
6-oz. can pitted ripe olives,
  drained and chopped
8 ozs. grated sharp cheddar
  cheese

1. Peel, pit and mash avocados with lemon juice, salt and pepper.
2. Combine sour cream, mayonnaise and taco seasoning mix.
3. To assemble spread beans on large serving platter. Top with avocado mixture and sour cream mixture.
4. Sprinkle with onion, tomatoes and olives. Cover with cheese.
5. Serve with tortilla chips.

Taco Dip

Irene P. Dietlin
New Hartford, CT
Cupid's Nine Patch

Makes 8 or more servings

2 8-oz. pkgs. cream cheese,
  softened
8-oz. jar hot taco sauce
8-oz. jar medium taco sauce
1 green pepper, diced
1 tomato, diced
1 medium onion, diced
  (optional)
½ cup grated sharp
  cheddar cheese

1. Combine cream cheese and sauces and spoon into 8-inch square baking dish. Sprinkle with diced vegetables and cheese.
2. Refrigerate several hours or overnight before serving.
3. Serve with tortilla chips.

Southwestern Layered Dip

Ann Sunday McDowell
Newtown, PA
Double Wedding Ring

Makes 30 servings

10½-oz. can jalapeño bean
  dip
1 cup sour cream
1 cup grated cheddar
  cheese
6-oz. can black olives,
  sliced
1 bunch green onions,
  sliced
½ cup chopped tomatoes
1-lb. bag tortilla chips

1. On a large platter layer ingredients, except tortilla chips, in the order listed.
2. Surround dip with tortilla chips and serve.

> During the winter when I made my first Lone Star quilt, we had a blizzard and were snowed in at home one day. A friend of one of my children was visiting. I had finished putting together the diamonds of the star and was working at adding the fill in.
>
> Each time I added a square or triangle, the young girl expressed surprise at how it all fit together. By the time I had finished, she was ecstatic with surprise and pleasure. To this day, I never put together a Lone Star without remembering that day and feeling a bit like a magician.
>
> —*Esther Becker, Gap, PA*

Chicken Nachos

Dawn Kouba
Albuquerque, NM
Enchanted View

Makes 6-8 appetizer servings

1 small bag tortilla chips
2 cups shredded, cooked chicken breast
1 cup picante sauce
2 cups grated Monterey Jack cheese
6-8 small dips sour cream
6-8 small dips guacamole

1. Line bottom of 10-inch pie plate with tortilla chips. Arrange chicken pieces over top. Pour picante sauce over chicken and chips. Top with grated cheese.
2. Cook under broiler until cheese melts. Top with dips of sour cream and guacamole and serve.

Note: Serve with a fruit salad as a main course for a delightful light supper. Serves 3-4 people.

Mexican Dip

Cyndie Marrara
Port Matilda, PA
Original

Makes 5 cups dip

28-oz. can tomatoes, drained and chopped
6-oz. can ripe olives, chopped
2 4-oz. cans chopped green chilies
8-10 green onions, chopped
3 Tbsp. olive oil
1½ Tbsp. wine vinegar
1 tsp. garlic salt

1. Mix all ingredients and refrigerate at least 24 hours before serving.
2. Use as a dip with corn or taco chips or as a relish for hot dogs and hamburgers.

Tortilla Roll-Ups

Sybil Turner
Bellville, TX
Tennessee Album
Judy Mocho
Albuquerque, NM
New Mexico Cow Quilt

Makes many appetizer servings

8-oz. carton sour cream
8-oz. pkg. cream cheese
4-oz. jar green chilies

Lemon juice to taste
½ tsp. cumin
1 pkg. flour tortillas
Picante sauce

1. Combine sour cream, cream cheese, green chilies, lemon juice and cumin. Spread mixture over each tortilla. Roll up tortillas and refrigerate several hours or overnight.
2. Slice into ¾-inch pieces and serve with picante sauce.

❖

Tortilla Rolls with Mustard

Elsie Long
Sterling, IL
Flying Geese

Makes many appetizer servings

Tortilla Rolls:
1 lb. cream cheese
1 lb. cooked ham, chopped
8-oz. can green chilies, chopped
8-oz. can black olives, chopped
12 flour tortillas

Mustard Dip:
1 cup malt vinegar
¼ cup dry mustard
1 cup sugar
3 eggs

1. To prepare tortilla rolls blend cream cheese, ham, chilies and olives.

Spread mixture evenly on each tortilla. Roll the tortillas jelly-roll style. Cover with plastic wrap and a damp cloth and refrigerate 4 hours.

2. To prepare mustard dip combine all ingredients in blender and mix well. Pour into top of a double boiler and cook 8-10 minutes over boiling water, stirring constantly. Refrigerate. Dip will thicken as it cools.

3. Immediately before serving, cut tortilla rolls into ½-inch slices and serve with mustard dip.

Buffalo Wings

Ruby Koehn
Bellville, TX
Pinwheel

Makes 12-15 servings

12-15 chicken wings
Salt and pepper to taste
1 cup ketchup
2 Tbsp. honey *or* brown sugar
½ tsp. garlic powder
4 Tbsp. soy sauce

1. Split each chicken wing at joint and discard tip. Place in a shallow baking pan. Salt and pepper to taste.

2. In a saucepan combine ketchup, honey, garlic powder and soy sauce and

bring to a boil. Pour over chicken wings.

3. Bake at 350° for 1 hour or until golden brown, turning halfway through baking time.

Sweet & Sour Green Chilies

Jackie Evans
Albuquerque, NM
Southwest Symphony

Makes 15-20 servings

1 cup sugar
1 cup vinegar
Garlic to taste
Dill to taste
Pinch cumin
10-12 green chilies

1. In a saucepan dissolve sugar and vinegar over medium heat. Add spices and mix well, tasting for preferred balance of flavors.

2. Cut chilies into medium-sized pieces. Add to sauce. Remove from heat and marinate overnight or at least several hours.

3. Serve chilies with crackers and cream cheese.

❖

Oven-Buttered Cornsticks

Judy Miller
Columbia, MD
Cape Hatteras Sunrise

Makes 20 servings

4 Tbsp. butter *or* margarine
2 cups Bisquick
8½-oz. can creamed corn

1. Turn oven to 450° and melt butter or margarine in 10" x 15" jelly roll pan.

2. In mixing bowl combine Bisquick and corn. Stir until soft dough forms. Knead on lightly floured surface for about 15 strokes.

3. Roll out into a 6" x 10" rectangle. Cut dough into 1" x 3" strips. Roll each strip in melted butter and arrange in single layer in pan.

4. Return pan to oven and bake 10-12 minutes. Serve with soup or chowder.

My husband does most of the cooking while I quilt.
—Joan Coale Klosek, Ellicott City, MD

Crisp Cornsticks

Doreen Copeland
Florence, SC
Flower Basket

Makes 10 cornsticks

1 cup cornmeal
¼ tsp. salt
¼ tsp. baking soda
4 Tbsp. cooking oil
1 cup buttermilk
2 Tbsp. light corn syrup

1. Sift cornmeal. Add salt and baking soda and mix. Stir in oil, buttermilk and corn syrup.
2. Spoon ingredients into greased cornstick-baking pan.
3. Bake at 400° for 30-40 minutes or until crisp.

Parmesan Potato Sticks

Sandy Brown
Connersville, IN
Double Wedding Ring

Makes 8 servings

2 lbs. potatoes
½ cup butter
½ cup bread crumbs
½ cup Parmesan cheese
¼ tsp. salt
⅛ tsp. black pepper
⅛ tsp. garlic powder

1. Cut each potato into quarters. Cut the quarter pieces into thirds.
2. Melt butter. Set aside.
3. Combine all remaining ingredients. Roll each potato piece in melted butter, then in the seasonings. Arrange on a baking sheet. Pour remaining butter and sprinkle remaining seasonings over pieces.
4. Bake at 400° for 30-35 minutes.

Parmesan Potato Rounds

Carolyn Shank
Dayton, VA
Sampler

Makes 6 servings

6 medium potatoes
⅓ cup butter *or* margarine, melted
¼ cup all-purpose flour
¼ cup grated Parmesan cheese
Salt and pepper to taste
Italian seasoning to taste

1. Slice potatoes into ¼-inch thick rounds.
2. Pour melted butter onto 10" x 15" jelly roll pan.
3. Combine flour, cheese, salt and pepper in a plastic bag. Add a few potato rounds at a time to the bag and shake to coat with flour mixture.
4. Arrange potatoes in single layer over butter in baking pan.
5. Bake at 350° for 30 minutes. Turn slices and sprinkle with Italian seasoning. Bake 30 minutes longer or until tender.

Stevenson's Deviled Eggs

SherylAnne Bratton
North Hills, PA
Steph's Quilt

Makes 24 servings

1 dozen large eggs
2 Tbsp. Dijon mustard
2 Tbsp. horseradish
1-2 cups mayonnaise
Paprika

1. After boiling, cooling and peeling eggs, cut in half and remove yolks into a large bowl.
2. Mash yolks and mix with horseradish, Dijon mustard and mayonnaise to desired consistency. Spoon into egg halves. Smooth, then sprinkle with paprika. Refrigerate until ready to serve.

Mini Pizzas

Rose Hankins
Stevensville, MD
Flying Geese

Makes 4 servings

4 English muffins, split
and toasted
¾ cup tomato sauce
½ cup grated Parmesan
cheese
½ cup cubed sharp cheese
½ tsp. basil
½ tsp. oregano
½ tsp. parsley
¼ lb. pepperoni

1. Divide tomato sauce
among toasted muffin
pieces and spread.
2. Divide cheeses and
spread.
3. Sprinkle herbs over
cheeses.
4. Slice pepperoni into 16
small pieces and arrange
evenly on each muffin.
5. Arrange muffins on
baking sheet.
6. Broil at 500° for 2-4
minutes. Serve.

Pizza Cups

Nancy Wall
Duncansville, PA
*Miniature Trip Around the
World*

Makes 10 servings

1 lb. ground beef
6-oz. can tomato paste
1 Tbsp. instant minced
onion
1 tsp. Italian seasoning
½ tsp. salt
10-oz. carton refrigerated
biscuits
½-¾ cup shredded
mozzarella cheese

1. Brown beef and drain
excess fat. Stir in tomato
paste, onion and season-
ings. Cook over low heat
for 5 minutes, stirring frequently. (Mixture will be
thick.)
2. Place biscuits into
greased muffin tins, pressing to cover bottoms and
sides.
3. Spoon about ¼ cup of
meat mixture into each bis-
cuit-lined cup and sprinkle
with cheese.
4. Bake at 400° for 12
minutes or until golden
brown.

Fresh Vegetable Pizza

Peggy Hamilton
Hillsboro, OH
Sue Dieringer-Boyer
Walkersville, MD
Alix Botsford, Seminole, OK

Makes 12-24 servings

2 pkgs. crescent rolls
2 8-oz. pkgs. cream cheese,
softened
1 cup mayonnaise
1 pkg. Hidden Valley
Ranch dressing
½ cup chopped onion
½ cup chopped cauliflower
½ cup chopped broccoli
½ cup chopped radishes
½ cup chopped celery
½ cup chopped green
pepper
½ cup chopped carrots
½ cup chopped tomato
(optional)
8 ozs. cheddar cheese,
grated

1. Press crescent rolls
into jelly roll pan.
2. Bake at 350° for 10
minutes. Set aside and cool.
3. Mix cream cheese,
mayonnaise and Hidden
Valley Ranch Dressing.
Spread over rolls and top
with the vegetables.
4. Sprinkle with cheddar
cheese and cut into 12 or 24
squares. Refrigerate until
ready to serve.

Shapleigh Luncheon Cheese

Geraldine A. Ebersole
Hershey, PA
Double Irish Chain

Makes 4 servings

4 slices dry bread
1 Tbsp. butter
½ lb. Swiss cheese
2 eggs, slightly beaten
1 cup light cream
1 tsp. salt *or* less
½ tsp. paprika
⅛ tsp. cayenne pepper

1. Spread bread with butter. Cut each slice bread into 8 thin strips. Arrange layers of strips across bottom of greased shallow baking pan.
2. Cut cheese into small pieces. Arrange cheese over bread and around the sides of the baking pan.
3. Combine all remaining ingredients and pour over cheese and bread.
4. Bake at 350° for 30-40 minutes or until top is golden.

Variations:
Add ¼ lb. cooked sausage, ¼ lb. sautéed mushrooms or 1 cup sliced , sautéed onions.

Spedini (Sandwiches)

Carol A. Findling
Beatrice, NE
Christmas Sampler

Makes 8 servings

1 loaf Italian *or* French bread, unsliced
¼ cup margarine, softened
1 clove garlic, minced
¼ tsp. oregano
¼ tsp. rosemary
12 slices cotto salami
24 pieces mozzarella cheese (see step 3)
2 eggs
⅔ cup milk
¼ tsp. salt
⅔ cup shredded Parmesan cheese

1. Cut ends from loaf of bread and slice loaf into 8 portions. Make 3 evenly spaced slashes crosswise in each slice, but do not cut through.
2. Combine margarine, garlic, oregano and rosemary. Spread on slash-cut bread surfaces.
3. Cut salami slices in half. Cut mozzarella cheese into 24 pieces, 1" x 1½" x ¼". Wrap each half slice salami around a piece of cheese and place one in each of the three crosswise slices of the bread. Thread a skewer through to hold pieces of salami and bread in place.

4. Combine eggs, milk and salt and dip each slice bread into mixture. Place on greased baking sheet and sprinkle with Parmesan cheese.
5. Bake at 400° for 6-8 minutes or until cheese melts and sandwich is heated through.

Note: Sandwiches may be prepared ahead of time, covered and refrigerated until ready to bake. (Hold the Parmesan cheese and sprinkle over sandwiches immediately before baking.) Bring to room temperature before baking. These are a great treat for the kids and especially good for cook-ahead meals.

Cheese Salad Sandwiches

Karen Unternahrer
Shipshewana, IN
Early American Sampler Quilt

Makes 15 servings

1 lb. mild cheddar cheese, shredded
1 Tbsp. sugar
Dash salt
1 Tbsp. relish
2 hard-boiled eggs, diced
1¼ cups mayonnaise
Bread *or* rolls

1. Combine all ingredients except bread or rolls

My friend Lenay and I are each mothers of two small children. We try to make time to quilt together at least one night a week. While we quilt, we also unwind, share our problems and sip tea often until long after midnight.

—Bea Gagliano, Lakewood, NJ

and mix well.

2. Spread on bread or rolls and serve as an appetizer or a main accompaniment to soup or salad.

Reuben Melt

Cora G. Napier
Connersville, IN
Around the Twist

Makes 4-6 servings

16-oz. can sauerkraut, drained
12-oz. can corned beef
8 ozs. cheddar cheese, shredded
8 ozs. Swiss cheese, shredded
1 cup mayonnaise

1. Mix together all ingredients and spoon into greased casserole dish.
2. Bake at 350° for 30 minutes. Cool slightly. Serve with nachos.

Pocket Salad Sandwich

Betty Krueger
Rogue River, OR
Crazy Patch

Makes 2 servings

2 pita pockets
½ cup shredded carrot
2 tsp. mayonnaise
¼ cucumber, thinly sliced
2 radishes, thinly sliced
1 tomato, thinly sliced
½ avocado, thinly sliced
2 lettuce leaves
2 spinach leaves
2 small handsful alfalfa sprouts
2 tsp. Honey Dijon Ranch dressing

1. Wrap pita bread in paper towels. Sprinkle lightly with water. Microwave on high for 15 seconds.
2. Mix shredded carrot with mayonnaise and spread inside pita pocket. Add thin slices of vegetables and avocado. Add lettuce and spinach leaves. Stuff with sprouts.
3. Top with Honey Dijon Ranch Dressing and press it down into the vegetables

with end of a spoon or similar object.

Note: Use a low-calorie mayonnaise and any raw vegetables of your choice for this delightful sandwich. Serve with extra carrot and celery sticks if desired.

Apple Raisin Sandwiches

Judy McKee
Beatrice, NE

Makes 15-20 servings

½ cup chopped raisins
1 small apple, finely chopped
4 ozs. cream cheese
⅛ tsp. cinnamon
1-1½ cups apple butter
1 loaf wheat bread

1. Combine all ingredients except bread, using enough apple butter to make spreading consistency.
2. Trim crusts off bread and save for bread crumbs.
3. Spread filling on bread, making sandwiches which are cut in either finger or triangle shapes.

Tuna Spread Sandwiches

Winnie Friese
Washington, NJ

Makes 12 servings

½ cup mayonnaise
1 Tbsp. lemon juice
½ tsp. salt
1 Tbsp. minced onion
½ cup minced celery
2 7-oz. cans tuna
6 wiener rolls, split

1. Combine mayonnaise, lemon juice and salt. Add onion, celery and tuna and mix well.
2. Spread mixture on wiener rolls, covering both halves out to edges of rolls.
3. Arrange on broiler pan tuna side up.
4. Broil at 500° for 2-4 minutes until browned.

Super Sandwich

Dusty Graham
Hagerstown, MD
Nine Patch Chain

Makes 6-8 servings

8"-10" round loaf
    pumpernickel bread
2 tsp. horseradish
¼ lb. roast beef
2 Tbsp. mayonnaise

4-6 slices Swiss cheese
2 Tbsp. sweet hot mustard
¼ lb. sliced ham
1 tomato, sliced
6 slices fried bacon
6 slices American cheese
½ sliced red onion
1 Tbsp. butter, softened

1. Slice bread into 6 layers horizontally. On the first slice combine horseradish and roast beef. Cover with another slice.
2. On second slice combine mayonnaise and Swiss cheese. Cover with another slice.
3. On third slice combine hot mustard and ham. Cover with another slice.
4. On fourth slice combine tomato and bacon. Cover with another slice.
5. On fifth slice combine American cheese and onion. Cover with another slice.
6. Rub top slice with soft butter and lay sandwich on baking sheet.
7. Bake, uncovered, at 400° for 10-15 minutes.
8. Slice into wedges and serve.

Citrus Fruit Dip

Dorothy Kauffman
Millersburg, OH
Double Wedding Ring

Makes 3 cups dip

6 ozs. prepared orange
    juice
3 ozs. lemonade
1 cup white sugar
1 egg
2 cups whipped topping

1. In a saucepan combine orange juice, lemonade, sugar and egg. Bring to a boil. Cook until thickened.
2. Cool and fold in whipped topping.
3. Serve with slices of fresh fruit.

Doris McCloskey's Fruit Dip

Doris McCloskey
Annapolis, MD
Dutch Windmill

Makes 8-10 servings

8-oz. carton sour cream
¼ cup brown sugar
10 macaroons, crumbled

1. Combine all ingredients and mix well.
2. Serve with an assortment of sliced fruits.

Joyce Niemann's Fruit Dip

Joyce Niemann
Fruitland Park, FL
Lap Sampler

Makes 12 servings

7-oz. jar marshmallow
cream
8-oz. pkg. cream cheese,
softened
¼ cup strawberry
preserves

1. Mix ingredients until smooth.
2. Serve with an assortment of sliced fruits.

Variations:
Substitute 1 tsp. lemon juice for the strawberry preserves.
Janice Yoskobich
Carmichaels, PA
Log Cabin

Substitute ¼ tsp. cinnamon and ¼ tsp. nutmeg for strawberry preserves.
Deb Koelsch
Lancaster, PA
Handy Andy

Apple Dip

Karen Unternahrer
Shipshewana, IN
Early American Sampler Quilt

Makes 2 cups dip

8-oz. pkg. cream cheese
¾ cup brown sugar
¼ cup butter
1 tsp. vanilla
Apples

1. In a saucepan melt all ingredients over medium heat except apples, stirring constantly. Cool.
2. Slice apples, dip and enjoy.

Hot Pepper Pecans

Gwen Oberg
Albuquerque, NM
View to a Zoo

Makes 4 cups pecans

4 Tbsp. butter *or* margarine
¼ cup Worcestershire
sauce
1 tsp. hot pepper sauce
4 cups pecan halves

1. Melt butter or margarine. Add Worcestershire sauce and pepper sauce.
2. Spread pecans on a foil-lined baking sheet. Coat with butter mixture.

3. Bake at 250° for 30 minutes or until pecans are toasted and crisp, stirring every 10 minutes.
4. When cooled, store in an airtight container.

❖

Hungarian Almonds

Lorraine Moore Lear
Del City, OK
Old Maid's Puzzle

Makes 2 cups almonds

1 egg white
2 tsp. garlic salt
1 Tbsp. paprika
¼ tsp. cayenne pepper
2 cups whole natural
almonds

1. In large bowl beat egg white until frothy. Mix in garlic salt, paprika and cayenne pepper to blend thoroughly.
2. Add almonds and toss to coat evenly. Spread in single layer on lightly greased baking sheet.
3. Bake at 300° for 20-25 minutes, stirring occasionally, until lightly toasted. Loosen from pan and cool.
4. Store in airtight container.

Caramel Popcorn

Lynne Fritz, Bel Air, MD
Shirley Norris
Walhonding, OH
Judy Mocho
Albuquerque, NM
Debra Jane Jackson
Rancho Cucamonga, CA

Makes about 20 1-cup servings

2 cups brown sugar
16 Tbsp. butter
½ cup light corn syrup
1 tsp. salt
1 tsp. baking soda
6 quarts popped popcorn
1-2 cups peanuts (optional)

1. In a saucepan combine brown sugar, butter, corn syrup and salt. Heat to boiling and boil 5 minutes, stirring frequently.
2. Remove from heat and stir in baking soda. Pour mixture over popcorn in a bowl. Add peanuts and spread onto 2 large baking sheets.
3. Bake at 200° for 1 hour, stirring at 15-minute intervals. Remove from oven, cool and store in tins or airtight containers.

Note: Do not use microwaved popcorn.

Taco-Flavored Oyster Crackers

Juanita Marner
Shipshewana, IN
Giant Dahlia

Makes many servings

1 pkg. dry taco seasoning
½ tsp. chili powder
½ tsp. oregano
½ tsp. garlic powder
2 12-oz. pkgs. oyster crackers
¾ cup cooking oil

1. Put all ingredients into a large paper bag and shake well.
2. Serve at snack time.

Toasty Cheese Crackers

Sherry Carroll
Delta, PA
Sampler

Makes 6 dozen crackers

2 cups shredded cheddar cheese
½ cup grated Parmesan cheese
½ cup butter *or* margarine, softened
3 Tbsp. water
1 cup all-purpose flour
¼ tsp. salt (optional)
1 cup uncooked oats
¾ tsp. oregano *or* basil

1. Beat together cheeses, butter and water until well blended. Add flour and salt and mix well. Stir in oats, mixing until well blended.

In 1976 a busload of quilters from northern New Jersey went to the Continental Quilting Congress near Washington D.C. At the beginning of the trip, we were each given a 15" square piece of backing, a 15" square of batting and various strips of fabric cut for a Log Cabin design.

After arriving at the convention, we attended lectures, workshops and luncheons, and, in our spare moments, hurried from room to room finishing the quilt blocks and sewing them together. With the exception of the binding, we finished the quilt. A local television station did a feature story on the "Quilt As You Go Bus Trip."

On our way home, everyone put their name in a box. The bus driver pulled a name, and it was mine! While it is not the best quilt ever made, I treasure it for all the memories it holds.

—*Elizabeth Boyton, Gordonville, PA*

2. Shape dough to form 12-inch long roll. Wrap securely and refrigerate at least 4 hours or overnight.

3. Cut into ¼-inch slices and flatten slightly. Arrange on lightly greased baking sheet.

4. Bake at 400° for 8-10 minutes or until edges are light golden brown. Remove immediately and cool on rack.

Note: For a smaller cocktail cracker, shape dough into four 6-8-inch long rolls and continue with step 3. For a nice gift, recipe makes enough crackers to fill a 1-lb. coffee can.

❖

Rusks

Marion Matson
Comfrey, MN
Amish Baskets

Makes 48 rusks

1 cup margarine
1¼ cups sugar
2 eggs
3¼ cups flour
1 tsp. baking soda
½ tsp. salt
1 cup sour milk
1 tsp. ground cardamom
1 tsp. almond flavoring
2 tsp. cinnamon
2 tsp. sugar

1. Cream together margarine and 1¼ cups sugar. Add eggs and mix.

2. Sift flour, baking soda and salt together. Add to creamed batter, alternating with sour milk. Add cardamom and almond flavoring. Pour into greased 9" x 13" baking pan.

3. Bake at 350° for 40 minutes. Cool.

4. When cooled, slice 4 the short way and 12 the long way. Spread on a baking sheet and sprinkle with cinnamon and sugar mixture.

5. Dry at 300° for 15 minutes. Turn rusks, sprinkle with cinnamon and sugar and dry 15 minutes longer. Turn the oven off, leaving the rusks in the oven until it cools completely, about 2 hours.

Note: Make your own sour milk by adding 1 Tbsp. lemon juice to a cup of milk.

Salads

Beef and Lentil Salad

Jay Conrad
Bedford, TX
Amish Bars

Makes 8 servings

1½ quarts water
1 tsp. salt
1 cup lentils
½ lb. roast beef
3 large bell peppers, sliced
3 scallions with tops, sliced
½ cup chopped fresh
   parsley
¼ cup chopped fresh dill
1 clove garlic, minced
2 Tbsp. olive oil
2 Tbsp. vinegar
1 tsp. Dijon mustard
Salt and pepper to taste
8 lettuce leaves
1-2 tomatoes
8 sprigs parsley
8 sprigs dill

1. Heat water and 1 tsp. salt in large saucepan to boiling. Add lentils, reduce heat and simmer until lentils are just tender, but not soft. Drain and cool.
2. Cut roast beef into narrow 2-inch strips.
3. Combine lentils, beef, peppers, scallions, chopped parsley and chopped dill in large bowl.
4. Whisk garlic, oil, vinegar and mustard together. Add to lentil and beef mixture and season to taste with salt and pepper. Refrigerate to chill.
5. Serve on lettuce leaves and garnish with tomato slices, parsley sprigs and dill sprigs. Accompany with rolls or muffins.

Turkey Salad

Jean Swift
Comfrey, MN
Starry Geese

Makes 6-8 servings

1 cup elbow macaroni
2 cups cooked turkey
1 cup diced celery
11-oz. can mandarin
   oranges, drained
⅓ cup slivered almonds
1 cup grapes
1 cup mayonnaise
Pinch salt
¾ cup whipping cream

1. Cook macaroni according to directions. Drain, rinse and cool.
2. Combine all ingredients except cream. Refrigerate overnight.
3. Whip cream. Stir into salad and serve.

Chicken Salad

Sharon Heide
Mountain Lake, MN
Ohio Star

Makes 10-15 servings

4 cups cooked chicken
4 cups grated carrots
4 cups finely chopped
   celery
1 medium onion, chopped

3 cups mayonnaise
2-3 cups shoestring
   potatoes

1. Combine chicken, carrots, celery and onion.
2. Stir mayonnaise into salad and mix well.
3. Immediately before serving, fold in shoestring potatoes.

A Favorite Luncheon Turkey Salad

Connee Sager
Tucson, AZ
Tulip Variation

Makes 12 or more servings

2½-3 lbs. turkey
20-oz. can water chestnuts
2 lbs. seedless grapes
2 cups sliced celery
2-3 cups toasted, slivered
   almonds
3 cups mayonnaise
1 Tbsp. curry powder
2 Tbsp. soy sauce
2 Tbsp. lemon juice
   (optional)
Lettuce
20-oz. can pineapple

chunks, drained
Fresh mint leaves
(optional)

1. Cook, cool and bone turkey. Cut into bite-sized pieces. Drain and slice water chestnuts. Remove grapes from stems.
2. Combine turkey, water chestnuts, grapes, celery and 1½-2 cups toasted almonds.
3. In a separate bowl mix mayonnaise, curry powder, soy sauce and lemon juice. Combine with turkey mixture. Chill for several hours or overnight.
4. Spoon onto a bed of lettuce arranged on individual serving plates. Sprinkle with remaining almonds and garnish with pineapple chunks and mint leaves.

Tuna Spinach Salad

Susan L. Schwarz
North Bethesda, MD
Paragon's Country Garden

Makes 6-8 servings

Salad:
6-8 slices bacon
1 lb. fresh spinach
1 cup water chestnuts,
   sliced
1 cup bean sprouts
3-4 hard-boiled eggs, sliced
7-oz. can tuna, drained and
   flaked

Dressing:
½ cup sugar *or* less
¼ cup vinegar
1 cup cooking oil
⅓ cup ketchup
1 Tbsp. Worcestershire
   sauce
1 medium onion, finely
   chopped

1. Fry, drain and crumble bacon. Combine all salad ingredients and refrigerate.
2. To prepare dressing combine sugar and vinegar in small saucepan over low heat until sugar dissolves. Remove from heat, combine all ingredients and shake well. Refrigerate until serving time.
3. Immediately before serving, combine dressing with salad and toss well.

Tuna Fruit Salad

Cindy Dellamonica
Lodi, CA

Makes 36 servings

Salad:
6 medium apples
¼ cup lemon juice
12 cups cooked shell
  macaroni
6 cups sliced celery
3 cups halved seedless
  grapes
1½ cups sliced green
  onions
6 7-oz. cans tuna, drained

Dressing:
4½ cups mayonnaise
4 Tbsp. curry powder
4 Tbsp. Dijon mustard

1. Core and wedge apples. Cut into bite-sized chunks and combine with lemon juice in large mixing bowl. Add all remaining salad ingredients and mix well.
2. Combine all dressing ingredients and pour over salad. Mix well. Refrigerate in airtight containers until ready to serve.

Shrimp Salad

Susan G. Sneer
Mountain Lake, MN
Amish Baskets Variation

Makes 12 or more servings

Dressing:
3 cups Miracle Whip salad
  dressing
6-oz. bottle chili sauce
1 onion, diced
3 pickles, diced
3 hard-boiled eggs, diced
1 tsp. Worcestershire sauce

Salad:
4 cups uncooked macaroni
½ cup diced celery
2 7-oz. cans shrimp
1 onion, diced
3 hard-boiled eggs, sliced
1 green pepper, diced
  (optional)

1. Combine all dressing ingredients and mix well.

Refrigerate overnight.
2. Cook macaroni according to directions. Drain and let cool. Add celery, shrimp, onion, eggs and green pepper if desired.
3. Mix together with the chilled dressing and refrigerate until ready to serve.

Variation:
Make a simple dressing with 2 cups mayonnaise and 1 cup French dressing. Mix well and stir into salad ingredients. Sprinkle with paprika and serve.

Donna Lantgen
Rapid City, SD
Dresden Plate

My grandmother, Doña Ana Wright Daugherty, was a beautiful and joyful woman who loved to quilt and cook. When I stayed with her, she occasionally would let me nap on a Victorian Crazy Quilt. I remember the feeling of deep pile velvet against my cheek and the outline of beautiful embroidery around the irregular patches of upholstery brocades, silks and velvets. The mysterious colors and textures of this rich quilt became my original inspiration when I too became a quilter.

I also cherish the memory of helping her make her famous biscuits. She always let me help even though I made a big mess of things. From her legacy I have learned to take pleasure in cooking and cleaning and sewing. Her art was her life, and her life was an art form that has greatly inspired me.

—*Katy J. Widger, Los Lunas, NM*

Shrimp Macaroni Salad

Gail Kozicki
Glen Mills, PA
Untitled

Makes 4-6 servings

Salad:
1½ cups uncooked
  macaroni
¾ cup diced celery
¼ cup sliced green onions
3 radishes, sliced thinly
2 4-oz. cans shrimp,
  drained and rinsed
Salt and pepper to taste
Salad greens

Dressing:
½ cup mayonnaise
1 Tbsp. vinegar
1 tsp. prepared mustard
½ tsp. celery seed

1. Cook, drain and cool macaroni.
2. Combine macaroni with all remaining salad ingredients except salad greens.
3. Combine all dressing ingredients and stir into salad. Chill several hours before serving.
3. Serve on a bed of salad greens.

Shrimp and Crab Salad

Charmaine Keith
Marion, KS
White on White

Makes 12 or more servings

4 cups cooked pasta
3 hard-boiled eggs, sliced
1-1½ cups small shrimp
1-1½ cups crab meat
8-oz. can black olives,
  diced
1 small onion, diced
3-4 stalks celery, diced
Salt to taste
Cajun seasoning to taste
1 cup mayonnaise

1. Combine pasta, eggs, shrimp and crab and refrigerate until cold.
2. In large bowl mix all ingredients, adding enough mayonnaise to hold salad together nicely.
3. Serve with garlic bread.

Note: Do not use canned shrimp as it will not flavor salad. Use small fresh shrimp, steamed in boiling water until pink and white color has appeared, about 3 to 5 minutes. The imitation crab meat will work very nicely. If your Cajun seasoning has salt in it, do not add extra salt.

Seafood Pasta Salad

Susan Orleman
Pittsburgh, PA
Island Stars

Makes 10 servings

16-oz. pkg. pasta
1 lb. fresh shrimp
½ lb. crab meat
1 cup frozen peas
3 green onions, chopped
3 medium tomatoes,
  chopped
¾ cup olive oil
¼ cup chopped fresh
  parsley
⅓ cup wine vinegar
1 tsp. dried oregano
1½ tsp. dried basil
½ tsp. garlic salt
½ tsp. coarsely ground
  pepper

1. Cook pasta according to package directions, omitting salt. Drain and rinse with cold water.
2. Steam and peel shrimp.
3. Combine all ingredients and toss gently. Chill and serve.

Summer Pasta Salad

Carol Trice
Wayne, PA
Baby Dresden

Makes 8 or more servings

16-oz. pkg. pasta
1 cup chopped tomatoes
1 cup chopped cucumbers
1 cup chopped green
  peppers
12-oz. bottle Italian salad
  dressing
½ bottle McCormick's
  Salad Supreme

1. Cook pasta according to package directions. Drain and rinse with cold water.
2. Stir chopped vegetables into pasta. Add Italian dressing and mix well.
3. Add McCormick's Salad Supreme and mix well.
4. Chill at least 3-4 hours to let flavors combine.

Note: Substitute your choice of chopped vegetables. Chopped chicken may also be added.

Pat's Pasta Salad

Barbara A. Nolan
Pleasant Valley, NY
Sampler

Makes 20 servings

1 lb. small pasta
2 Tbsp. flour
¾ cup sugar
2 tsp. salt *or* less
2 eggs
2 15-oz. cans pineapple
  chunks
2 11-oz. cans mandarin
  oranges, drained
2 9-oz. cartons whipped
  topping
1 medium jar maraschino
  cherries

1. Cook pasta 6-8 minutes in boiling water. Do not overcook. Drain and rinse with cold water.
2. In a saucepan combine flour, sugar and salt. Add eggs and juice from pineapple. Cook until thickened. Cool.
3. Mix cooled sauce, pineapple chunks and oranges with pasta. Refrigerate overnight.
4. Fold whipped topping and cherries into pasta salad and mix thoroughly.
5. Garnish with fruit of choice.

Note: This may be very watery at first, but it will firm up as it stands. May be made several days ahead of time.

Easy Carry Macaroni Salad

Marion Nanopoulos
Oxford, PA
Bermuda Triangles

Makes 6 servings

8-oz. pkg. elbow macaroni
1 cup mayonnaise
1 Tbsp. vinegar
1 Tbsp. prepared mustard
1 tsp. salt
¼ tsp. pepper
1 Tbsp. celery seed
1 cup diced celery
½ cup diced onions
10-oz. pkg. frozen peas

1. Cook macaroni according to package directions. Drain and rinse.
2. Combine all ingredients except peas in airtight container. Chill thoroughly.
3. Make a well in center and pour frozen peas into well. Cover and carry to picnic or fellowship meal.
4. Immediately before serving, stir to mix well.

Note: Frozen peas help keep salad safely cold while waiting for picnic to begin.

Spaghetti Salad

Barbara Wenders
Moscow, ID
Universal Garden

Makes 12 servings

Salad:
7-oz. pkg. angel hair
   spaghetti
1 green pepper
1 red pepper
1-2 green onions
1 large tomato
1 zucchini
3 stalks celery
¼ cup Parmesan cheese

Dressing:
¼ cup red wine vinegar
¼ cup olive oil
2 Tbsp. dry Italian
   dressing mix
1 Tbsp. parsley
1 Tbsp. sugar

1. To prepare salad cook angel hair, rinse and cool. Dice vegetables.
2. To prepare dressing combine all ingredients and chill.
3. Toss pasta with vegetables. Sprinkle with dressing and toss again. Add Parmesan cheese and chill overnight.

Curried Rice Salad

Gwen Oberg
Albuquerque, NM
View to a Zoo

Makes 6-8 servings

½ cup uncooked rice
1 Tbsp. vinegar
2 Tbsp. cooking oil
¾ cup mayonnaise
1 tsp. salt *or* less
¾ tsp. curry powder
¼ cup chopped onion
1 cup chopped celery
10-oz. pkg. frozen peas

1. Cook rice according to directions.
2. Meanwhile, combine vinegar, cooking oil, mayonnaise, salt and curry powder. Add cooked rice to this mixture and stir in onion while rice is still hot. Chill.
3. Fold in celery and peas and serve.

Barley Salad

Paula Lederkramer
Levittown, NY
Spectrum II &
Island in the Sun

Makes 8 servings

4 cups cooked barley
¼ cup olive oil
3 Tbsp. lemon juice

2 cloves garlic, minced
½ cup chopped dill
2 cups diced tomatoes
2 cups diced cucumbers
½ cup diced scallions
Salt and pepper to taste

1. Toss barley in large bowl with olive oil, lemon juice and garlic. Add dill.
2. Toss in tomatoes, cucumbers and scallions. Season with salt and pepper.
3. Let salad rest at least 1 hour to blend flavors. Garnish with dill and serve.

Potato and Egg Salad

Diana Huntress Deem
Bethesda, MD
Love in the Cabin

Makes 8-10 servings

6-8 medium red potatoes
3 hard-boiled eggs
2 medium dill pickles
1 cup mayonnaise
1 tsp. dry mustard

1. Cook potatoes in water to cover. Cool and dice.
2. Chop eggs and pickles into very small pieces. Combine with potatoes in serving bowl.
3. Thoroughly mix mayonnaise and mustard. Stir into potato salad and mix well. Chill until ready to serve.

Potato Salad

Alma Mullet
Walnut Creek, OH
Triple Irish Chain

Makes 6-8 servings

Salad:
6 boiled potatoes, diced
2 small onions, diced
3 hard-boiled eggs, diced
1 stalk celery, finely
  chopped
1 small sweet pickle,
  finely chopped

Dressing:
2 Tbsp. flour
½ cup vinegar
3 Tbsp. prepared mustard
3 Tbsp. sugar
2 tsp. salt
3 eggs, separated
1 cup sour cream
Season to taste

1. Combine all salad ingredients. Set aside.
2. To prepare dressing combine all ingredients except egg whites and sour cream in a saucepan. Bring to a boil, stirring constantly until thickened. Cool mixture.
3. Beat egg whites and sour cream together. Fold into dressing mixture. Season to taste.
4. Pour cooled dressing over salad and serve.

Old-Fashioned Potato Salad

Katie's Quilts and Wall Hangings, Millersburg, OH
Elsie Schlabach
Millersburg, OH
Gertrude W. Byler
Smicksburg, PA

Makes 20-24 servings

Salad:
4 lbs. potatoes
12 hard-boiled eggs, diced
1 medium onion, chopped
2 cups chopped celery

Dressing:
3 cups mayonnaise
3 Tbsp. prepared mustard
¼ cup vinegar
1¾ cups white sugar
4 tsp. salt *or* less
½ cup milk

1. Boil potatoes in jackets. Cool and shred. Add all other salad ingredients and toss.
2. Combine all dressing ingredients and mix well.
3. Pour dressing over potato salad and refrigerate at least overnight before serving (will keep up to 1 week).

Mexican Salad

Betty L. Richards
Rapid City, SD
Patti Boston, Coshocton, OH
Judy Berry, Columbia, MD

Makes 10-12 servings

1 head lettuce, shredded
2 tomatoes, chopped
1 medium onion, chopped
1 lb. cheddar cheese,
  shredded
16-oz. can pinto *or* kidney
  beans, drained
12-oz. bottle Catalina
  dressing
15-oz. pkg. corn *or* taco
  chips

1. Toss lettuce, tomatoes and onion in large bowl. Add cheese and beans.
2. Immediately before serving, toss with dressing.
3. Serve with chips.

My mother died of cancer in 1987 after being sick for a very long time. I don't think I could have gotten through the many hours I spent at her bedside if it had not been for quilting. I look now at the quilts I made during that time (most were wall hangings so I could carry them with me), and I remember our conversations, our shared worries and our laughter. Those quilts are my link to her. Indeed, quilts are more than just coverings for beds and walls, they are living memories which join us to our past.

—*Mary Puskar, Baltimore, MD*

Taco Salad

MaryJane S. Pozarycki
Neptune City, NJ
Fancy Nine Patch

Makes 6-8 servings

1 head lettuce, shredded
2-3 tomatoes, wedged
1 cucumber, thinly sliced
½-1 cup chopped onion
8-oz. bottle Italian salad
   dressing
1 lb. ground beef
1 pkg. dry taco seasoning
8 ozs. cheddar cheese,
   grated
6-oz. pkg. taco chips,
   crumbled

1. In a large bowl combine lettuce, tomatoes, cucumber, onion and salad dressing.
2. Brown ground beef. Drain excess fat. Stir in taco seasoning and cool.
3. Fold ground beef and cheese into salad. Immediately before serving, add taco chips and mix well.

Variation:
Add 16-oz. can chickpeas, drained, to salad along with cheese.

Jacquelyn Kreitzer
Mechanicsburg, PA
Lap Sampler

Seven-Layer Salad

Lori Drohman
Rogue River, OR
Fan & Jacob's Ladder
Esther S. Martin
Ephrata, PA
Nine Patch

Makes 8 servings

Salad:
1 head lettuce
1 cup chopped celery
4 hard-boiled eggs, sliced
10-oz. pkg. frozen peas
½ green pepper, sliced
1 medium onion, sliced
1 cup grated carrots
3-oz. jar bacon bits

Dressing:
2 cups mayonnaise
2 Tbsp. sugar
4 ozs. cheddar cheese,
   grated

1. Tear lettuce and arrange in 9" x 13" pan. Layer remaining salad ingredients in the order listed.
2. To prepare dressing combine mayonnaise and sugar and spread over salad. Top with grated cheddar cheese.
3. Refrigerate 8-10 hours before serving.

Wilted Lettuce Salad

Marjory Garman
Florence, SC
Tree of Life & Queen Anne Star
Winnie Friese
Washington, NJ
Heart and Hands

Makes 8-10 servings

1 large bunch leaf lettuce
1 small onion, thinly sliced
3 slices lowfat bacon
2 tsp. sugar
¼ tsp. salt *or less*
Pepper to taste
¼ cup vinegar
1 egg, slightly beaten

1. Tear lettuce into pieces in large bowl. Add onion slices which have been separated. Set aside.
2. Fry bacon and reserve drippings. Crumble bacon slices and set aside.
3. Stir sugar, salt, pepper, vinegar and egg into bacon drippings. Heat to boiling and pour over lettuce immediately. Toss. Add bacon bits and toss again.
4. Serve warm.

Greek Peasant Salad

Joan T. Schneider
Seaford, NY
Double Irish Chain

Makes 6-8 servings

Salad:
1 large head romaine
    lettuce
2 medium tomatoes,
    wedged
1 large cucumber, sliced
6-8 radishes, thinly sliced
4-6 green onions, sliced
6 ozs. feta cheese, coarsely
    crumbled
¼ lb. Greek black olives
1 tsp. minced fresh mint
    (optional)

Dressing:
3 Tbsp. lemon juice
2 Tbsp. red wine vinegar
1 clove garlic, crushed
½ tsp. minced fresh
    oregano

1. Wash, drain and chill
lettuce. Tear into large
bowl. Add vegetables,
cheese and olives. Sprinkle
with mint.
2. Blend all dressing in-
gredients in small bowl
with whisk. Pour over
salad and toss lightly. Serve
immediately.

Pam's Caesar Salad

Pamela R. Kerschner
Stevensville, MD
Bunny Trail

Makes 12-15 servings

Dressing:
1 cup olive oil
⅓ cup red wine vinegar
3 Tbsp. fresh lemon juice
2 tsp. salt *or* less
1½ tsp. freshly ground
    black pepper
2 cloves garlic, peeled and
    halved

Salad:
3 large heads romaine
    lettuce
1 lb. mushrooms
16-oz. can pitted, ripe
    olives
¾ cup grated Parmesan
    cheese
½ box croutons

1. To prepare dressing
measure all ingredients into
container with tight-fitting
lid. Shake to blend. Refrigerate to chill.
2. Bring dressing to
room temperature. Remove
garlic pieces and discard.
3. Wash, drain and dry
romaine. Tear into large
mixing bowl.
4. Wash and dry mush-
rooms. Slice thinly into lettuce.
5. Drain and slice olives
into salad. Sprinkle with
Parmesan cheese.
6. Pour dressing over

salad and toss well to coat
all ingredients. Add croutons, toss and serve immediately.

Three-Bean Salad

Barbara F. Shie
Colorado Springs, CO
Pineapple

Makes 6-8 servings

Salad:
16-oz. can string beans,
    drained
16-oz. can wax beans,
    drained
16-oz. can kidney beans,
    drained
4-oz. can diced pimentos
2 small onions, diced
1 green pepper, diced

Dressing:
⅓ cup cooking oil
⅔ cup vinegar
⅔ cup sugar
½ tsp. pepper
1 tsp. salt *or* less
2 tsp. celery seeds

1. Combine all salad in-
gredients and set aside.
2. Combine all dressing
ingredients and pour over
salad. Toss well and refrigerate in covered container.
Better if prepared several
days in advance.

Variation:
I add a 16-oz. can black-

eyed peas and call this Four-Bean Salad. I also substitute the following dressing: ½ cup sugar, ½ cup vinegar, ½ cup cooking oil, 2 Tbsp. snipped parsley, ½ tsp. dried basil and ½ tsp. salt.

Shirley Norris
Walhonding, OH
Double Irish Chain

Going Away Salad

Judith Ann Govotsos
Monrovia, MD
Irish Chain

Makes 10-12 servings

Salad:
16-oz. can kidney beans, drained
16-oz. can wax beans, drained
16-oz. can chickpeas, drained
16-oz. can string beans, drained
1 large onion, thinly sliced
1 cucumber, thinly sliced
2 carrots, thinly sliced
4-5 cups shredded cabbage
3 stalks celery, diced

Dressing:
1 cup cooking oil
1⅓ cups vinegar
1 cup sugar
1 tsp. salt
½ tsp. pepper

1. Combine all salad ingredients and mix well.

2. Combine all dressing ingredients and mix well. Toss with salad and refrigerate up to one week before serving.

Frozen Slaw

Susie Braun, Rapid City, SD
Joan Kelly, Arnprior, ON
Rosalyn J. Clem
Silver Spring, MD
Anna Oberholtzer, Lititz, PA

Makes 6-10 servings

Salad:
1 medium head cabbage, finely shredded
1 tsp. salt
1 carrot, finely chopped
1 green pepper, finely chopped

Syrup:
1 cup vinegar

2 cups white sugar
¼ cup water
1 tsp. celery seed
1 tsp. mustard seed

1. Sprinkle salt over cabbage and let stand 1 hour at room temperature. Squeeze out any extra juices from cabbage. Add carrot and green pepper to cabbage.

2. Meanwhile, combine all syrup ingredients in medium saucepan and bring to a boil. Boil for 1 minute. Let cool to lukewarm and pour over cabbage, carrot and pepper mixture. Spoon into container and freeze before using.

Note: This mixture may be refrozen or it keeps well in the refrigerator. When you need to take a dish to a potluck, simply take out of freezer and leave. Works especially well in hot weather.

My mother grew up in Missouri among avid quilters, and all of her family quilts were very traditional. When she and my father retired, they moved to Tucson, Arizona. During the time of their 40th wedding anniversary, they planned a trip to West Virginia to visit my family. While I had not yet completed a full-size quilt, I decided to make them a Moon Over Mountain quilt—a Southwest pattern and very different from the other quilts in our family.

At the party Mom opened the package and just sat there. (She didn't know I had started to quilt.) Finding it hard to believe that I had made the quilt and with tears streaming down her face, she asked, "How did you know how?"

—Carol Weaver, Houston, TX

Red Cabbage Slaw

Virginia Dunkline
Florence, SC
Log Cabin

Makes 10-12 servings

Salad:
½ head red cabbage, grated
4 green onions, chopped
1 pkg. chicken-flavored
  Ramen noodles
½ cup toasted sliced
  almonds
2 Tbsp. sesame seed

Dressing:
2 Tbsp. sugar
½ cup cooking oil
1 tsp. salt
1 Tbsp. vinegar
½ tsp. pepper
Seasoning pkg. of Ramen
  noodles

1. Combine all salad ingredients and set aside.
2. Combine all dressing ingredients and mix well. Stir into cabbage mixture immediately before serving.

Variation:
To serve as a main dish add 3 diced, cooked chicken breasts to salad ingredients.
Doris Morelock
Alexandria, VA
The Links of Friendship

South River Cabbage Salad

Marsha Sands
Ocean City, MD
Amish Sparkle Star

Makes 6 servings

Salad:
½ head cabbage, thinly
  sliced
½ green pepper, thinly
  sliced
1 carrot, grated
1 celery stalk, chopped
1 apple, chopped
1 Tbsp. finely chopped
  onion

Dressing:
1 cup mayonnaise
1½ Tbsp. Worcestershire
  sauce
½ tsp. onion salt
2 Tbsp. prepared mustard
2 Tbsp. cider vinegar
½ cup sugar
½ tsp. pepper
½ tsp. celery seed

1. Combine all salad ingredients and set aside.
2. Combine all dressing ingredients and beat until thoroughly mixed. Chill.
3. Immediately before serving, toss dressing with vegetables.

Jellied Coleslaw

Joan Lemmler
Albuquerque, NM
Bearry Agee

Makes 8 servings

Salad:
3-oz. pkg. lime gelatin
3-oz. pkg. lemon gelatin
2 cups boiling water
12-14 ice cubes
1 tsp. salt
⅛ tsp. pepper
¼ tsp. garlic powder
3 Tbsp. cider vinegar
⅔ cup sour cream *or* yogurt
¼ cup finely sliced green
  onion
1 cup diced cucumber
½ cup diced green pepper
1½ cups finely shredded
  cabbage

Garnish:
8 leaves lettuce
8 slices cucumber
8 radish roses

1. Pour boiling water over lime and lemon gelatin in a large bowl. Stir until gelatin is dissolved. Add ice cubes and stir until mixture starts to set. Remove and discard any small pieces of ice. Add salt, pepper, garlic powder, vinegar and sour cream. Stir until smooth.
2. Stir in all vegetables. (If mixture has not set enough to hold vegetables, refrigerate for five minutes. Stir again.)

3. Pour into 8 individual molds or an oblong pan which has been lightly greased. Chill until well set.

4. To serve unmold or cut into eight servings. Serve on lettuce leaves with cucumber slices and radish roses.

Creamy Coleslaw

Dottie Geraci
Burtonsville, MD
Rosie Stars

Makes 6-8 servings

3-oz. pkg. lemon gelatin
¼ tsp. salt
1 cup boiling water
1 Tbsp. vinegar
½ cup cold water
½ cup mayonnaise
½ cup sour cream
1 tsp. grated onion
1 Tbsp. prepared mustard
3 cups finely shredded cabbage
2 Tbsp. chopped green pepper
1 Tbsp. chopped parsley

1. Dissolve gelatin and salt in boiling water. Add vinegar and cold water and mix well. Stir in all remaining ingredients, blending thoroughly.

2. Pour into mold or serving dish and chill until firm. Serve.

Broccoli Garden Salad

Susan Harms
Wichita, KS
Sampler

Makes 8 servings

Salad:
1 head broccoli
2-3 tomatoes
1 cucumber
1 green pepper

Dressing:
¼ cup sugar
½ tsp. paprika
½ tsp. onion powder
¼ cup vinegar
½ tsp. salt
½ tsp. celery seed
½ cup cooking oil

1. Wash, drain and dice broccoli flowerets and stem into serving dish. Dice tomatoes, cucumber and green pepper into dish and toss.

2. Combine all dressing ingredients and mix well. Pour over salad, toss and refrigerate at least 1 hour before serving.

Broccoli Cauliflower Salad

Edna Stoltzfus
Leola, PA
Log Cabin

Makes 20 servings

Salad:
8-10 slices bacon
1 head broccoli
1 head cauliflower
1 cup grated cheese
1 small onion, diced

Dressing:
½ cup sour cream
½ cup mayonnaise
½ cup sugar

1. Fry, drain and crumble bacon.

2. Chop broccoli and cauliflower into large serving dish. Add bacon, cheese and onion and toss.

3. Thoroughly mix all dressing ingredients. Pour over salad and mix well. Serve.

My chili has often been a lifesaver on days when all I want to do is quilt. I literally throw the ingredients into a crockpot in the morning and get right to my quilting.

When supper time rolls around, the members of my family simply help themselves. And I never have to interrupt my day of quilting to "get supper started."

—*Grace Ketcham, Pennsville, NJ*

Fresh Broccoli Salad

Beatrice Orgish
Richardson, TX
Bear Paw

Makes 8 servings

Salad:
2 bunches fresh broccoli
10 slices bacon, cooked
**   and crumbled**
⅔ cup raisins
¼-½ purple onion,
**   chopped**

Dressing:
1 cup mayonnaise
⅓ cup sugar
2 Tbsp. red wine vinegar

1. Wash and cut broccoli into bite-sized pieces.
2. Combine broccoli, bacon, raisins and onion in a large bowl.
3. In a separate bowl mix mayonnaise, sugar and vinegar. Pour dressing over salad and toss.
4. Refrigerate at least 2 hours before serving, tossing occasionally.

Variations:
Substitute ½-¾ cup sliced almonds for onion.
Jean H. Robinson
Cinnaminson, NJ
Little School Girl

Add 1 cup frozen peas and 1 cup sunflower seeds.
Laura Heller
Delanco, NJ
This Old House

Substitute 6 ozs. grated mozzarella cheese for raisins.
Barbara Sparks
Glen Burnie, MD
Study in Blue and White

Omit raisins and substitute bacon bits for bacon.
Rayann Rohrer
Allentown, PA
Mode of Transportation

Crunchy Salad

Darlene S. Rosenberry
Fayetteville, PA
Swan

Makes 6 servings

Salad:
1 lb. fresh broccoli
1 small head cauliflower
2-3 carrots, sliced
½ cup chopped celery
2 onions, sliced

Dressing:
⅔ cup mayonnaise
⅓ cup cooking oil
⅓ cup vinegar
¼ cup sugar
1 tsp. salt

1. Break broccoli and cauliflower into bite-sized pieces. Include broccoli stems.
2. Combine all salad ingredients and set aside.
3. Combine all dressing ingredients and mix well. Pour dressing over salad. Refrigerate at least 2 hours before serving.

Parmesan Salad

Ruth Day
Sturgis, SD
Double Jacob's Ladder

Makes 6 servings

Salad:
1 bunch broccoli
1 head cauliflower
6-8 slices bacon
1 medium onion, finely
**   chopped**

Dressing:
1 cup mayonnaise
¼ cup Parmesan cheese
¼ cup sugar

1. Break broccoli and cauliflower into bite-sized pieces. Include thinly sliced broccoli stem.
2. Fry, drain and crumble bacon.
3. Combine all salad ingredients and set aside.
4. Combine all dressing ingredients and mix well. Toss with salad and serve.

Several years ago I decided to serve caramel corn to a group of women who came to my home for a quilting bee. Needless to say, we had to suspend all quilting activity while we ate the popcorn.

—*Judy Mocho, Albuquerque, NM*

Hungarian Cucumber Salad

Maureen Csikasz
Wakefield, MA
Trip Around the World

Makes 4 servings

2 cucumbers
1 Tbsp. salt *or* less
½ cup water
¼ cup vinegar
⅛ cup sugar
Paprika

1. Peel and grate cucumbers. Sprinkle with salt and let stand 1 hour.
2. Squeeze excess juice out of cucumbers. Place cucumbers in serving bowl. Pour water, vinegar and sugar over cucumbers and mix lightly. Chill in refrigerator.
3. Sprinkle with paprika and serve.

Cucumber Salad

Colleen Kern
Oakland, NJ
Tumbling Blocks

Makes 4 servings

1 Tbsp. dehydrated onion flakes
¼ tsp. dried parsley
1 tsp. sugar
1 tsp. salt
1 Tbsp. lemon juice
1 tsp. celery seed
¼ cup vinegar
¼ tsp. Accent (optional)
⅛ tsp. pepper
2 cucumbers, peeled and sliced

1. Combine all ingredients in a bowl and stir well.
2. Refrigerate for several hours before serving.

Marinated Cucumbers

Teresa M. Prete
East Falmouth, MA
Double Wedding Ring

Makes 10-12 servings

1¼ cups wine vinegar
1 cup water
3 Tbsp. sugar
1 Tbsp. crushed dill weed
2 cloves garlic, crushed
Salt and pepper to taste
6 large cucumbers

1. Combine vinegar, water, sugar, dill, garlic, salt and pepper in medium saucepan. After bringing to a boil, lower heat and simmer for 5 minutes.
2. Peel cucumbers and slice thin pieces into a noncorrosive bowl.
3. Pour marinade over cucumbers and refrigerate at least 24 hours before serving.
4. Drain and serve on lettuce leaves.

Marinated Carrot Salad

Florence Heard
St. Marys, ON
Double Irish Chain

Makes 6-8 servings

2 lbs. carrots
1 medium onion
1 medium green pepper
½ cup tomato soup
¼ cup sugar
½ cup cooking oil
⅓ cup vinegar
½ tsp. dry mustard
½ tsp. salt
¼ tsp. pepper

1. Peel and cut carrots into ¼-inch diagonal slices. Cook in boiling salted water until just tender, about 6 to 8 minutes. (Do not overcook.) Drain.
2. Slice onion thinly and separate. Seed and cut green pepper into thin strips. Add onion rings and green pepper strips to carrots.
3. In a small jar combine all remaining ingredients. Shake to blend. Pour over vegetables. Marinate at least 12-24 hours in refrigerator.
4. To serve lift vegetables out of dressing and transfer to a serving bowl.

Marinated Mushrooms

Marlene Fonken
Upland, CA
Crazy Patch

Makes 8-10 servings

2 4-oz. jars whole mushrooms, drained
2 pkgs. artificial sweetener
1 tsp. dry mustard
¼ tsp. salt
⅓ cup water
⅓ cup red wine vinegar

1. In a small saucepan combine all ingredients except mushrooms. Bring to a boil and pour over mushrooms.
2. Cover and refrigerate at least 24 hours before serving.

Zucchini Couscous

Freda Gail Stern
Dallas, TX
Harley's Feathered Star

Makes 4 servings

1 cup instant couscous
½ cup boiling water
2 Tbsp. olive oil
2 cups diced zucchini
1 Tbsp. minced fresh mint leaves
2 Tbsp. minced parsley
¼ cup fresh lemon juice
Salt and pepper to taste

1. Cover couscous with boiling water in heatproof bowl. Gently separate grains with a fork. Stir in 1 Tbsp. olive oil. Refrigerate and continue stirring frequently until cooled, about 30 minutes.
2. Meanwhile, combine zucchini, mint, parsley, lemon juice and remaining olive oil.
3. Fold zucchini mixture into completely cooled couscous and chill another 30 minutes before serving. Season with salt and pepper.

Spinach Strawberry Salad

Deb Koelsch
Lancaster, PA
Handy Andy & Clown

Makes 6 servings

Salad:
12 ozs. fresh spinach
1 quart strawberries
2 tsp. sesame seed

Dressing:
½ cup cooking oil
¼ cup vinegar
¼ tsp. Worcestershire sauce
½ cup sugar
¼ tsp. paprika
1½ tsp. grated onion

1. Wash and drain spinach. Tear bite-sized pieces into serving bowl. Add strawberries and sesame seed and toss.

2. To prepare dressing blend together all ingredients.

3. Toss dressing with salad and serve immediately.

❖

Grandma Bartel's Cheese Salad

Cheryl Bartel
Hillsboro, KS
Traditional Sampler

Makes 10 servings

2 20-oz. cans pineapple chunks
3 egg yolks, beaten
½ cup sugar
1 heaping Tbsp. flour
½ lb. Velveeta cheese, cubed
1 small pkg. marshmallows

---

1. Drain pineapples and reserve juice.

2. In a saucepan combine egg yolks, sugar, flour and pineapple juice. Cook until clear, stirring frequently.

3. Remove from heat and add pineapple chunks, cheese and marshmallows and toss well.

❖

Cranberry Gelatin Salad

Marge Jarrett
Gaithersburg, MD
Grandmother's Flower Garden

Makes 12-16 servings

1 lb. fresh cranberries
2 cups ground apples
1½ cups sugar
1 tsp. lemon juice
6-oz. pkg. raspberry gelatin
½ cup chopped walnuts
½ cup chopped celery

---

1. Grind cranberries and apples separately in food grinder.

2. Combine cranberries, apples, sugar and lemon juice and let stand several hours, stirring occasionally.

3. Prepare gelatin according to package directions. When cooled, but not set, stir in fruit mixture, walnuts and celery.

4. Pour into serving dish and refrigerate until set.

Variation:
Omit apples. Add 1 cup sour cream along with walnuts and celery.
Julianna Csikasz
Wakefield, MA
Patchwork Baby Quilt

Our grandson, Brandon, stayed with us two days a week for about three years. He liked to watch me quilt. When he was two, he would stick quilting pins in rows and call that quilting. By the time he was three, he wanted a needle and thread. I did not knot the thread, and he could "sew" a long time. He wised up to me and asked for a knot in his thread. The last quilt he "helped" me with before going to nursery school was a Cat Quilt for his mother. I let his stitches in the quilt, and, of course, it has become a family conversation piece. One is never too young to learn to quilt!

—Violette Denney, Carrollton, GA

Frosted Cranberry Salad

Minnie A. Stoltzfus
Lancaster, PA
Log Cabin

Makes 12-15 servings

1 lb. cranberries
3 cups water
1 cup sugar
20-oz. can crushed
  pineapple
2 6-oz. pkgs. strawberry
  gelatin
3 cups boiling water
1 cup pineapple juice
¼ cup sugar
1 egg yolk
2 Tbsp. flour
1 cup butter
½ cup chopped nuts

1. Grind cranberries with 3 cups water in blender. Drain well. Add sugar and let stand 2 hours.
2. Drain pineapple, reserving juice. Add pineapple to cranberries and mix well.
3. Dissolve gelatin in boiling water. Cool. Stir cranberry mixture into gelatin and let set completely.
4. Add enough water to reserved pineapple juice to make 1 cup.
5. Combine juice, sugar, egg yolk, flour and butter in saucepan. Bring to a boil. Cool.
6. Spread cooled sauce over cranberry and pineapple gelatin. Chill.
7. Immediately before serving, sprinkle with nuts.

Cranberry Holiday Salad

Shirley Norris
Walhonding, OH
Double Irish Chain

Makes 12 servings

6-oz. pkg. raspberry gelatin
1 cup boiling water
16-oz. can whole berry
  cranberry sauce
20-oz. can crushed
  pineapple, drained
½ cup chopped walnuts
8-oz. pkg. cream cheese,
  softened
1 cup sour cream
¼ cup chopped walnuts

1. Combine gelatin and boiling water in a large bowl. Stir in cranberry sauce and break up into gelatin mixture. Add pineapple and ½ cup walnuts and mix well. Pour into 9" x 13" pan. Refrigerate until set.
2. Beat together cream cheese and sour cream and spread over salad. Sprinkle with ¼ cup walnuts and serve.

Easy Cranberry Salad

Ruth Liebelt
Rapid City, SD
Americana

Makes 10-12 servings

2 6-oz. pkgs. cherry gelatin
2 cups boiling water
16-oz. can whole cranberry
  sauce
16-oz. container sour cream

1. In a large bowl dissolve gelatin in boiling water. Stir in cranberries and refrigerate.
2. When starting to set, add sour cream, beating lightly with electric beater or whisk until well mixed.
3. Pour into mold and refrigerate overnight.
4. Unmold and serve.

Cranberry Frozen Salad

Margaret Jarrett
Anderson, IN
Country Love

Makes 10-12 servings

8-oz. pkg. cream cheese,
  softened
1 cup sugar
1 pkg. frozen, cranberry
  orange relish

1 cup chopped nuts
15-oz. can crushed
   pineapple, drained
1 tsp. lemon juice
1 cup whipping cream

1. Cream together cream cheese and sugar. Add cranberry orange relish and fold in nuts. Add pineapple and lemon juice and mix well.

2. Beat whipping cream until stiff. Fold into salad mixture. Chill in refrigerator at least overnight. May be frozen before serving if desired.

Cranberry Salad

Nancy George
De Pere, WI
Hearts and Strings

Makes 4-6 servings

4 cups fresh cranberries
1¼ cups sugar
2 cups halved red grapes
1 cup pineapple tidbits
½ cup chopped walnuts
1 cup whipped topping

1. Put cranberries through coarse grinder. Sprinkle with sugar and let stand overnight. Drain well.

2. Add grapes, pineapple and walnuts to cranberries and mix well. Fold in whipped topping and serve.

❖

Blueberry Salad

Tommie Freeman
Carrollton, GA
Olympic Quilt

Makes 10-12 servings

2 3-oz. pkgs. blackberry
**   gelatin**
2 cups boiling water
15-oz. can blueberries
8-oz. can crushed
**   pineapple**
8-oz. pkg. cream cheese
½ cup sugar
1 cup sour cream
½ tsp. vanilla
1 cup chopped pecans

1. Dissolve gelatin in boiling water.

2. Drain blueberries and pineapple, reserving liquid. Add enough water to liquid to make 1½ cups. Stir liquid into gelatin mixture. Stir in blueberries and pineapple and pour into 9" x 13" casserole dish. Refrigerate until set.

3. Cream together cream cheese and sugar. Add sour cream and vanilla and mix well. Spread over salad. Sprinkle with chopped pecans and serve.

❖

Raspberry Crown Salad

Anita Falk
Mountain Lake, MN
Double Irish Chain

Makes 8-10 servings

3-oz. pkg. raspberry gelatin
2 cups boiling water
¾ cup cranberry juice
1 cup diced apples
¼ cup chopped celery
¼ cup chopped walnuts
3-oz. pkg. lemon gelatin
1 cup whipped topping
½ cup mayonnaise

1. Dissolve raspberry gelatin in 1 cup boiling water. Add cranberry juice and chill about 1 hour, until slightly thickened. Fold in apples, celery and walnuts. Spoon into 6-cup ring mold and chill until set, about 15 minutes.

2. Dissolve lemon gelatin in 1 cup boiling water. Chill until slightly thickened, about 45 minutes.

3. Combine whipped topping and mayonnaise and fold into lemon gelatin. Spoon onto raspberry gelatin. Chill until firm, at least 4 hours.

4. Unmold and serve.

Mom's Cider Salad

LuAnne S. Taylor
Canton, PA
Log Cabin Barnraising

Makes 8 servings

3-oz. pkg. lemon gelatin
2 cups hot cider
2 Tbsp. lemon juice
1 cup chopped red apples
½ cup broken walnuts
½ cup sliced, pitted dates
1 Tbsp. grated orange rind
   (optional)
8 lettuce leaves

1. Dissolve gelatin in hot cider. Add lemon juice and chill until partially set.
2. Fold in apples, walnuts, dates and orange rind. Turn into 1-quart mold. Chill until firm.
3. Serve on lettuce leaves.

Grape Salad

Ann Harrison
Garland, TX
Strawberry Patch

Makes 10-12 servings

2 Tbsp. butter *or* margarine
2 Tbsp. flour
1 cup milk
1 large bag marshmallows
2 lbs. seedless green grapes
15-oz. can crushed
   pineapple, drained
1 cup chopped pecans

1. Melt butter in saucepan. Add flour and stir until bubbly. Add milk and heat over low temperature until mixture thickens, stirring frequently. Add marshmallows and continue heating, stirring constantly until marshmallows are melted.
2. Remove from heat and stir in grapes, pineapple and pecans.
3. Refrigerate several hours before serving.

Pineapple Salad

Marilyn Maurstad
Beatrice, NE
Ohio Star Variation
Mary Brubacker
Barnett, MO
Broken Star

Makes 8-10 servings

3-oz. pkg. lime gelatin
3-oz. pkg. lemon gelatin
2 cups boiling water
1 cup crushed pineapple
½ cup sugar
1½ Tbsp. lemon juice
½ pint whipping cream
1 cup grated mild cheddar
   cheese

1. Dissolve gelatins in boiling water. Chill until partially set, about 45-50 minutes.
2. Combine undrained pineapple, sugar and lemon juice. Fold into partially set gelatin. Chill another 15-20 minutes.
3. Meanwhile, whip cream. Combine whipped cream and cheese and fold into partially set gelatin.
4. Pour into glass serving dish and chill until firm. Serve.

When I was expecting our first child, we were enjoying a weekend visit from my parents and paternal grandmother from Iowa and my maternal grandmother from Pennsylvania. My mother-in-law suggested on the spur of the moment that we quilt a baby quilt while "we have all these quilting grandmas together." So we five women spent the next several days around the quilt anticipating the arrival of a new generation in our family. We sent the quilt to Texas where my husband's only living grandmother sewed the binding on, and I had a baby quilt stitched and bound with love by six women from three generations.

—*Karen Unternahrer, Shipshewana, IN*

Pineapple Custard Salad

Betty Caudle
Colorado Springs, CO
Double Wedding Ring

Makes 15-20 servings

6-oz. pkg. lemon gelatin
2 cups boiling water
1½ cups cold water
20-oz. can crushed
   pineapple
4 bananas, diced
2 cups miniature
   marshmallows
¾ cup sugar
3 Tbsp. flour
2 eggs, beaten
1½ cups pineapple juice
3 Tbsp. butter
3-oz. pkg. cream cheese
1 cup whipped topping
¼ cup grated cheddar
   cheese

1. Dissolve gelatin in boiling water. Stir in cold water and let set until syrupy.
2. Drain pineapple, reserving juice.
3. Stir pineapple, bananas and marshmallows into partially set gelatin. Chill until firm.
4. Meanwhile, combine sugar, flour, eggs, pineapple juice and butter in top of double boiler. Cook until thickened, stirring occasionally. Cool.
5. Cream cream cheese with mixer. Combine cream cheese and whipped topping and fold into cooled custard mix. Spread over firm gelatin and sprinkle with grated cheese.

Dump Salad

Joyce Niemann
Fruitland Park, FL
Lap Sampler

Makes 6 servings

8-oz. can crushed
   pineapple, well drained
3-oz. pkg. orange *or* lime
   gelatin
8-oz. carton cottage cheese
4-oz. carton whipped
   topping
6 lettuce leaves

1. Combine pineapple and dry gelatin and mix until gelatin has dissolved. Dump in cottage cheese and whipped topping and stir.
2. Refrigerate until serving time.
3. Serve on 6 individual plates on bed of lettuce.

Lazy Day Salad

Dorothy Shank
Sterling, IL
Anniversary Quilt

Makes 8-10 servings

16-oz. can crushed
   pineapple, drained
16-oz. can fruit cocktail,
   drained
2 11-oz. cans mandarin
   oranges, drained
1 small pkg. instant vanilla
   pudding
8-oz. carton whipped
   topping
1 cup chopped pecans

1. Combine pineapple, fruit cocktail, oranges, dry pudding and whipped topping. Mix well and chill.
2. Sprinkle pecans over top and serve.

Sawdust Salad

Melissa Myers
Indian Head, MD
Bow Tie

Makes 12 servings

3-oz. pkg. orange gelatin
3-oz. pkg. lemon gelatin
16-oz. can crushed
    pineapple, drained
3-4 bananas
1-2 cups miniature
    marshmallows
1 small pkg. instant vanilla
    pudding
8-oz. pkg. cream cheese
8-oz. carton whipped
    topping
½ cup grated cheese *or*
    grated coconut

1. Mix lemon and orange gelatins and prepare according to package directions. Stir in crushed pineapple after gelatin has slightly set. Pour into 9" x 13" pan and let set completely.
2. Slice bananas over gelatin. Spread marshmallows over bananas.
3. Prepare pudding according to package directions. Spread over marshmallows.
4. Beat together cream cheese and whipped topping. Spread over pudding layer.
5. Top with grated cheese or coconut and serve.

Orange Salad

Mildred Kennel
Atglen, PA
Sailboat

Makes 10-12 servings

3-oz. pkg. orange gelatin
24-oz. carton cottage cheese
20-oz. can crushed
    pineapple *or* fruit
    cocktail, drained
11-oz. can mandarin
    oranges, drained
8-oz. carton whipped
    topping

1. Reserve 1 cup juice from pineapple and oranges. Bring to a boil and combine with orange gelatin. Chill until partially set.
2. Fold all remaining ingredients into partially set gelatin.
3. Refrigerate until firm and serve.

Orange Gelatin Salad

Vivian Angstadt
Mertztown, PA
Dahlia

Makes 10 servings

6-oz. pkg. orange gelatin
½ cup sugar
½ cup boiling water
2 cups whipped topping
8-oz. pkg. cream cheese
11-oz. can mandarin
    oranges

1. Dissolve gelatin and sugar in boiling water. Let cool until starting to set.
2. Beat together whipped topping and cream cheese. Stir until smooth.
3. When gelatin has slightly set, fold in oranges with their juice. Fold in whipped topping mixture.
4. Refrigerate overnight before serving.

Orange Buttermilk Salad

Audrey L. Kneer
Williamsfield, IL
Snowball Nine Patch

Makes 8-10 servings

**8-oz. can crushed
   pineapple
6-oz. pkg. orange gelatin
2 cups buttermilk
8-oz. carton whipped
   topping
½ cup chopped nuts**

1. Bring pineapple with juice to a boil. Stir in gelatin and cool to room temperature.
2. Stir in buttermilk. Fold in whipped topping and nuts.
3. Chill at least 4 hours before serving.

Gingerale Salad

Sarah S. King
Gordonville, PA
Giant Dahlia

Makes 12-15 servings

**Layer 1:
2 Tbsp. unflavored gelatin
2½ Tbsp. cold water
1 cup boiling water
¾ cup sugar
2 Tbsp. lemon juice
2 cups gingerale
8-oz. can crushed
   pineapple
1 cup diced apples**

**Layer 2:
2 Tbsp. flour
½ cup sugar
2 eggs, beaten
1½ Tbsp. butter
1 cup pineapple juice
8-oz. container whipped
   topping
1 cup chopped nuts
   (optional)**

1. To prepare first layer dissolve gelatin in cold water. Add boiling water and sugar and stir until dissolved. Add lemon juice and gingerale. Chill until partially set.
2. Drain pineapple and reserve juice. Fold pineapple and apples into gelatin. Pour into pan or mold and chill until set.
3. To prepare second layer combine flour and sugar in a saucepan. Add eggs, butter and 1 cup pineapple juice (add water to make 1 cup if necessary). Heat through, stirring constantly. Cool completely.
4. Fold in whipped topping. Spoon over first layer and sprinkle with nuts if desired. Serve.

Soups

Zucchini Soup

Janet S. Gillespie
Gilbertsville, KY
Log Cabin Schoolhouse

Makes 4 servings

2 tsp. cooking oil
1 cup chopped onion
1 clove garlic, minced
4 medium zucchini,
   coarsely chopped
4 tsp. chicken-flavored
   bouillon granules
1 Tbsp. lemon juice
3 cups water
2 tsp. dill
½ cup sour cream

1. In large saucepan heat oil over medium-low heat. sauté onion and garlic about 5 minutes or until soft.

2. Stir in zucchini, chicken bouillon granules, lemon juice and water and bring to a boil. Reduce heat and simmer 15 minutes.

3. Purée mixture in food processor or blender. Pour into serving dish and quickly whisk in dill and sour cream. Serve.

Cheese Broccoli Soup

Lola Kennel
Strang, NE
Broken Star & Appliqued Roses

Makes 4-6 servings

1 small onion, chopped
2 Tbsp. butter
3 Tbsp. flour
2 cups milk
2 chicken bouillon cubes
1½ cups boiling water
2 cups shredded cheese
½ tsp. salt
½ tsp. thyme
1 Tbsp. garlic salt
Dash pepper
1 cup cooked, chopped
   broccoli

1. Sauté onion in butter until tender. Stir in flour and heat until bubbly.

Gradually add milk and heat slowly, stirring constantly.

2. Dissolve bouillon cubes in boiling water. Add to white sauce with cheese, salt, thyme, garlic salt and pepper and heat through.

3. Stir in cooked broccoli and serve.

Broccoli Soup

Amanda Schlabach
Millersburg, OH
*Wedding Ring
& Lancaster Rose*

Makes 4 servings

2 cups water
2 medium potatoes
10-oz. pkg. frozen broccoli
12-oz. can evaporated milk
1 cup grated sharp cheese
1 tsp. seasoning salt

1. Bring water to a boil. Slice potatoes and put into water. Add broccoli and

cook until tender.

2. Add the remaining ingredients and simmer for 10 minutes on very low heat because it burns easily.

Sweet and Sour Cabbage Soup

Freda Gail Stern
Dallas, TX
Harley's Feathered Star

Makes 10 servings

3-4-lb. chuck roast with bone
9 cups water
2-lb. head cabbage, shredded
1½ cups diced onion
3-4 carrots, sliced
2 stalks celery, diced
2 16-oz. cans tomatoes
8 ginger snaps
1 tsp. salt
½ tsp. celery salt
½ tsp. dill weed
Freshly ground pepper to taste
⅓ cup white sugar
¼ cup light brown sugar
1 tsp. sour salt (citric acid)

1. In large soup kettle combine chuck roast and water and bring to a boil. Simmer for ½ hour. Skim water.
2. Add cabbage, onion, carrots, celery, tomatoes, ginger snaps and all seasonings except sugars and sour

salt. Bring to a boil. Lower heat and simmer 3-4 hours.

3. Add sugars and sour salt. Cook over medium heat for 15 minutes. Taste and adjust seasoning as desired.

4. Cool and refrigerate for at least one day before serving.

5. Before reheating remove bone, cutting meat into bite-sized pieces. Reheat and serve.

Russian Cabbage Soup

Dottie Geraci
Burtonsville, MD
Rosie Star

Makes 10-12 servings

Beef Stock:
1-lb. brisket
5-10 beef marrow bones, cracked
4 quarts water
1 large onion, quartered
1 tsp. salt
1 large carrot, sliced
2 celery tops, diced
6 sprigs parsley
2 bay leaves

Soup:
4 Tbsp. butter
2 cups onions, thinly sliced
2 lbs. cabbage, shredded
1 Tbsp. parsley
1 cup diced celery
2 carrots, sliced

3 medium potatoes, diced
3 tomatoes, chopped
1 tsp. salt
Freshly ground pepper to taste
Sour cream

1. At least one day before preparing soup bring brisket, bones and water to a boil in a heavy pot. Skim off foam. Add remaining stock ingredients. Reduce heat and simmer 1-1½ hours. Remove meat, dice and set aside.

2. Simmer stock another 1-2 hours. Strain stock and refrigerate.

3. Before preparing soup, remove layer of fat from top of refrigerated beef stock.

4. To prepare soup melt butter in large soup kettle. Add onions and cook 8-10 minutes until soft. Stir in cabbage, parsley, celery and carrots. Cover and simmer 15 minutes.

5. Add beef stock, diced beef and potatoes to soup kettle. Simmer another 30-40 minutes. Add tomatoes and cook 10 minutes. Add salt and pepper to taste.

6. Serve with sour cream.

Country Cabbage Soup

Bea Marxen
Bellville, TX
Baltimore Album

Makes 4-6 servings

½ lb. ground beef
4 cups shredded green
  cabbage
1 cup finely diced potatoes
1 cup finely diced carrots
½ cup chopped onion
3 Tbsp. butter
1 Tbsp. flour
1½ cups beef broth
1½ cups Hidden Valley
  Ranch dressing

1. Brown beef in large saucepan and drain excess fat.
2. Add cabbage, potatoes, carrots and onion. Stir in butter and cook until potatoes are tender but not brown, about 5 minutes. Stir in flour.
3. Add remaining ingredients and simmer about 20 minutes. Serve.

Hearty French Market Bean Soup

Mitzi McGlynchey
Downingtown, PA
Bear Paw

Makes 10-12 servings

1 lb. assorted beans
2 quarts water
1 quart chicken stock
1 Tbsp. salt
1 ham hock
2 bay leaves
½ tsp. dried thyme
28-oz. can tomatoes,
  chopped
2 cups chopped onion
2 cups chopped celery
1 clove garlic, mashed
8 ozs. smoked sausage,
  sliced
8 ozs. chicken breast, diced

1. Wash and soak beans at least 2 hours, preferably overnight.
2. In a large soup kettle combine beans, water, stock, salt, ham hock, bay leaves and thyme. Cover and simmer for 2½-3 hours.
3. Add tomatoes, onion and celery. Cover and simmer 1½ hours.
4. Add garlic, sausage and chicken. Cover and simmer 40 minutes. Serve.

Black Bean Soup

Kelly Wagoner
Albuquerque, NM
Rainbows in Your Rafters

Makes 3 quarts soup

3 cups dry black beans
6-8 cups water
1 Tbsp. cooking oil
3 Tbsp. honey
4 carrots, chopped
1 large onion, chopped
3 stalks celery, chopped
1 green bell pepper,
  chopped
Salt and pepper (optional)
1 whole orange

1. Soak washed beans 2-3 hours or overnight. Cook beans in water, oil and honey until tender. (To speed process, precook beans for 5 minutes in pressure cooker.) Put through blender.
2. Return blended beans to soup pot. Add vegetables and orange which has been cut in half. Simmer 45 minutes to 1 hour or until vegetables are tender. Gently squeeze out orange halves into soup and discard shells. Serve.

Note: This wonderful vegetarian's soup is delightful served with homemade whole wheat bread. Better the second day.

Refried Bean Soup

Betty Krueger
Rogue River, OR
Crazy Patch

Makes 4-6 servings

½ cup chopped onion
¼ cup chopped celery
2 cloves garlic, minced
1 tsp. olive oil
2 16-oz. cans refried beans
1 cup canned tomatoes, chopped
2 cups water
1 cup grated cheddar cheese
1 bag tortilla chips

1. Sauté onion, celery and garlic in olive oil until tender.
2. In a saucepan combine refried beans, canned tomatoes and water. Heat over medium heat. Adjust water to desired consistency.
3. Add sautéed vegetables and simmer together about 5 minutes.
4. Top with grated cheese and serve with tortilla chips.

Bean and Potato Soup

Jan Carroll
Morton, IL
Columbus Challenge

Makes 6 servings

1 lb. mixed dried beans
16-oz. can chicken broth
3-5 stalks celery, diced
1 onion, chopped
1 carrot, grated
1 bay leaf
5-7 new potatoes, diced
4 cups water
8-oz. can tomato sauce

1. Prepare beans according to directions, soaking for at least 2 hours.
2. Combine all ingredients except tomato sauce in a Dutch oven or large soup kettle. Simmer 2-6 hours. After 2 hours add tomato sauce and heat through. Remove bay leaf before serving.
3. If desired, add more water during last half hour to dilute soup to desired consistency.

Potato Soup

Silva Beachy
Millersburg, OH
Lone Star

Makes 6-8 servings

6-8 slices bacon
4 large potatoes, diced
¼ tsp. salt (optional)
1 onion, chopped
2 carrots, diced
½ cup butter
¾ cup flour
4 cups milk
½ cup grated cheese

1. Fry bacon until crisp. Crumble and set aside.
2. To bacon drippings add potatoes, onion and carrots. Add enough water to cover vegetables. Boil until potatoes are tender.
3. Meanwhile, melt butter in separate saucepan. Add flour and stir until smooth, cooking about 1 minute. Add milk, blending until smooth, and cook until mixture thickens, stirring constantly.
4. Add white sauce to cooked vegetables and heat through. (For a thinner soup add more milk.)
5. Immediately before serving, add reserved bacon. Garnish with grated cheese.

My grandmother was a quilter and I have many memories of sitting beside her, listening and watching as she sewed her quilts. We used those quilts on our beds, as ground cover at picnics, to turn chairs into rainy day caves and to make tents out of clotheslines. Today they are my heirlooms, but they certainly were not handled with white gloves.

—*Grace K. Bruce, Albuquerque, NM*

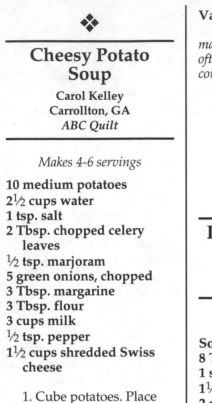

Cheesy Potato Soup

Carol Kelley
Carrollton, GA
ABC Quilt

Makes 4-6 servings

10 medium potatoes
2½ cups water
1 tsp. salt
2 Tbsp. chopped celery
  leaves
½ tsp. marjoram
5 green onions, chopped
3 Tbsp. margarine
3 Tbsp. flour
3 cups milk
½ tsp. pepper
1½ cups shredded Swiss
  cheese

1. Cube potatoes. Place in large, heavy kettle with water, salt, celery leaves, marjoram and white part of onions. Bring to a boil. Reduce heat and simmer 30 minutes.

2. Remove from heat and mash undrained vegetables. Set aside.

3. In another saucepan melt margarine and blend in flour. Cook until mixture bubbles, stirring constantly. Slowly add milk and cook until thickened, stirring constantly.

4. Stir white sauce into potato mixture. Add green onion tops, pepper and cheese. Heat over medium to low heat until cheese melts. Serve.

Variation:
I always use a blender to mash the vegetables. Also I often serve with crumbled bacon bits on top.
Grace Ketcham
Pennsville, NJ
Hearts and Flowers

Potato Rivel Soup

Linda Baker
Arnold, MD
Tree of Life

Makes 4 servings

Soup:
8 Tbsp. butter
1 small onion, diced
1½ quarts water
2 medium potatoes, cubed
2 stalks celery, diced
1 large onion, diced
1 tsp. celery seed
Salt and pepper to taste

Rivels:
1 cup minus 2 Tbsp. flour
Dash salt and pepper
1 egg

1. Melt butter in 3-quart pan until browned. Add small onion and brown until very dark. Discard onion. Add water and bring to a boil. Add vegetables and celery seed and bring to a boil.

2. To prepare rivels put flour in a bowl. Stir in salt and pepper. Make a well and drop egg into well. Stir with a fork until crumbly.

3. Drop rivels, one tablespoon at a time, into boiling soup. Simmer for 20-30 minutes.

4. Season with salt and pepper and serve.

Wild Rice Soup

Lee Ann Hazlett
Freeport, IL
Snowbound

Makes 6 servings

½ lb. bacon
1 onion, diced
½ cup chopped celery
3 Tbsp. butter *or* margarine
3 Tbsp. flour
½ tsp. thyme
½ tsp. paprika
1 Tbsp. Worcestershire
  sauce
10¾-oz. can chicken broth
2 cups milk
1 cup cooked wild rice

1. Fry, drain and crumble bacon. Set aside.

2. Sauté onion and celery in butter. Stir in flour, thyme and paprika and heat until bubbly. Add Worcestershire sauce, chicken broth and milk and heat, stirring until thickened.

3. Fold in wild rice and bacon and serve.

Elegant Wild Rice Soup

Jean Swift
Comfrey, MN
Starry Geese

Makes 6 servings

2 Tbsp. butter
1 Tbsp. minced onion
¼ cup flour
4 cups chicken broth
2 cups cooked wild rice
½ tsp. salt
1 cup half-and-half
2 Tbsp. dry sherry
  (optional)
Minced parsley *or* chives

1. Melt butter in saucepan and sauté onion until tender. Blend in flour, stirring constantly. Gradually add broth and cook, stirring constantly until mixture thickens slightly.
2. Stir in rice and salt and simmer about 5 minutes.
3. Blend in half-and-half and sherry and heat to serving temperature.
4. Garnish with minced parsley or chives and serve.

Crab Corn Bisque

Judy Miller
Columbia, MD
Cape Hatteras Sunrise

Makes 6 servings

2 Tbsp. margarine
¼ cup chopped onion
¼ cup chopped bell pepper
¼ cup chopped celery
¼ tsp. thyme
10¾-oz. can cream of potato soup
1½ cups milk
17-oz. can creamed corn
12-oz. can imitation crab meat

1. Melt margarine in a 3-quart casserole dish in microwave on high.
2. Add chopped vegetables and thyme and cover with plastic wrap which has several slits in top. Cook in microwave on high for 5 minutes, stirring one time.
3. Stir in all remaining ingredients, cover with vented plastic wrap and microwave on high for 7 minutes or until boiling hot. Serve.

Cream of Corn Crab Soup

Jul Hoober
New Holland, PA
Roman Stripe

Makes 10-12 servings

8-oz. pkg. cream cheese
3 cups sour cream
2 7-oz. cans crab meat
Juice of ½ lemon
Salt and pepper to taste
¼ tsp. garlic powder
4 Tbsp. butter
4 Tbsp. flour
2-3 cups milk
1½-2 cups corn
1-2 cups croutons

1. Beat cream cheese until smooth. Add sour cream, crab, lemon juice and seasonings and mix well.
2. In a large saucepan melt butter. Add flour and cook until bubbly. Turn to low heat and slowly add milk, stirring constantly to make a smooth white sauce. Add corn and cream cheese mixture and heat through, stirring until smooth.
3. Serve with croutons.

> Even though I am legally blind, I was able to piece a Lone Star wall hanging in Christmas colors last summer. I put masking tape on my sewing machine to indicate where the fabric should be as I stitched it.
>
> —*Mary Elizabeth Bartlet, Schenectady, NY*

Seafood Soup

Irene Dewar
Pickering, ON
Barns

Makes 6 servings

1 Tbsp. butter
2 Tbsp. green onions, minced
2 Tbsp. lemon juice
½ bay leaf
¼ tsp. dried thyme
2 cups whipping cream
1½ cups chicken stock
1 tsp. salt
1½ tsp. ground pepper
7-oz. can shrimp *or* fish flakes
1 tsp. cornstarch
1 Tbsp. water
2 Tbsp. sherry (optional)
1 Tbsp. parsley, chopped

1. Melt butter in large saucepan. Sauté onions. Add lemon juice, bay leaf and thyme and cook about 3-4 minutes until liquid is reduced, stirring frequently.
2. Blend in cream, chicken stock, salt, pepper and seafood. Slowly bring just to a boil. Reduce heat immediately.
3. Dissolve cornstarch in water and stir into soup. Simmer for 15 minutes.
4. Add sherry if desired and simmer an additional 5 minutes. Remove bay leaf. Ladle soup into heated bowls. Sprinkle with parsley and serve.

Oyster Stew

Juanita Marner
Shipshewana, IN
Giant Dahlia Tablecloth

Makes 2-4 servings

8-oz. can oysters
2 Tbsp. margarine
1-1½ cups milk
¼ tsp. celery seed
Dash cayenne pepper
Dash paprika

1. Drain and reserve liquid from oysters.
2. Place margarine in 1-quart casserole dish. Microwave on high until melted, 30-45 seconds. Add oysters and cover. Microwave on high until edges are curled, 2-4 minutes.
3. Add enough milk to oyster liquid to measure 1½ cups. Add milk mixture, celery seed and cayenne pepper to oysters and cover. Microwave on medium high (70% power) until mixture is hot, 4 to 5 minutes. Sprinkle with paprika and serve.

Hot and Sour Soup

Marlene Fonken
Upland, CA
Crazy Patch

Makes 12 servings

10 ozs. boneless, skinless chicken breast
6½ cups chicken broth
2 cups shredded Chinese cabbage
2 cups shredded carrots
2 cups sliced fresh mushrooms
1 Tbsp. soy sauce
12 ozs. tofu
¼ cup rice vinegar
½ tsp. pepper
¼ cup cornstarch
¼ cup water
4-5 green onion tops, diced

1. Cut uncooked chicken breast into strips.
2. Combine chicken breast, chicken broth, cabbage, carrots, mushrooms and soy sauce and bring to a boil. Reduce heat and simmer for 5 minutes.
3. Cut tofu into strips.
4. Add tofu, rice vinegar and pepper to chicken soup and bring to a boil again. Boil for 1 minute.
5. Combine cornstarch and water and stir into soup. Heat, stirring until slightly thickened.
6. Immediately before serving, sprinkle with green onion tops.

Chicken Soup

Elaine Untracht Pawelko
Monroe Township, NJ
Bride's Bouquet

Makes 8 servings

5-lb. stewing hen
Water to cover
1 Tbsp. salt *or* less
1 large onion, diced
3 ribs celery, chopped
2 carrots, diced
1 small parsnip, diced
2 small turnips, sliced
1-2 leeks, diced
1 small handful fresh dill
  sprigs

1. Rinse chicken and trim off excess fat. Place in soup pot. Add giblets from hen. Add water to cover and salt. Cover pot and heat to boiling. Uncover and skim.
2. Add vegetables to pot. Cover and simmer over low heat for 2 hours. Remove chicken from soup. Debone and cut meat into bite-sized pieces. Return chicken to broth.
3. Add dill sprigs and heat through.

Note: Soup is best when made a day in advance. Before reheating, remove excess fat which has formed on top.

Cheesy Turkey Chowder

Mrs. Mahlon Miller
Hutchinson, KS

Makes 6 servings

2 turkey wings *or* 1 turkey
  drumstick
1 tsp. salt
1 medium onion, chopped
1 cup chopped carrots
1 cup chopped celery
1 cup chopped potatoes
2 cups milk
6 Tbsp. flour
4 Tbsp. butter
1 cup shredded cheddar
  cheese

1. In a large saucepan cook turkey, salt and onion in water to cover. Simmer until meat is tender.
2. Remove meat from broth. Cool, debone and dice into small pieces. Set aside.
3. Add water to make 4 cups broth. Add carrots, celery and potatoes and simmer until tender.
4. Gradually blend milk into flour until mixture is smooth. Stir milk and flour mixture into turkey broth. Add butter and cheese and cook over medium heat until thickened, stirring constantly.
5. Add turkey meat to chowder and heat through. Serve.

Beef Chili with Zucchini

Sue Gierhart
Voorhees, NJ
Friendship Quilt

Makes 6 servings

¾ lb. lean ground meat
1½ cups chopped onions
1½ lbs. zucchini
16-oz. can red kidney beans
28-oz. can tomatoes
6-oz. can tomato paste
½ cup water
1 Tbsp. chili powder
1 tsp. cumin
4 cups cooked brown rice
¾ cup shredded sharp
  cheddar cheese
6 green onions, minced

1. Cook ground meat and onions in 4-quart Dutch oven over medium-high heat, stirring frequently.
2. Cut zucchini into small pieces. Drain and rinse kidney beans.
3. When meat is browned, add zucchini, beans, tomatoes, tomato paste, water, chili powder and cumin. Stir gently just until blended. Cover and simmer for 10 minutes. Uncover and simmer 15 minutes longer, stirring occasionally.
4. Spoon over rice. Sprinkle with cheese and green onions. Serve.

Amish Chili

Catherine Esh
Spring Mills, PA
Pillow Tops

Makes 6 servings

1 lb. lean ground beef
½ cup chopped onion
½ cup chopped celery
3 Tbsp. flour
¼ cup brown sugar
¼ cup ketchup
4 cups tomato juice
2-3 Tbsp. chili powder
16-oz. can kidney beans
Salt and pepper to taste

1. Brown ground beef, onion and celery. Drain excess fat. Add flour and heat through, stirring constantly. Add all remaining ingredients and mix well.
2. Cover and simmer 30 minutes. Serve.

Chili California

Piecemakers Country Store
Costa Mesa, CA
Cover Quilt for Calendar

Makes 6-8 servings

1 cup chopped onion
½ cup chopped celery
1 cup diced jicama
½ cup sliced carrots
1 cup chopped green
pepper
2 cloves garlic, minced
2 Tbsp. olive oil
2 beef bouillon cubes
1½ tsp. cumin
1½ tsp. chili powder
8-oz. can no-salt tomato sauce
2 16-oz. cans no-salt whole tomatoes, undrained
½ cup water
16-oz. can pinto beans, drained
16-oz. can chili beans, undrained
½ cup shredded cheddar cheese

1. In a Dutch oven sauté onion, celery, jicama, carrots, green pepper and garlic in oil until crisp tender. Add bouillon cubes, cumin, chili powder, tomato sauce, tomatoes and water. Bring to a boil.
2. Cover and simmer for 20 minutes, stirring occasionally. Uncover and simmer to desired thickness and until vegetables are tender, 10-20 minutes.
3. Stir in beans and heat through.
4. Sprinkle cheese over top and serve immediately.

Note: This is a low-calorie chili which has lost none of its good full flavor.

Crockpot Chili

Grace Ketcham
Pennsville, NJ
Hearts and Flowers

Makes 6 servings

1 lb. ground meat
1 medium onion, chopped
2 tsp. chili powder
2 bay leaves
1 tsp. Worcestershire sauce
15-oz. can tomato sauce
16-oz. can pork and beans
16-oz. can chili beans
1-2 hot peppers, chopped
1 cup grated cheddar cheese

1. In a skillet brown ground meat and drain excess fat.
2. Combine all ingredients except cheese in a crockpot.
3. Cover and cook approximately 2 hours on high heat, stirring occasionally. Reduce heat and cook on low another 3-4 hours, stirring occasionally.
4. Serve with grated cheddar cheese.

> **Each Tuesday I attend the meeting of the Bloomingdale Grange Quilters where we spend time quilting and enjoying a potluck lunch. Believe it or not, our dues are still only 10 cents a year.**
>
> —*Eleanor Larson, Glen Lyon, PA*

Crockpot Chili Con Carne

Katherine A. Schwartz
Freeport, IL
Double Irish Chain

Makes 8-10 servings

2 lbs. ground beef
2 cups chopped onion
2 cloves garlic, crushed
3 Tbsp. chili powder
1 tsp. salt
1 tsp. paprika
1 tsp. oregano
1 tsp. ground cumin
$\frac{1}{2}$ tsp. cayenne pepper
$\frac{1}{2}$ cup beef stock *or* tomato juice
28-oz. can tomatoes
16-oz. can red kidney beans
8-oz. pkg. macaroni

1. Brown beef in hot skillet. Drain excess fat.
2. Combine all ingredients except macaroni in crockpot, stirring well. Cook on low 8-10 hours or on high for 5 hours.
3. About 20 minutes before serving, prepare macaroni according to package directions.
4. Serve chili over macaroni.

Taco Soup

Judy Miller
Hutchinson, KS
Star of the East
Marjorie Miller
Partridge, KS
Crib Quilt

Makes 6-8 servings

$1\frac{1}{2}$ lbs. ground beef
$\frac{1}{2}$ cup chopped onion
28-oz. can whole tomatoes, undrained
16-oz. can kidney beans, undrained
17-oz. can corn, undrained
8-oz. can tomato sauce
1 pkg. dry taco seasoning
1-2 cups water
Salt and pepper to taste
1 cup shredded cheese
1 small bag nacho chips, crushed
1 cup sour cream

1. Brown beef in heavy kettle. Drain excess fat and add onion. Cook until onions are tender.
2. Add all remaining ingredients except cheese, nacho chips and sour cream. Simmer for 15 minutes.
3. Ladle into bowls and top with shredded cheese, nacho chips and sour cream. Serve.

Ham Chowder

Betty Sereno
Terra Alta, WV
String Star

Makes 6 servings

2 cups diced potatoes
1 cup green beans
1 carrot, diced
2 cups water
$1\frac{1}{2}$ tsp. salt *or* less
4 Tbsp. margarine
2 cups diced ham
1 cup chopped onion
2 $10\frac{3}{4}$-oz. cans cream of mushroom soup
3 cups milk
Pepper to taste

1. In a saucepan combine potatoes, green beans, carrot, water and salt. Cook until potatoes and carrot are tender.
2. Heat margarine in skillet and sauté ham and onion. Add to potato mixture.
3. Add cream of mushroom soup and milk. Blend and heat through. Season to taste and serve.

Mom's Vegetable Beef Soup

Janis Landefeld
Baltimore, MD
Antique Nine Patch

Makes 8 large servings

1¼ lbs. ground beef
3 ribs celery, sliced
3 carrots, sliced
1 medium onion, chopped
5 beef bouillon cubes
5 cups boiling water
16-oz. can tomatoes, undrained
1 tsp. dried basil
Salt and pepper to taste
1 Tbsp. Kitchen Bouquet
2 cups frozen vegetables
3-4 cups cooked barley *or* cooked pasta

1. Combine ground beef, celery, carrots and onion in large soup pot. Cook over medium high heat until ground beef is completely browned. Drain excess fat.
2. Dissolve bouillon cubes in boiling water.
3. Add bouillon, tomatoes, basil, salt, pepper, Kitchen Bouquet and vegetables to soup pot. Simmer about 20 minutes.
4. Immediately before serving, stir in cooked pasta or barley. Serve with a loaf of homemade bread.
5. For thinner soup add more bouillon broth.

Hamburger Vegetable Soup

Ruth Ann Penner
Hillsboro, KS
Rocking Horse Applique

Makes 6 servings

1¼ lbs. ground beef
1½ quarts water
½ cup chopped celery
2 cups diced potatoes
1 large onion, chopped
1 cup chopped carrots
Salt and pepper to taste
10¾-oz. can tomato soup
½ cup minute rice

1. Bring raw hamburger to a good boil in 1½ quarts water. Add celery, potatoes, onion, carrots, salt and pepper. Simmer 45-60 minutes.
2. Add tomato soup and rice and simmer another 2-3 minutes. Serve.

Variation:
Substitute 46-oz. can V-8 juice for water. Omit potatoes. Substitute 10¾-oz. can cream of celery soup for tomato soup. Add dash of sugar and basil. Follow other directions and heat through.
Judi Robb
Manhattan, KS
President's Sampler

Creamy Vegetable Soup

Christine H. Weaver
Reinholds, PA
Applique Table Runner

Makes 4-6 servings

1 Tbsp. margarine
3 medium carrots, thinly sliced
1 medium pepper, chopped
1 medium onion, chopped
16-oz. can whole tomatoes, chopped
3-4 potatoes
2 cups water
1 tsp. chicken bouillon
1½ cups skim milk
1 Tbsp. prepared mustard

1. In heavy frying pan over medium heat melt margarine. Add very thin carrots and peppers and sauté until lightly browned. Add onions and sauté until vegetables have softened.
2. Drain juice from tomatoes and add chopped tomatoes to vegetables. Continue cooking over medium heat.
3. Meanwhile, in soup kettle dissolve chicken bouillon in water. Cook potatoes in chicken broth until softened. Pour into food processor and blend until smooth.
4. Return to kettle and add milk, mustard and vegetables. Heat over low heat. Do *not* bring to a boil. Serve when heated through.

Cheeseburger Soup

Barbara Miller
Partridge, KS

Makes 6-8 servings

1 lb. ground beef
3 cups chicken broth
½ cup grated carrots
¼ cup chopped onion
⅓ cup chopped celery
2 cups cooked rice
2 10¾-oz. cans cheddar cheese soup
2 soup cans milk
8-oz. carton sour cream
Salt and pepper to taste

1. Brown ground beef. Drain excess fat.
2. In large kettle combine broth, carrots, onion and celery. Bring to boil and simmer 10 minutes. Add ground beef, rice, soup and milk. Stir in sour cream and heat mixture through. Do not bring to a boil. (Thin with a little water if desired.)
3. Season to taste and serve.

Summer Minestrone Soup

Dorothy Reise
Severna Park, MD
Beverly's Baskets with Tulips

Makes 6 servings

4 slices bacon, diced
1¼ Tbsp. olive oil
1 onion, chopped
1 clove garlic, crushed
2 carrots, chopped
2 stalks celery, chopped
5 cups water
5 beef bouillon cubes
1 large potato, diced
16-oz. can whole tomatoes
½ cup frozen peas
1½ Tbsp. tomato paste
½ cup uncooked macaroni
1½ Tbsp. chopped parsley
½ tsp. chopped oregano
Salt and pepper to taste
Grated Parmesan cheese

1. Sauté bacon briefly. Drain excess fat.
2. Heat oil in a large saucepan. Add onion, garlic, carrots, celery and bacon. Cook until onion is soft and transparent.
3. Dissolve bouillon cubes in water to make a stock.
4. Add stock, remaining vegetables and tomato paste to saucepan. Cover and cook over low heat for about 40 minutes.
5. Add macaroni, parsley and oregano and cook about 15-20 minutes longer. Add salt and pepper to taste. Serve with grated Parmesan cheese.

Note: Add sliced zucchini or string beans to vegetables when in season.

Minestrone

Pat Garrow
Lodi, CA
Irish Chain

Makes 8-10 servings

2 garlic cloves, crushed
4 green onions, finely chopped
2 Tbsp. chopped fresh parsley
2 carrots, sliced
1 large onion, chopped
4 celery stalks, diced
¼ cup olive oil
28-oz. can whole tomatoes, undrained
2 quarts water
16-oz. can refried beans
1 cup uncooked pasta
Salt and pepper to taste

1. In large saucepan sauté garlic, onions, parsley, carrots, onion and celery in olive oil.
2. Chop tomatoes. Add chopped tomatoes with juice, water and beans to saucepan with vegetables and cook on low for 2 hours, stirring frequently.
3. Stir in pasta and cook 1 more hour, stirring occasionally. Season to taste and serve.

Herbed Cheese Topping for Minestrone

Frances D. Bents
Annapolis, MD
Barbara's Bridal Sampler

Makes 6 servings

1 cup Parmesan cheese
4 Tbsp. butter, softened
¼ cup finely ground walnuts
1 clove garlic, minced
1½ Tbsp. minced parsley
½ tsp. chervil
½ tsp. basil
½ tsp. marjoram

1. Combine all ingredients in blender or small bowl and blend or mix until just smooth.
2. Serve minestrone in individual bowls. Top each serving with herbed cheese topping.

Cheddar Chowder

Lena Hoover
Narvon, PA
Plain White
Emma Martin
Lititz, PA
Irish Chain & Log Cabin Star

Makes 6 servings

2 cups water
2 cups diced potatoes
½ cup diced carrots
½ cup diced celery
¼ cup chopped onion
1 tsp. salt
¼ tsp. pepper
4 Tbsp. butter
½ cup flour
2 cups milk
¼ cup grated cheddar cheese
1 cup cubed ham *or* hot dogs

1. Combine water, potatoes, carrots, celery, onion, salt and pepper in large kettle and cook 10-12 minutes.
2. Meanwhile, prepare a white sauce in small saucepan by melting butter. Stir in flour until smooth. Slowly add milk and cook until thickened. Stir in cheese until melted.
3. Drain vegetables thoroughly and stir in white sauce. Add ham or hot dogs and heat until almost boiling point. Serve.

Cheese Soup

Katy J. Widger
Los Lunas, NM
Nikki's Ecology Quilt

Makes 8 servings

2 Tbsp. butter *or* margarine
¾ cup finely chopped onion
1 clove garlic, minced
½ lb. cheddar cheese, grated
½ lb. Swiss *or* Stilton cheese, grated
⅓ cup flour
3 cups chicken broth
1 cup half-and-half
⅓ cup dry white wine (optional)
Salt and pepper to taste
1 bay leaf

1. Melt butter in large, heavy saucepan. Sauté onion and garlic until onion is wilted.
2. On a piece of waxed paper sprinkle grated cheeses and flour. Add to saucepan, stirring to mix cheeses, flour, onion and garlic thoroughly and quickly. Remove from heat.
3. Gradually add chicken broth, half-and-half and wine if desired. Bring to a boil slowly over medium heat. Add salt, pepper and bay leaf. Simmer for 10 minutes. Remove bay leaf and serve.

Baked Onion Soup

Jean Harris Robinson
Cinnaminson, NJ
Little School Girl

Makes 10-12 servings

Beef Broth:
4 small beef and 2 small
    veal bones
2 carrots, chopped
4 sprigs parsley
1 Tbsp. salt (optional)
8 peppercorns
2 quarts water

Soup:
Beef broth
5 beef bouillon cubes
Water
4 large onions, very thinly
    sliced
½ lb. butter
1 loaf French bread, very
    thinly sliced
1 lb. Swiss cheese, very
    thinly sliced
15-20 sprigs parsley

1. To prepare broth combine all ingredients in a large pot and bring to a boil. Skim, then simmer for approximately 3 hours. Strain through a sieve. Cool broth and store in refrigerator overnight. Discard layer of hardened fat that will form on top of broth.

2. To prepare soup reheat broth to warm. Stir in bouillon cubes which have been dissolved in a little warm water. Add enough water to make two quarts broth.

3. In separate pan sauté onions in butter until soft and golden. Set aside.

4. In three 2-quart casserole dishes arrange the following as if you were preparing lasagna: 1 cup broth, layer of onions, layer of bread and layer of cheese. Repeat layers until casserole dishes are full, ending with layers of cheese.

5. Divide remaining broth over the three casseroles. Store in refrigerator until ready to bake.

6. Bake at 350 F. for 1 hour.

7. This soup will be thick. Spoon into small shallow bowls or mugs. Add sprig of parsley for garnish.

Note: This recipe may be made with 4-5 cans beef or chicken broth, but the extra flavor in the homemade broth is well worth the effort.

Some years ago I inadvertently left an air-soluble fabric marking pen lying on the kitchen table. (This was before I realized that these pens eventually cause deterioration.) Unknown to me my husband came in from the barn for the checkbook to pay the Dairy Herd Improvement Association for the monthly testing of our Holsteins. You guessed it, he grabbed my marking pen to write a fairly sizable check. The DHIA tester slipped the check into his case along with many other checks from his work and turned them over to the treasurer of the association.

The following week I received a call from the bank saying they had a completely blank check from DHIA which had come through on our account. I immediately guessed what probably had happened and tried to explain it. I promised to advise my husband of the problem, and have him bring a properly written check to the bank later that day.

When I told Lawrence about the matter, he was upset (mostly at me for having such a pen around for the unsuspecting) and advised me that he did not write a bad check. You can well guess who had to rewrite the check and take it to town! Fellow quilters on hearing the story have often remarked, tongue in cheek, that we probably found a far better use for that pen than its intended use for marking quilts.

—Ann Reimer, Beatrice, NE

Easy French Onion Soup

Mary Puskar
Baltimore, MD
Chinese Coins

Makes 6-8 servings

4 cups sliced onions
¼ cup margarine
¼ cup flour
6 cups water
¼ cup beef bouillon granules
6 slices French bread, cubed
1 cup grated mozzarella cheese

1. In a large saucepan sauté onions in margarine. Cook over low heat until onions are tender, stirring occasionally. Sprinkle with flour and cook for 2 minutes, stirring constantly.
2. Add water and beef bouillon. Heat until boiling, cover and simmer another 20 minutes.
3. Ladle soup into ovenproof bowls and top with French bread. Top with grated cheese and place under broiler until cheese melts and is bubbly. Serve immediately.

Elaine Good's Tomato Soup

Elaine W. Good
Lititz, PA
Antique Six-Pointed Star

Makes 6 servings

2 Tbsp. margarine
2 Tbsp. flour
2 cups milk
1 quart home-canned tomato juice

1. In a 2-quart saucepan melt margarine and stir in flour. Gradually add milk, stirring until smooth. Heat on medium until hot and just barely boiling.
2. In a separate saucepan heat tomato juice to boiling. When both liquids are same temperature, add tomato juice carefully to milk mixture, stirring well. Remove from heat. Serve.

Note: Everyone has a favorite way to make tomato juice. Our family enjoys a combination of celery, peppers, onions and tomatoes processed into a juice which is then seasoned and canned. We love this soup served with toasted cheese sandwiches. Making it has rescued many a meal when I gave more time to quilting than I should have and had to rush to get food on the table.

Helen Gerber's Tomato Soup

Helen Gerber
Stoughton, WI
Spring Tulips

Makes 8 servings

28-oz. can tomatoes, undrained
1 small onion, sliced
2 stalks celery, chopped
6 Tbsp. butter *or* margarine
6 Tbsp. flour
4 cups milk
½ Tbsp. dill weed
Pepper to taste
¾ cup shredded cheddar cheese

1. Cut tomatoes into bite-sized pieces. In saucepan bring tomatoes, onion and celery to a boil. Boil for 5 minutes.
2. In large soup kettle

Once a month our quilting group of twelve women meets to work on our own projects and share a potluck lunch. Because we sometimes discuss how much bother it is to prepare a dish, we recently decided to vote on abandoning the potluck. However, everyone voted to continue because we so enjoy eating each other's food!

—Carolee Kidd, Albuquerque, NM

melt butter. Blend in flour and cook until smooth and bubbly. Gradually add milk, stirring constantly.

3. Slowly add hot tomato mixture to white sauce, stirring constantly. Season with dill weed and pepper.

4. Immediately before serving, top with cheddar cheese.

❖

Creamy Tomato Soup

**Flossie Sultzaberger
Mechanicsburg, PA**
Nine Patch

Makes 4 servings

**2 Tbsp. finely chopped
   onion
3 Tbsp. butter *or* margarine
1½ lbs. ripe tomatoes
¼ cup water
1 Tbsp. minced fresh basil
1 Tbsp. sugar
2 Tbsp. all-purpose flour
½ tsp. salt
¼ tsp. white pepper
2 cups milk**

1. In microwave-safe bowl combine onion with 1 Tbsp. butter. Microwave on high 2 minutes or until onion has softened.

2. Peel, seed and chop tomatoes. Reserve ¼ cup for garnish. Add remaining tomatoes to onion mixture with water, basil and sugar.

Stir and microwave on high 4½-5 minutes until tomatoes are softened, stirring once more.

3. In 2-quart bowl microwave 2 Tbsp. butter on high 30 seconds. Whisk in flour, salt and pepper. Stir in milk. Microwave on high 4-5 minutes or until thickened, stirring frequently.

4. In food processor or blender process tomato mixture slowly, pouring in milk mixture.

5. Garnish with reserved chopped tomato and serve hot or chilled.

❖

Puréed Carrot Soup

**Kathy Hardis Fraeman
Olney, MD**
Star Over My Sofa

Makes 4-6 servings

**1½ Tbsp. cooking oil
1-2 cups coarsely chopped
   leeks
1 clove garlic, minced
4 cups coarsely chopped
   carrots
1 large potato, coarsely
   chopped
4-6 cups water *or* chicken
   stock
½ tsp. salt
Pepper to taste
1 cup croutons**

1. In a large soup kettle heat oil. Sauté leeks and garlic until softened, but not browned.

2. Add carrots, potato and enough liquid to barely cover. Simmer about 30 minutes until vegetables are softened.

3. Purée soup in blender. Return to soup pot and add remaining liquid to desired consistency. Mix well and heat through.

4. Serve hot or cold with croutons.

Split Pea Soup

Barbara Forrester Landis
Lititz, PA
Jacob's Ladder

Makes 8 servings

1 lb. dry green split peas
1 ham hock
1 cup chopped onion
1 tsp. chicken bouillon
   granules
8 cups water
½ tsp. salt
¼ tsp. pepper
1 cup sliced carrots
1 cup chopped celery
½ cup milk *or* light cream
2 Tbsp. butter *or* margarine

1. In a kettle combine peas, ham hock, onion, bouillon granules, water, salt and pepper. Bring to a boil. Cover and simmer 1½ hours, stirring frequently.
2. Remove ham bone, debone and return meat to soup. Add carrots and celery and simmer another 30 minutes.
3. Stir milk and butter into soup and heat through. Serve.

Pumpkin Soup

Winnie Friese
Washington, NJ
Hearts and Hands

Makes 6 servings

1 quart chicken stock
29-oz. can pumpkin
12-oz. can evaporated milk
¼ cup whole milk
1 cup chopped onion
8 Tbsp. margarine
1 Tbsp. flour
¼ tsp. nutmeg
¼ tsp. ginger

1. In a large saucepan heat chicken stock. Add pumpkin, evaporated milk and whole milk and continue heating.
2. Sauté onion in margarine. Add flour, nutmeg and ginger and cook until bubbly. Stir into soup and heat mixture until piping hot. Do NOT boil. Serve.

Gazpacho

Ann Foss
Brooklyn, NY

Makes 8 servings

4 cups tomato juice
2 beef bouillon cubes
2 large tomatoes
½ cup chopped cucumbers
¼ cup chopped green
   pepper
¼ cup chopped onion
¼ cup wine vinegar
2 Tbsp. cooking oil
½ tsp. salt
1 tsp. Worcestershire sauce
6 drops Tabasco

1. Bring tomato juice to a boil in large saucepan. Add beef cubes and stir to dissolve. Remove from heat and cool.
2. Peel, seed and dice tomatoes. Do not peel cucumbers.
3. Add tomatoes, cucumbers and all remaining ingredients to cooled broth and mix well.
4. Refrigerate and serve in chilled bowls or mugs.

Breads, Rolls and Muffins

❖

Homemade White Bread

Mary Esther Yoder
Partridge, KS
Double Irish Chain
Candy Horton
Greenfield, OH
Cecil's Fan

Makes 2 large loaves

1½ Tbsp. yeast
1 tsp. sugar
2 cups lukewarm water
⅓ cup cooking oil
⅓ cup white sugar
1 Tbsp. salt
5-6 cups flour

1. Sprinkle yeast and sugar into 1 cup lukewarm water. Let stand for 10 minutes.

2. Pour yeast mixture into large bowl and add all ingredients, kneading well. If dough is too sticky, add a little more flour. Place in greased bowl and cover with cloth.

3. Let rise 1 hour or until doubled in size. Punch down. Let rise again until doubled in size.

4. Form dough into 2 loaves and place into large greased loaf pans. Let rise again until nicely rounded in pan.

5. Bake at 350° on lower oven rack for 25 minutes. Remove from oven and butter tops lightly. Immediately remove bread from pans.

❖

Brown Honey Bread

Verna Keim
Millersburg, OH
Star Spin

Makes 5 loaves

3 pkgs. yeast
½ cup warm water
½ cup honey
¼ cup cooking oil
½ cup brown sugar
4 tsp. salt *or* less
4½ cups hot water

2½ cups whole wheat flour
11 cups white flour

1. Dissolve yeast in warm water.

2. In a large bowl combine honey, oil, sugar and salt. Add hot water and mix well. Add yeast mixture and stir.

3. Stir in whole wheat flour and mix well. Gradually add enough white flour to make a stiff dough. Knead well. Place in greased bowl, turning to grease all sides.

4. Let rise until doubled in bulk. Punch down.

5. Divide dough into 5 equal loaves. Place in greased loaf pans and let rise again until doubled in bulk.

6. Bake at 350° for 40 minutes or until done.

Limpa (Swedish Rye Bread)

Joyce Niemann
Fruitland Park, FL
Lap Sampler

Makes 3 loaves

4 cups water
½ cup light molasses
½ cup shortening
¼ cup light corn syrup
1½ tsp. anise seeds
1½ tsp. grated orange rind
½ tsp. fennel seeds
½ tsp. caraway seeds
2 pkgs. dry yeast
¼ cup lukewarm water
1 egg
5 cups rye flour
1 cup sugar
1 Tbsp. salt
½ tsp. freshly crushed cardamom seeds
7-8 cups all purpose flour

1. Heat 4 cups water to boiling. Stir in molasses, shortening, corn syrup, anise, orange rind, fennel and caraway. Cool to lukewarm. Reserve ⅓ cup of this mixture.

2. Sprinkle yeast over ¼ cup lukewarm water (105-115°) in a large mixing bowl, stirring until dissolved. Stir in molasses mixture. Beat in egg.

3. Combine rye flour, sugar, salt and cardamom and beat into molasses mixture.

4. Stir in flour, 1 cup at a time, until dough no longer clings to side of bowl. Turn out onto lightly floured surface and knead until smooth and elastic, about 15 minutes. Put into a large greased bowl, turning to grease all sides.

5. Cover and let rise in warm place until doubled in size, about 1 hour. Punch down and turn onto lightly floured board.

6. Divide dough into 3 parts. Shape each piece into a smooth ball. Place each ball in center of a greased 8-inch square baking pan. Cover and let rise until doubled in size, about 1 hour.

7. Bake at 350° for 35-40 minutes or until loaves sound hollow when lightly tapped. Remove from pans and immediately brush tops with reserved molasses mixture.

Daily Bread

Cleda Cox
Estes Park, CO
The Eagle

Makes 6 loaves

2 pkgs. dry yeast*
6 cups lukewarm water
½ cup honey
¼ cup molasses
1 cup non-fat dry milk
½ cup oat bran
¼ cup wheat bran
¼ cup wheat germ
4 tsp. salt
½ cup cooking oil
4 cups whole wheat flour
10-12 cups bread flour

*Do not use fast-acting yeast.

1. Dissolve yeast in lukewarm water. Add honey, molasses, dry milk, oat and wheat bran, wheat germ, salt and oil.

2. Stir in all of the whole wheat flour. Stir in 7 cups of the white flour and mix as well as you can.

3. Put 3 cups of remaining flour on large bread board or table top and place dough in the middle of flour. Knead flour into dough until dough no longer sticks to the table or hands, at least fifteen minutes. (Dough should be elastic and feel spongy and alive to touch.)

4. Place dough in large well-greased container. Cover and let rise in a slightly warm place until doubled in size, about 1½ hours. Punch down and divide dough into 6 pieces.

5. Place dough in greased 7" x 3" loaf pans. Oil top of each loaf. Cover with a cloth and let rise in a warm place until dough is about 1½" above the pan top. (Do not let rise to full height of loaf or it will fall as it cools.)

6. Bake at 400° for 10 minutes. Reduce oven temperature to 350° and bake another 35 minutes. (If

> I belong to a quilting group called UFO (unfinished objects). We meet twice a month to work on our personal projects and to enjoy food, laughter, learning and good company. The first meeting of the month we usually have a potluck. I have learned so much from the varied levels of experience among us. Everyone is willing to encourage, share and teach others.
>
> —*Mary Saunders, Albuquerque, NM*

loaves appear to brown too quickly during baking, cover loosely with a piece of aluminum foil.) Remove loaves from pan and brush entire loaf with melted butter. Freeze any extra loaves.

Note: It is difficult to predict exactly how much white flour to use. The amount varies with the dryness of the flour and the humidity. Knead in flour until dough no longer sticks to your hands or table surface. Never allow any of the dough or ingredients to be hotter than lukewarm as heat kills the yeast action. In altitudes of 5000' and higher reduce the yeast to 1½ packages.

Whole Grain Bread

Edna Nisly
Partridge, KS
Encircled Tulips

Makes 3 loaves

2 cups quick oatmeal
2½ cups boiling water
½ cup honey

½ **cup cooking oil**
2 Tbsp. salt *or* less
4 eggs
1 cup warm water
2 Tbsp. yeast
9½ cups whole wheat flour

1. Pour boiling water over oatmeal and let stand until cooled to lukewarm. Add honey, oil, salt and eggs. Beat one minute.
2. Dissolve yeast in warm water and add to the oatmeal mixture. Add 5 cups of flour and beat 2 minutes.
3. Add more flour and continue mixing until dough becomes too stiff for mixer. Finish mixing by hand. (Dough should be very sticky.) Turn into greased bowl, turning to grease all sides.
4. Cover and let rise until doubled in size, about 1½ hours. Knead and let rise again until doubled in size, about 45 minutes.
5. Punch down and shape into loaves. Place in greased loaf pans. Let rise again until doubled in size.
6. Bake at 350° for 35 minutes until golden brown.

Mom's Oatmeal Bread

Debra M. Zeida
Waquoit, MA
Pennsylvania Bride

Makes 2 loaves

1 heaping cup oats
2 tsp. salt
½ **cup molasses**
4 tsp. bacon drippings *or* **margarine**
2 cups boiling water
1 yeast cake
⅓ **cup warm water**
5⅓ cups flour

1. Combine oats, salt, molasses and bacon drippings. Pour boiling water over mixture and let stand until cool.
2. Dissolve yeast in ⅓ cup warm water. Add to oatmeal mixture. Add flour and knead thoroughly. If dough is too sticky, add a little more flour. Place in greased bowl.
3. Let stand until doubled in size. Knead and shape into 2 loaves. Place in greased loaf pans. Let rise again to double size.
4. Bake at 375° for 45 minutes. Remove from pans and grease tops with butter.

Oatmeal Bread

Helen Gerber
Stoughton, WI
Spring Tulips

Makes 3 loaves

1 cup brown sugar
⅓ cup shortening
3 cups boiling water
1¾ cups quick oats
1 pkg. yeast
½ cup warm water
1 Tbsp. salt *or* less
7-8 cups flour

1. Dissolve sugar and shortening in boiling water and immediately pour over oats. Stir well and let cool to 100-110°.
2. Soak yeast in ½ cup warm water until dissolved. Add yeast to oatmeal mixture. With an electric mixer beat in salt and three cups of flour.
3. Mix in remaining flour with a spoon and by hand until dough is no longer sticky. Do not knead. Place in covered bowl and let rise about 1½ hours.
4. Shape into 3 loaves and place into greased loaf pans. Cover and let rise until doubled in size, about 1 hour.
5. Bake at 350° for 35-40 minutes. Brush tops with melted butter to provide a soft crust.

❖

Oatmeal Raisin Bread

Susan M. Miller
Centreville, MD
Strip-Pieced Triangles

Makes 2 loaves

½ cup warm water
2 pkgs. yeast
1¾ cups warm milk
¼ cup brown sugar, firmly packed
1 Tbsp. salt *or* less
3 Tbsp. margarine
5-6 cups flour
1 cup rolled oats
1 cup raisins

1. Measure warm water into large warmed bowl. Sprinkle yeast on top and stir until dissolved. Add warm milk, sugar, salt and margarine. Add 2 cups flour and beat with electric beater until smooth, about 1 minute.
2. Add 1 cup flour and oats. Beat vigorously with spoon until smooth, about 150 strokes. Add enough flour to make a soft dough. Turn out onto lightly floured board and knead until smooth and elastic, about 8-10 minutes. Cover with plastic wrap and a cloth. Let rest 20 minutes.
3. Divide dough in half and roll each into an 8" x 12" rectangle. Sprinkle ½ cup raisins over each rectangle. Shape into loaves by rolling up and tucking ends

under. Place into greased loaf pans and cover loosely with plastic wrap. Let rise in warm place until doubled in size, about 1 hour.
4. Bake at 400° for 30-40 minutes or until done.

Dilly Casserole Bread

Betty Caudle
Colorado Springs, CO
Double Wedding Ring

Makes 8-12 servings

1 pkg. yeast
¼ cup warm water
1 cup cottage cheese
2 Tbsp. sugar
1 Tbsp. minced onion flakes
1 Tbsp. butter
2 Tbsp. dill seed
1 tsp. salt
¼ tsp. baking soda
1 egg
2¼-2½ cups flour

1. Soften yeast in water.
2. Heat cottage cheese to lukewarm. In a mixing bowl combine cottage cheese, sugar, onion, butter, dill seed, salt, baking soda, egg and softened yeast.
3. Add flour to form a stiff dough, beating well after each addition. Cover and let rise in warm place until light and doubled in size. Stir down.

4. Turn into well-greased 2-quart casserole dish. Let rise again.

5. Bake at 350° for 40-50 minutes. Brush top with butter and sprinkle with salt.

Snails Trail Bread

Eileen Plementos
Williams Lake, BC
Drunkard's Path

Makes 2 loaves

1 tsp. honey
½ cup lukewarm water
4 tsp. active dry yeast
1½ cups warm water
¼ cup margarine, melted
1 egg, beaten
¼ cup honey
2 tsp. salt
2 Tbsp. lemon juice
5½-6 cups flour
1 Tbsp. margarine, melted
¼ cup brown sugar
1 tsp. cinnamon

1. Dissolve 1 tsp. honey in ½ cup lukewarm water. Sprinkle yeast into honey water. Let stand for 10 minutes, then stir well.

2. Measure 1½ cups warm water into large bowl. Add ¼ cup melted margarine, egg, ¼ cup honey, salt and lemon juice. Add yeast mixture and stir. Add 2 cups flour and mix until smooth. Add suffi-

cient additional flour to make a soft, workable dough.

3. Turn dough onto lightly floured surface. Knead 8-10 minutes or until dough is smooth and elastic. Form into ball and place into greased bowl, turning to grease all sides.

4. Cover and let rise until doubled in size, about 50 minutes. Punch down and form two round balls. Cover and let rest for 20 minutes.

5. Roll out each piece of dough into 7" x 15" rectangle. Spread each piece with melted margarine.

6. Combine brown sugar and cinnamon and sprinkle ½ of sugar mixture over each rectangle. Roll up like a jelly roll, beginning at the narrow end and sealing edges. Place, sealed edges down, in greased loaf pans. Cover and let rise for 45-50 minutes.

7. Bake at 375° for 30-35 minutes or until bread sounds hollow when tapped. Remove from pans and cool on wire racks, turning after 10 minutes to cool completely.

English Muffin Bread

Maryellen Mross
Bartonsville, PA
Hearts and Flowers

Makes 2 loaves

2 pkgs. dry yeast
6 cups flour
1 Tbsp. sugar
2 tsp. salt
¼ tsp. baking soda
2 cups milk
½ cup water
Yellow cornmeal

1. Combine yeast, 3 cups flour, sugar, salt and baking soda.

2. Heat milk and water until very warm. Add to dry mixture and beat well. Add remaining 3 cups flour to make a stiff batter.

3. Grease 2 loaf pans and dust insides with cornmeal. Spoon dough into pans and sprinkle with cornmeal. Cover and let rise for 45 minutes.

4. Bake at 400° for 25-30 minutes. Cool on wire rack. Slice, toast and enjoy.

During Easter vacation I received an anguished call from my daughter. She was so upset, I was sure something had happened to one of her family. When she was finally able to talk, she told me what had happened. Her daughter had volunteered to take care of the class bunny over school vacation. Fearing the bunny might get cold, Lindsey covered his cage with her special carrousel quilt. The next morning the family discovered, to their dismay, that bunny had liked the quilt so much that he ate big chunks of it by pulling it into the cage. My daughter was sure she would be severely reprimanded by me. I was so grateful that all her family members were alive and healthy that I reminded her, "Yes, a quilt is a treasured possession, but it is still a thing—not a being—and it may be repaired or replaced." Today Lindsey's repaired carrousel quilt includes a label which tells the story of Peter Rabbit's Easter breakfast.

—M. Jeanne Osborne, Sanford, ME

Cream Cheese Bread

Marilyn Mowry
Irving, TX
Airplanes, Airplanes

Makes 4 small loaves

Bread:
1 cup sour cream
½ cup sugar
1 tsp. salt
½ cup margarine *or* butter, melted
2 pkgs. dry yeast
½ cup warm water
2 eggs
4 cups sifted flour

Cream Cheese Mixture:
2 8-oz. pkgs. cream cheese
¾ cup sugar
1 egg, beaten

⅛ tsp. salt
2 tsp. vanilla

Glaze:
2 cups powdered sugar
4 Tbsp. milk
2 tsp. vanilla

1. To prepare bread stir sour cream over low heat in pan. Add sugar, salt and melted margarine.

2. Sprinkle yeast over warm water in large bowl and let dissolve. Add sour cream mixture, 1 egg and flour and mix together. Cover tightly and refrigerate overnight.

3. Divide dough into 4 parts and roll each piece into an 8" x 12" rectangle.

4. To prepare cream cheese mixture combine all ingredients and mix until smooth. Spread ¼ of mixture onto each rectangle of

dough.

5. Roll up starting with long side. Tuck under ends. Slit each roll diagonally across top (2-3 times). Arrange on greased baking sheet. Cover and let rise in warm place for 1 hour.

6. Bake at 350° for 12-15 minutes or until browned.

7. To prepare glaze combine all ingredients and mix until smooth. While loaves are still warm, cover with glaze.

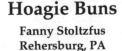

Hoagie Buns

Fanny Stoltzfus
Rehersburg, PA
Sunshine and Shadow

Makes 6 rolls

4½-5½ cups unsifted bread flour
1 Tbsp. sugar
1 Tbsp. salt
2 Tbsp. yeast
1 Tbsp. softened butter
1¾ cups very warm tap water
Cooking oil

1. Combine 1½ cups flour, sugar, salt and yeast. Add butter and mix well.

2. Gradually add remaining flour, alternating with tap water. Knead until smooth, 10-15 minutes.

3. Cover with plastic wrap and let rest for 20 min-

utes. Shape into six large hoagie buns and place on 2 greased baking sheets. Brush dough with cooking oil.

4. Cover loosely with plastic wrap and refrigerate from 2 to 24 hours.

5. Remove from refrigerator and let stand at room temperature 10 minutes. Slit top of each bun.

6. Bake at 425° for 15 minutes.

Sourdough Dinner Rolls

Elaine W. Good
Lititz, PA
Reproduction Center Diamond

Makes 24 rolls

1 cup sourdough starter
1 cup warm water (115°)
½ tsp. baking soda
½ cup cooking oil
1 egg
1 tsp. salt
¼ cup sugar
4½-5 cups white bread flour

1. Combine starter, water and baking soda in a plastic or glass bowl, stirring with a plastic or wooden spoon. Do not use metal.

2. Combine oil and egg and stir into starter mixture. Add salt and sugar.

3. Add flour, 1 or 2 cups

at a time, and stir until dough cleans the bowl. Turn out onto floured surface, cover with bowl and let rest 10 minutes. Knead thoroughly.

4. Shape dough into 24 rolls and place in a greased 9" x 13" baking pan (may be metal).

5. Cover with damp cloth and let rise in a warm place for several hours. (I use my oven with the light turned on.)

6. Bake at 350° for 20 5minutes.

Note: I received my first starter from a friend. If you do not have sourdough starter, you may begin your own. (See sourdough starter recipe below.)

Sourdough Starter

Elaine W. Good
Lititz, PA
Antique Six-Pointed Star

---

1 Tbsp. yeast
2 cups warm water
2 cups unbleached flour
¼ cup sugar

1. Dissolve yeast in warm water in a 2-quart glass jar, crock or plastic container. Do not use metal. Let stand 10 minutes.

2. Stir in flour and sugar. Cover and let stand at room temperature until bubbly

and slightly sour smelling. This will take a day or two.

3. After measuring the amount you need for a recipe, feed your starter with 1 cup unbleached flour, 1 cup milk and ¼ cup sugar.

4. Store at room temperature, stirring it down every day and using it at least once a week.

5. If you cannot use starter, but it needs to be fed, replenish with a "half feed" occasionally. Add ½ cup flour, ½ cup milk and 2 Tbsp. sugar.

6. If the quantity does grow out of its container, simply freeze some or all of the starter. You may do this whenever you are weary of its company or if you plan to be gone for awhile.

7. Bring starter to room temperature, and it is ready to use again.

Squash Yeast Rolls

Alma C. Ranck
Paradise, PA
Trip Around the World

Makes 28 rolls

5½-6 cups flour
⅓ cup dry milk
2 pkgs. dry yeast
½ tsp. mace
12-oz. pkg. frozen squash,
  cooked
1 cup water
½ cup sugar
3 Tbsp. shortening
2 tsp. salt

1. Stir together 2 cups flour, dry milk, yeast and mace. Set aside.
2. In a saucepan combine squash, water, sugar, shortening and salt. Heat slowly until warm (120-130°), stirring to blend.
3. Add liquid ingredients to flour and yeast mixture. Beat until smooth, about 1 minute on medium speed or 300 strokes by hand. Beat 2 minutes at high speed.
4. Stir in remaining flour to make a moderately soft dough. Turn out onto lightly floured board and knead until smooth, about 5-10 minutes. Place in greased bowl, turning to grease all sides.
5. Cover and let rise in warm place (80-85°) until doubled in size, about 1½ hours. Punch down. Let rise again for about 10 minutes.
6. Divide dough into fourths and shape each portion into 7 rolls. Place on greased sheet pan. Cover and let rise in warm place until doubled in size, about 30 minutes.
7. Bake at 350° for 25-35 minutes or until done. Brush tops lightly with butter and cover rolls.

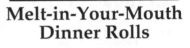

Dinner Rolls

Lillian McAninch
Leesburg, FL
My First Quilt

Makes 40 small rolls

2 pkgs. dry yeast
½ cup warm water
½ cup sugar
2 eggs
1 tsp. salt
⅔ cup margarine
1 cup mashed potatoes
1 cup milk, room
  temperature
6½ cups flour
1-2 Tbsp. margarine,
  melted

1. Dissolve yeast in warm water. Set aside.
2. Beat together sugar and eggs. Add salt, margarine, potatoes, milk, yeast and 3 cups flour. Beat at least 10 strokes.
3. Add remaining flour and knead until smooth. Place in a greased bowl.
4. Let rise in warm place until almost doubled in size. Punch down.
5. Divide dough into 5 parts and roll each out into a circle. Cut into 8 wedges. Roll up each wedge, starting at wide edge. Place on greased sheet pans. Let rise again until doubled in size. Brush tops with melted margarine.
6. Bake at 375° for 10 minutes. Brush tops again with melted margarine.

Melt-in-Your-Mouth Dinner Rolls

L. Jean Moore
Anderson, IN
Family Sampler

Makes 16 or more rolls

1 pkg. yeast
½ cup warm water
1 Tbsp. sugar
1 tsp. baking powder
1 cup milk
⅓ cup margarine
⅓ cup sugar
Dash salt
2 eggs, beaten
4½ cups flour

1. Dissolve yeast in warm water. Add sugar and baking powder and let stand for 20 minutes.
2. Scald milk. Add margarine, sugar and salt. Stir in yeast. Cool and add

eggs. Gradually add flour until well mixed.

3. Cover and refrigerate overnight.

4. About 2 hours before serving, roll out dough. Cut with biscuit cutter, score with knife across middle and fold over. Place in greased baking pans with rolls touching.

5. Bake at 425° for 10 minutes.

Quick Light Rolls

Ella Miller
Fredericksburg, OH
Crystalis

Makes 2 dozen rolls

1 cup milk
5 Tbsp. sugar
1 tsp. salt
1 pkg. dry yeast
1 cup lukewarm water
5 cups enriched flour
6 Tbsp. lard, melted

1. Scald milk, add sugar and salt and cool to luke-warm.

2. Dissolve yeast in warm water. Add to cooled milk mixture.

3. Sift flour. Add 2½ cups to yeast mixture, beating until smooth.

4. Add melted lard and remaining flour. Knead well and let rise until doubled in bulk, about 1½

hours. Shape into rolls, cover and let rise about 1 hour or until doubled in size. Place into greased muffin tins.

5. Bake at 350° for 15 minutes.

Yogurt Crescent Rolls

Carolyn Shank
Dayton, VA
Sampler

Makes 4 dozen rolls

⅓ cup cooking oil
8-oz. carton plain lowfat yogurt
½ cup sugar
2 pkgs. dry yeast
½ cup warm water
1 egg
1 egg white
4 cups flour
1 tsp. salt
Vegetable cooking spray

1. Combine oil, yogurt and sugar and set aside.

2. In large mixing bowl dissolve yeast in warm water. Let stand for 5 minutes.

3. Stir in yogurt mixture, egg and egg white.

4. In separate bowl combine flour and salt. Stir 2 cups flour into yogurt mixture and beat at medium speed until smooth. Gradually stir in remaining flour mixture.

5. Cover and refrigerate 8 hours or overnight. Punch dough down and divide into 4 equal parts. On a floured surface roll each into a 10-inch circle. Coat circles of dough with cooking spray. Cut each circle into 12 wedges.

6. Roll up each wedge, beginning with wide end. Arrange on greased baking sheets with point side down. Cover and let rise in warm place, free from drafts, about 45 minutes or until doubled in bulk.

7. Bake at 375° for 10-12 minutes or until golden brown.

Childhood memories of food and quilts have always gone together for me. My grandmother had a beautiful quilt bordered in green with white panels of red and pink tulips which she used as a picnic tablecloth. We would lay the quilt on a grassy hill and arrange our bounty of fried chicken, potato salad and lemon ice tea on it, enjoying the ever-blooming flowers on our table year round.

—*Barbara Sparks, Glen Burnie, MD*

Whole Wheat Butterhorns

Joanne Spatz
Lebanon, PA
The Chief

Makes 18-24 rolls

2¾ cups all-purpose flour
2 pkgs. dry yeast
1¾ cups water
⅓ cup brown sugar,
    packed
½ cup butter
2 Tbsp. honey
2 tsp. salt
2 cups whole wheat flour

1. In a large mixing bowl combine 1½ cups flour and yeast.

2. In a saucepan combine water, brown sugar, 3 Tbsp. butter, honey and salt and heat to about 130°. Stir into flour and yeast mixture. Beat on low for 30 seconds and on high for about 3 minutes.

3. Stir in whole wheat flour and enough all-purpose flour to make a soft dough. Turn out onto lightly floured surface and knead until smooth and elastic, about 6-8 minutes. Place in greased bowl.

4. Cover and let rise in warm place until doubled in size, about 1½ hours. Punch down.

5. Divide dough into thirds, shaping each piece into a ball. Cover and let rest 10 minutes.

6. On a lightly floured surface, roll balls out into circles, 12 inches in diameter. Cut each circle into 6-8 wedges. Roll wedges into crescent shape, starting at wide end. Place on greased baking sheets.

7. Cover and let rise until doubled in size, about 1 hour. Melt remaining butter and brush tops of crescents.

8. Bake at 400° for 10-15 minutes until golden brown. Brush tops with butter and serve.

Zwieback

Judy Miller
Hutchinson, KS
Star of the East

Makes about 4 dozen Zwieback

2 cups milk
1 cup shortening
2 tsp. salt
4 Tbsp. sugar
1 yeast cake
2 tsp. sugar
1 cup lukewarm water
2 eggs, beaten (optional)
8-10 cups sifted flour

1. Scald milk. Add shortening, salt and 4 Tbsp. sugar. Cool to lukewarm.

2. Crumble yeast in a small bowl. Add 2 tsp. sugar and warm water. Put in a warm place until spongy.

3. Add yeast mixture and beaten eggs to lukewarm milk mixture. Mix well and gradually stir in flour. Knead until very soft and smooth.

4. Cover and let rise in a warm place until doubled in bulk.

5. Pinch off balls of dough about the size of a small egg, and arrange about an inch apart on a greased baking sheet. Put a similar ball, but slightly smaller, on top of each bottom ball. Press down with thumb. Let rise until doubled in bulk, about 1 hour.

6. Bake at 375-400° for 15-20 minutes.

Semmel

Ann Reimer
Beatrice, NE
Joshua's Star Log Cabin

Makes 16 Semmel

1 pkg. yeast
3 cups lukewarm water
6 cups flour
1 scant Tbsp. salt

1. Dissolve yeast in water in a large mixing bowl. Add salt and 3 cups flour. Mix for 5 minutes. Add remaining flour and beat with a wooden or plastic spoon another 5 minutes

or until dough is shiny in appearance and blisters begin to form on the surface. (Yes, your arm will be tired!)

2. Cover and let rise for 1 hour. Stir down and place on greased baking sheet in large spoonsful, no more than 8 to a sheet. (It is wise to also grease the spoon as this dough is quite stiff.)

3. Bake at 400° for 20-25 minutes or until Semmel are very lightly browned. Remove and serve immediately.

4. Bake only as many as are needed each time. Cover and refrigerate remaining dough which will keep several days.

Note: The outside of the Semmel will be very hard while the inside is soft and somewhat moist. To open, insert a knife and cut each Semmel in half, horizontally. Serve with butter, honey, jelly, peanut butter, ham or cheese. Semmel (pronounced ZEM mel) is German for "hard roll." This particular recipe seems to be unique to the Beatrice, Nebraska, Mennonite community.

Angel Yeast Biscuits

Betty Sereno
Terra Alta, WV
String Star

Makes 20 biscuits

1 pkg. dry yeast
½ cup warm water
5 cups flour
1 tsp. baking soda
3 tsp. baking powder
3 Tbsp. sugar
¾ cup shortening
2 cups buttermilk

1. Dissolve yeast in warm water. Set aside.

2. Sift together all dry ingredients. Cut shortening into dry mixture until well mixed. Add buttermilk and yeast and work together with a large spoon.

3. Place dough in a large, greased bowl. Cover and refrigerate until ready to use. Take out only as much dough as needed and roll to about ½-inch thickness on a floured board. Cut with a biscuit cutter.

4. Arrange on a baking sheet and let rise until doubled in size.

5. Bake at 400° for 10-15 minutes.

Soft Pretzels

Genny Morrow
Lancaster, PA
Irish Chain
Esther L. Lantz
Leola, PA
Irish Chain

Makes 12 pretzels

1 pkg. fast-acting yeast
1½ cups warm water
¼ cup brown sugar
4-4½ cups flour
Baking soda
Kosher salt

1. In a mixing bowl combine yeast, warm water and brown sugar. Let stand for 5 minutes. Add flour and beat with a dough hook until smooth.

2. Let stand 5 minutes while you bring a deep saucepan full of water to a boil. (For every cup of water add 2 Tbsp. baking soda.)

3. Divide dough into 12 even pieces. Roll each piece into long rope and twist into pretzel shape.

4. Drop each pretzel into boiling water and boil for 10 seconds. Remove with a slotted spoon. Arrange pretzels on a greased baking sheet and sprinkle with kosher salt.

5. Bake at 450° about 8 minutes or until browned.

Pizza Sticks

Marilyn Yoder
Mt. Hope, OH
Rubic's Cube

Makes about 3 dozen sticks

2 pkgs. yeast
2 cups lukewarm water
$\frac{1}{2}$ cup sugar
1 egg, beaten
3 Tbsp. oil
1 tsp. salt
5 cups flour

1. Dissolve yeast in warm water. Add sugar and let stand 5 minutes.
2. Beat together egg, oil and salt. Stir into yeast mixture. Gradually add flour to make a soft dough and knead well, 8-10 minutes. Place in greased bowl and cover with towel. Let rise in warm place until doubled in size.
3. Punch down and shape into 6-inch long sticks. Let rise in warm place until doubled in bulk. Arrange on greased baking sheets.
4. Bake at 450° for 8-10 minutes. Serve with hot pizza sauce.

Raised Doughnuts

Alma Mullet
Walnut Creek, OH
Triple Irish Chain

Makes 3 dozen doughnuts

$1\frac{1}{4}$ cups milk
$\frac{1}{4}$ cup shortening
1 tsp. salt
1 small cake yeast
$4\frac{1}{2}$-5 cups flour, sifted
$\frac{3}{4}$ cup white sugar
$\frac{1}{4}$ tsp. nutmeg
3 eggs, beaten

1. In a saucepan scald milk. Add shortening and salt. Remove from heat and cool to lukewarm. Add crumbled yeast and stir. Pour into a mixing bowl.
2. Gradually add $2\frac{2}{3}$ cups flour, beating thoroughly. Place in a warm spot and let stand until full of bubbles.
3. In a separate bowl combine sugar, nutmeg and eggs. Pour into milk and yeast mixture and mix well. Add remaining flour and knead until well mixed.
4. Cover and let rise in a warm place for about 1 hour.
5. Turn out onto lightly floured board and roll out until about $\frac{1}{2}$-inch thick. Cut dough with a doughnut cutter. Let rise on a board until tops are springy when touched.
6. Deep-fry in fat at 365° Drain doughnuts in colan-der and lay out to cool. Dip in choice of sugar or glaze and serve.

Overnight Sweet Rolls

Esther Becker
Gap, PA
Log Cabin Star

Makes 18 servings

4 cups flour
$\frac{1}{4}$ cup sugar
1 tsp. salt
1 cup margarine
1 pkg. yeast
$\frac{1}{4}$ cup very warm water
1 cup milk
2 eggs, beaten
Soft margarine
1 cup sugar
1 tsp. cinnamon
$1\frac{1}{2}$ cups powdered sugar
2-3 Tbsp. milk
2 tsp. grated orange rind (optional)

1. In a large bowl combine flour, $\frac{1}{4}$ cup sugar and salt. Cut 1 cup margarine into dry ingredients.
2. Sprinkle yeast into very warm water and stir until dissolved.
3. Scald 1 cup milk and cool to lukewarm. Add yeast, milk and eggs to flour mixture. Toss until well mixed. Cover tightly and refrigerate overnight.
4. Divide dough in half.

Roll each half into a 12" x 18" rectangle. Spread with soft margarine.

5. Combine 1 cup sugar and cinnamon. Sprinkle over rolled out dough. Roll up and cut into 1-inch pieces. Arrange in baking dish.

6. Bake at 400° for 15 minutes.

7. Combine powdered sugar and 2-3 Tbsp. milk. Drizzle over hot rolls. If desired, sprinkle with grated orange rind. Serve.

Hungarian Begli

Berta Stegmeier
Silver Spring, MD
Friends and Food 1991

Makes 8 dozen servings

Dough:
2 pkgs. yeast
1 cup sugar
1 cup warm milk
10 cups all-purpose flour
1½ lbs. butter, softened
4 eggs
8-oz. carton sour cream

1. Dissolve yeast and 1 Tbsp. sugar in warm milk.

2. With hands mix flour, butter, remaining sugar, 2 eggs, sour cream and yeast mixture. Knead dough approximately 10 minutes or until smooth and elastic. (Add more flour if mixture is too sticky. Add more sour cream if mixture is too dry.)

3. Divide dough into 8 balls. Cover with cloth and let rise for 1 hour.

4. Roll out each dough ball to a ⅛-inch thick rectangle. Spread rolled dough with choice of filling. (See filling recipes which follow.)

5. Roll up dough, beginning at wide side. Tuck in ends of roll. Arrange on greased baking sheet.

6. Bake at 350° for 15 minutes.

7. Beat remaining 2 eggs. Remove begli from oven and brush well with beaten egg.

8. Return to oven and bake another 25 minutes. Cool and slice each roll into 12 pieces before serving.

Poppy Seed Filling

1 cup water
2½ cups sugar
8 Tbsp. butter
1 lb. ground poppy seeds

1. In a saucepan bring water, sugar and butter to a boil. Remove from heat and stir poppy seeds into mixture. Cool.

2. Spread evenly over rolls of begli dough. Makes enough for 4 rolls.

Walnut Filling

½ cup water
½ cup sugar
4 Tbsp. butter
1 lb. ground walnuts

1. In a saucepan bring water, sugar and butter to a boil. Remove from heat and stir in walnuts. Cool.

2. Spread evenly over rolls of begli dough. Makes enough for 3 rolls.

Apricot Filling

1 lb. dried apricots
Water
Sugar

1. Place apricots in saucepan. Add enough water to cover apricots. Simmer until apricots are soft and mushy. Add sugar to taste. Cool.

2. Spread evenly over rolls of begli dough. Makes enough for 5 rolls.

When my husband interrupted his farming career to return to the classroom in the middle of a school year, our five-year-old son, who was accustomed to spending his days with Daddy, did not know quite what to do with me. One day I suggested we make a quilt. He happily ran from the ironing board to the sewing machine, bringing me tools and patches and making appropriate remarks about how the quilt was turning out. Patching redeemed that bleak January and February and we went on to find a reasonable daily rhythm. Today he still picks out his favorite patches from the quilt which is now used on his sister's bed.

—*Elaine W. Good, Lititz, PA*

Crispy Rolls

Nancy George
De Pere, WI
Hearts and Strings

Makes 24 large rolls

Dough:
1 pkg. dry yeast
¼ cup warm water
4 cups flour
1 tsp. salt
¼ cup sugar
16 Tbsp. butter
2 eggs, beaten
1 cup warm milk
1 Tbsp. cinnamon
1 Tbsp. white sugar

Frosting:
1 cup powdered sugar
1 Tbsp. milk
½ tsp. vanilla

1. Dissolve yeast in warm water. Set aside.
2. In a large bowl combine flour, salt and sugar. Cut in butter.
3. Combine eggs, yeast mixture and milk. Stir into the flour and butter mixture. Combine lightly. Cover tightly and refrigerate overnight.
4. Divide dough in half. Roll each piece into a 12" x 18" rectangle and sprinkle with cinnamon and sugar. Roll up like jelly roll and cut each roll into 12 pieces. Arrange pieces on greased baking sheet and press down with hand.
5. Bake at 400° for 12 minutes. Frost while warm with powdered sugar frosting.
6. To prepare frosting combine all ingredients and mix until smooth.

Irish Soda Bread

Irene Scheid
Wood Haven, NY
Memories Quilt

Makes 1 round loaf

3 cups flour, sifted
4 tsp. baking powder
1 tsp. salt
1 cup sugar
1 cup raisins
1 cup boiling water
2 tsp. caraway seeds (optional)
1 egg
1 cup milk
3 Tbsp. shortening

1. Combine flour, baking powder, salt and sugar and mix.
2. Pour boiling water over raisins. Let stand until cool. Drain and pat dry.
3. Add raisins and caraway seeds to dry ingredients.
4. In another bowl mix egg, milk and shortening. Combine all ingredients, adding more milk if needed. Form into round loaf and place on greased baking sheet.
5. Bake at 350° for 1 hour or until done. Store in tightly closed plastic bag to prevent hardening.

Irish Pan Bread

Grace Moore
Lodi, CA

Makes 1 large round loaf

5 cups flour, sifted
1 cup sugar
1 Tbsp. baking powder
1 tsp. baking soda
1½ tsp. salt
8 Tbsp. butter
2½ cups buttermilk
1 egg, lightly beaten
2½ cups seedless raisins
3 Tbsp. caraway seeds
1 Tbsp. sugar
1 Tbsp. buttermilk

1. Sift together flour, 1 cup sugar, baking powder, baking soda and salt. Cut in butter until texture is coarse. Add 2½ cups buttermilk and egg to dry mixture, along with raisins and caraway seeds, blending only until moistened.
2. Generously grease a large, heavy iron skillet. Turn batter into skillet.
3. Bake at 350° for 1 hour or until firm and browned. Remove from oven. Sprinkle with 1 Tbsp. sugar and drizzle with 1 Tbsp. buttermilk to form a crust as bread cools. Cool on a wire rack.

Mama's Cornbread

Tommie Freeman
Carrollton, GA
Olympic Quilt

Makes 6-8 servings

1 egg
2 cups buttermilk
1½ cups self-rising cornmeal
½ cup self-rising flour
1 tsp. sugar
¼ cup cooking oil

1. Break egg into 2-quart bowl and add buttermilk. Add cornmeal, flour and sugar and mix well.
2. Grease a medium iron skillet and heat it. Pour oil into cornmeal mixture and mix well. Pour mixture into hot skillet.
3. Bake at 400° for about 30 minutes or until golden brown.

Grandma's Johnny Cake

Marie E. Fuller
Ashfield, MA
Little Red Schoolhouse Anniversary

Makes 10-12 servings

1 cup cornmeal
1 cup flour
½ cup sugar
1 tsp. cream of tartar
½ tsp. baking soda
½ tsp. salt
2 Tbsp. butter
1 cup milk
1 egg

1. Mix together all dry ingredients. Cut in butter with pastry blender or two knives until well mixed.
2. In separate bowl combine milk and egg. Add to dry ingredients and stir until just moistened. Pour into greased 9-inch square baking pan.
3. Bake at 400° for 20 minutes.

Onion Cheese Cornbread

Mary Lou Kirtland
Berkeley Heights, NJ
Bear Paw

Makes 8-10 servings

4 Tbsp. margarine
1 large Spanish onion,
   thinly sliced
¾ cup sour cream
1 cup shredded cheddar
   cheese
1 pkg. cornbread mix
8-oz. can cream-style corn
⅓ cup milk
1 egg

1. In frying pan melt margarine and sauté onion until transparent. Add sour cream and ½ cup shredded cheese and mix well.
2. In mixing bowl blend cornbread mix, cream-style corn, milk and egg. Spread into greased 9-inch square baking pan.
3. Spread onion mixture over cornbread. Sprinkle with remaining cheese.
4. Bake at 425° for 35-40 minutes. Serve hot.

Tin Can Bread

Trudy Kutter
Corfu, NY
Cake Stand

Makes 4 loaves

1 Tbsp. margarine
2-2½ cups raisin, date and
   nut mixture
1 tsp. baking soda
1 cup boiling water
2 eggs
1 cup sugar
1 tsp. lemon *or* orange
   extract
2 cups flour
2 tsp. baking powder
½ tsp. salt

1. Prepare 4 16-oz. tin cans by washing them thoroughly and removing the paper labels. Dry, grease and flour lightly.
2. Combine margarine, raisin mixture and baking soda. Pour boiling water over and let cool to room temperature.
3. Beat eggs until light. Gradually add sugar and extract.
4. Stir together dry ingredients and add to egg mixture. Stir in cooled raisin mixture. Spoon into 4 tin cans.
5. Bake at 325° for 55 minutes. Remove by turning cans upside down so loaves will fall out. Cool on wire rack. Serve with cream cheese or butter.

Pork and Bean Bread

Martha J. Lewis
Carlisle, PA
Sampler

Makes 2 loaves

3 eggs
1 cup cooking oil
2 cups sugar
16-oz. can pork and beans,
   undrained
1 cup applesauce
1 tsp. vanilla
2 cups flour
1 tsp. baking soda
½ tsp. baking powder
1 tsp. cinnamon
½ tsp. allspice
½ tsp. salt
1 cup chopped nuts

1. Blend together eggs, oil and sugar.
2. Pour pork and beans into separate bowl and mash. Add to egg and sugar mixture. Add applesauce, vanilla and all dry ingredients and mix thoroughly. Fold in nuts. Spoon into 2 greased loaf pans.
3. Bake at 325° for 60-70 minutes. Serve warm.

Poppy Seed Bread

Sue Hertzler Schrag
Beatrice, NE
Star Spin

Makes 2 loaves

Dough:
3 cups flour
1½ tsp. salt
1½ tsp. baking powder
2¼ cups sugar
3 eggs
1½ cups milk
1⅛ cups cooking oil
1½ Tbsp. poppy seeds
1½ tsp. vanilla
1½ tsp. almond flavoring
1½ tsp. butter flavoring

Glaze:
¾ cup sugar
¼ cup orange juice
½ tsp. vanilla
1½ tsp. almond flavoring
1½ tsp. butter flavoring

1. Combine all dough ingredients and beat 2 minutes with mixer. Spoon into 2 large greased loaf pans.
2. Bake at 350° for 1 hour or until toothpick comes out clean. Remove from oven and cool 5 minutes.
3. To prepare glaze combine all ingredients and mix well. Pour glaze over slightly cooled bread and return to oven for 10 minutes. Remove and cool 5 minutes before turning bread out of pans.

Beet Bread

Abbie Christie
Berkeley Heights, NJ
Bow Ties for Andy

Makes 10-12 servings

3-ozs. unsweetened chocolate
1 cup cooking oil
1¾ cups sugar
3 large eggs
2 cups puréed beets
1 tsp. vanilla
2 cups flour
2 tsp. baking soda
½ tsp. salt

1. Melt chocolate with ¼ cup oil. Cool slightly.
2. Beat sugar and eggs with mixer until light and fluffy. Slowly beat in remaining ¾ cup oil, beets, chocolate and vanilla.
3. Sift together flour, baking soda and salt. Slowly add to batter, stirring well. Spoon into greased and floured 12-cup bundt pan.
4. Bake at 375° for 1 hour. Cool 15 minutes in pan.

Zucchini Bread

Carol Weaver
Houston, TX
Cover Up Clowns
Mary Ellen Roseberry
Mount Joy, PA
Sampler

Makes 2 loaves

2 eggs
1 cup cooking oil
1 cup brown sugar
1 cup white sugar
2 cups grated zucchini
2 Tbsp. vanilla
3 cups flour
1 tsp. baking soda
¼ tsp. baking powder
1 tsp. cinnamon
½ cup chopped nuts *or* raisins (optional)

1. Beat eggs. Add oil, sugars, zucchini and vanilla and mix lightly.
2. Combine flour, baking soda, baking powder and cinnamon. Add slowly to batter and mix lightly. If desired, fold in nuts or raisins.
3. Pour batter into 2 medium greased and floured loaf pans.
4. Bake at 350° for 1 hour or until toothpick inserted in center comes out clean.

Variation:
Add 1 tsp. nutmeg and about 3 tsp. cinnamon, according to taste.
Sue Shelenberger
Conneaut, OH
Ohio Star Challenge

Rita's Date Bread

M. Jeanne Osborne
Sanford, ME
Pieced Star for Lucas

Makes 1 loaf

1 cup sugar
½ cup margarine
½ cup sour cream
1 tsp. vanilla
3 mashed bananas
2 eggs
2 cups flour
1 tsp. baking soda
¼ tsp. salt
1 cup chopped dates
½ cup chopped raisins
½ cup chopped walnuts

1. Combine all ingredients and mix well. Pour batter into greased loaf pan.
2. Bake at 350° for 45-60 minutes. .

❖

Aunt Mabel's Date Nut Bread

Betty K. Fulmer
Quakertown, PA
North Carolina Lily

Makes 1 loaf

2 cups boiling water
8-oz. pkg. pitted dates, chopped
2 tsp. butter
2 tsp. baking soda

1 egg, beaten
2⅔ cups flour
1½ cups sugar *or* less
½ tsp. salt
1 tsp. vanilla
½ cup broken walnuts

1. In a large bowl pour boiling water over dates. Cool to warm. Add butter and baking soda and continue cooling. Stir in beaten egg.
2. In separate bowl sift together flour, sugar and salt. Add to date mixture with vanilla and nuts. Stir by hand to avoid breaking up walnuts. Pour into a greased and floured loaf pan. Let stand for 20 minutes.
3. Bake at 350° for 60-70 minutes, testing for doneness with toothpick.

❖

Nut Bread

Connie Weaver
Bethlehem, PA
Log Cabin

Makes 1 loaf

2 cups flour
2½ tsp. baking powder
¾ tsp. salt
½ cup sugar
½ cup chopped nuts
1 cup milk
1 egg, beaten
5 Tbsp. shortening, melted

1. Sift together all dry ingredients. Add nuts.
2. Combine milk, egg and shortening. Add to dry ingredients, stirring until well mixed. Pour into greased loaf pan and let stand about 20 minutes.
3. Bake at 350° for about 1 hour, testing for doneness with toothpick.

Banana Nut Bread

Celia LoPinto
San Francisco, CA
Eileen Plementos
Williams Lake, BC
Mrs. Enos C. Yoder
Haven, KS
Carolee Kidd
Albuquerque, NM

Makes 1 loaf

½ cup shortening
1 cup sugar
2 eggs
2 cups all-purpose flour
1 tsp. baking soda
1 cup mashed ripe bananas
¼ cup chopped walnuts

1. Cream shortening and sugar together. Add eggs, one at a time, beating after each addition.
2. Sift together flour and baking soda. Add to batter, alternating with bananas. Mix until dough is moistened. Fold in walnuts and pour into greased loaf pan.

3. Bake at 350° for 45-55 minutes or until done.

Pumpkin Banana Bread

Lois Stoltzfus
Honey Brook, PA
Dresden Plate

Makes 1 loaf

½ cup sugar
1 large banana, mashed
¾ cup cooking oil
1 cup mashed pumpkin
2 eggs
2 cups all-purpose flour
1 tsp. baking soda
½ tsp. baking powder
½ tsp. salt
2 tsp. vanilla

1. Mix sugar, banana, oil, pumpkin and eggs in large bowl. Stir in remaining ingredients until just mixed. Pour into greased loaf pan.
2. Bake at 325° for 60-70 minutes or until wooden pick inserted in center comes out clean.
3. Let cool 10 minutes. Remove from pan and cool completely before slicing.

Spicy Pumpkin Bread

Thelma Swody
Stonington, CT
Edna Nisly, Partridge, KS
Patricia Segal
Mechanicsburg, PA

Makes 2 loaves

¾ cup butter
2½ cups sugar
4 eggs
16-oz. can pumpkin
⅔ cup water
3½ cups unbleached flour
2 tsp. baking soda
1½ tsp. salt
1½ tsp. baking powder
1 tsp. cinnamon
1 tsp. ground cloves
⅔ cup chopped nuts

1. In large bowl cream together butter, sugar and 2 eggs. Add remaining eggs, one at a time, beating thoroughly. Stir in pumpkin and water.
2. In separate bowl combine all remaining ingredients except nuts and mix well. Add to pumpkin mixture, a little at a time, and stir until batter is thoroughly blended. Fold in nuts. Spoon batter into 2 greased and floured loaf pans.
3. Bake at 350° for 1 hour and 10 minutes or until toothpick inserted in center comes out clean. Cool 15 minutes before removing from pan.

Applesauce Fruit Bread

Philip S. Pipero
Brooklyn, NY

Makes 1 loaf

1½ cups all-purpose flour
1 cup applesauce
½ cup brown sugar
⅓ cup cooking oil
2 eggs
1½ tsp. salt
1 tsp. baking soda
1 tsp. baking powder
1 tsp. cinnamon
1½ cups quick oats
1 cup seedless raisins
½ cup candied fruit

1. Using medium speed on mixer, mix together flour, applesauce, brown sugar, oil, eggs, salt, baking soda, baking powder and cinnamon until well blended. Stir in oats, raisins and candied fruit. Spoon into greased 9" x 5" loaf pan.
2. Bake at 350° for 1 hour or until toothpick inserted in center comes out clean.

Orange Bread

Thelma Swody
Stonington, CT
Sunnybrook Farm

Makes 2 loaves

1 cup sugar
1/2 cup butter
2 eggs
1 cup sour cream
Rind of 1 orange, grated
2 cups flour
1 tsp. baking soda
1/2 cup sugar
Juice of 1 orange

1. Cream together 1 cup sugar and butter. Add eggs, sour cream and rind of orange.
2. Sift together flour and baking soda. Mix into creamed ingredients. Spoon into 2 greased medium loaf pans.
3. Bake at 350° for 50 minutes.
4. Mix together 1/2 cup sugar and orange juice and pour over bread while still hot. Cool 10 minutes and invert. Enjoy!

Hawaiian Bread

Jennifer L. Rhodes
Lancaster, PA
White on White

Makes 2 loaves

28-oz. can crushed
   pineapple, undrained
10-oz. pkg. moist flaked
   coconut
4 eggs
1 1/2 cups sugar
4 cups flour
2 tsp. salt (optional)
2 tsp. baking soda

1. Combine all ingredients and mix well. Pour into 2 greased loaf pans.
2. Bake at 325° for 1 hour or until toothpick inserted in center comes out clean.

Lemon Bread

Maureen Csikasz
Wakefield, MA
Trip Around the World

Makes 8 servings

Batter:
1/2 cup shortening
1 cup sugar
2 eggs, beaten
1 1/2 cups flour
1/2 tsp. salt
1 tsp. baking powder
1/2 cup milk

1/2 cup chopped nuts
   (optional)
Rind of 1 lemon, grated

Topping:
Juice of 1 lemon
1/2 cup sugar

1. Cream together shortening and sugar. Add eggs and mix well.
2. Sift together flour, salt and baking powder. Add to creamed mixture, alternating with milk. Fold in nuts and lemon rind. Spoon into greased loaf pan.
3. Bake at 350° for 45-60 minutes.
4. To prepare topping combine lemon juice and sugar and mix well. After bread is baked, turn out onto plate right side up and cool about 10 minutes. Pour topping over bread. Cool completely.

Variation:
Add 1/4 tsp. almond extract to ingredients in step 1. Pour batter into 8" x 4" Corning-style baking pan. Here in the mountains I bake this recipe at 325° for 70 minutes or until toothpick comes out clean when inserted in center.

Sue Seeley
Black Forest, CO
Flying Geese

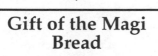

Gift of the Magi Bread

Arlene C. Kelly
Clarence, NY
Feathered Star Sampler

Makes 2 loaves

½ cup butter
1 cup sugar
2 eggs
1 tsp. vanilla
2 cups flour
1 tsp. baking soda
Pinch salt
1 cup mashed ripe bananas
11-oz. can mandarin
   oranges, drained
6-oz. pkg. mini chocolate
   chips
1 cup shredded coconut
⅔ cup sliced almonds or
   chopped walnuts
½ cup chopped
   maraschino cherries
½ cup chopped dates

1. Cream together butter and sugar. Add eggs and vanilla and beat until fluffy.
2. Sift together flour, baking soda and salt. Add to creamed mixture, alternating with bananas. Stir in orange segments, chocolate chips, coconut, almonds, cherries and dates. Pour into 2 greased loaf pans.
3. Bake at 350° for 1-1¼ hours.

Note: Occasionally I make 8 mini loaves with this batter. Bake at 350° for 45 minutes.

Cinnamon Monkey Bread

JoAnn Pelletier
Longmeadow, MA
Six Quilts in 14 Days

Makes 1 loaf

1 loaf frozen bread dough
8 Tbsp. butter *or* margarine
½ cup sugar
4-5 tsp. cinnamon

1. Thaw frozen bread dough and cut into 18-24 pieces.
2. Melt butter.
3. Mix sugar and cinnamon together.
4. Dip pieces of dough into melted butter and into cinnamon–sugar mixture.
5. Arrange coated pieces of dough in large loaf pan. Cover and let rise until pan is filled, about 1½ hours.
6. Bake at 350° for 25 minutes. Transfer hot bread with syrup into large casserole dish and serve.

Pailful of Muffins

Pauline Morrison
St. Marys, ON
Signature Quilt

Makes 60 muffins

2 cups boiling water
2 cups natural bran
1 cup soft margarine
2½ cups white sugar
½ cup molasses
4 eggs
4 cups buttermilk
5 cups all-purpose flour
2 Tbsp. baking soda
2 tsp. salt
2 cups All-Bran
2 cups oat bran
2 cups raisins

1. Pour boiling water over natural bran. Set aside.
2. Cream together margarine, sugar and molasses. Add eggs and buttermilk and beat until smooth. Add bran mixture.
3. In a separate bowl combine flour, baking soda and salt. Stir well and add to bran mixture. Stir in All-Bran, oat bran and raisins and mix until blended.
4. Refrigerate until ready to use. This batter will keep up to 2 months in airtight container.
5. When ready to use, fill greased muffin tins ½-⅔ full.

Raisin Bran Muffins

Rose Fitzgerald
Delaware, OH
Connee Sager, Tucson, AZ
Susie Braun, Rapid City, SD
Lori Drohman
Rogue River, OR
Cyndie Marrara
Port Matilda, PA

Makes 6 dozen muffins

4 eggs, beaten
1 quart buttermilk
5 tsp. baking soda
3 cups sugar
5 cups unsifted flour
1 cup cooking oil
15-oz. box raisin bran flakes

1. Combine all ingredients well and refrigerate at least overnight. Batter will keep as long as six weeks.
2. Spoon desired amount of batter into greased muffin tins.
3. Bake at 400° for 15 minutes.

Variation:
Instead of raisin bran flakes pour 2 cups boiling water over 2 cups 100% bran cereal and let cool. Stir in 4 cups All-Bran and add raisins as desired. Mix with other ingredients and proceed as given.
Ruth Liebelt
Rapid City, SD
Americana

Best Bran Muffins

Margaret M. McTigue
Scarsdale, NY
Village Squares

Makes 12 small muffins

1 Tbsp. molasses
¼ cup brown sugar
½ cup butter *or* margarine
1 tsp. baking soda
1 cup milk
½ cup flour
2 cups bran flakes
½ cup raisins
1 egg

1. Cream together molasses, brown sugar and butter. Stir in all remaining ingredients and let stand several minutes to soften bran flakes. Mix well.
2. Spoon into greased muffin tins.
3. Bake at 400° for 15-20 minutes, watching closely to prevent burning.

No-Fat Bran Muffins

Violette Denney
Carrollton, GA
1991 Sampler

Makes 12 muffins

1½ cups All-Bran
1¼ cups milk
1 egg
½ cup applesauce
1¼ cups self-rising flour
½ cup sugar
⅔ cup raisins (optional)

1. In a large bowl combine All-Bran and milk. Let stand about 3 minutes or until cereal softens.
2. Add egg and applesauce and mix well. Add flour and sugar. Fold in raisins.
3. Divide batter evenly into 12 lightly greased muffin-pan cups.
4. Bake at 400° about 20 minutes or until golden brown. Serve warm.

My mother-in-law has made a practice of giving each of her grandchildren a quilt on their sixth birthday. She also presents each child with a memories scrapbook covering the events of the first six years of their lives. They anticipate this birthday for months and feel so special when it finally arrives.

—*Rebecca MeyerKorth, Wamego, KS*

Company Muffins

Joan Kelly
Arnprior, ON
Sampler

Makes 18 muffins

1 cup all-purpose flour
1 cup oat bran
2 tsp. baking soda
1 tsp. baking powder
½ tsp. salt
2 tsp. cinnamon
1 cup brown sugar
2 large tart apples
1½ cups finely shredded
   carrots
½ cup raisins (optional)
1 cup chopped pecans
¼ cup cooking oil
½ cup skim milk
2 eggs, lightly beaten
1 tsp. vanilla

1. Combine flour, oat bran, baking soda, baking powder, salt and cinnamon in a large bowl. Add brown sugar and stir.

2. Peel, core and shred apples. Add apples, carrots, raisins and pecans to dry mixture and mix well. Make a well in the center and add oil, milk, eggs and vanilla. Stir until just moistened.

3. Using a ¼-cup measure, scoop muffin batter into greased muffin tins.

4. Bake at 375° for 18-20 minutes or until nicely browned.

Apple Raisin Muffins

Susan M. Miller
Centreville, MD
Strip-Pieced Triangles

Makes 12 muffins

¾ cup cooking oil
1 cup sugar
2 eggs
1 tsp. vanilla
2 cups flour
¾ tsp. baking soda
1 tsp. cinnamon
½ tsp. salt
1½ cups diced apples
½ cup raisins
½ cup chopped walnuts

1. In a large bowl beat oil and sugar with electric mixer for 2 minutes. Add eggs and vanilla and beat 1 minute.

2. In separate bowl stir together flour, baking soda, cinnamon and salt. Add to creamed mixture and stir until just moist. Fold in apples, raisins and walnuts. Fill 12 greased muffin cups ¾ full.

3. Bake at 400° for 25-30 minutes or until done. Remove from pan and cool on rack. May be served warm or cold.

Spicy Whole Wheat Zucchini Muffins

Sue Gierhart
Voorhees, NJ
Friendship

Makes 12 muffins

1 cup whole wheat flour
¾ cup unbleached white
   flour
¼ cup wheat germ
¼ cup sugar
1 Tbsp. baking powder
¼ tsp. baking soda
½ tsp. cinnamon
¼ tsp. allspice
Dash salt
1 cup milk
1 egg, lightly beaten
¼ cup cooking oil
1 cup grated, unpeeled
   zucchini
⅓ cup raisins

1. In mixing bowl combine flours, wheat germ, sugar, baking powder, baking soda, spices and salt.

2. Pour milk into 2-cup (or larger) measuring cup. Add egg and oil and blend well.

3. Pour milk mixture over dry ingredients and add zucchini and raisins. Stir just enough to moisten. Do not over mix.

4. Spoon batter into greased muffin cups.

5. Bake at 400° for 20-22 minutes.

Pineapple Zucchini Muffins

Marsha Sands
Ocean City, MD
Amish Sparkle Star
Sara Wolf
Washington, PA
Rolling Stones

Makes 2 dozen muffins

3 eggs
1 cup sugar
2 tsp. vanilla
1 cup cooking oil
2 cups grated zucchini,
   drained
3 cups flour
1 tsp. baking powder
1 tsp. baking soda
1 tsp. salt
1 cup crushed pineapple,
   drained
½ cup raisins
1 cup chopped nuts

1. Beat together eggs, sugar, vanilla and oil until fluffy. Add zucchini.
2. Combine flour, baking powder, baking soda and salt. Stir into zucchini mixture. Fold in pineapple, raisins and nuts. Spoon batter evenly into greased muffin tins.
3. Bake at 375° for 25 minutes or until done.

Banana Muffins

Marlene Fonken
Upland, CA
Crazy Patch

Makes 12 muffins

¼ cup shortening
1 cup sugar
1 egg
3 bananas, mashed
1 tsp. baking soda
1¼ cups flour
½ cup chopped nuts
   (optional)

1. Cream together shortening, sugar and egg. Add bananas and mix well. Add baking soda and flour and mix well. Fold in nuts. Spoon into 12 greased muffin cups.
2. Bake at 375° for 15 minutes.

Cranberry Orange Muffins

Susan Harms
Wichita, KS
Sampler

Makes 12 muffins

1 cup fresh cranberries,
   chopped
½ cup sugar
1 tsp. grated orange peel
1¾ cups all-purpose flour

2½ tsp. baking powder
¾ tsp. salt
1 egg, beaten
¼ cup orange juice
½ cup milk
⅓ cup cooking oil

1. Mix cranberries, sugar and orange peel. Set aside.
2. Sift together flour, baking powder and salt in large bowl.
3. In separate bowl combine egg, orange juice, milk and cooking oil. Add to dry ingredients, stirring until just moistened. Fold in cranberry mixture. Fill 12 greased muffin cups ⅔ full.
4. Bake at 400° for 20-25 minutes. Serve warm.

Whole Wheat Oat Blueberry Muffins

Betty Ann Sheganoski
Bayonne, NJ
Schoolhouse

Makes 12 muffins

2 eggs
3 Tbsp. sunflower oil
½ cup honey
¾ cup buttermilk
¾ tsp. vanilla
¾ cup oats
1¾ cups whole wheat flour
1⅓ tsp. baking soda
1⅓ tsp. baking powder
1 tsp. cinnamon
1¾ cups blueberries

1. Combine eggs, oil, honey, buttermilk, vanilla and oats and soak for 10 minutes.

2. In a separate bowl combine all dry ingredients. Pour dry ingredients into wet ingredients and mix well. Fold in blueberries. Spoon into greased muffin tins.

3. Bake at 375° for 18-20 minutes.

Sweet Blueberry Muffins

Maryellen Mross
Bartonsville, PA
Hearts and Flowers

Makes 24 muffins

Batter:
2 eggs
1 cup milk
½ cup cooking oil
3 cups flour
1 cup sugar
4 tsp. baking powder
1 tsp. salt
2 cups fresh *or* frozen
  blueberries

Crumbs:
1 cup flour
½ cup sugar
¼ cup butter

1. To prepare batter combine eggs, milk and oil in a bowl.

2. In separate bowl com-

bine flour, sugar, baking powder and salt.

3. Stir wet ingredients into dry ingredients until just moistened. Fold in blueberries. Spoon batter into 24 paper-lined muffin cups.

4. To prepare crumbs crumble all ingredients together. Sprinkle crumbs over each muffin.

5. Bake at 400° for 20-30 minutes.

Raspberry Streusel Muffins

Blanche Cahill
Willow Grove, PA
Variegated Star

Makes 12 muffins

Batter:
8 Tbsp. butter
½ cup sugar
1 large egg
2 cups flour
½ tsp. baking soda
½ tsp. baking powder
½ tsp. cinnamon
¼ tsp. salt
½ cup milk
½ cup sour cream
1 tsp. vanilla
1 cup fresh raspberries
Powdered sugar

Topping:
½ cup flour
½ cup quick oats
⅓ cup sugar

½ tsp. cinnamon
⅛ tsp. salt
6 Tbsp. butter

1. To prepare batter cream together butter and sugar until light and fluffy in large bowl. Add egg and beat until blended.

2. In medium bowl combine flour, baking soda, baking powder, cinnamon and salt.

3. In a small bowl combine milk, sour cream and vanilla.

4. Add flour mixture to creamed mixture, alternating with milk mixture. Beat only until all ingredients are combined. Gently fold in raspberries.

5. To prepare topping combine all dry ingredients in a medium bowl. With pastry blender or two knives cut in butter until mixture resembles crumbs. Rub briefly between fingers to blend butter.

6. Spoon muffin batter into greased tins, filling ⅔ full. Sprinkle top with streusel mix. Leftover streusel may be frozen for later use.

7. Bake at 400° for 20-25 minutes until cake tester comes out clean. Cool on rack and sprinkle with powdered sugar.

Lemon Nut Muffins

Trudi Cook
Newtown Square, PA
Amish Flower Garden

Makes 12 muffins

Batter:
1¾ cups flour
1 cup chopped walnuts
⅓ cup sugar
2 tsp. baking powder
1 tsp. grated lemon rind
½ tsp. salt
1 egg
½ cup milk
⅓ cup butter *or* margarine, melted
¼ cup sour cream

Streusel Topping:
3 Tbsp. flour
3 Tbsp. brown sugar
3 Tbsp. wheat germ
2 Tbsp. softened butter *or* margarine
1 tsp. grated lemon rind

1. To prepare batter combine flour, walnuts, sugar, baking powder, lemon rind and salt in large bowl.
2. In a small bowl beat egg with fork. Stir in milk, butter and sour cream. Add to flour mixture, stirring until just blended.
3. To prepare streusel topping combine all ingredients and mix until crumbly.
4. Fill greased muffin tins ⅔ full with batter. Sprinkle with streusel topping.

5. Bake at 400° for 15-20 minutes or until toothpick inserted in center comes out clean.

Sweet Potato Muffins

Teresa M. Prete
East Falmouth, MA
Double Wedding Ring

Makes 6 muffins

¾ cup flour
1½ tsp. baking powder
½ tsp. cinnamon
Dash nutmeg
6 ozs. cooked and peeled sweet potato, mashed
½ cup maple syrup
1 egg, beaten
2 Tbsp. cooking oil

1. In medium bowl combine flour, baking powder, cinnamon and nutmeg.
2. In small bowl combine remaining ingredients, mixing until egg is thoroughly combined. Stir into dry ingredients until just moistened. Spoon batter into 6 greased muffin cups.
3. Bake at 400° for 20-25 minutes. Cool muffins on wire rack.

Savory Cheese Muffins

Florence Heard
St. Marys, ON
Double Irish Chain

Makes 12 muffins

2 cups all-purpose flour
2 Tbsp. baking powder
½ tsp. salt
½ cup softened butter
¼ cup sugar
2 eggs
1 cup milk
1 cup grated cheddar cheese
1 tsp. basil

1. Sift together flour, baking powder and salt.
2. Cream together butter and sugar. Add eggs and beat well. Gradually add dry ingredients, alternating with milk. Quickly fold in cheese and basil. Spoon into greased muffin tins.
3. Bake at 350° for 25-30 minutes.

Cornmeal Muffins

Janet Groff
Stevens, PA
Country Love

Makes 12 muffins

1 cup all-purpose flour
1 cup yellow cornmeal
⅓ cup sugar
1 Tbsp. baking powder
1 tsp. salt
2 Tbsp. finely chopped
    onion
1 cup cream-style corn
½ cup mayonnaise
3 Tbsp. cooking oil
1 egg

1. In a large mixing bowl combine all dry ingredients.
2. Make a well in the center and add all remaining ingredients. Stir until lightly mixed.
3. Spoon into 12 greased muffin tins.
4. Bake at 400° for 20 minutes.

Southern Gal Biscuits

Donna Miller
Partridge, KS
Star Spin

Makes 6 biscuits

2 cups flour
4 tsp. baking powder
½ tsp. salt
2 Tbsp. sugar
½ tsp. cream of tartar
½ cup shortening
¾ cup milk
1 egg

1. Sift together flour, baking powder, salt, sugar and cream of tartar. Add shortening and mix well. Add milk and egg. Stir to stiff dough.
2. Roll out to 1-inch thickness. Cut biscuits with cookie cutter and arrange on greased baking sheet.
3. Bake at 450° for 10-15 minutes.

Drop Biscuits

Marlene Blackman
St. Marys, ON
Mountain Trails

Makes 8 biscuits

2 cups all-purpose flour
4 tsp. baking powder
2 Tbsp. white sugar
½ tsp. salt
5 Tbsp. shortening
¼ cup raisins (optional)
1 cup milk

1. Sift dry ingredients into bowl. Add shortening and work in with pastry blender. Add raisins if desired. Add milk all at once. Stir until flour is moistened.
2. With a greased tablespoon drop mixture onto ungreased baking sheet to make 8 biscuits.
3. Bake at 450° for 12 minutes or until golden.

When our rotary exchange student, Belen Pereira, prepared to return to her home in Argentina, she remarked that she would have two memories of me—my special bean salad recipe and my habit of cutting cloth into little pieces only to sew them back together again.

—*Shirley Norris, Walhonding, OH*

Meat Main Dishes

❖

Old-Fashioned Pot Roast

Elaine Untracht Pawelko
Monroe Township, NJ
Bride's Bouquet

Makes 6 servings

4-lb. beef brisket
1½ cups water
2 onions, sliced
1 clove garlic, minced
1 carrot, shredded
1 stalk celery, diced
1 green pepper, diced
2 tsp. salt
½ tsp. paprika
2 bay leaves

1. Heat heavy pot and braise meat until browned on all sides. (Meat will stick to pot.) Remove meat from pot.

2. Pour water into pot and heat to boiling. Scrape off browned bits from bottom of pot to form gravy. Return meat to pot. Add all remaining ingredients.

3. Simmer 1 ½-2 hours or until meat is tender.

4. Slice meat thinly and serve with strained gravy.

❖

Company Pot Roast

Lee Ann Hazlett
Freeport, IL
Snowbound

Makes 4-6 servings

3-lb. roast
1-2 Tbsp. cooking oil
2 onions, quartered
1½ cups water
1 beef bouillon cube
2 Tbsp. sugar
½-1 tsp. cinnamon
⅓ cup dry sherry (optional)
¼ cup soy sauce
4 potatoes, peeled and halved
1½ Tbsp. cornstarch
¼ cup cold water

1. In Dutch oven brown the roast in oil. Add all remaining ingredients except potatoes, cornstarch and cold water.

2. Cover and simmer until meat is tender, about 2 hours. Add water as needed.

3. Add potatoes and simmer another 45-60 minutes. Spoon juices over vegetables occasionally while cooking.

4. When tender, remove meat and vegetables onto warming platter.

5. Dissolve cornstarch in cold water and add to juices in Dutch oven. Stir until slightly thickened. Serve gravy with meat and vegetables.

Note: Prepare in crockpot by combining all ingredients except cornstarch and water. Cook on medium for 6-8 hours. Immediately before serving, prepare gravy with cornstarch and water.

94

Baked Steak in Mushroom Gravy

Shirley Liby
Muncie, IN
At Loose Ends

Makes 4-6 servings

3-5 lb. cut round steak
Cooking oil
½ cup flour
2 10¾-oz. cans cream of
  mushroom soup
8-oz. jar sliced
  mushrooms, drained
2 cups milk
Salt and pepper to taste

1. Trim all fat from meat and cut into 3-inch square pieces. Prepare skillet with scant amount cooking oil. Dredge meat in flour and brown on both sides.
2. Pour 1 can cream of mushroom soup into Dutch oven. Arrange meat over soup. Pour remaining soup over meat and add mushrooms, milk and seasonings.
3. Cover and bake at 300° for 2 hours.

Variation:
Add 3 sliced onions and 2 large chopped potatoes in step 2.

SherylAnne Bratton
North Hills, PA
Steph's Quilt

Round Steak in Tomato Sauce

Anna Tompkins
Greenfield, OH
Card Trick

Makes 6-8 servings

2-3 lb. round steak
Flour
1 Tbsp. cooking oil
½ cup water
16-oz. can tomatoes
1 stalk celery, diced
1 small onion, diced
1 small mango, diced
1 Tbsp. sugar

1. Flour and brown steak in cooking oil in a heavy skillet. Add water and cook on medium heat for ½ hour.
2. Prepare vegetables and pour over meat. Stir in sugar.
3. Cook for 2 hours on medium heat. Serve.

Baked Chuck Roast

Mary Ellen Esh
Gordonville, PA
Giant Dahlia

Makes 10-12 servings

5-lb. chuck roast
1 pkg. dry onion soup mix
2 12-oz. cans Coca Cola

1. Place chuck roast in roasting pan. Sprinkle with onion soup mix. Pour Coca Cola over roast.
2. Cover and seal tightly with aluminum foil.
3. Bake at 250° for 4 hours or until tender.

Variation:
Substitute 3-6 carrots, sliced, 10¾-oz. can mushroom soup and dash garlic salt for Coca Cola. Bake at 250° for 4 hours.

Barbara Neuhauser
Parkesburg, PA
Baby Quilt

My sister and I decided to make a quilt for our father's 50th birthday. Determined to make the project a joint effort, even though we lived 300 miles apart, we divided the piecing duties and worked separately on the top. When it came to the actual quilting, we needed a way to transport the quilt several times between our homes in Victoria and Brownsville, Texas. Dad solved the problem.

As a pilot he made numerous trips between our towns, so we packed our project and disguised it as anything but a quilt. Without ever suspecting anything, he flew it back and forth several times. He was thrilled with the quilt and its story.

—*Susan Thomson, Houston, TX*

Barbecued Brisket

Dorothy Dyer
Lee's Summit, MO
Lover's Heart

Makes 25-30 servings

10-12-lb. brisket
½ cup Italian dressing
2 tsp. liquid smoke
½ cup brown sugar
1 tsp. celery salt
1 tsp. salt
1 Tbsp. Worcestershire
sauce
½ tsp. pepper
¼ tsp. chili powder
½ tsp. garlic powder
12-oz. jar barbecue sauce

1. Pierce meat with fork on both sides. Place meat on large piece of aluminum foil in roaster.
2. Combine all remaining ingredients except barbecue sauce and pour over both sides of meat. Close foil tightly and refrigerate at least 12 hours to marinate.
3. Preheat oven to 300°. Place roaster in oven. Reduce oven temperature to 275° and bake about 5 hours.
4. Cool meat completely and slice diagonally across the grain. Arrange sliced meat in foil-lined baking pan. Pour barbecue sauce over meat.
5. Before serving, bake at 325° for about 20 minutes.

Pepper Steak

Elaine A. Halos
Comfrey, MN
Log Cabin & Amish Basket

Makes 6 servings

2 lbs. beef pot roast, cubed
2 Tbsp. cooking oil
¾ cup water
Salt and pepper to taste
2 beef bouillon cubes
¾ cup chopped onion
1½ cups sliced green
peppers
½ cup chopped
mushrooms (optional)
1½ cups chopped celery
5 Tbsp. soy sauce
1½ cups water
1½ Tbsp. cornstarch
4 tomatoes

1. Brown beef slightly in oil. Add water, salt, pepper and bouillon cubes and simmer for 1 hour or until tender. Add more water if necessary.
2. Add vegetables, cover and heat through.
3. Combine soy sauce, water and cornstarch. Pour over mixture and cook for about 15 minutes.
4. Chop each tomato into 8 wedges. Arrange wedges over top of meat and vegetables. Cover and cook about 5 minutes or until tomatoes are soft.
5. Serve over cooked rice.

Hungarian Gulyas

Maureen Csikasz
Wakefield, MA
Trip Around the World

Makes 4-6 servings

2 lbs. beef *or* pork
4 Tbsp. cooking oil
2 onions, coarsely chopped
4 Tbsp. sweet paprika
Salt to taste
¼ tsp. caraway seed
1 clove garlic, chopped
½ green pepper
4-6 Tbsp. sour cream
Parsley

1. Cut meat into 2-inch pieces. Brown in oil. Add onion and cook until onion is transparent.
2. Add paprika, salt, caraway seed and garlic. Lay ½ whole green pepper on top.
3. Cover and cook slowly for approximately 1 hour or until meat is tender. Add water if needed.
4. Garnish with sour cream and parsley and serve with noodles or potatoes.

Rouladen

Margaret Morris
Middle Village, NY
Grandma's Flower Garden

Makes 4 servings

2-lb. piece flank steak
3 tsp. Dijon mustard
½ tsp. salt
¼ tsp. pepper
2 large pickles
3 slices bacon
1 large onion, chopped
¼ cup cooking oil
1½ cups hot beef broth
4 peppercorns
½ bay leaf
1 Tbsp. cornstarch
¼ cup water

1. Lay steak on flat surface. (If flank steak is too thick, slice lengthwise through middle to make thinner pieces.) Pound meat until flat. Cut up into 6" x 8" pieces. Spread each piece with mustard, salt and pepper.

2. Cut pickles into long thin strips. Cut bacon into smaller slices. Divide pickles, bacon and onion evenly over steak. Roll up and secure with toothpick or thread.

3. Heat oil in heavy saucepan. Add steak rolls and brown well on all sides, about 15 minutes. Pour hot beef broth, peppercorns and bay leaf into saucepan. Cover and simmer for 1 hour and 20 minutes.

4. Remove beef rolls, discarding toothpicks or thread and arrange on platter.

5. Blend cornstarch with water. Stir into broth mixture in saucepan and bring to a boil. Cook until thickened and bubbly.

6. Remove bay leaf and peppercorns and serve gravy with Rouladen.

Beef Birds

Carolyn Callis
Houston, TX
Ohio Star

Makes 8 servings

2½ lbs. round steak
8-10 slices bacon
1 lb. ground pork sausage
2-3 Tbsp. chopped onion
1 lb. small white onions
2 lbs. mushrooms
10¾-oz. can beef stock
2-3 cups red wine
   (optional)
½ cup flour
1 bay leaf
1 Tbsp. chopped parsley

1. Have grocer slice steak into ¼-inch slices. Cut meat slices into 8-10 3" x 6" pieces. Spread one meat slice over each bacon slice.

2. Combine sausage and 2-3 Tbsp. onion. Spread evenly on each slice of meat and bacon. Roll up and tie

with twine. Place in hot skillet and brown lightly. Remove to casserole dish and surround with white onions and mushrooms.

3. In a saucepan heat beef stock. Add wine. (Substitute with water or more beef stock if desired.) Gradually add flour and heat until thickened. Pour gravy over meat and vegetables in casserole dish. Add bay leaf.

4. Cover and bake at 350° for 2 hours.

5. Remove twine and bay leaf. Pour gravy into separate serving dish. Arrange meat and vegetables on platter and sprinkle with parsley.

Beef Pot Pie

Jean H. Robinson
Cinnaminson, NJ
Little School Girl

Makes 12 servings

3 lbs. beef cubes
Flour
3 Tbsp. olive oil
2 onions, chopped
5 carrots, chopped
4 cups water
1½ cups frozen peas
Enough pastry to cover
ingredients in 9" x 13" pan

1. Cut beef cubes into small pieces and dust with flour. Brown in Dutch oven in olive oil.
2. Stir in onions and carrots and sauté lightly. Add water. Cover and cook 1 hour.
3. Add peas and cook several minutes longer. Remove from heat. Pour into 9" x 13" baking pan. Cover with pastry.
4. Bake at 350° for 45 minutes.

Beef Casserole

Dottie Geraci
Burtonsville, MD
Rosie Stars

Makes 6-8 servings

2 lbs. beef cubes
Salt and pepper to taste
2 large onions, sliced
2 Tbsp. olive oil
4-oz. can sliced mushrooms
4 medium potatoes, thinly
sliced
10¾-oz. can cream of
mushroom soup
¾ cup milk
¾ cup sour cream
1 tsp. salt
¼ tsp. pepper
2 cups shredded cheddar
cheese
½ cup fine dry bread
crumbs (optional)

1. Season meat with salt and pepper. In large skillet cook and stir meat and onions in olive oil until meat is brown and onions are tender. Drain oil.
2. Drain mushrooms, reserving liquid. Add enough water to mushroom liquid to make 1 cup. Stir mushrooms and liquid into meat and onions. Heat to boiling. Reduce heat, cover and simmer 1-1½ hours.
3. Pour meat mixture into 9" x 13" baking dish. Arrange potatoes over meat.
4. Combine soup, milk, sour cream, 1 tsp. salt and ¼ tsp. pepper. Pour over

potatoes and sprinkle with cheese.
5. Bake, uncovered, at 350° for 1 hour. Sprinkle with bread crumbs if desired. Bake, uncovered, until potatoes are tender and crumbs are browned, about 20-30 minutes.

❖

Beef Stroganoff

Frani Shaffer
West Caln, PA
Rose of Sharon
Judi Robb
Manhattan, KS
Inner City

Makes 4 servings

2 lbs. lean sirloin steak
1 large onion, diced
2 10¾-oz. cans cream of
mushroom soup
¼ cup water
2 Tbsp. parsley
1 tsp. salt
1 tsp. pepper
1 pint sour cream
1 pkg. egg noodles

1. Cut steak into 1-inch strips. (If steak is partially frozen, it is easier to slice.)
2. Sauté strips of steak with diced onion in hot skillet until just slightly pink. Stir in soup and water and simmer for 10 minutes over low heat.
3. Meanwhile, prepare noodles according to pack-

age directions.

4. Add seasonings and sour cream to steak, stirring until blended. Serve steak with cooked noodles.

Stir-Fry Beef with Snow Pea Pods

Cynda Leininger
Mechanicsburg, PA

Makes 2-4 servings

1 lb. top round beef
2 Tbsp. soy sauce
2 Tbsp. dry sherry
 (optional)
2 Tbsp. cooking oil
16 snow pea pods
8-12 water chestnuts, sliced
½ cup chicken broth
1 Tbsp. cornstarch
2 Tbsp. cold water
Walnuts

1. Freeze meat partially. Slice into thin pieces.

2. Combine 1 Tbsp. soy sauce and 1 Tbsp. sherry in small bowl. Substitute extra soy sauce for sherry if desired. Add beef and marinate for 30 minutes.

3. Heat oil in wok or skillet. Stir-fry snow peas 1-2 minutes. Set aside.

4. Stir-fry water chestnuts 1 minute. Set aside.

5. Stir-fry beef 3-4 minutes. Add snow peas, water chestnuts, chicken broth, 1 Tbsp. soy sauce and 1 Tbsp.

sherry and heat through, stirring constantly.

6. Dissolve cornstarch in water. Add to mixture and heat until sauce thickens and is clear.

7. Garnish with walnuts and serve with rice.

Crockpot Beef Stew

Anna S. Petersheim
Paradise, PA
Shadow Star

Makes 8-10 servings

1½ lbs. cubed beef *or*
 venison
¼ cup chopped onion
4 medium potatoes, sliced
1 stalk celery, diced
2 carrots, sliced
Salt and pepper to taste
½ tsp. Worcestershire
 sauce
8-oz. can tomato sauce

1. Layer ingredients in crockpot in order given.

2. Cook on high for ½ hour. Turn to low and cook another 6-8 hours.

Oven Beef Burgundy

Mary Mitchell
Battle Creek, MI

Makes 4-6 servings

3 lbs. beef chuck roast, cut
 into cubes
10¾-oz. can cream of
 mushroom soup
1 scant soup can dry red
 wine (optional)
8-oz. jar whole
 mushrooms, undrained
1-2 onions, cut into chunks
Salt and pepper to taste
¼ cup cold water
¼ cup flour

1. Place all ingredients except water and flour in 3-quart casserole dish. (If desired, substitute beef stock for wine.)

2. Cover and bake at 350° for 3 hours. Stir once or twice during baking time.

3. Combine water and flour to make flour paste. If paste is not smooth, add more water. During last 5 minutes of baking time, stir flour paste into mixture to thicken.

4. Serve over hot noodles.

Variation:
Substitute 8-oz. can tomato sauce and 1 pkg. dry onion soup mix for mushroom soup. Use ½ cup red wine if desired.
Susan G. Sneer
Mountain Lake, MN
Double Irish Chain

Caesar Stew

Charmaine Caesar
Lancaster, PA
Grandmother's Memories

Makes 6 servings

1½ lbs. beef cubes
4 Tbsp. flour
½ tsp. salt
¼ tsp. pepper
2 Tbsp. shortening
2 medium onions, diced
1 cup red wine (optional)
2 bay leaves
3 10¾-oz. cans beef broth
3 cups diced potatoes
2 lbs. carrots, finely
  chopped
2 Tbsp. Worcestershire
  sauce
1 lb. fresh green beans,
  thinly sliced
12-ozs. fresh mushrooms,
  sliced
28-oz. can whole tomatoes,
  chopped

1. Coat meat with flour, salt and pepper mixture.
2. Heat shortening in skillet and brown meat. Put meat in stew pot with onions, wine and bay leaves. (Substitute water for wine if desired.)
3. Simmer for 1-1½ hours until meat is tender. Add remaining ingredients except tomatoes, cover and cook on slow simmer until vegetables are tender.
4. Add mushrooms and simmer for ½ hour.
5. Stir in tomatoes and heat through.

Buffalo Stew

Katy J. Widger
Los Lunas, NM
Nikki's Ecology Quilt

Makes 4 servings

1 lb. buffalo meat, cut in
  small cubes
Salt and pepper to taste
1 Tbsp. olive oil
½ cup chopped onion
1 clove garlic, minced
10¾-oz. can chicken broth
½ cup red wine (optional)
¼ cup ketchup
1 Tbsp. Kitchen Bouquet
1-2 Tbsp. flour
½ cup chicken broth
1 cup sliced fresh
  mushrooms

1. Salt and pepper the meat.
2. Heat oil in saucepan and sauté meat. Add onion and garlic and sauté until clear.
3. Reserve ½ cup chicken broth. Add remaining chicken broth, wine, ketchup and Kitchen Bouquet to ingredients. Heat slowly.
4. Combine flour and chicken broth and add gradually to stew, stirring to thicken. Add mushrooms.
5. Simmer until meat is tender, about 35-40 minutes. Serve with crusty bread and a green salad.

Meatloaf and Piquant Sauce

Barbara G. Mann
Beatrice, NE
Double Irish Chain

Makes 5 servings

Meatloaf:
2 eggs, beaten
1 cup milk
⅔ cup bread *or* cracker
  crumbs
1½ lbs. ground beef
¼ cup chopped onion
½ tsp. sage
⅛ tsp. pepper
1 tsp. salt

Sauce:
6 Tbsp. brown sugar
½ cup ketchup
½ tsp. nutmeg
2 tsp. dry mustard

1. To prepare meatloaf beat eggs in small bowl. Add milk and crumbs and stir together with fork. Set aside.
2. In medium bowl combine ground beef, onion and seasonings. Add milk and crumb mixture and stir well. Pack meatloaf into greased loaf or baking pan.
3. To prepare sauce combine all ingredients and beat together with a fork. Spread sauce over meatloaf.
4. Bake at 350° for 1 hour.

Surprise Meatloaf

M. Jeanne Osborne
Sanford, ME
Gwen's Tulips

Makes 6-8 servings

2½ lbs. lean ground beef
Salt and pepper to taste
½ tsp. garlic salt
2 eggs
⅔ cup bread crumbs
1 Tbsp. parsley flakes
10-oz. pkg. chopped
    spinach, thawed
8-oz. carton lowfat sour
    cream
1 cup shredded lowfat
    mozzarella cheese

1. Mix together ground beef, salt, pepper, garlic salt, eggs, bread crumbs and parsley flakes. Roll out into ½-inch thick rectangle.
2. Combine spinach, sour cream and cheese and spread over meat mixture. Roll up in jelly roll fashion and place in a large loaf pan.
3. Bake at 350° for 1 hour.

Celery Meatloaf

P. Helen Hall
Arnprior, ON
Sampler

Makes 4 servings

1 lb. lean ground beef
2 slices day-old bread,
    cubed
10¾-oz. can cream of
    celery soup
1 medium onion, chopped
1 egg
1 Tbsp. soy sauce
Dash pepper

1. Combine all ingredients in bowl and mix well. Spoon into loaf pan or casserole dish.
2. Bake at 400° for 1 hour.

Surprise Mini Loaves

Esther Becker
Gap, PA
Log Cabin Star

Makes 12-15 servings

1½ cups soft bread crumbs
½ cup milk
3 eggs, beaten
1 pkg. dry onion soup mix
3 lbs. lean ground beef
12-oz. bottle barbecue
    sauce
1½ cups water
½ cup brown sugar
16-oz. can sauerkraut
16-oz. can whole berry
    cranberry sauce

1. Combine bread crumbs, milk, eggs, onion soup and ground beef. Shape into 4 small loaves.
2. In a saucepan combine all remaining ingredients. Simmer for 5 minutes. Pour over loaves in a baking pan.
3. Cover and bake at 350° for 1½ hours.

A highlight of my young quilting years was being featured with my mother and grandmother as three generations of quilters at a quilt show in my home community of Freeman, SD. Though we now live 500 miles apart, my mother and I still frequently consult each other on quilting patterns and materials.

—*Lois Landis, Sterling, IL*

Sara Stoltzfus's Meatballs

Sara Ann Stoltzfus
Spring Mills, PA
Wedding Ring

Makes 20-24 meatballs

Meatballs:
2 lbs. ground beef
½ tsp. salt *or* less
1 tsp. pepper *or* less
1 tsp. dry mustard
1 medium onion, chopped
1 egg
1 cup applesauce
2 cups oatmeal *or* cornflakes

Sauce:
1 cup water
1 cup ketchup
2 10¾-oz. cans mushroom *or* celery soup
Pinch brown sugar

1. Combine all meatball ingredients and form into balls. Arrange in 9" x 13" baking pan.
2. Combine all sauce ingredients and cook until well mixed. Pour over meatballs.
3. Bake at 350° for 1 hour.

❖

Barbecued Meatballs

Mrs. Melvin A. Yoder
Hutchinson, KS
Barbara Stoltzfus, Kinzer, PA
Amanda Schlabach
Millersburg, OH

Makes 80 small meatballs

Meatballs:
3 lbs. ground beef
12-oz. can evaporated milk
2 cups quick oatmeal

At the time Atlanta was lobbying for the chance to host the 1996 Summer Olympics, my son was enthusiastically involved. I too became excited at the prospect and decided to express my emotion with an original quilt design.

"My Olympic Quilt" became a family project, involving my daugher, my husband's aunt and my mother. I incorporated Olympic symbols and various other designs that represent the city of Atlanta and the state of Georgia. It is done in gold, red, blue, green and black and is my way of documenting this major event in the history of Atlanta. I find myself wondering if 100 years from now my quilt will be discoverd somewhere and people will wonder about the 1996 Summer Olympics and the quilter who was so interested in the event.

—*Tommie Freeman, Carrollton, GA*

2 eggs
½ cup chopped onion
½ tsp. garlic powder
2 tsp. salt
½ tsp. pepper
2 tsp. chili powder

Sauce:
2 cups ketchup
1 cup water
1 cup brown sugar
½ cup chopped onion
2 Tbsp. liquid smoke

1. Combine all meatball ingredients and shape into balls about the size of a walnut. Arrange in flat baking pans, one layer to a pan.
2. Combine all sauce ingredients and pour over meatballs.
3. Bake at 350° for 1 hour.

❖

Frankie Greeley's Meatballs

Frankie Greeley
Arnprior, ON
Sampler

Makes 35-40 meatballs

Meatballs:
1 lb. ground beef
1 lb. ground pork
1 cup milk
2 eggs
1 tsp. salt
1 cup bread crumbs

Sauce:
1½ cups brown sugar

¾ cup white vinegar
½-1 tsp. garlic powder
¾ cup water
1 tsp. dry mustard

1. Combine all meatball ingredients and form into balls.
2. Combine all sauce ingredients and pour over meatballs in casserole dish.
3. Bake at 350° for 40 minutes.

❖

Busy Day Barbecued Meatballs

Karen M. Rusten
Waseca, MN
Ocean Waves

Makes 20-25 meatballs

Meatballs:
1½ lbs. ground beef
1 egg, slightly beaten
½ cup soft bread crumbs
1 tsp. salt
Pepper to taste

Sauce:
1 cup ketchup
1 Tbsp. Worcestershire sauce
2 Tbsp. brown sugar
2 Tbsp. vinegar
¼ tsp. salt
Dash pepper

1. Combine all meatball ingredients. Shape into 1-inch balls.
2. Mix sauce ingredients well. Pour over meatballs in a glass baking pan. Refrigerate until baking time.
3. Bake at 350° for 1 hour and 15 minutes. Baste once or twice while baking. Do not brown the meatballs first.

❖

Piquant Meatballs

MaryBeth Gower
Northampton, PA
Cut Glass Dishes

Makes 20 meatballs

Meatballs:
1½ lbs. ground meat
¼ cup dry bread crumbs
⅓ cup chopped onion
¼ cup milk
1 egg
1 Tbsp. parsley
1 tsp. salt *or less*
⅛ tsp. pepper
1 Tbsp. Worcestershire sauce

Sauce:
5 ozs. grape jelly
12-oz. jar chili sauce

1. Combine all meatball ingredients gently. Shape into small balls. Arrange on a non-stick jelly roll pan.
2. Bake at 350° for 30 minutes.
3. Meanwhile, combine sauce ingredients in a sauce-pan and heat through.
4. Drain meatballs and spoon into sauce.
5. Serve with toothpicks as an appetizer.

❖

Sophisticated Meatballs

Rosaria V. Strachan
Old Greenwich, CT
Nine Patch

Makes 20-24 meatballs

1 lb. ground beef
⅓ cup dry bread crumbs
⅓ cup milk
1 egg, beaten
2 Tbsp. chopped onion
½ tsp. salt
Pepper to taste
2 Tbsp. cooking oil
10¾-oz. can mushroom soup
8-oz. pkg. cream cheese, softened
½ cup water

1. Combine beef, bread crumbs, milk, egg, onion, salt and pepper and shape into balls.
2. Brown meatballs in cooking oil. Cover and cook 15 minutes over low heat. Remove balls, pour off drippings and stir in mushroom soup, cream cheese and water. Heat through.
3. Serve in a chafing dish to keep warm.

Sweet and Sour Meatballs

Sarah S. King
Gordonville, PA
Giant Dahlia

Makes 20-24 meatballs

1 egg, beaten
1/3 cup milk
1/2 cup bread crumbs
1 lb. ground beef
1 small onion, chopped
1 clove garlic, chopped
3/4 tsp. salt
1/4 tsp. seasoning salt
1/4 tsp. pepper
Cooking oil
2 carrots, cut in strips
1 onion, cut in chunks
1 bell pepper, cut in strips
10-oz. jar sweet and sour
 sauce

1. In mixing bowl combine egg, milk and bread crumbs. Add ground beef, chopped onion, garlic and seasonings and mix well. Shape into small balls.
2. In small amount of cooking oil brown meatballs lightly.
3. Meanwhile, stir-fry carrots, onion chunks and pepper over medium heat until just soft.
4. In a saucepan combine all ingredients and heat through. Delicious when served with rice.

Variation:
 Omit stir-fried vegetables and serve meatballs with fol-

lowing sauce. Combine 15-oz. can cranberry sauce, 12-oz. bottle chili sauce, 2 Tbsp. brown sugar and 2 Tbsp. lemon juice. Pour over meatballs and heat to boiling point, stirring frequently. Lower heat and simmer for 1 hour, stirring occasionally.
 Elsie F. Porter
 Baltimore, MD
 Nine Patch Star

❖

Sweet and Sour Sauce

Sara Harter Fredette
Williamsburg, MA
Jer Bear's Bait Shop

Makes 2½ cups sauce

1 cup ketchup
1/2 cup vinegar
1/2 cup sugar
1 cup chopped onion
1 green pepper, chopped
3 Tbsp. Worcestershire
 sauce

1. Combine all sauce ingredients and pour over meatball recipe of choice.
2. Bake at 350° for 1 hour.

❖

Swedish Meatballs

Philip S. Pipero
Brooklyn, NY

Makes 48 small meatballs

1 lb. ground beef
1 lb. ground pork
1/2 cup dry bread crumbs
1/2 cup milk
1 egg, slightly beaten
1 Tbsp. chopped onion
1 tsp. salt
1 tsp. sugar
1/4 tsp. pepper
1/2 tsp. ground allspice
1/4 cup butter *or* margarine
2 Tbsp. flour
2 cups milk *or* cream
Salt and pepper to taste

1. Combine ground beef and pork with bread crumbs, 1/2 cup milk, egg, onion and seasonings. Shape into 48 small meatballs.
2. Brown meatballs in butter or margarine, shaking skillet so they brown uniformly. Cover pan tightly and steam about 15 minutes. Remove meatballs from skillet and keep warm.
3. Prepare a gravy by blending flour with drippings in pan. Add milk or cream and cook until thickened, stirring constantly. Season to taste.
4. Place meatballs on large platter and serve with gravy.

Barbecued Beef or Pork

Joyce Niemann
Fruitland Park, FL
Lap Sampler

Makes 6-8 servings

2 lbs. beef *or* pork roast
Water to cover
14-oz. bottle ketchup
3 green peppers, chopped
2 onions, diced
2 Tbsp. dry mustard
2 Tbsp. brown sugar
2 Tbsp. vinegar

1. Cook meat with just enough water to cover, simmering until it pulls apart easily, about 2 hours. Cool meat and shred by hand.
2. Mix all remaining ingredients and stir into meat in skillet. Heat through.
3. Serve with hamburger rolls.

Shredded Beef Barbecue

Kathy Hardis Fraeman
Olney, MD
Star Over My Sofa

Makes 8-10 servings

1 medium onion, chopped
1 small green pepper, chopped

1 Tbsp. cooking oil
3 lbs. cubed chuck roast
28-oz. jar spaghetti sauce
20-oz. bottle ketchup
2 Tbsp. Worcestershire sauce
2 tsp. dry mustard
Salt and pepper to taste
8-10 hamburger buns

1. Sauté onion and pepper with a small amount of oil.
2. Cut chuck roast into very small pieces. Add to skillet and sauté until brown. Add remaining ingredients except buns and simmer for approximately 3 hours.
3. Mash with potato masher until beef is in threads. Spoon onto buns.

Sloppy Joes

Doris Morelock
Alexandria, VA
The Links of Friendship

Makes 10-12 servings

2 lbs. ground beef
2 onions, chopped
2 green peppers, chopped
1 cup chopped celery
20-oz. bottle ketchup
½ cup brown sugar
⅓ cup mustard
2 tsp. Worcestershire sauce
1 tsp. chili powder
Salt and pepper
10-12 hamburger buns

1. Brown beef. Drain all excess fat. Add remaining ingredients except hamburger buns and cook 1 hour.
2. Serve over hamburger buns.

❖

Barbecue Beef

Nancy Graves
Manhattan, KS
My President's Quilt
Betty J. Kilroy
Ellicott City, MD
Twelve Days of Christmas

Makes 8 servings

1½ lbs. ground beef
1 onion, chopped
½ tsp. salt
½ tsp. pepper
14-oz. bottle ketchup
1 Tbsp. prepared mustard
1 Tbsp. vinegar
4 Tbsp. sugar
½ cup water
1 tsp. salt
¼ tsp. pepper
¼ tsp. paprika

1. Brown ground beef, onion, ½ tsp. salt and ½ tsp. pepper. Drain excess fat.
2. Add all remaining ingredients and heat through.
3. Serve on hamburger rolls.

> I'm still quite new at quilting, but last summer my mother remembered having some patches which had been made by my grandmother more than 50 years ago. She gave them to me and I created a full-size bedspread. When I gave the spread to my parents as a surprise, they were both speechless.
>
> —*Kim Marlor, Owings Mills, MD*

oughly and shape into 12 large patties.

3. Heat ¼ cup butter in large skillet. Cook patties over medium heat until well browned on both sides, turning once (about 5-6 minutes on each side for medium rare).

Beef Burgers

Lucille Z. Brubacker
Barnett, MO
Country Love

Makes 6 servings

**4 cups chopped beef *or*
  chicken**
1 Tbsp. prepared mustard
**2 Tbsp. Worcestershire
  sauce**
1½ cups ketchup
6 hamburger buns
Mayonnaise
6 slices American cheese

1. Cook beef or chicken until tender and chop into small pieces.

2. In a saucepan combine beef, mustard, Worcestershire sauce and ketchup and simmer for 10 minutes. Add water if needed.

3. Spread hamburger buns with mayonnaise, a layer of beef and a slice of cheese.

4. Put under broiler until cheese melts. Serve.

Farmhouse Hamburgers

Inez E. Dillon
Tucson, AZ
Seven Sisters

Makes 12 hamburgers

1 Tbsp. diced onion
1 tsp. butter *or* margarine
2 lbs. lean ground beef
2 eggs
**2 Tbsp. drained, prepared
  horseradish**
1 tsp. salt
Dash pepper
¼ tsp. sugar
1 Tbsp. lemon juice
**½ cup finely chopped
  pickled beets**
**½ cup cream *or* evaporated
  milk**
**1½ cups whole wheat
  bread crumbs**
¼ cup butter *or* margarine

1. Sauté onion lightly in 1 tsp. butter. Combine onion, ground beef, eggs, horseradish, seasonings, lemon juice and beets.

2. Combine cream and bread crumbs; let stand 5 minutes and add to other ingredients. Mix thor-

Open-Face Hamburgers

Ann Reimer
Beatrice, NE
Joshua's Star Log Cabin

Makes 6 servings

1 lb. hamburger
¼ cup milk
¾ cup cubed cheese
½ cup chili sauce
½ tsp. dry mustard
1 tsp. salt
½ tsp. pepper
¼ tsp. allspice
**6 hamburger rolls, cut in
  half**

1. Combine hamburger, milk, cheese, chili sauce and spices.

2. Lightly butter each half hamburger roll. Spread mixture on rolls.

3. Place under broiler for 7-8 minutes or until nicely browned. (If you prefer hamburger well done, turn oven to 350° and bake an extra 5 minutes.) Serve immediately.

Hamburgers with Sweet and Sour Sauce

Grace K. Bruce
Albuquerque, NM
Card Trick

Makes 6 servings

8-oz. can shredded sauerkraut, drained
¼ cup cranberry sauce
¼ cup chili sauce
¼ cup water
3 Tbsp. brown sugar
1 egg, lightly beaten
1 pkg. dry onion soup mix
¼ cup water
1½ lbs. ground beef
6 hamburger rolls

1. In a saucepan combine sauerkraut, cranberry sauce, chili sauce, ¼ cup water and brown sugar and bring to a boil. Reduce heat and simmer 20 minutes, stirring occasionally.
2. In a bowl combine egg, onion soup, and ¼ cup water and let stand 5 minutes. Add ground beef and mix well. Shape into 6 patties.
3. Grill to desired degree of doneness and place hamburger patties on rolls. Serve with sweet and sour sauce.

Hamburger-Stuffed Bread

Patti Boston
Coshocton, OH
Flywheel

Makes 4-6 servings

1 round loaf unsliced bread
1 lb. ground beef
1 green pepper, diced
½ cup diced celery
1 tsp. salt
1 Tbsp. Worcestershire sauce
10¾-oz. can cheddar cheese soup
2 slices cheddar cheese

1. Cut top off bread lengthwise. Gently hollow out inside, forming a ¼-½-inch thick crust shell. Reserve hollowed-out bread.
2. Brown ground beef and drain excess fat. Add all remaining ingredients except cheese slices. Simmer for 4-5 minutes.
3. Tear hollowed-out bread into small pieces, making 2 cups. Add bread to meat mixture. Fill bread crust shell with meat and bread mixture.
4. Cut cheese slices in half diagonally. Place over top of bread crust shell. Place on baking sheet.
5. Bake at 350° for 8-10 minutes or until cheese melts. Replace top of bread and serve.

Ground Meat Cornbread

Molly Wilson
Gonzales, TX
Marriage Quilt

Makes 6 servings

1 lb. ground beef
1 large onion, chopped
1 cup cornmeal
1 cup milk
½ tsp. baking soda
¾ tsp. salt
2 eggs
16-oz. can cream-style corn

1. Cook ground beef and onion together in a skillet. Drain excess fat and set aside.
2. Combine all other ingredients in a large bowl.
3. Pour ½ of cornbread mixture, into large rectangular baking pan. Top with meat mixture. Pour remaining cornbread mixture over meat.
4. Bake at 450° for about 45 minutes or until cornbread is done.

Sue's Casserole

Sue Dieringer-Boyer
Walkersville, MD
Stage Quilts for **Quilters**

Makes 8 servings

1 lb. ground meat
1 clove garlic, minced
1 tsp. salt
½ tsp. freshly ground
**   black pepper**
1 tsp. sugar
3 8-oz. cans tomato sauce
6-oz. can tomato paste
4-oz. pkg. cream cheese,
**   softened**
1 cup sour cream *or* plain
**   yogurt**
8 ozs. noodles
1 cup shredded cheese

1. Brown ground meat in large skillet. Drain all excess fat.

2. Add garlic, salt, pepper, sugar, tomato sauce and tomato paste. Mix well and bring to a boil, stirring frequently.

3. Reduce heat and simmer, uncovered, for 15 minutes.

4. In a bowl mix cream cheese and sour cream.

5. Cook noodles and drain.

6. Remove meat sauce from heat. Carefully stir in cream cheese and sour cream mixture. Toss in cooked noodles.

7. Pour contents into a large rectangular baking dish or split into 2 dishes if necessary. Sprinkle shredded cheese on top.

8. Bake at 350° for 15-20 minutes or until bubbly.

Meatza

Rachel Pellman
Lancaster, PA
Panel for the AIDS Quilt

Makes 6 servings

1 lb. lean ground beef *or*
**   turkey**
⅔ cup milk
½ cup bread crumbs
1 tsp. garlic salt
½ cup ketchup
4-oz. jar sliced
**   mushrooms, drained**
1 cup shredded cheese
2 Tbsp. Parmesan cheese
¼ tsp. oregano

1. Combine ground meat, milk, bread crumbs and garlic salt. Pat into 9-inch pie plate, covering sides and bottom.

2. Spread ketchup over meat mixture. Layer mushrooms over ketchup. Add cheeses and top with oregano.

3. Bake at 375° for 25-35 minutes. Drain excess fat before serving.

Ground Beef Stroganoff

Marion Matson
Comfrey, MN
Amish Baskets
Anita Falk
Mountain Lake, MN
Double Irish Chain

Makes 4-6 servings

1 lb. lean ground beef
½ cup chopped onion
4-oz. jar mushroom stems
**   and pieces, drained**
⅛ tsp. garlic powder
½ tsp. dry mustard
½ cup mayonnaise
½ cup sour cream
½ cup beef bouillon
Cooked noodles or rice

1. Sauté ground beef, onion, mushrooms, garlic powder and mustard until beef is browned. Drain excess fat.

2. Combine mayonnaise, sour cream and bouillon and stir into meat mixture. Cook over low heat until heated through.

3. Serve over noodles or rice.

During the spring of 1991 I quilted a Double Irish Chain with appliqued hearts for my daughter's bed. She was four years old and I lost count of the times she asked, "Is it finished yet?"

To my surprise she insisted on taking the finished quilt to her preschool for "Show and Tell." We managed to fold that full-size quilt into a 17" x 21" "Show and Tell" bag. Her peers rewarded her with lots of oohs and aahs.

—*Judy Steiner Buller, Beatrice, NE*

❖

Italian Casserole

Jacquelyn Kreitzer
Mechanicsburg, PA
Lap Sampler

Makes 4 servings

1 lb. ground beef
1 small onion, chopped
1 clove garlic, minced
½ tsp. salt
10¾-oz. can tomato soup
⅓ cup water
2 cups cooked wide
　noodles
1 cup shredded cheese

1. Brown ground beef with onion, garlic and salt. Drain excess fat.
2. Combine all ingredients except cheese in 1-quart casserole dish. Sprinkle cheese over top.
3. Bake at 350° for 30 minutes.

❖

Hamburger Stew

Vera Mae Zimmerman
Stevens, PA
Broken Star

Makes 4-6 servings

1 lb. ground beef
1 tsp. salt
⅛ tsp. pepper
½ cup chopped celery
¾ cup chopped onion
⅓ cup uncooked rice
¼ tsp. chili powder
1 tsp. Worcestershire sauce
1 cup chopped carrots
2 cups tomato juice

1. Brown ground beef, salt, pepper, celery and onion. Drain excess fat.
2. Add all remaining ingredients and cook over low heat about 1 hour, stirring occasionally. Add water as needed.

❖

Haystack Supper

Juanita Marner
Shipshewana, IN
Giant Dahlia Tablecloth

Makes 10-12 servings

3 lbs. ground beef
3 pints spaghetti sauce
2 10¾-oz. cans cheddar
　cheese soup
3 soup cans milk
½ lb. soda crackers,
　crushed
2 cups cooked rice
2 heads lettuce, chopped
2 pkgs. corn chips, crushed
4 tomatoes, diced
2 cups chopped nuts
2 cups sliced olives

1. Brown ground beef and drain all excess fat. Stir in spaghetti sauce and simmer until beef is cooked.
2. Combine soup and milk and heat thoroughly.
3. Serve each ingredient in separate serving dish and let guests create own haystack with choice of ingredients.

Pizza Rice Casserole

Mrs. Mahlon Miller
Hutchinson, Kansas

Makes 6 servings

⅔ cup uncooked rice
¾ lb. ground beef
1 onion, chopped
2 cups tomato sauce
¼ tsp. garlic salt
1 tsp. sugar
1 tsp. salt
Dash pepper
¼ tsp. oregano
1 tsp. parsley flakes
1½ cups cottage cheese
½ cup shredded cheese

1. Cook rice according to directions.
2. Brown ground beef and onion in large skillet. Drain excess fat. Add tomato sauce, garlic salt, sugar, salt, pepper, oregano and parsley. Cover and simmer 15 minutes.
3. Combine cottage cheese and rice. Put ⅓ of rice mixture in greased 2-quart casserole. Top with ⅓ of meat-tomato sauce. Continue to alternate layers, ending with tomato sauce. Sprinkle with shredded cheese.
4. Bake at 325° for 30 minutes or until hot and bubbly.

Chinese Hamburger Casserole

Karen M. Rusten, Waseca, MN
Mrs. Mahlon Miller
Hutchinson, KS
Esther S. Martin, Ephrata, PA

Makes 8-10 servings

1 lb. ground beef
2 medium onions, chopped
2 cups diced celery
1 cup uncooked rice
10¾-oz. can mushroom soup
10¾-oz. can cream of chicken soup
2 cups water
4 Tbsp. soy sauce
15-oz. can bean sprouts, undrained
Salt and pepper to taste
10-oz. can chow mein noodles

1. Brown ground beef and drain excess fat. Add remaining ingredients except chow mein noodles and blend well. Spoon into large casserole dish and sprinkle with chow mein noodles.
2. Bake at 350° for 1½ hours.

Note: For a family gathering, put into crockpot on low and let simmer for 8-12 hours. Immediately before serving, add chow mein noodles.

Shepherd's Pie

Cora G. Napier
Connersville, IN
Around the Twist

Makes 4-6 servings

1 lb. ground beef
1 onion, diced
16-oz. can tomato juice
2 10-oz. pkgs. frozen mixed vegetables
Salt and pepper to taste
Dash garlic
2 cups mashed potatoes
2 Tbsp. Parmesan cheese

1. Brown ground beef and onion. Drain excess fat. Add all remaining ingredients except mashed potatoes and cheese. Simmer 10 minutes or until vegetables are lightly cooked. Pour into casserole dish.
2. Spread mashed potatoes over top (instant potatoes may be used). Sprinkle with Parmesan cheese.
3. Bake at 325° for 25 minutes or until browned.

Börek

Susan Melton
Olney, MD

Makes 8 servings

10-oz. pkg. frozen chopped
  spinach
1 medium onion, chopped
1 lb. ground beef
Salt and pepper to taste
2 eggs, beaten
1-2 loaves frozen bread
  dough
8 slices mozzarella cheese
1 Tbsp. yogurt *or* sour
  cream
1 Tbsp. olive oil

1. Thaw spinach in fry-
ing pan. Add onion,
ground beef, salt and pepper and brown. Drain well.
Mix in eggs and set aside.
2. Roll out dough into 4
equal circles to make top
and bottom crust for 2 8"
meat pies. Place bottom
crusts in pie plates.
3. Spoon half of the meat
mixture into one pie, top
with cheese and cover with
top crust. Pinch edges
closed. Combine yogurt
and olive oil. Brush over
top crust. Repeat for second
pie.
4. Bake at 350° for 20
minutes. Increase oven temperature to 400° and bake
another 10 minutes. Serve
with sour cream.

Chinese Pork Roast

Priscilla M. Wade
Voorhees, NJ
Bear Paw

Makes 4-6 servings

2 lbs. boneless pork loin
2 Tbsp. soy sauce
½ tsp. ground ginger
¼ cup dry sherry
2 Tbsp. honey

1. Place pork loin in
roasting pan.
2. Combine soy sauce
and ginger and pour over
pork.
3. Bake at 325° for 1
hour, basting frequently.
4. Combine sherry and
honey and pour over pork.
5. Bake another 30 min-
utes, basting frequently.
6. Remove from oven
and let stand for 10-15 minutes under foil.
7. Slice and serve with
pan juices on the side.

Wiener Schnitzel with Sage

B. Helen Plauschinn
Pickering, ON
Miniature Tulip

Makes 4 servings

⅓ cup all-purpose flour
1 Tbsp. salt
½ tsp. pepper
1 egg
2 Tbsp. water
⅔ cup plain bread crumbs
¼ cup lightly packed sage
  leaves
1 lb. veal *or* pork cutlets
2 Tbsp. cooking oil
Lemon wedges

1. On large plate com-
bine flour, salt and pepper.
2. In large bowl beat egg
with 2 Tbsp. water.
3. On another large plate
combine bread crumbs and
sage.
4. Dredge cutlets in flour
mixture. Dip into egg.
Dredge in bread crumb mixture.
5. Heat 1 Tbsp. oil in
large non-stick skillet. Sauté
half the meat 2-4 minutes
on each side. Repeat with
remaining oil and meat.
Place on serving platter.
Garnish with lemon
wedges.

> **My young daughter, upon overhearing a comment about
> the number of quilts I produce, remarked with great
> sadness, "My mother used to cook."**
>
> —*Paula Lederkramer, Levittown, NY*

Veal with Mushrooms and Peppers

Eunice B. Heyman
Baltimore, MD
Joanne's Anniversary Quilt

Makes 4 servings

4 Tbsp. olive oil
1 lb. veal cubes
Flour
12 mushrooms, quartered
1 green pepper, sliced
1 medium onion, sliced
1 Tbsp. dried oregano
½ tsp. allspice
¼ tsp. dried red pepper
¾ cup dry Marsala wine
3 large cloves garlic, minced
½ cup chicken broth

1. Heat 2 Tbsp. oil in heavy, oven-proof skillet over medium-high heat. Dredge veal in flour and sauté in oil until lightly browned, about 5 minutes. Transfer veal to plate.
2. Add remaining 2 Tbsp. oil to skillet and sauté mushrooms, pepper, onion, oregano, allspice and red pepper until onions and mushrooms have begun to brown lightly, about 5 minutes.
3. Stir in Marsala and garlic and boil until skillet is almost dry, about 5 minutes.
4. Return veal and any juices that have accumulated to skillet. Mix in chicken broth and bring to a boil.

5. Cover skillet and bake at 350° for 1 hour or until veal is very tender. Serve over rice.

Company Baked Pork Chops

Vivian K. Lee
Marysville, KS
Charm Quilt

Makes 6 servings

6 large pork chops
Salt and pepper to taste
¼ cup brown sugar
½ cup ketchup
¾ cup cold water
6 large slices onion

1. Season each pork chop and arrange in large baking dish.
2. Combine sugar, ketchup and water. Pour sauce over pork chops. Place 1 onion slice directly on each pork chop.
3. Cover and bake at 375° for 45-60 minutes. Baste pork chops with sauce.

4. Bake, uncovered, another 30 minutes or until done.

Yummy Pork Chops

Judy Berry
Columbia, MD
Original

Makes 4 servings

4 lean pork chops
1 Tbsp. cooking oil
1 medium onion, diced
1 cup sliced mushrooms
¼ cup water
2 tsp. dry mustard
½ tsp. salt
½ cup sour cream

1. Brown pork chops in cooking oil. Top with onions and mushrooms.
2. Combine water, mustard and salt and pour over pork chops. Bring to boil and turn down to simmer, cooking 60-75 minutes or until pork chops are done.
3. Remove chops and

My mother often hosted quilting parties in the summertime. Two quilts would be set up in the front yard, and on the appointed day aunts, cousins and neighbors arrived for the quilting bee. We little girls were given the task of making lemonade to serve to the women. Our arms would be worn out from pounding enough lemons for several gallons of lemonade.

—*Kathryn M. Geissinger, Ephrata, PA*

keep warm. Add sour cream to liquid in skillet and heat through.

4. Serve pork chops with sauce over rice or noodles.

into 2 Tbsp. cold water. Pour slowly into skillet, stirring constantly. Cook until sauce thickens. Spoon sauce over chops and serve.

3. Drain pineapple and reserve pineapple chunks. Combine pineapple juice, water, cornstarch, brown sugar, salt, curry powder, lemon rind, tomato sauce, vinegar and soy sauce and mix well. Add to skillet and heat, stirring constantly until sauce thickens. Add pineapple chunks and simmer to heat.

4. Arrange pork chops in 9" x 13" greased baking pan. Pour sauce over chops.

5. Cover tightly and bake at 350° for 45 minutes. Remove cover and sprinkle with pecans. Bake, uncovered, for another 15 minutes.

Pork Chops a la Orange

Barbara Aston
Sharon Hill, PA
Sampler

Sweet and Sour Pork Chops

Joan Lemmler
Albuquerque, NM
Bearry Agee

Makes 4 servings

4 pork chops
1½ Tbsp. flour
2 tsp. seasoning salt
1 tsp. paprika
¼ tsp. pepper
¼ Tbsp. cooking oil
½ cup orange juice *or* more
4 whole cloves
4 thin orange slices
2 Tbsp. cold water

1. Combine flour, seasoning salt, paprika and pepper. Reserve 1 tsp. mixture. Coat chops with remaining flour mixture.

2. Heat oil in skillet and brown chops. Add orange juice and cloves.

3. Cover and simmer for 45 minutes or until tender, turning occasionally.

4. Add orange slices and cook 5 minutes longer. Remove chops and orange slices to serving platter. Remove cloves and discard.

5. Blend reserved flour

Makes 6 servings

6 1-inch thick pork chops
½ tsp. salt
2 Tbsp. cooking oil
¼ cup chopped onion
¼ medium green pepper, thinly sliced
1 large clove garlic, minced
15¼-oz. can pineapple chunks
½ cup water
2 Tbsp. cornstarch
1 Tbsp. brown sugar
½ tsp. salt
½ tsp. curry powder
1 tsp. grated lemon rind
3 Tbsp. tomato sauce
2 Tbsp. cider vinegar
1 Tbsp. soy sauce
½ cup pecan halves

1. Sprinkle chops with salt. Brown in oil. Remove and reserve.

2. Drain all but 2 Tbsp. drippings from pan. Sauté onion, pepper and garlic until soft.

Sweet and Sour Pork

Adelle Horst Ward
Scotia, NY
Double Nine Patch

Makes 4-6 servings

Meat Marinade:
1 lb. pork cubes
1 egg yolk
1 Tbsp. cornstarch
1 Tbsp. soy sauce
Dash pepper
Cooking oil
5 Tbsp. cornstarch

Sweet and Sour Sauce:
5 Tbsp. sugar
1 Tbsp. cornstarch
½ tsp. salt
2 Tbsp. vinegar
2 Tbsp. soy sauce
½ cup water
1 green pepper, sliced
1 medium carrot, thinly diced
1 cup bamboo shoots
½ cup water chestnuts

1. To prepare meat marinade combine pork cubes, egg yolk, 1 Tbsp. cornstarch, soy sauce and pepper. Marinate 6-8 hours.
2. Prepare cooking oil in saucepan for deep frying. Dip pork cubes in 5 Tbsp. cornstarch and deep fry.
3. In a separate saucepan prepare sauce by combining sugar, cornstarch, salt, vinegar, soy sauce and water. Bring to a boil. Cook until thickened, stirring frequently. Stir in vegetable pieces and meat and heat through.
4. Serve over rice.

Pork Chops and Stuffing

Peggy Smith
Hamlin, KY
Evening View Through the Window

Makes 4 servings

4 pork chops
1 Tbsp. cooking oil
3 cups soft bread cubes
2 Tbsp. chopped onion
¼ cup melted margarine
¼ cup water
¼ tsp. poultry seasoning
10¾-oz. can cream of mushroom soup
⅓ cup water

1. Heat cooking oil in oven-proof skillet and brown pork chops. Pour off all drippings.
2. Mix bread cubes, onion, margarine, ¼ cup water and poultry seasoning. Place a mound of stuffing on each pork chop.
3. Blend cream of mushroom soup with ⅓ cup water. Pour over chops and stuffing.
4. Bake, uncovered, at 350° for 1 hour.

Pork Chop Casserole

Betty A. Gray
Ellicott City, MD
Carrousel Crib Quilt

Makes 4 servings

4 loin pork chops
1 tsp. salt
⅛ tsp. pepper
Flour
2 Tbsp. shortening
⅔ cup uncooked rice
3 cups boiling water
4 thick slices tomato
4 rings green pepper
4 thin slices onion

1. Wipe chops with damp cloth, sprinkle with seasonings and dredge with flour.
2. Heat shortening in skillet and brown pork chops. Arrange in greased casserole dish.
3. Wash rice and cook 5 minutes in water.
4. Place slice of tomato, ring of green pepper and slice of onion on each chop. Pour rice with water around chops.
5. Cover and bake at 350° for 1 hour or until rice and chops are tender. Add more water if necessary.

Pork Barbecue

Sue Hertzler Schrag
Beatrice, NE
Star Spin

Makes 10-12 servings

3-4-lb. pork roast
½ tsp. salt
½ cup water
1½ Tbsp. Worcestershire
  sauce
¼ cup chopped onion
4 Tbsp. brown sugar
1 cup ketchup
¼ cup white vinegar
⅛ tsp. pepper
1 Tbsp. mustard
10-12 hamburger buns

1. Cook and flake pork roast.
2. In a saucepan combine all remaining ingredients except buns. Bring to a boil. Add meat and reheat.
3. Serve on hamburger buns.

Canadian Spareribs

Katherine S. Lombard
Deerfield, NH
Amish Center Square

Makes 6 servings

3 lbs. spareribs
1 lb. brown sugar
12-oz. bottle soy sauce
2 onions, sliced
1 clove garlic, chopped
¼ tsp. black pepper

1. Arrange spareribs in a roasting pan.
2. Combine all other ingredients and pour over meat.
3. Cover and bake at 350° for 2 hours. Uncover and bake another 20 minutes. Serve.

Barbecued Spareribs

Theresa M. Leppert
Schellsburg, PA
Grandmother's Flower Garden

Makes 6 servings

5 lbs. spareribs
1½ cups ketchup
1½ cups water
4 Tbsp. brown sugar
1 Tbsp. soy sauce
1 Tbsp. lemon juice
½ cup pineapple juice

1. In large skillet brown ribs.
2. In large saucepan combine all remaining ingredients and bring to a boil. Simmer for 10 minutes.
3. Place ½ of ribs in a crockpot, pour ½ of sauce on top of meat. Repeat layers.
4. Cover and cook on low for 8 to 10 hours or on high for 5 or 6 hours.

Note: To bake in oven place in large casserole dish, cover and bake at 350° for 1½-2 hours.

I discovered the world of quilts when my husband and I visited Lancaster County, PA on our honeymoon in 1977. After a long search we bought a Bridal Wreath quilt from an Old Order Mennonite woman. Fourteen years later we returned to this woman's shop and found it was now operated by her daughter. The daughter pointed out a Log Cabin quilt as the last one her mother had made. My husband gave me the Log Cabin quilt for our fourteenth wedding anniversary.

—*Debra M. Zeida, Waquoit, MA*

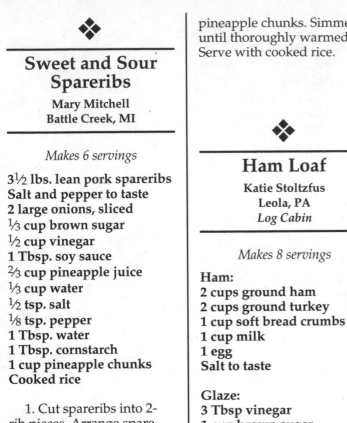

Sweet and Sour Spareribs

**Mary Mitchell
Battle Creek, MI**

Makes 6 servings

3½ lbs. lean pork spareribs
Salt and pepper to taste
2 large onions, sliced
⅓ cup brown sugar
½ cup vinegar
1 Tbsp. soy sauce
⅔ cup pineapple juice
⅓ cup water
½ tsp. salt
⅛ tsp. pepper
1 Tbsp. water
1 Tbsp. cornstarch
1 cup pineapple chunks
Cooked rice

1. Cut spareribs into 2-rib pieces. Arrange spareribs on oven broiler pan and sprinkle with salt and pepper. Broil, turning once, until deep brown on both sides.
2. Sauté onions in large Dutch oven with 2 Tbsp. pork drippings from broiler pan. Add brown sugar, vinegar, soy sauce, pineapple juice, ⅓ cup water, salt, pepper and ribs.
3. Cover and simmer over low heat for 2 hours. Remove ribs.
4. Combine 1 Tbsp. water and cornstarch to make a paste. Thicken sauce with cornstarch. Replace ribs in sauce and add

pineapple chunks. Simmer until thoroughly warmed. Serve with cooked rice.

Ham Loaf

**Katie Stoltzfus
Leola, PA
*Log Cabin***

Makes 8 servings

Ham:
2 cups ground ham
2 cups ground turkey
1 cup soft bread crumbs
1 cup milk
1 egg
Salt to taste

Glaze:
3 Tbsp vinegar
1 cup brown sugar
1 tsp. dry mustard
3 Tbsp. water

1. Combine all ham ingredients and mix well. Pat into a loaf pan.
2. To prepare glaze combine vinegar, sugar, mustard and water in saucepan and bring to a boil. Pour sauce over ham loaf.
3. Bake, uncovered, at 350° for 1 hour.

Grandma White's Easy Ham

**E. Michaella Keener
Upper Darby, PA
*Micki's Dream***

Makes 2-4 servings

2-4 slices ham, 1-inch thick
1 small onion, sliced
½-1 cup milk
1-2 Tbsp. butter
Pepper to taste

1. Arrange ham slices in baking dish. Pour milk into dish until it measures half the depth of the ham slices. Arrange onion slices over ham. Dot with butter and pepper to taste.
2. Bake at 350° for 45 minutes or until done.

Overnight Ham Casserole

**Mrs. Crist H. Yoder
Hutchinson, KS
*Star of the West***

1 cup uncooked macaroni
10¾-oz. can cream of
    mushroom soup
1 cup milk
1 cup shredded cheese
½ cup diced onion
1 cup chopped ham
3 Tbsp. butter

In New Mexico green chilies are a very popular casserole ingredient. Several years ago our quilters' meeting fell on St. Patrick's Day. We thought it would be fun to each bring a "green" food dish to the potluck luncheon. We are still amused that twenty New Mexicans brought "green" food dishes without a single green chili dish. Each of us was sure someone else would bring green chilies, so we came with almost every other imaginable green vegetable and even a green jello salad.

—*Carol Price, Los Lunas, NM*

1. Mix together all ingredients and refrigerate overnight, stirring occasionally before going to bed.

2. Bake at 350° for 1½-2 hours.

Sausage with Spicy Kraut

Judy Steiner Buller
Beatrice, NE
Log Cabin Star Spin

Makes 4-6 servings

1 lb. bag sauerkraut
1 apple, chopped
5 cloves
2 Tbsp. brown sugar
1½ lbs. link sausages

1. In a saucepan combine all ingredients except sausage.

2. Cut sausages into ½-inch lengths and brown in a skillet.

Place sausages on top of other ingredients.

3. Cover saucepan and simmer for ½ hour. Remove cloves before serving.

Sausage and Rice

Betty J. Kilroy
Ellicott City, MD
Twelve Days of Christmas

Makes 4 servings

1½ cups uncooked rice
1 lb. sausage
1 cup diced onion
1 cup diced celery
14-oz. jar spaghetti sauce
½ cup water
1 cup sliced green pepper
1 cup sliced mushrooms

1. Prepare rice according to directions.

2. Brown sausage and drain all excess fat. In a skillet combine sausage, onion, celery, spaghetti sauce and water. Simmer until celery and onions are tender.

3. Add green pepper and mushrooms and simmer until pepper is tender and sauce is thickened.

4. Serve sausage and vegetables over rice.

❖

Sausage Pie

Elizabeth Boyton
Gordonville, PA
Irish Chain

Makes 8 servings

1 lb. Italian sausage
6 eggs, beaten
2 10-oz. pkgs. spinach, thawed and drained
1 lb. mozzarella cheese, shredded
⅔ cup ricotta cheese
½ tsp. salt
⅛ tsp. pepper
⅛ tsp. garlic powder
1 10" unbaked pastry shell

1. Remove sausage meat from skin. Brown, crumble and drain.

2. Combine all ingredients except pastry shell and mix well. Spoon mixture into pastry shell.

3. Bake at 375° for 60-75 minutes or until knife inserted in center comes out clean. Let stand 10 minutes before serving.

4. Serve with a tossed salad.

Corned Beef Casserole

Margaret Jarrett
Anderson, IN
Country Love

Makes 8-10 servings

8-10 potatoes, sliced
Salt and pepper to taste
1 cup grated cheddar
  cheese
1 small onion, chopped
10¾-oz. can cream of
  mushroom soup
10¾-oz. can cream of
  chicken soup
12-oz. can corned beef
2 cups milk
½ cup buttered bread
  crumbs

1. Slice potatoes into greased 9" x 13" baking dish until you have a 2- or 3-inch layer. Season to taste and add cheese and onion. Pour soups over mixture. Crumble corned beef over all and add milk. Sprinkle bread crumbs over top.
2. Bake at 350° for 1 hour or until potatoes are done.

Variation:
Use 1 medium package noodles, cooked according to directions, instead of potatoes. Drain noodles before placing in baking dish.
Suellen Fletcher
Noblesville, IN
Double Irish Chain

Wiener Bavarian

Dorothy M. VanDeest
Memphis, TN
The Bearish and Bullish Dow

Makes 8-10 servings

10¾-oz. can cream of
  mushroom soup
¾ cup mayonnaise
1-lb. pkg. all-beef wieners
16-oz. can shredded
  sauerkraut
1 tsp. caraway seed
4 cups diced, cooked
  potatoes
½ cup bread crumbs
¼ tsp. paprika

1. Combine soup and mayonnaise.
2. Slice wieners lengthwise once and cut into small pieces. Combine wieners, sauerkraut and caraway seed with ½ of the mayonnaise mixture. Spread into a 9" x 13" baking pan.
3. Combine remaining ½ mayonnaise mixture with potatoes. Spread over wieners. Sprinkle with bread crumbs and paprika.
4. Bake at 350° for 35-40 minutes.

Oven-Fried Fish

Trudy Kutter
Corfu, NY
Cake Stand

Makes 4 servings

1 lb. skinless, boneless
  lean fish
4 tsp. cooking oil
1 Tbsp. lemon juice
4 Tbsp. plain *or* seasoned
  bread crumbs
Salt, pepper, paprika and
  parsley to taste
4 lemon wedges

1. Choose thin fillets and cut into four pieces.
2. Mix oil and lemon juice in shallow plate. Mix crumbs and dry seasonings on separate plate.
3. Turn fillets lightly in oil mixture, then press into crumb mixture until lightly coated. Arrange fillets on greased baking sheet.
4. Bake on center rack at 450-500° for 6 to 10 minutes, until fish is cooked through and coating is crisp.
5. Garnish with lemon wedges and parsley. Serve.

Shrimp and Beef Curry

Connee Sager
Tucson, AZ
Tulip Variation

Makes 8-10 servings

½ lb. lean ground beef
2 Tbsp. dried bread crumbs
1 egg, beaten
1¼ cups chopped onion
½ tsp. salt
⅛ tsp. pepper
2 Tbsp. butter *or* margarine
1 cup diced celery
3 Tbsp. cooking oil
½ lb. shelled, deveined shrimp
2 Tbsp. margarine
1 tsp. salt
⅛ tsp. pepper
1½ tsp. curry *or* less
2 cups chicken broth
4 cups cooked rice

1. Combine beef, bread crumbs, egg, ¼ cup onion, ½ tsp. salt and ⅛ tsp. pepper. Form into tiny meatballs, using heaping teaspoon of mixture for each. Set aside.

2. In large skillet heat 2 Tbsp. butter or margarine. Sauté 1 cup chopped onion and celery until golden. Remove from skillet.

3. Heat oil in skillet. Add raw shrimp and sauté 3-5 minutes until cooked. Remove from skillet.

4. Brown meatballs by rotating skillet over heat. Remove meatballs and set aside.

5. Melt 2 Tbsp. margarine in skillet and add 1 tsp. salt, ⅛ tsp. pepper, curry and chicken broth. Bring to a boil. Add rice, cover and remove from heat. Let stand until rice soaks up chicken broth mixture.

6. Add celery, onion mixture, shrimp and meatballs to rice mixture. Cover and heat until piping hot.

7. Serve with vegetable, tossed salad and rolls.

Sour Cream Shrimp Curry

Dorothy Reise
Severna Park, MD
Beverly's Baskets with Tulips

Makes 4 servings

Curry:
2 Tbsp. butter
⅓ cup chopped onion
¼ cup chopped green peppers
1 clove garlic, minced
1 cup sour cream
1 tsp. curry powder
¼ tsp. salt
Pepper to taste
1¼ lbs. cooked, cleaned shrimp
Cooked rice

Condiments:
4 hard-boiled eggs, chopped
1 green pepper, finely chopped
1-2 cups raisins
1 cup chutney
1-2 cups chopped parsley
1-2 cups crumbled, cooked bacon
1-2 cups chopped nuts
1-2 cups shredded coconut
1-2 cups banana chunks
1-2 cups pineapple chunks
1-2 cups chopped tomatoes

1. In a heavy saucepan sauté ⅓ cup onion, ¼ cup green peppers and garlic in butter until onion is tender, but not browned. Stir in sour cream, curry powder, salt and pepper. Add cooked and cleaned shrimp. Refrigerate.

2. When ready to serve, reheat slowly over low heat and serve over hot cooked rice with condiments. Let guests choose which condiments they desire.

Shrimp Scampi

Becki Bryant
Mechanicsburg, PA
State Flowers

Makes 4 servings

1¼ lbs. shelled, deveined
  shrimp
3 Tbsp. lemon juice
1 Tbsp. + 1 tsp. margarine,
  melted
2 small garlic cloves,
  mashed
½ tsp. pepper
½ tsp. salt
½ tsp. paprika
Parsley sprigs

1. In each of 4 individual oven-proof casserole dishes arrange 5 ozs. shrimp.
2. In a small bowl combine remaining ingredients except parsley.
3. Pour ¼ of mixture over each portion of shrimp and toss to coat.
4. Broil 3 to 4 inches from heat source until shrimp are golden brown, 1-2 minutes. Garnish with parsley and serve.

We take turns providing refreshments for our quilt club meetings. I found a recipe for double orange sugar cookies held together with orange marmalade and dipped into melted chocolate. I was sure I would enjoy the compliments of other members of the group. Although I followed the recipe faithfully and tried it with variations two other times, I had three flops. At the eleventh hour I teamed up with Betty Crocker and humbly took a pan of brownies to the meeting.

—*Margaret M. McTigue, Scarsdale, NY*

Spicy Garlic Shrimp

Ann Stutts
Grants Pass, OR
Ocean Waves

Makes 4 servings

2 lbs. shrimp
½ cup dry sherry (optional)
¼ cup freshly squeezed
  lemon juice
1 Tbsp. olive oil
3 cloves garlic, minced
2 tsp. paprika
1 tsp. cayenne pepper
Lemon wedges (optional)

1. Peel and devein shrimp. Arrange in shallow glass baking dish.
2. In a bowl combine sherry, lemon juice, olive oil, garlic, paprika and cayenne pepper. Pour over shrimp. Cover and marinate in refrigerator for 8 hours, turning occasionally.
3. Place shrimp in large skillet with marinade. Turn to medium heat and cook until done, stirring occasionally.

4. Remove shrimp from marinade and arrange on serving platter. Serve with lemon wedges.

Baked Shrimp

Ann Harrison
Garland, TX
Strawberry Patch

Makes 4 servings

Cocktail Sauce:
½ cup chili sauce
½ cup ketchup
2 Tbsp. lemon juice
2 Tbsp. horseradish
2 Tbsp. Worcestershire
  sauce

Shrimp:
5 lbs. medium, unshelled
  shrimp
1 lb. margarine
16-oz. bottle Italian
  dressing
⅓ cup lemon juice
¼ cup Worcestershire
  sauce

½ tsp. garlic salt
Salt and pepper to taste

1. Combine all cocktail sauce ingredients and refrigerate at least one day before serving.
2. Wash shrimp several times and devein. Place in 9" x 13" baking pan.
3. In a saucepan combine margarine, Italian dressing, lemon juice, Worcestershire sauce, garlic salt, salt and pepper. Heat over low heat until margarine is melted. Pour sauce over shrimp and stir.
4. Cover and bake at 350° for 45-75 minutes, depending on size of shrimp. Stir every 15 minutes while baking.
5. Shrimp peels easily when done. Serve with cocktail sauce.

Seafood Casserole

Flossie Sultzaberger
Mechanicsburg, PA
Nine Patch

Makes 8-10 servings

8-oz. pkg. egg noodles
1 lb. shrimp, shelled, deveined and cooked
7½-oz. can crab meat, drained, boned and flaked
5-oz. can water chestnuts, drained and sliced
¼ cup coarsely chopped

pimento
2 Tbsp. butter *or* margarine
3 Tbsp. finely chopped onion
¼ cup finely chopped green pepper
4-oz. jar sliced mushrooms, drained
2 Tbsp. butter *or* margarine
2 Tbsp. all-purpose flour
1 tsp. salt
½ cup dry sherry (optional)
3 cups light cream

1. Cook noodles according to directions. Drain and set aside.
2. Combine shrimp, crab meat, water chestnuts and pimento in large mixing bowl.
3. Heat 2 Tbsp. butter in medium saucepan. Add onion, green pepper and mushrooms and sauté gently 5 minutes or until tender. Add to seafood mixture in bowl.
4. Heat 2 Tbsp. butter in same saucepan. Stir in flour and salt, cooking for 1 minute. Remove pan from heat and gradually stir in sherry and cream. Cook over medium heat, stirring constantly until mixture comes to a boil and is slightly thickened.
5. Add to vegetable seafood mixture. Stir in noodles. Spoon into lightly greased 2½-quart baking dish.
6. Bake at 400° for 25 minutes or until bubbly.

Cheese Crab Imperial

Jean Shaner
York, PA
Whig Rose

Makes 6 servings

½ cup chopped celery
½ cup chopped onion
3 Tbsp. butter
4 slices bread, cubed
1 cup milk
2 eggs, beaten
1 lb. backfin crab meat
1 Tbsp. Worcestershire sauce
½ cup mayonnaise
1 tsp. Old Bay seasoning
1 tsp. dry mustard
1 Tbsp. lemon juice
1 cup grated cheese
Parsley to taste

1. Sauté celery and onion in butter.
2. Soak together bread, milk and egg.
3. In a 2-quart baking dish combine all ingredients except parsley and mix well. Mixture will be very moist. Sprinkle with parsley.
4. Bake at 350° for 30 minutes or until browned on top.

Crab Burgers

Dawn Kouba
Albuquerque, NM
Enchanted View

Makes 6 servings

1 lb. cooked crab meat
3 ribs celery, chopped
½ small onion, chopped
1-1½ cups grated cheddar
  cheese
½ cup mayonnaise
6 onion hamburger rolls
Margarine

1. Clean and pick over
thawed crab meat. Tear
into small pieces.
2. Combine crab meat,
celery, onion, cheese and
mayonnaise in bowl. Mix
well. Add enough mayon-
naise to bind ingredients together.
3. Split onion rolls apart.
Spread generously with
margarine.
4. Arrange rolls on
cookie sheet. Place heaping
tablespoon of crab mixture
on each roll.
5. Broil until cheese
melts and edges of rolls are
browned. Serve immedi-
ately.

Crab Casserole

Donna Joy
Silver Spring, MD

Makes 10-12 servings

10 slices white bread,
  cubed
1 lb. crab meat
1 cup mayonnaise
1 cup chopped celery
½ small onion, chopped
1 medium green pepper,
  sliced
1 Tbsp. fresh parsley
1 tsp. grated lemon rind
Salt and pepper to taste
4 eggs
3 cups milk
10¾-oz. can mushroom
  soup
1 cup Parmesan cheese

1. Put ½ of bread cubes
in bottom of 9" x 13" baking
pan.
2. Combine crab meat,
mayonnaise, celery, onion,
green pepper, parsley,
lemon rind, salt and pep-
per. Arrange mixture over
bread cubes. Put remaining
½ of bread cubes over crab
mixture.
3. Combine eggs and
milk and beat well. Pour
over crab mixture. Cover
and refrigerate overnight.
4. Cover and bake at 350°
for 1 hour.
5. Heat mushroom soup
slightly. Add cheese and mix
well. Remove crab casserole
from oven and pour mush-
room and cheese over dish.

6. Bake at 425° for 5-10
minutes until cheese is
melted.

Crab Cakes

Shirley R. McFadden
Mary Pearce Rufenacht
Annapolis, MD
Trip Around the World

Makes 4-5 servings

1 lb. backfin crab meat
2 slices bread
Dash red pepper
1 Tbsp. parsley
2 Tbsp. mayonnaise
1 Tbsp. prepared mustard
1 egg, slightly beaten
1 Tbsp. butter

1. Pick through crabmeat
to be sure there are no
shells.
2. Toast bread and crum-
ble into very small pieces.
3. Mix all ingredients except butter and form into
about 8 2-inch cakes.
4. Heat butter in skillet
and fry cakes over medium
heat until lightly browned
on both sides.

My mother-in-law tells the story of one unusual potluck quilting bee. After happily quilting for several hours, the seven women decided to break for lunch. In the kitchen they each uncovered their dishes and dicovered seven different ways to prepare and serve beans!

—*Carolyn Shank, Dayton, VA*

Salmon Patties

Esther L. Lantz
Leola, PA
Irish Chain

Makes 6 servings

15-oz. can salmon
1 egg
1/3 cup chopped onion
1/2 cup flour
1 1/2 tsp. baking powder
1/2 Tbsp. shortening

1. Drain salmon, reserving 2 Tbsp. liquid.
2. Combine salmon, egg and onion. Stir in flour.
3. Stir baking powder into salmon liquid and add to salmon and onion mixture. Form mixture into 6 patties.
4. Heat shortening on skillet and fry each patty on both sides until golden brown. Serve.

Salmon Steaks a la Irla

Susan L. Schwarz
North Bethesda, MD
Paragon's Country Garden

Makes 4 servings

4 salmon steaks
1/2 lb. mushrooms, sliced
2 Tbsp. butter
3 Tbsp. flour
1 tsp. onion salt
1/4 tsp. pepper
4 bay leaves
1/4 cup lemon juice
1 1/4 cups light cream
Paprika

1. Sauté mushrooms in butter. Spread mushrooms into greased baking dish.
2. Combine flour, onion salt and pepper. Dip steaks in flour mixture and arrange over mushrooms.
3. Put one bay leaf on top of each steak. Pour lemon juice and cream over all.
4. Bake at 400° for 30 minutes. Remove bay leaves. Immediately before serving, sprinkle with paprika.

Baked Salmon

Audrey Romonosky
Poughkeepsie, NY
Double Irish Chain

Makes 4 servings

1 1/2 lbs. salmon fillets
1 egg, beaten
3/4 cup Italian seasoned bread crumbs
4 Tbsp. margarine *or* butter, melted
2 Tbsp. lemon juice

1. Cut salmon fillets into 4 equal pieces. Dip into egg and then bread crumbs. Arrange fillets in greased baking pan.
2. Combine margarine and lemon juice. Pour evenly over salmon.
3. Bake at 400° about 10 minutes or until salmon flakes easily when touched with fork.

Six of us get together every Monday for quilting, fellowship and eating. The hostess provides coffee which is ready at 9:00 a.m. when we arrive. Each person brings her own sandwich and beverage for lunch, and the hostess provides the dessert. We have an unwritten law to always try something new and different. So far there have been no flops (at least not that have been shared), and there have been numerous quite successful recipes.

—*Myrtle Mansfield, Alfred, ME*

Salmon Casserole

Florence Heard
St. Marys, ON
Double Irish Chain

Makes 4-6 servings

1 cup uncooked macaroni
8-oz. can salmon
2 Tbsp. butter
¼ cup minced onion
1 Tbsp. flour
¼ tsp. salt
1 cup milk
2 tsp. lemon juice
2 Tbsp. finely chopped
    parsley
1 cup shredded Jack cheese

1. Cook macaroni in boiling water until tender; drain and rinse in cold water.
2. Drain salmon and save liquid. Break salmon into bite-sized pieces.
3. Melt butter in saucepan and sauté onion until transparent. Blend in flour and salt, stirring constantly.
4. Add milk to salmon liquid to make 1 cup. Stir into mixture in saucepan and cook until smooth and thick, stirring constantly.
5. Add lemon juice and parsley and mix well.
6. Spoon macaroni into greased casserole dish. Add salmon and sprinkle with ¾ cup cheese. Pour sauce over other ingredients and sprinkle with remaining cheese.
7. Bake at 375° for 25 minutes or until hot and lightly browned.

Tuna Casserole

Cora G. Napier
Connersville, IN
Around the Twist

Makes 4-6 servings

4 Tbsp. margarine
½ cup chopped onion
½ cup chopped celery
6½-oz. can tuna, undrained
1 cup milk
½ cup mayonnaise
10¾-oz. can cream of
    mushroom soup
8 ozs. egg noodles
½ cup bread crumbs

1. In large skillet sauté onion and celery with 2 Tbsp. margarine. Add flaked tuna with liquid, milk, mayonnaise and cream of mushroom soup and heat through.
2. Cook noodles according to package directions. Drain.
3. Mix noodles with everything else and pour into a well-greased 2-quart baking dish.
4. Melt remaining 2 Tbsp. margarine. Toss bread crumbs in margarine and arrange over other ingredients.
5. Bake at 350° for 25-30 minutes or until lightly browned and bubbly.

Turkey Casserole

Doreen Copeland
Florence, SC
Sailboat & Flower Basket

Makes 12 servings

2 10¾-oz. cans cream of
    mushroom soup
1½ cups milk
2 Tbsp. prepared mustard
½ tsp. rosemary
4 cups cooked, diced turkey
½ pkg. frozen peas
2 cups cooked rice
Buttered bread crumbs

1. Blend soup, milk, mustard, rosemary, turkey and peas.

2. Pour over rice in 3-quart casserole dish. Edge with bread crumbs.

3. Bake at 350° for 25 minutes.

Shenandoah Turkey Casserole

Carolyn Shank
Dayton, VA
Sampler

Makes 4-6 servings

2 cups Pepperidge Farm stuffing
¼ cup blanched almonds, slivered
2 cups diced, cooked turkey
10-oz. pkg. French-cut green beans, thawed
10¾-oz. can cream of mushroom soup
½ soup can milk
¼ cup hot water
2 Tbsp. melted butter

1. Spread 1⅓ cups stuffing into greased 7" x 11" baking dish. Sprinkle with almonds, turkey and green beans.

2. Combine soup and milk and pour over top.

3. Moisten remaining dressing with hot water and melted butter and spread over top.

4. Bake at 300° for 40 minutes.

Turkey Sauerbraten

M. Jeanne Osborne
Sanford, ME
Gwen's Tulips

Makes 6 servings

½ cup red wine vinegar
1½ cups water
1½ bay leaves
12 crushed gingersnaps
2 pkgs. dry onion soup mix
2 Tbsp. brown sugar
½ tsp. black pepper
1 lb. sliced, cooked turkey
Noodles

1. In a blender mix thoroughly vinegar, water, bay leaves and gingersnaps. Pour into a 9" x 13" baking dish and add onion soup, brown sugar and pepper and mix well.

2. Coat both sides of each slice of turkey with sauerbraten mixture. Lay turkey slices over sauerbraten.

3. Cover and bake at 350° for 30 minutes or until heated through. Serve with cooked noodles.

Tasty Chicken Breasts

Judy Berry
Columbia, MD
My First Quilt
Marjorie Miller
Conneaut Lake, PA
Wedding Ring Variation

Makes 4 servings

4 boneless chicken breasts
8 slices mozzarella cheese
10¾-oz. can cream of mushroom soup
10¾-oz. can cream of chicken soup
1 cup sour cream
Lemon pepper
1 cup fine seasoned bread crumbs
Paprika

1. Cut breasts in half. Pound to flatten a bit. Place one slice cheese on each half breast. Roll up and place in baking dish.

2. Combine soups and sour cream and pour over chicken breasts. Season to taste with lemon pepper. Sprinkle with crumbs and paprika.

3. Bake at 350° for 1½ hours.

Peach-Stuffed Chicken Breasts

Philip S. Pipero
Brooklyn, NY

Makes 6-8 servings

6 whole chicken breasts,
    boned and skinned
1 tsp. salt
1/8 tsp. ground pepper
1/2 cup butter *or* margarine
3 fresh ripe peaches,
    peeled and diced
1/2 cup chopped onion
1/2 cup chopped cashews
1/8 tsp. ground ginger

1. Place each chicken breast on a piece of wax paper. Flatten to 1/4-inch thickness with a meat mallet or rolling pin. Sprinkle insides of breasts with salt and pepper. Set aside.
2. Combine peaches, onion, cashews and ginger, stirring well. Place 1/4 cup filling on each breast. Fold sides over filling and secure with a toothpick.
3. Melt butter in a 9" x 13" baking pan and place breasts top side down in butter.
4. Bake at 375° for 25 minutes, turn chicken and bake an additional 20 minutes.
5. Serve with a peach sauce.

Peach Sauce

Dawn J. Ranck
Strasburg, PA
Friendship Quilt

Makes 2 cups sauce

1/2 cup white sugar
2 Tbsp. cornstarch
1/2 tsp. nutmeg
2 Tbsp. lemon juice
1 1/2 cups water
1/2 cup chopped, fresh
    peaches

1. Combine sugar and cornstarch in saucepan. Add nutmeg, lemon juice and water. Heat, stirring until thickened.
2. Stir in peaches and heat through. Serve with peach-stuffed chicken breasts.

Note: Substitute canned peaches for fresh peaches. Use peach juice for part of liquid.

Baked Chicken

Anna S. Petersheim
Paradise, PA
Shadow Star

Makes 3 servings

3 skinless chicken breasts
3 Tbsp. lowfat plain yogurt
10 3/4-oz. can cream of
    chicken soup
Salt, pepper and parsley to
    taste
1 1/2 cups sliced mushrooms
3 Tbsp. sour cream

1. Place chicken breasts in lightly greased baking dish. Spread yogurt, chicken soup and seasonings over chicken.
2. Bake at 350° for 1 hour or until done, basting several times with sauce.
3. Remove from oven and spread mushrooms and sour cream over chicken pieces. Bake 5 more minutes or until heated through.

My friend and I planned a bridal shower for a mutual friend. Tired of the usual boring games, I invited each person who attended the shower to design one block for a sampler wall hanging. It was great fun watching persons who thought they had no talent use my supplies and suggestions to piece together wonderful designs. I had a hard time parting with the finished wall hanging!

—*Rebecca Eldredge, Honolulu, HI*

Chicken on the Run

Pat Higgins
Norman, OK
Sugar Loaf

Makes 2 servings

2 chicken breasts
¼ cup sliced onion
¼ tomato, sliced
1 medium potato, sliced
1 small carrot, sliced
1 stalk celery, chopped
¼ tsp. pepper
⅛ tsp. tarragon
1 tsp. lemon juice

1. Wrap all ingredients in tin foil.
2. Bake at 350° for 1 hour.

❖

Herbed Chicken

LaVerne A. Olsen
Willow Street, PA
Log Cabin Star

Makes 6 servings

10¾-oz. can cream of celery soup
¼ cup soy sauce
¼ cup wine vinegar
¼ cup water
½ tsp. minced garlic
1 tsp. powdered ginger
½ tsp. oregano
1 Tbsp. brown sugar

3 chicken breasts, split into halves
3-4 cups cooked rice

1. Combine all ingredients except chicken and rice and mix well.
2. Arrange chicken pieces in large casserole dish and pour soup mixture over chicken.
3. Cover and bake at 375° for 1 hour and 15 minutes. Uncover and bake 15 minutes longer.
4. Serve over rice, separating gravy from chicken pieces if desired.

Bengal Tigers Chicken

Ann Judge
Queenstown, MD
Sampler

Makes 4-6 servings

4 chicken breasts
1 Tbsp. butter
10¾-oz. can cream of chicken soup
1 cup mayonnaise
1 Tbsp. lemon juice
1 tsp. curry powder
½ cup shredded cheddar cheese
½ cup Pepperidge Farm stuffing
2 Tbsp. butter

1. Skin, bone and split chicken breasts. Place

chicken in single layer in 9" x 13" baking dish. Dot each piece with butter.
2. Combine soup, mayonnaise, lemon juice, curry and cheese. Spread over chicken. Sprinkle stuffing on top and dot with butter.
3. Bake at 300° for 1½ hours.

❖

Chicken and Rice with Mushrooms

Alana Robbins
Los Lunas, NM
Double Wedding Ring

Makes 4-6 servings

4 chicken breasts
2½-3 cups uncooked rice
10¾-oz. can onion soup
10¾-oz. can cream of chicken soup
2 soup cans water
4-5 large fresh mushrooms, sliced
Salt and pepper to taste
Poultry seasoning to taste

1. Put rice into deep casserole dish. Place chicken on top of rice. Add both cans of soup. Add both cans of water and put mushrooms on top.
2. Season with salt and pepper and several dashes of poultry seasoning.
3. Cover and bake at 325° for 1½ hours.

Chicken Cheese Rolls

Marybeth Romeo
Roanoke, VA
Triple Rail

Makes 6 servings

3 large chicken breasts,
boned and split
8-oz. pkg. cream cheese
2 Tbsp. chives
1 Tbsp. butter *or* margarine
6 slices bacon

1. Place chicken breasts between waxed paper and pound to ½-inch thickness.
2. Cream cream cheese and chives together.
3. Spread each chicken breast with 3 Tbsp. cream cheese. Dot with ½ tsp. butter. Fold ends over filling. Wrap 1 slice bacon around each roll. Place seam side down in shallow baking pan.
4. Bake at 400° on top rack of oven for 40 minutes or until juices run clear. Broil 5 minutes to brown bacon.

Carlene Horne's Chicken

Carlene Horne
Bedford, NH
Refrigerator Quilt

Makes 3 servings

1 lb. boneless, skinless
chicken breasts
15-oz. can unsweetened
pineapple chunks
3 Tbsp. soy sauce
1 cup pineapple juice
¼ tsp. garlic powder
1½ tsp. ground ginger
1 small onion, chopped
1 cup snow pea pods

1. Place chicken in a baking dish.
2. Drain pineapple chunks and reserve juice. Arrange pineapple chunks over chicken.
3. In a small bowl, combine soy sauce, pineapple juice, garlic powder and ginger. Pour over chicken.
4. Sauté onion and pea pods until lightly browned. Arrange over chicken.
5. Cover and bake at 350° for 1 hour.

Creamed Chicken with Broccoli and Rice

Bea Gagliano
Lakewood, NJ
Mariner's Compass

Makes 4 servings

1 lb. boneless, skinless
chicken breasts
1 Tbsp. butter *or* margarine
¼ cup milk
10¾-oz. can cream of
broccoli soup
1 pkg. Uncle Ben's white
rice

1. Brown chicken pieces in butter until golden brown.
2. While chicken browns, combine milk and soup. Pour into frying pan with chicken and simmer for 30 minutes or until chicken is completely cooked.
3. Cook rice according to package directions. Serve chicken over rice.

❖

Microwave Chicken

Doris C. McCloskey
Annapolis, MD
Dutch Windmill

Makes 4 servings

4 chicken breasts, skinned and boned
¼ cup grated Parmesan cheese
¼ cup bread crumbs
1 Tbsp. parsley
¼ tsp. garlic powder
1 tsp. oregano
2 Tbsp. margarine

1. Combine cheese, crumbs, parsley, garlic and oregano in bag and shake well.
2. Melt margarine and brush chicken with margarine.
3. Shake chicken pieces in bag with seasonings.
4. Arrange chicken in a glass pie plate and cover with a paper towel.
5. Microwave on high for 6-7 minutes. Let stand 5 minutes before serving.

❖

Chicken and Lime

Marjorie Mills
Bethesda, MD
Scrap Quilt

Makes 3 servings

6 chicken thighs *or* 3 large chicken breast halves
2 Tbsp. cooking oil
1 medium onion, chopped
1 clove garlic, minced
⅛ tsp. hot red pepper
½ tsp. ground cumin
½ tsp. crushed coriander seeds
¼ tsp. turmeric
2 Tbsp. soy sauce
2 limes

1. Heat oil in large skillet. Skin chicken and brown over medium heat. Add onion and garlic and cook 2 minutes. Add all other ingredients except limes. Reduce heat, cover and cook until tender, about 20-25 minutes.
2. Immediately before serving, add the juice of 2 limes, about 2 Tbsp. Heat through.
3. Garnish with lime quarters and serve.

❖

Flaming Chicken Bombay

Irene Dewar
Pickering, ON
Barns

Makes 8 servings

2 Tbsp. butter
2 Tbsp. cooking oil
4-5 lbs. chicken pieces
Salt and pepper to taste
2 onions, chopped
1 green pepper, chopped
1½ tsp. curry powder
1 tsp. salt
¼ tsp. pepper
¾ tsp. thyme
1 tsp. sugar
½ cup raisins
1½ cups uncooked rice
1 cup water
28-oz. can tomatoes, undrained

1. Heat butter and oil in large electric frying pan. Brown chicken, seasoning with salt and pepper. Remove chicken and set aside.
2. Sauté onion and pepper in frying pan.
3. In a bowl combine curry, salt, pepper, thyme, sugar and raisins and mix well. Stir in rice, water and tomatoes with juice.
4. Return chicken to frying pan. Spoon rice mixture over chicken.
5. Cover and cook for 1 hour or until chicken is thoroughly cooked. Stir occasionally, adding water if necessary.

Chicken Dulce

Jackie Evans
Albuquerque, NM
Southwest Symphony

Makes 10-12 servings

12 chicken thighs
16-oz. can whole berry
cranberry sauce
½ cup French dressing
1 pkg. dry onion soup mix

1. Arrange chicken pieces in greased 9" x 13" baking dish.
2. Mix together cranberry sauce, French dressing and onion soup mix. Pour over chicken and marinate in refrigerator for 1½ hours.
3. Bake, uncovered, at 350° for 1½ hours.

Curried Chicken and Rice

Erma Zimmerman
Goshen, IN
Crayon Color Nursery Quilt

Makes 4-6 servings

8-10 pieces chicken,
skinned
¼ cup flour
1 Tbsp. curry powder
1 tsp. salt
½ tsp. pepper

4 Tbsp. margarine
1 cup uncooked rice
3 chicken bouillon cubes
3 cups boiling water
1 large red onion, sliced
1 cup raisins

1. Mix together flour, curry powder, salt and pepper. Roll chicken in mixture. Brown chicken in margarine in deep skillet.
2. After chicken is browned, pour grease from skillet. Add rice which has been washed.
3. Dissolve chicken bouillon cubes in boiling water. Pour over rice and chicken, making sure rice is covered with liquid. Slice onion over top and add raisins. Simmer until chicken is tender and liquid is absorbed.

Parmesan Chicken

Eleanor Larson
Glen Lyon, PA
Basket & Autograph

Makes 6-8 servings

2 cups bread crumbs
½ cup parsley flakes
1 cup Parmesan cheese
Dash salt and pepper
1 Tbsp. garlic powder
8 Tbsp. margarine, melted
4 chicken legs and thighs
2 chicken breasts
4 chicken wings

1. Combine bread crumbs, parsley flakes, cheese, salt, pepper and garlic powder.
2. Dip each chicken piece in melted margarine, then in bread crumb mix. Arrange on ungreased baking sheet. Sprinkle any remaining margarine and crumb mixture over chicken.
3. Bake at 350° for 20 minutes. Turn chicken pieces and bake another 20 minutes.

Oven-Fried Chicken

Emma Martin
Lititz, PA
Irish Chain & Log Cabin

Makes 6-8 servings

4-5-lb. whole chicken
2-3 cups finely crushed
Rice Krispies
1 cup finely crushed
cracker crumbs
½ tsp. pepper
1 tsp. poultry seasoning
½ tsp. garlic powder
Dash chili powder
½ cup butter, melted

1. Cut chicken into serving pieces.
2. Combine the Rice Krispies, cracker crumbs and seasonings.
3. Dip chicken pieces into the melted butter, then

dip into crumbs. Arrange chicken in a baking dish.

4. Bake at 350° for approximately 1 hour or until chicken is tender.

Paradise Island Chicken

Rebecca Eldredge
Honolulu, HI
Kohala Beauty

Makes 4-6 servings

1 whole chicken, cut up
½ cup soy sauce
2 Tbsp. brown sugar
1 tsp. cooking oil
1 tsp. sesame oil
½ cup orange juice
1 large clove garlic
½ tsp. fresh ginger

1. Arrange chicken in shallow baking dish.
2. Combine all remaining ingredients and pour over chicken. Marinate overnight or at least several hours.
3. Grill chicken, basting with marinade frequently.

Barbecue Chicken

Violette Denney
Carrollton, GA
1991 Sampler

Makes 4-6 servings

1 medium chicken, cut up
18-oz. bottle barbecue sauce
8-oz. can Coca Cola
9-oz. bottle ketchup

1. Brown chicken pieces lightly in a large frying pan.
2. Combine all remaining ingredients and mix well. Pour sauce over chicken.
3. Cook slowly for about 1 hour or until chicken is tender. Serve.

Barbecued Chicken in Oven

Mildred Kennel
Atglen, PA
Sailboat

Makes 8 servings

8 chicken halves
Salt and pepper to taste
2 Tbsp. Worcestershire sauce
2 Tbsp. brown sugar
1 cup vinegar
½ cup ketchup
1 Tbsp. mustard
½ cup cooking oil
¾ cup margarine

1. Season chicken pieces and place in shallow baking pan.
2. Combine remaining ingredients in saucepan and bring to a boil.
3. Baste chicken pieces with sauce.
4. Bake at 350° for 1 hour, basting every 15 minutes.

Variation:

Substitute 2 tsp. chili powder and 2 tsp. paprika for mustard. Substitute 4 Tbsp. vinegar, 2 Tbsp. lemon juice and 8 Tbsp. water for vinegar. Delete cooking oil and margarine.
Grace Ketcham
Pennsville, NJ
Hearts and Flowers

Add ½ cup chopped onion, ½ cup chopped celery and ¼ cup green pepper to sauce in step 2.

Carol Trice
Wayne, PA
Baby Dresden

Brunswick Chicken Bake

Sherry Carroll
Delta, PA
Sampler

Makes 6 servings

2 ½-3-lb. fryer chicken, cut up
2 Tbsp. cooking oil
1 large onion, chopped
2 Tbsp. flour
6-oz. pkg. Italian salad dressing mix
16-oz. can stewed tomatoes
1 bay leaf
10-oz. pkg. frozen succotash

1. In a skillet brown chicken in oil. Arrange chicken in large baking dish.
2. Reserve 2 Tbsp. drippings and cook onion till tender. Stir in flour and salad dressing mix. Add tomatoes and bay leaf and cook until thickened and bubbly. Stir in vegetables and heat through. Pour mixture over chicken.
3. Cover and bake at 350° for one hour. Remove bay leaf and serve.

Chicken Turnovers

Julie Lynch Arnsberger
Gaithersburg, MD
Trip Around the World

Makes 8 servings

2 Tbsp. cooking oil
8 medium chicken thighs
1 cup water
1 chicken bouillon cube
3 Tbsp. all-purpose flour
¾ tsp. salt
⅛ tsp. pepper
1½ cups milk
8-oz. pkg. pork sausage links
2 8-oz. pkgs. crescent dinner rolls
1 egg, slightly beaten

1. Heat cooking oil in 10-inch skillet over medium heat. Cook chicken thighs until browned on all sides.
2. Remove chicken to saucepan. Add water and bouillon cube and heat to boiling. Reduce heat to low, cover and simmer 25 minutes.
3. Meanwhile, stir flour, salt and pepper into drippings in skillet and cook until bubbly. Gradually stir in milk, stirring until thickened. Remove skillet from heat. Set aside.
4. Prepare sausage according to package directions. Drain all excess fat.
5. Carefully remove bone from each chicken thigh, leaving meat in one piece. Place one sausage link in opening left by bone.
6. On lightly floured surface separate dough from each crescent roll package into 4 rectangles. Pinch diagonal perforations together. With lightly floured rolling pin roll each dough piece into a 6" x 8" rectangle.
7. Place sausage-stuffed thigh in center of each dough piece and top with 1 Tbsp. gravy mixture. Fold dough over stuffed thigh so long edges meet and press gently to seal.
8. Place turnovers, seam side down, on large baking sheet, sealing all edges. Brush each turnover with egg.
9. Bake at 375° for 15 minutes or until lightly browned.
10. Meanwhile, heat remaining gravy mixture. Serve gravy with turnovers.

Hungarian Chicken Paprikas

Julianna Csikasz
Wakefield, MA
Baby Patchwork

Makes 6-8 servings

3-lb. chicken, cut up
2 onions, finely chopped
3 Tbsp. cooking oil
4 Tbsp. sweet paprika
Salt to taste
½ green pepper

½ cup sour cream
(optional)
Dash hot pepper (optional)

1. Wash chicken well and drain.

2. Brown onions in oil. Add paprika and chicken pieces and sprinkle with salt. (If needed, add a bit of water.) Add green pepper (whole piece).

3. Cover and cook slowly about 45 minutes or until chicken is tender. Pour sour cream and hot pepper over chicken and heat for one minute only.

4. Serve with fresh boiled noodles, potatoes or rice.

Sweet and Sour Chicken Wings

Linda Roberta Pond
Los Alamos, NM
Not the Same Old Cat

Makes 4-6 servings

**10-12 chicken wings
14-oz. bottle ketchup
8-oz. can tomato sauce
1 cup vinegar
1 cup white sugar
1 tsp. dry mustard
1 tsp. ginger**

1. Arrange chicken wings in 9" x 13" baking pan.

2. Combine all other in-

gredients in a saucepan and bring to a boil. Pour sauce over chicken wings.

3. Bake at 325° for 1½-2 hours, turning wings several times.

Oriental Chicken Wings

Joan Coale Klosek
Ellicott City, MD
AIDS Baby Quilt

Makes 4-6 servings

**½ cup ketchup
½ cup soy sauce
½ tsp. garlic powder
1 Tbsp. ginger
3 Tbsp. brown sugar
3 lbs. chicken wings
¼ cup white sugar**

1. Combine ketchup, soy sauce, garlic powder, ginger and brown sugar. Refrigerate overnight to blend flavors.

2. Separate chicken wings at joints, discarding tips. Place in bowl and sprinkle with white sugar. Let stand for 1½ hours.

3. Dip chicken wings in marinade and arrange on 10" x 15" jelly roll pan. Pour remaining marinade over wings and let stand for 1½ hours.

4. Bake at 375° for 1½ hours, basting several times.

Chicken Kabobs

Ellen Crockett
Springfield, VA
With a Little Help From My Friends

Makes 4 servings

**Chicken:
1 lb. boneless, skinless chicken breasts
4 small onions, quartered
8-10 mushrooms
8-10 cherry tomatoes, halved
4 bell peppers, cut in chunks**

**Marinade:
¼ cup cooking oil
1 tsp. oregano
1 tsp. garlic
2 Tbsp. lemon juice
1 tsp. soy sauce**

1. Cut uncooked chicken into 1-inch cubes.

2. Combine all marinade ingredients and pour into large ziploc bag. Add chicken and marinate at least 2 hours, turning bag at least twice.

3. Form kabobs by alternating chicken with vegetables on wooden or metal skewers.

4. Cook either on an outdoor grill or under the broiler, about 5-10 minutes per side or until chicken is cooked through and vegetables are desired degree of tenderness.

Burmese Chicken

U Khin
Rocky Ridge, MD
Miniature House

Makes 6 servings

2-3 lbs. chicken
¼ tsp. turmeric
1½ tsp. salt
2 large onions, finely diced
2 cloves garlic, minced
½-inch piece ginger,
   minced
1 tsp. chili powder
   (optional)
2 Tbsp. soy sauce
1 tomato, crushed
   (optional)
3 Tbsp. cooking oil
¼ cup water

1. Cut chicken from bones with sharp knife and cut into small pieces.
2. Throw all ingredients into wok or large pot. Cover and cook over medium heat, simmering about 15-20 minutes.
3. Add ½ cup more water and cook until chicken is tender, about 40-45 minutes. Stir occasionally.
4. Serve with cooked pasta or rice.

Curried Chicken

Julie Rizzello
Glenelg, MD
Baltimore Album Applique

Makes 4 servings

4 chicken breasts
2 small onions, chopped
2 Tbsp. margarine
1 cup sliced mushrooms
1 cup raisins
1 tsp. curry powder
10¾-oz. can cream of
   chicken soup

1. Cook chicken breasts and cut into 1-inch pieces.
2. Sauté onions in margarine. Add mushrooms, raisins and curry powder and heat, stirring until blended.
3. Add chicken and heat through. Stir in soup and heat until bubbly.
4. May be served with noodles or rice.

Chicken Deluxe

Karen Moore
Fairfax, VA
Amish Nine Patch

Makes 10 servings

2 cups Pepperidge Farm
   stuffing
8 Tbsp. butter *or*
   margarine, melted
10¾-oz. can cream of
   celery soup
2 cups diced, cooked
   chicken
1 cup chicken broth
½ cup milk
¾ cup peas
1 Tbsp. minced onion

1. Mix 1 cup stuffing with melted butter. Pat into bottom of 2-quart casserole dish.
3. Combine all other ingredients and spoon over stuffing. Top with remaining 1 cup stuffing.
4. Bake at 425° for 15-20 minutes until bubbly.

Barbara Swartz's Chicken Casserole

Barbara J. Swartz
Mercer, PA
Sampler

Makes 4-6 servings

4 chicken breasts
2-3 slices fresh bread
2 eggs, beaten
½ cup milk
1 tsp. Worcestershire sauce
2 tsp. poultry seasoning
1 tsp. salt

1. Skin and cook chicken. Cool, bone and cut into small pieces. Reserve broth.
2. Crumb bread by tearing into tiny pieces. Reserve 1 slice for topping.

3. Mix chicken, bread, eggs, milk, Worcestershire sauce and seasonings in a casserole dish. Sprinkle bread crumbs from reserved slice bread over dish.

4. Bake at 350° for 60-90 minutes.

5. Prepare gravy with reserved chicken broth. Serve.

❖

Ruby Cook's Chicken Casserole

Ruby I. Cook
Newtown Square, PA
White on White

Makes 6 servings

2 cups cooked, diced chicken
10¾-oz. can mushroom soup
8-oz. can pineapple chunks with juice
1 cup diced celery
3-4 cups cooked rice
2 Tbsp. chopped onion
1 Tbsp. soy sauce
1 green pepper, chopped
½ cup crushed potato chips

1. Combine all ingredients except potato chips in a 5-quart casserole dish. Sprinkle with potato chips.

2. Bake at 350° for 50 minutes.

❖

Chicken and Rice Pilaf

Bertha Penner
Beatrice, NE
Tree of Life Quilt

Makes 6 servings

1 whole chicken
5-6 cups water
1 tsp. salt
½ Tbsp. whole allspice
1 Tbsp. lard *or* shortening
1 onion
2 cups uncooked rice
4 cups chicken broth
4 small carrots, sliced
1 tsp. salt
¼ tsp. pepper

1. Cook chicken in water, salt and allspice until done. Cool, bone and dice chicken. Set diced chicken aside. Skim broth and set aside.

2. In a large skillet sauté onion in lard. Add chicken, rice, broth, carrots, salt and pepper.

3. Cook over medium heat until mixture boils. Turn to low heat, cover tightly and cook for about 1 hour. Serve.

❖

Rice and Chicken Parmesan

Lorraine Moore Lear
Del City, OK
Old Maid's Puzzle

Makes 6 servings

2 lbs. chicken pieces
4 cups water
2 tsp. Mrs. Dash seasoning
1 cup chicken broth
2 cups brown rice
1 cup diced celery
1 medium onion, chopped
2 8-oz. cartons sour cream
½-1 cup Parmesan cheese

1. Cook chicken in water with Mrs. Dash seasoning. When cooked, remove chicken, cool and debone.

2. Skim broth. Cook rice, celery and onion in chicken broth according to directions on rice package.

3. Combine chicken pieces with rice mixture and sour cream. Arrange in 9" x 13" casserole dish and sprinkle with Parmesan cheese.

4. Bake at 300° for 15-20 minutes or until heated through.

When my husband and I moved off our farm, I began making quilts for our six grandchildren. In September of 1981 we bought a frame, and I began making quilts to sell. As of April 1992 I am working on my 112th quilt.

—Evelyn Becker, Paradise, PA

> **Our group of five quilters meets every Monday morning to quilt, chat and share "Monday muffins and dessert." We range in age from 43 to 78 and have solved many problems from the personal to the global!**
>
> —*Marilyn Wallace, Alfred, ME*

Omit butter. Substitute 2 cups chicken broth and 1 cup milk for the 4 cups milk. Add 2 diced hard-boiled eggs.
Mary Beth Gower
Northampton, PA
Cut Glass Dishes

Convent Pie

Julie Lynch Arnsberger
Gaithersburg, MD
Trip Around the World

Makes 6-8 servings

¾ cup uncooked macaroni
1 cup milk
½ cup grated cheese
1 cup bread cubes
3 eggs
10¾-oz. can cream of
    mushroom soup
1 Tbsp. minced onion
1 tsp. salt
⅓ cup butter, melted
1 Tbsp. chopped parsley
    (optional)
4-oz. jar mushroom pieces,
    undrained
2 cups diced, cooked
    chicken *or* turkey

1. Cook, drain and rinse macaroni.
2. Add all remaining ingredients to macaroni and mix well. Spoon into greased 9" x 13" casserole dish.
3. Bake at 350° for 1 hour.

Chicken Supreme

Joanne Spatz
Lebanon, PA
Love Rings

Makes 10-12 servings

4 cups diced, cooked
    chicken
4 cups uncooked macaroni
4 cups milk
2 cups grated cheese
3 10¾-oz. cans cream of
    chicken soup
½ cup chopped onion
1 tsp. salt
½ tsp. pepper
6 Tbsp. butter

1. Combine all ingredients except half of cheese. Place in large greased casserole dish and refrigerate overnight.
2. Remove from refrigerator and bake at 350° for 75 minutes, stirring occasionally. Top with remaining cheese and bake 15 minutes longer.

Variation:
Substitute cream of mushroom soup for the chicken soup. Omit the butter.
Marjorie Miller
Conneaut Lake, PA
Wedding Ring Variation

Chicken Divan

Janet Groff
Stevens, PA
Country Love

Makes 10-12 servings

2 10-oz. pkgs. broccoli
4-6 cups chopped, cooked
    chicken breast
10¾-oz. can cream of
    chicken soup
10¾-oz. can cream of
    mushroom soup
½ cup mayonnaise
1 tsp. lemon juice
1 cup grated cheese
1 cup bread crumbs

1. Cook broccoli according to package directions.
2. In an 8" x 12" baking dish layer broccoli and chicken.
3. Combine soups, mayonnaise and lemon juice and pour over chicken. Sprinkle with cheese and bread crumbs.
4. Bake at 350° for 35-40 minutes.

Variations:
Use 6 whole chicken

breasts, cut in half. Layer broccoli into baking dish without cooking it. Arrange chicken breasts over broccoli. Continue with steps 3 and 4.

Barbara Forrester Landis
Lititz, PA
Jacob's Ladder

Add ½ tsp. curry powder to mixture in step 3.
Mitzi McGlynchey
Downingtown, PA
Trip Around the World

❖

Chicken Corn Casserole

Lois Niebauer
Pedricktown, NJ
Christopher's Bear

Makes 4-6 servings

2 Tbsp. butter
¼ cup flour
½ tsp. salt
Dash pepper
1½ cups chicken broth
2 cups diced, cooked chicken
1½ cups corn
½ cup shredded cheddar cheese
3 Tbsp. chopped pimento
1 small can Durkee onions, crushed

1. Melt butter and stir in flour, seasonings and chicken broth, cooking and stirring occasionally until thickened.

2. Add chicken, corn, cheese, pimento and ⅔ of onions and mix well. Pour into an 8" x 12" baking dish and sprinkle remaining onions over ingredients.

3. Bake at 325° for 35 minutes.

❖

Chicken Au Gratin Casserole

L.W. Weaver
Ephrata, PA
Country Love

Makes 6 servings

1 quart green beans
1 cup diced, cooked chicken
10¾-oz. can cream of chicken soup
¼ cup water
Salt and pepper to taste
2 cups soft bread cubes
⅓ cup butter, melted
½ cup grated cheese

1. Place green beans and chicken in a casserole dish.

2. In a saucepan combine chicken soup and water and heat to boiling. Pour over chicken and season to taste.

3. Combine bread cubes, butter and cheese. Toss lightly and sprinkle over chicken.

4. Bake at 350° for 30 minutes or until brown.

❖

Pineapple Chicken Stir-fry

Jean H. Robinson
Cinnaminson, NJ
Little School Girl

Makes 4 servings

2 lbs. boneless chicken breasts
2 Tbsp. olive oil
½ cup chopped onion (optional)
8-oz. can unsweetened pineapple chunks
3 Tbsp. teriyaki sauce (optional)
4 Tbsp. cornstarch
2 Tbsp. brown sugar
2 medium carrots, thinly chopped
6-oz. pkg. pea pods

1. Cook, bone and cut chicken into chunks.

2. In a medium skillet or wok stir-fry chicken chunks in oil over medium heat. Add onion and sauté.

3. In a small bowl combine pineapple juice and teriyaki sauce. Add enough water to make 1½ cups liquid. Stir in cornstarch and brown sugar and set aside.

4. Add carrots to chicken and onion. Cook for 5 minutes, stirring occasionally. Stir in liquid, pea pods and pineapple chunks. Cook and stir 2 more minutes.

5. Serve with noodles, rice or spaghetti.

Savory Crust Chicken Bake

Jul Hoober
New Holland, PA
Roman Stripe

Makes 6-8 servings

Crust:
½ cup butter *or* margarine
1 cup sour cream
1 egg
1 cup flour
1 tsp. salt
1 tsp. baking powder
½ tsp. sage *or* thyme

Filling:
½ cup chopped carrots
½ cup chopped onion
½ cup chopped celery
2 Tbsp. butter *or* margarine
2 cups chopped, cooked chicken
10¾-oz. can cream of chicken soup
4-oz. jar mushrooms, drained
½-1 cup shredded cheddar cheese

1. To prepare crust cream butter and sour cream. Add egg and dry ingredients and mix at low speed. Spread crust into 9-inch greased pie plate.
2. To prepare filling sauté vegetables in butter until tender. Add chicken, soup and mushrooms and heat through.
3. Spoon filling into crust. Top with cheese.
4. Bake at 400° for 25-30 minutes. Cut into wedges and serve.

❖

Chicken Pies

Irene P. Dietlin
New Hartford, CT
Cupid's Nine Patch

Makes 8 servings

4 cups minced, cooked chicken
2 cups minced carrots
1 cup minced onions
1 cup minced celery
2 Tbsp. olive oil
2 cups shredded cheese
½ cup chopped fresh parsley
3 Tbsp. chopped fresh basil
Salt and pepper to taste
1 pkg. fresh phyllo dough
1 Tbsp. unsalted butter, melted

1. In a large frying pan sauté minced vegetables in olive oil for one hour. Remove from heat and cover with waxed paper for one hour (to steam).
2. In a large bowl combine cooled vegetables and chicken. (Be sure to drain vegetables well to avoid a wet filling.)
3. Toss cheese, herbs and spices together and add to chicken mixture.
4. Stack 2 pieces phyllo dough and spread lightly with butter. Put about ¾ cup filling on dough and fold into triangle shape. Continue with remaining pieces of dough. Arrange on baking sheet.
5. Bake at 375° for 15-20 minutes. Cool on racks.

Note: Cover dough with damp towel while working with it to prevent dough from drying.

❖

Savory Chicken Crescent Squares

Sherry Sommers
Millersburg, OH
Lady's Fan

Makes 2-4 servings

3-oz. pkg. cream cheese, softened
3 Tbsp. margarine, softened
2 cups diced, cooked chicken
¼ tsp. salt
⅛ tsp. pepper
2 Tbsp. milk
1 tsp. minced onion
8-oz. pkg. crescent rolls
1 Tbsp. margarine, melted
¾ cup seasoned croutons

1. Cream together cream cheese and 3 Tbsp. margarine. Add chicken, salt, pepper, milk and onion and mix well.
2. Separate crescent rolls into 4 rectangles. Press perforations firmly to seal.

Spoon ½ cup meat mixture into center of each rectangle. Pull corners of dough to top and twist slightly. Seal edges.

3. Arrange in small rectangular baking dish. Brush tops with 1 Tbsp. margarine. Sprinkle with croutons.

4. Bake at 350° for 20-25 minutes.

Mom's Chicken Pot Pie

Hazel Lightcap Propst
Oxford, PA
Amish Sunshine and Shadows

Makes 10-12 servings

Stew:
3-4-lb. whole chicken
2 quarts water
2 potatoes, chopped
2 carrots, chopped
1 onion, chopped

Pot Pie Dough:
2 cups flour
2 eggs
2-3 Tbsp. milk

1. Cook chicken in water until tender. Remove chicken from broth and let cool.

2. Add potatoes, carrots and onion to broth and cook until tender.

3. Meanwhile, prepare pot pie dough by combining all ingredients by hand.

Roll dough out as thin as possible and cut into 2-inch squares.

4. Skim broth and bring to a full, rolling boil. Drop dough squares into broth, a few at a time. Keep broth boiling until all squares are in broth. Cover and cook about 20 minutes until tender.

5. Bone and dice chicken. At end of cooking time return chicken to broth and quickly heat through. Serve.

Chicken Pot Pie

Joyce McFarland
Woodbridge, VA
Patchwork Pals

Makes 4-6 servings

Chicken Mixture:
1 carrot, sliced
2 potatoes, diced
¼ cup butter
¼ cup flour
1 cup chicken broth
1 cup milk
1 tsp. sage
½ tsp. thyme
½ tsp. salt
⅛ tsp. pepper
2 cups diced, cooked chicken
½ cup frozen peas

Pastry:
1 cup flour
½ tsp. salt
⅓ cup soft butter

3-5 Tbsp. water
2 Tbsp. milk

1. Cook carrot and potatoes until soft.

2. Meanwhile, melt butter in medium saucepan. Add flour and cook over medium heat 1 minute, stirring constantly. Add broth, milk and seasonings and bring to a boil. Cook, stirring until thickened.

3. Stir in chicken, peas, carrot and potatoes. Pour into a 10-inch pie pan.

4. To prepare pastry mix flour and salt in small bowl. Cut in butter until mixture resembles coarse crumbs. Sprinkle with water and toss with a fork until moist. Press into a ball.

5. Roll out onto well-floured surface. Lay over top of chicken ingredients in pie pan. Cut several slits for steam and flute edge. Brush top of crust with milk. Place pie pan onto another baking pan because dish almost always runs over.

6. Bake at 450° for 20 minutes.

Hot Chicken Salad

Sally Thorpe
Roanoke Rapids, NC
Storm at Sea

Makes 6 servings

2 cups diced, cooked
  chicken
10¾-oz. can cream of
  chicken soup
1 cup chopped celery
1 tsp. chopped onion
½ cup chopped nuts
  (optional)
1 tsp. salt
¼ tsp. pepper
1 Tbsp. minced green
  pepper
2 Tbsp. lemon juice
½ cup mayonnaise
1 hard-boiled egg, chopped
1 cup Pepperidge Farm
  stuffing
2 Tbsp. butter

1. Combine all ingredients except stuffing and butter. Spoon into casserole dish. Sprinkle dressing over top and dot with butter.
2. Bake at 350° for 15-20 minutes.

Georgia Chicken Stew

Marsha Sands
Ocean City, MD
Window of Miracles
Carol Kelley
Carrollton, GA

Makes 8-10 servings

1 whole chicken
16-oz. can whole tomatoes
2 chicken bouillon cubes
10¾-oz. can tomato soup
1 bay leaf
2 Tbsp. Worcestershire
  sauce
1 tsp. paprika
2 Tbsp. vinegar
1 tsp. sage
3 sprinkles garlic salt
4 Tbsp. margarine
1 large onion, chopped
10-oz. pkg. frozen limas
10-oz. pkg. frozen corn
6 large potatoes, cubed

1. Cook chicken in 3-4 cups water. Cool and bone chicken. Boil broth down to about 2 cups.
2. Return chicken pieces to broth and add tomatoes which have been chopped. Add all other ingredients except potatoes and cook until thickened, stirring occasionally. Remove bay leaf.
3. Meanwhile, cook potatoes in a separate saucepan until softened. Drain and, immediately before serving, stir into stew.

Creamy Cajun Chicken with Pasta

Denise S. Rominger
Cranbury, NJ
Crazy Patch

Makes 4 servings

1 tsp. minced garlic
2 Tbsp. butter
12 ozs. boneless, skinless
  chicken breasts, cubed
1 Tbsp. Cajun spices
⅓ cup chopped green
  onions
1 cup heavy cream
12 ozs. thin spaghetti
2 Tbsp. fresh parsley
Freshly grated Parmesan
  cheese

1. In a skillet cook garlic in butter for approximately 30 seconds on medium heat. Stir in chicken and Cajun spices and cook until lightly browned. Stir in onions and cook 1 minute. Add cream and turn heat to high, boil until slightly thickened.
2. Meanwhile, cook and drain spaghetti according to directions.
3. In a serving dish combine chicken mixture with pasta and parsley. Serve with Parmesan cheese.

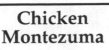

Chicken Montezuma

Dorothy M. VanDeest
Memphis, TN
The Bearish and Bullish Dow

Makes 10-12 servings

1 large onion, chopped
4 Tbsp. margarine
12 soft corn tortillas
2 10¾-oz. cans cream of
    mushroom soup
10¾-oz. can cream of
    chicken soup
16-oz. can stewed tomatoes
3 cups diced, cooked
    chicken
1½ cups grated Parmesan
    or cheddar cheese

1. Sauté onion in margarine.
2. Tear tortillas into small pieces.
3. Combine all ingredients except ½ cup cheese and pour into 9" x 13" baking pan. Top with remaining cheese.
4. Bake at 350° for 20 minutes.

Sonora Chicken Casserole

Ruth Day
Sturgis, SD
Double Jacob's Ladder

Makes 6-8 servings

4 whole chicken breasts
10¾-oz. can cream of
    chicken soup
10¾-oz. can cream of
    mushroom soup
15-oz. can chili without
    beans
1 small onion, finely
    chopped
½ lb. sharp cheddar
    cheese, grated
½ lb. Monterey Jack
    cheese, grated
½ cup milk
6 tortillas, torn into pieces
14-oz. can chili salsa

1. Cook, cool and bone chicken. Dice into small pieces.
2. In a large bowl combine all remaining ingredients. Add cooked chicken.
3. Bake at 350° 25-30 mintues or until hot and bubbly.

Mexican Chicken

Elizabeth J. Yoder
Millersburg, OH
Log Cabin

Makes 6-8 servings

1 whole chicken
1 tsp. garlic salt
Crushed red pepper
1 large onion, chopped
½ lb. cheese, grated
½ bag taco chips
8-oz. can whole tomatoes
10¾-oz. can cream of
    mushroom soup
10¾-oz. can cream of
    chicken soup

1. Cook, cool and bone chicken. Place in large casserole dish. Sprinkle with garlic salt and red pepper. Add onion and cheese.
2. Crush half of taco chips and sprinkle over ingredients.
3. Combine the tomatoes and soups and pour over other ingredients and mix lightly.
4. Crush remaining chips and sprinkle over top.
5. Bake at 400° for 45 minutes.

My mother-in-law, Catherine Seeley, taught me how to quilt many years ago. On our trips to Ithaca, NY she would reminisce about her family while we sat around the quilt talking and drinking tea. I learned so much about my husband and his family during those special times.

—*Sue Seeley, Black Forest, CO*

Chicken Enchiladas

Sue Hertzler Schrag
Beatrice, NE
Star Spin

Makes 10-12 servings

½ cup chopped onion
4 Tbsp. margarine
¼ cup flour
2 cups chicken broth
1 tsp. chicken bouillon
8-oz. carton sour cream,
  room temperature
3 cups slivered, cooked
  chicken
2 cups shredded cheddar
  cheese
4-oz. can chopped green
  chilies, drained
1 tsp. chili powder
10-12 flour tortillas

1. In saucepan sauté onion in margarine until tender. Stir in flour and add chicken broth and bouillon. Cook and stir until thickened. Remove from heat and stir in sour cream.
2. In large bowl combine 1 cup cooked sauce, chicken, 1 cup cheese, chilies and chili powder. Mix well.
3. Fill each tortilla with equal portions of chicken mixture. Roll up and arrange in greased 9" x 13" pan. Spoon remaining sauce over tortillas. Sprinkle with remaining cheese.
4. Bake at 350° for 25 minutes.

Cheesy Enchiladas

Silva Beachy
Millersburg, OH
Lone Star

Makes 10-12 servings

Enchiladas:
2 lbs. ground beef
1 medium onion, chopped
2 Tbsp. flour
1 tsp. salt
1 cup canned tomatoes
⅛ tsp. pepper
½ tsp. cumin
½ tsp. oregano
10-12 flour tortillas
2 cups grated cheese

Cheese sauce:
8 Tbsp. margarine
4 Tbsp. flour
3 cups milk
8 ozs. Velveeta cheese
8-oz. carton sour cream

1. Brown ground beef and onion and drain excess fat. Add flour and salt, stirring until heated through. Add tomatoes with juice and seasonings, stirring until heated through.
2. Spread meat mixture and grated cheese on each tortilla. Roll up and place in greased 9" x 13" baking pan.
3. To prepare cheese sauce melt margarine in a saucepan. Stir in flour until bubbly. Gradually add milk, stirring constantly until thickened. Stir in Velveeta cheese and sour cream and heat through.

Pour cheese sauce over enchiladas.
4. Bake at 350° for 20-30 minutes. Serve.

Enchiladas

Barbara Miller
Partridge, KS

Makes 6 servings

1 lb. ground beef
1 onion, chopped
16-oz. can refried beans
2 Tbsp. dry taco seasoning
2 tsp. salt *or* less
¼ tsp. pepper
1 Tbsp. chili powder
8-oz. can tomato sauce
6-8 corn tortillas
1½ cups grated cheddar
  cheese
1 cup water

1. Brown beef and onion and drain excess fat. Add refried beans, taco seasoning, salt, pepper and chili powder and mix well.
2. Heat tomato sauce in saucepan. Dip tortillas in heated tomato sauce, one at a time.
3. Fill tortillas evenly with beef mixture and 1 cup cheese. Fold and arrange in 7" x 11" baking pan. Pour remaining tomato sauce and water over tortillas. Top with ½ cup cheese.
4. Bake at 350° for 20-25 minutes.

Chimichangas

Ada Miller
Sugarcreek, OH
Log Cabin Broken Star

Makes 12 servings

¼ cup bacon drippings
2 cups chopped, cooked
   beef
1 medium onion, diced
2 cloves garlic, minced
2 medium tomatoes,
   chopped
2 4-oz. cans green chilies
1 tsp. salt
1½ tsp. dried oregano
1-2 tsp. chili powder
2 Tbsp. minced fresh
   cilantro
12 flour tortillas, warmed
1 Tbsp. cooking oil
1½ cups shredded cheddar
   cheese
1 cup sour cream
1 cup guacamole
1 cup salsa
2 cups shredded lettuce
1 cup sliced ripe olives
1 cup chopped tomatoes

1. In a skillet melt bacon drippings over medium heat. Sauté meat, onion, garlic, tomatoes and chilies until the onion softens. Add salt, oregano, chili powder and cilantro and simmer 2-3 minutes.

2. Place a scant ½ cup meat filling on each tortilla. Fold, envelope-style, like a burrito.

3. Fry, seam side down, in hot oil (360-375°) until crispy and brown. Turn and brown other side. Drain briefly on a paper towel.

4. Place on a serving plate and top with shredded cheese, a dollop of sour cream, guacamole and salsa.

5. Arrange shredded lettuce topped with tomatoes and olives on another serving plate. Serve chimichangas with lettuce.

❖

White Enchiladas Casserole

Gwen Oberg
Albuquerque, NM
View to a Zoo

Makes 4-6 servings

1 small pkg. tortilla chips
8-oz. carton sour cream
10¾-oz. can cream of
   chicken soup
½ cup milk
4-oz. can chopped green
   chilies
½ cup chopped onion
2 cups diced, cooked
   chicken
1 cup grated cheddar
   cheese

1. In a greased, shallow casserole dish spread tortilla chips and mash down slightly.

2. Mix together all remaining ingredients except cheese. Pour over chips. Sprinkle cheese over top.

3. Cover and bake at 350° for 30 minutes. Uncover and bake another 10-15 minutes.

❖

Tortillas de Harina (White Flour Tortillas)

Judy Mocho
Albuquerque, NM
New Mexico Beef and Batting Cow Quilt

Makes 8-12 tortillas

4 cups flour
2 tsp. salt
2 tsp. baking powder
4 Tbsp. shortening
1½ cups warm water

1. Combine dry ingredients, then cut in shortening. Add water, a few drops at a time, and work dough with hands until manageable.

2. Knead dough 15-20 times. Let rest for 10 minutes. Form dough into balls the size of an egg. Roll each piece out into a 6-inch circle.

3. Set electric skillet at 425°. Place each tortilla in skillet and cook 2 minutes on each side, or until done.

4. Use these inexpensive homemade tortillas instead of packaged tortillas.

Inez Dillon's Taco Casserole

Inez E. Dillon
Tucson, AZ
Seven Sisters

Makes 20-25 servings

5 lbs. ground beef
4 tsp. dehydrated onion
2 Tbsp. oregano
1 Tbsp. celery seed
1 Tbsp. crushed chili
  peppers
2 Tbsp. cumin
1 Tbsp. paprika
2 Tbsp. chili powder
1 tsp. salt
2 Tbsp. parsley flakes
2 10-oz. cans peeled green
  chilies, undrained
42-oz. can peeled whole
  tomatoes, undrained
10-oz. can hot enchilada
  sauce
2 medium jalapeños, diced
1 cup uncooked rice
2 lbs. cottage cheese
1½ lbs. Monterey Jack
  cheese, shredded
2 pkgs. flour tortillas
1 pkg. taco chips
2 lbs. longhorn cheese,
  shredded

1. Brown meat in large frying pan and drain all fat.
2. Put meat into deep saucepan or large pressure cooker. Add all remaining ingredients except the cheeses, tortillas and taco chips.
3. Cook in deep pan for 1½ hours, stirring occasionally. If using pressure cooker, steam for 40 minutes.
4. Line three 2½-quart casserole dishes with the flour tortillas on the sides and bottoms. Add meat mixture, cottage cheese and Monterey Jack cheese in layers. When dishes are full, push taco chips into top of ingredients so they stick up. Top with final layer of shredded longhorn cheese.
5. Bake at 350° for 30 minutes or until all cheese has melted.

Mexican Casserole

Marge Slabaugh
Kalona, IA
Tulip Quilt

Makes 6 servings

1 Tbsp. cooking oil
½ cup chopped onion
2 cloves garlic, minced
1½ lbs. lean ground beef
28-oz. can stewed tomatoes
1 pkg. dry taco seasoning
4-oz. can sliced green
  chilies

> My son Andy is a Miami Dolphins football fan. When I went to purchase fabric for a Bow Tie quilt I planned to make for him, the sales people at the store questioned my strange color choices—orange, white and aqua. My son is now 25 and quite proud of his Dolphins Bow Tie quilt.
>
> —*Abbie Christie, Berkeley Heights, NJ*

2 ½-oz. can chopped black
  olives
16-oz. can refried beans
½ cup shredded
  mozzarella cheese
1 pint sour cream
8-oz. pkg. cheese-flavored
  tortilla chips
½ cup shredded cheddar
  cheese

1. Heat oil in large skillet over medium heat. Add onion and garlic and sauté. Add meat and cook until browned, stirring frequently. Blend in tomatoes, taco seasoning, chilies and olives and simmer for about 10 minutes.
2. Spread refried beans into greased 9" x 13" baking dish. Add meat mixture, mozzarella cheese and sour cream. Top with tortilla chips.
3. Bake at 350° for 30 minutes or until heated through. Sprinkle with cheddar cheese. Continue baking until cheese melts. Let stand 15 minutes before serving.

Black Eyes of Texas

Becki Bryant
Mechanicsburg, PA
State Flowers

Makes 8 servings

1 onion, chopped
1 Tbsp. cooking oil
1½ lbs. lean ground beef
½ tsp. garlic powder
16-oz. can black-eyed peas, drained
16-oz. can chilies and tomatoes, undrained
10-oz. can enchilada sauce
1 jalapeño pepper, finely chopped (optional)
12 corn tortillas
2 cups grated cheddar cheese

1. In a large saucepan sauté onion in oil until soft. Add meat and brown. Drain off excess fat. Stir in garlic powder, black-eyed peas, tomatoes, enchilada sauce and jalapeño pepper. Heat through, stirring occasionally.
2. Cut each tortilla into strips. Spread ⅓ of tortilla strips on bottom of 9" x 13" baking pan. Cover with ⅓ of meat mixture. Repeat layers 2 more times. Cover with grated cheese.
3. Cover and bake for 30-35 minutes. Serve with Spanish rice, tortilla chips and a fresh salad.

White Pizza

Eunice B. Heyman
Baltimore, MD
Joanne's Anniversary Quilt

Makes 6 servings

1 pizza shell
1 tsp. olive oil
½ lb. mushrooms, sliced
1 Tbsp. olive oil
1½ cups grated Swedish Fontina cheese
1 cup grated mozzarella cheese
1 pkg. Italian salad dressing mix
½-¾ cup grated Parmesan cheese

1. Place pizza shell in baking pan and brush with 1 tsp. olive oil.
2. Sauté mushrooms in 1 Tbsp. olive oil.
3. Sprinkle Fontina and mozzarella cheese into shell. Follow with mushrooms and salad dressing mix. Top with Parmesan cheese.
4. Bake at 400° for 15-20 minutes or until cheeses have completely melted.
5. Cut into wedges and serve.

Pizza Buns

Jean Turner
Williams Lake, BC
Harlequin Hearts

Makes 10-12 servings

1 lb. cheddar cheese, grated
8-oz. jar sliced mushrooms, drained
8-oz. can tomato sauce
2 green onions, chopped
⅓ cup cooking oil
Salt to taste
⅓ tsp. basil
⅓ tsp. rosemary
⅓ tsp. oregano
12 hamburger buns, split

1. Mix all ingredients except hamburger buns.
2. Spread mixture evenly over buns and arrange on baking sheets.
3. Broil at 500° until cheese bubbles. Mixture freezes well.

Pasta Main Dishes

❖

Garden Lasagna

Mary Hooley
Lodi, CA

Makes 10-12 servings

16-oz. pkg. lasagna noodles
4 Tbsp. margarine
¼ cup flour
3 cups milk
1 cup grated Parmesan cheese
½ tsp. white pepper
1 onion, chopped
1 Tbsp. margarine
10-oz. pkg. frozen spinach

1. Cook lasagna noodles according to package directions. Drain.

2. Melt 4 Tbsp. margarine in a saucepan. Stir in flour until bubbly. Gradually pour in milk, stirring constantly over low heat until sauce thickens. Stir in Parmesan cheese and pepper and mix well.

3. Sauté onion in 1 Tbsp. margarine. Add spinach which has been thawed and chopped. Cook until onion is transparent.

4. In greased 9" x 13" baking dish layer ⅓ of lasagna, ⅓ of sauce and ⅓ of spinach mixture. Repeat layers 2 more times, ending with spinach mixture.

5. Bake at 350° for 25 minutes. Let stand about 15 minutes before serving.

❖

Crab Meat Lasagna

Carol L. Trice
Wayne, PA
Baby Dresden

Makes 8 servings

½ lb. lasagna noodles
1 tsp. olive oil
8-oz. pkg. cream cheese, softened
2 cups cottage cheese
2 10 ¾-oz. cans cream of mushroom soup
1 egg
1 large onion, chopped
1 clove garlic, chopped
1 tsp. basil
1 tsp. salt
2 cups crab meat
2 cups grated sharp cheddar cheese

1. Cook lasagna in water and olive oil according to package directions. Drain.

2. Combine cream cheese, cottage cheese, mushroom soup, egg, onion, garlic, basil and salt and mix well. Fold in crabmeat.

3. In a lightly greased 9" x 13" baking pan layer ½ of lasagna noodles, ½ of crab meat mixture and ½ of cheddar cheese. Repeat layers.

4. Bake at 350° for 1 hour. Let stand 15 minutes before serving.

Chicken Lasagna

Joan Lemmler
Albuquerque, NM
Bearry Agee

Makes 6-8 servings

½-lb. pkg. lasagna noodles
⅓ cup chopped onion
⅓ cup chopped green
  pepper
1 Tbsp. margarine
10¾-oz. can cream of
  chicken soup
1 cup milk
4-oz. jar sliced mushrooms
½ tsp. poultry seasoning
3-4 cups diced, cooked
  chicken
2 3-oz. pkgs. cream cheese,
  softened
1 cup cottage cheese
¼ cup sliced green olives
¼ cup snipped parsley
½ cup buttered bread
  crumbs

1. Cook noodles until firm to the bite in boiling, salted water. Drain well. Cover with cold water and set aside. Drain before adding to casserole dish.
2. Sauté onion and green pepper in margarine until transparent. Add chicken soup, milk, mushrooms, poultry seasoning and chicken. Simmer until heated through.
3. Beat together cream cheese and cottage cheese. Stir in olives and parsley.
4. Spread ⅓ cup soup mixture across bottom of lightly greased 7" x 12" baking pan. Layer with ½ of noodles, ½ of cheese mixture and ½ of remaining soup mixture. Repeat layers. Top with bread crumbs.
5. Bake at 375° for 45 minutes until hot and bubbly. Let stand for 10 minutes before cutting into squares to serve.

Green Chile Chicken Lasagna

Dawn Kouba
Albuquerque, NM
Enchanted View

Makes 4 servings

2 whole chicken breasts
6 lasagna noodles
10¾-oz. can cream of
  chicken soup
1 cup plain yogurt
4-oz. jar chopped green
  chilies
8 ozs. Monterey Jack
  cheese, sliced
½ cup grated Parmesan
  cheese

1. Boil chicken until tender. Skin, bone and shred meat into bite-sized pieces.
2. Cook noodles according to package directions. Drain.
3. Combine soup, yogurt and green chilies in small bowl and mix well.
4. In bottom of lightly greased 9-inch square baking dish layer ½ of noodles (torn to fit pan). Cover with ½ of soup and yogurt mixture. Add ½ of sliced Monterey Jack cheese. Repeat layers. Top with Parmesan cheese.
5. Bake, uncovered, at 350° for 30 minutes.

My family had just moved and was getting settled in our new house. My mother-in-law and two sisters-in-law were coming for lunch. I was sure the quiche I had planned would be a hit. I had not used the oven before and when the liquid ingredients began running over the edges of the pans it was too late to level my new stove. The house filled with black smoke.

I worked as quickly as I could to scrape the mess from the oven, made aluminum foil wedges to level the pie plates and reset the oven. Luckily, it was a breezy day and with both the front and back doors open, the black cloud cleared out of my house just in time for me to greet my guests.

—Ann Sunday McDowell, Newtown, PA

Lasagna

Polly Gilmore
St. Joseph, MI
Under Direction of My Sister

Makes 6-8 servings

16-oz. carton cottage cheese
1 tsp. Italian seasoning
1 tsp. garlic powder
(optional)
1 egg
10-oz. pkg. frozen,
chopped spinach
32-oz. jar spaghetti sauce
16-oz. pkg. lasagna noodles
1 lb. mozzarella cheese,
grated
$1/2$-$3/4$ cup water

1. Mix together cottage cheese, seasoning and garlic powder. Beat in egg.
2. Thaw and thoroughly drain spinach. Add to cottage cheese mixture and mix well. Set aside.
3. In bottom of 10" x 14" glass baking dish spread thin layer spaghetti sauce. Layer with $1/3$ of dry noodles, $1/3$ of cottage cheese mixture and $1/3$ of grated cheese. Pour $1/3$ of remaining spaghetti sauce over all. Repeat layers 2 more times, ending with grated cheese. Set aside 60-75 minutes before baking.
4. When ready to bake, pour water around edges.
5. Bake at 325° for 1 hour. Let stand in warm place 10-15 minutes before serving.

Lazy Lasagna

Cathy Mazur
Williams Lake, BC
Bear Paw

Makes 6 servings

3 cups uncooked penne
pasta
$1\frac{1}{2}$ lbs. ground beef
1 clove garlic, minced
8-oz. can tomato sauce
6-oz. can tomato paste
1 tsp. oregano
1 tsp. marjoram
1 tsp. basil
$1/2$ tsp. salt
1 tsp. pepper
1 cup cottage cheese
1 cup sour cream
3 green onions, sliced
$1/4$ cup grated Parmesan
cheese
1 cup grated mozzarella
cheese

1. Cook pasta and drain.
2. Brown ground beef and garlic. Drain off excess fat. Stir in tomato sauce, tomato paste and seasonings. Bring to a boil and simmer for 5 minutes, stirring occasionally. Pour into greased 9" x 13" baking dish.
3. Combine pasta, cottage cheese, sour cream, green onions and Parmesan cheese. Pour over meat sauce mixture. Sprinkle with mozzarella cheese.
4. Bake at 350° for 30-35 minutes or until hot and bubbly.

Mexican Lasagna

Marlene Fonken
Upland, CA
Crazy Patch

Makes 8 servings

1 lb. ground turkey
2 cups canned tomatoes,
diced
2 cups tomato sauce
4-oz. jar diced green chilies
1 pkg. dry taco seasoning
4 egg whites
$1\frac{1}{2}$ cups lowfat ricotta
cheese
8 corn tortillas
10 ozs. Monterey Jack
cheese, shredded

1. Cook ground turkey. Add tomatoes, tomato sauce, chilies and taco seasoning mix. Bring to a boil and simmer approximately 15 minutes.
2. In small bowl whisk egg whites. Add ricotta cheese and mix well.
3. Spread $1/2$ of meat mixture into 9" x 13" baking dish. Top with 4 tortillas. Spread $1/2$ of ricotta cheese over top. Repeat layers. Spread Monterey Jack cheese over all.
4. Bake at 350° for 20-30 minutes. Let stand 10 minutes before serving.

Taco Lasagna

Ruth Meyer
Linn, KS
Cat Walk

Makes 6-8 servings

1½ lbs. ground beef
1 pkg. dry taco seasoning
8 ozs. cheddar cheese, grated
16-oz. can refried beans
5 flour tortillas
8-oz. jar picante sauce

1. Brown ground beef. Drain off excess fat. Stir in taco seasoning.
2. In a greased deep casserole dish layer ½ of ground beef, 1 tortilla, ½ of cheese, 1 tortilla, ½ of beans, 1 tortilla, ½ to ground beef, 1 tortilla, ½ of beans, 1 tortilla and ½ of cheese. Pour picante sauce over all.
3. Bake at 350° for 40 minutes.

Note: If tortillas are too large for casserole dish, use fewer and tear to fit dish.

Spinach-Stuffed Shells

Ann Foss
Brooklyn, NY

Makes 10 servings

12-oz. pkg. jumbo shells
2 10-oz. pkgs. frozen, chopped spinach
15-oz. carton ricotta cheese
8 ozs. mozzarella cheese, shredded
1 tsp. salt
¼ tsp. pepper
½ lb. ground beef *or* turkey
32-oz. jar spaghetti sauce

1. Cook shells according to package directions. Drain.
2. Prepare spinach according to package directions. Cool slightly. Stir in ricotta cheese, mozzarella cheese, salt and pepper.
3. When shells are cool enough to handle, stuff each one with 1 Tbsp. spinach-cheese mixture. Arrange in shallow baking pan.
4. In skillet over medium heat cook ground beef or turkey until browned. Drain any excess fat. Stir in spaghetti sauce and heat through. Pour meat sauce over stuffed shells.
5. Bake at 350° for 30 minutes or until bubbly.

Stuffed Pasta Shells

Sandi Monterastelli
Ontario, CA
Lover's Knot

Makes 4-6 servings

18 jumbo pasta shells
½ lb. ground beef
½ lb. ground turkey
1 onion, chopped
1 clove garlic, minced
2 cups shredded mozzarella cheese
½ cup seasoned bread crumbs
2 Tbsp. parsley flakes
1 egg, beaten
2 15-oz. jars spaghetti sauce
½ cup Parmesan cheese

1. Cook pasta shells according to package directions. Drain.
2. Brown ground beef, turkey, onion and garlic. Drain excess fat. Stir in mozzarella, bread crumbs, parsley and egg.
3. Stuff shells with meat mixture.
4. Pour 1 jar spaghetti sauce into large casserole dish. Arrange stuffed shells over sauce. Pour remaining jar spaghetti sauce over all. Top with Parmesan cheese.
5. Bake at 350° for 30 minutes or until heated through.

Manicotti

Marcia S. Myer
Manheim, PA
Dresden Plate

Makes 8-10 servings

Sauce:
6 Tbsp. olive oil
1 clove garlic, minced
1 medium onion, minced
2 Tbsp. chopped parsley
32-oz. can whole tomatoes
16-oz. can tomato sauce
1 tsp. salt
Dash pepper
1 tsp. sugar
½ tsp. basil
½ cup Parmesan cheese

Filling:
15-oz. carton ricotta cheese
¼ lb. mozzarella cheese, grated
1 Tbsp. chopped parsley
3 Tbsp. Parmesan cheese
1 egg, lightly beaten
1 pkg. manicotti shells

1. To prepare sauce heat olive oil in heavy saucepan. Add garlic, onion and parsley and sauté until golden. Add tomatoes, tomato sauce, salt, pepper, sugar and basil and bring to a boil. Simmer, uncovered, for 20 minutes.

2. Combine all filling ingredients except manicotti shells. Fill uncooked shells with cheese filling, using a teaspoon or small knife.

3. Pour a thin layer of sauce into bottom of 9" x 13" baking pan. Arrange filled manicotti shells in single layer across dish. Add all remaining sauce to completely cover shells. Cover with aluminum foil.

4. Bake at 400° for 40 minutes. Remove aluminum foil, sprinkle dish with ½ cup Parmesan cheese. Return to oven and bake another 5-10 minutes.

Fettucine with Cheese Sauce

Jennifer Hall
Delta, PA
Heart and Home

Makes 8 servings

12-oz. pkg. green fettucine noodles
15-oz. carton lowfat ricotta cheese
½ cup skim milk
3 Tbsp. Parmesan cheese
⅛ cup basil leaves

1. Fill large saucepan with cold water. Bring to a boil. Add fettucine and cook until firm to the bite. Drain.

2. In a separate saucepan combine ricotta cheese, milk and Parmesan cheese. Add basil leaves and cook over low heat until warm, stirring occasionally.

3. Pour cheese sauce over drained fettucine and serve.

Linguini with Tuna Sauce

Robin Liberty
Bradenton, FL

Makes 8 servings

1 large onion, diced
1 clove garlic, minced
1 Tbsp. cooking oil
2 7-oz. cans tuna, undrained
1 tsp. oregano
1 tsp. Italian seasoning
Pepper to taste
32-oz. jar spaghetti sauce
1 lb. linguini

1. In a saucepan sauté onion and garlic in oil until onions are golden. Stir in tuna. Add oregano, Italian Seasoning and pepper and mix well. Pour in spaghetti sauce, stirring until well mixed.

2. Simmer on low for 10-15 minutes.

3. Cook linguini according to package directions. Drain.

4. Pour sauce over linguini and serve.

Ziti with Sausage

Catherine Wenzel
Center Moriches, NY
Crazy Cats

Makes 8-10 servings

3 cups uncooked ziti
1/2 lb. Italian sausage, sliced
8 Tbsp. butter *or* margarine
1 cup sliced mushrooms
1 cup sliced green pepper
1/2 cup chopped onion
1/2 cup all-purpose flour
2 1/4 cups milk
2 cups shredded cheddar cheese
1/2 cup grated Parmesan cheese
1/2 tsp. pepper

1. Cook ziti according to package directions. Drain.
2. In saucepan brown sausage. Remove from pan and drain fat.
3. Melt butter in saucepan and sauté mushrooms, green pepper and onion until tender but not browned. Blend flour into vegetable mixture, stirring until bubbly. Gradually add milk and cook over medium-low heat, stirring constantly, until mixture begins to boil. Boil and stir for 1 minute. Blend in 1 1/2 cups cheddar cheese, Parmesan cheese and pepper, stirring until cheeses are melted and mixture is smooth.
4. Stir hot, cooked ziti and sausage into vegetable cheese sauce. Pour into greased 2-quart casserole dish. Top with remaining 1/2 cup cheddar cheese.
5. Bake at 350° for 30 minutes or until hot and bubbly.

Linguini in Peanut Sauce

Joy Moir
Holtsville, NY
Winter Cactus

Makes 6 servings

1 lb. linguini
1/2 cup hot water
1/2 cup peanut butter
2 tsp. soy sauce
2 tsp. red wine vinegar
2 scallions, chopped
2 cloves garlic, crushed
1 tsp. sugar
Red pepper to taste

1. Cook linguini according to package directions. Drain.
2. In a separate bowl combine hot water and peanut butter. Stir in soy sauce, vinegar, scallions, garlic, sugar and red pepper and mix well.
3. Combine drained pasta with sauce and toss well. Serve hot or at room temperature.

Thai Noodles with Peanut Sauce

Arline M. Rubin
New York, NY
First Sampler

Makes 4 servings

Pasta:
1/2 lb. spaghetti *or* noodles
1 lb. tofu
1/2 cup chopped scallions

Sauce:
1/2 cup roasted peanuts
8 cloves garlic, minced
6 Tbsp. cooking oil
6 Tbsp. water
6 Tbsp. soy sauce
1 1/2-2 Tbsp. hot Chinese oil *or* cayenne pepper
2 Tbsp. honey *or* sugar
4 Tbsp. vinegar
1/2 cup crunchy peanut butter

1. Cook spaghetti or noodles according to package directions. Drain.
2. Cut tofu into 1/2-inch cubes.
3. In a saucepan combine all sauce ingredients. Bring to a boil. Reduce heat and simmer for 5 minutes. Add cooked spaghetti and tofu. Remove to serving dish and garnish with scallions.

Pasta Pesto Florentine

Marybeth Romeo
Roanoke, VA
Triple Rail

Makes 4-6 servings

½ cup walnuts
3 cloves garlic
10-oz. pkg. frozen, chopped spinach
½ cup grated Parmesan cheese
½ cup olive oil
1 cup water
½ tsp. salt *or more*
1 tsp. dried basil

1. In food processor process walnuts and garlic until smooth.
2. Thaw and drain spinach. Add spinach and all remaining ingredients to walnuts and garlic and process until smooth.
3. Spoon over choice of cooked pasta. Serve hot or cold.

Chicken Spaghetti

Nancy Graves
Manhattan, KS
My President's Quilt

Makes 10 servings

1 whole chicken
1½ quarts water
1 medium onion, chopped
1 green pepper, chopped
2 Tbsp. butter
12-oz. pkg. spaghetti
1 lb. Velveeta cheese, cubed
Salt and pepper to taste

1. Boil chicken in water until tender. Remove chicken from kettle, cool and bone. Set aside.
2. In a skillet sauté onion and green pepper in butter. Set aside.
3. Skim fat off chicken broth. Bring to a boil and cook spaghetti in broth. Do not drain. Add Velveeta cheese and stir until melted. Add chicken, onion mixture, salt and pepper and mix well.
4. Pour mixture into lightly greased 9" x 13" baking pan.

5. Bake at 350° for 30 minutes or until heated through.

Variation:
Omit Velveeta cheese. Season with ¼ tsp. chili powder and ¼ tsp. garlic salt.
Ann Harrison
Garland, TX
Strawberry Patch

Spaghetti Pie

Marilyn Mowry
Irving, TX
Airplanes, Airplanes, Airplanes

Makes 4-6 servings

6-oz. pkg. spaghetti
2 eggs, beaten
¼ cup Parmesan cheese
2 Tbsp. butter *or* margarine
⅓ cup chopped onion
1 cup sour cream
1 lb. Italian sausage
6-oz. can tomato paste
1 cup water
3-4 slices mozzarella cheese

1. Break spaghetti into small pieces. Cook in boiling salted water. Drain.
2. While spaghetti is warm, add eggs and Parmesan cheese. Pour into wellgreased 10-inch pie pan. Pat mixture up around sides with a spoon.
3. In a saucepan melt butter. Sauté onion until limp. Add sour cream and heat

I come from a small farming and ranching community near Adrian, TX. Once or twice a month the women of the community got together for an all-day quilting bee. They sat around the quilt talking about their children, their relatives and the women who were not there on that particular day. We children loved the opportunity to run wild and free, playing games and climbing trees.

—Linda Roberta Pond, Los Alamos, NM

through. Spoon over spaghetti crust.

4. Remove sausage from casing. Crumble and cook in skillet until browned. Drain excess fat. Stir in tomato paste and water. Bring to a boil and simmer for 10 minutes. Spoon sausage mixture over sour cream mixture.

5. Bake at 350° for 25 minutes. Arrange mozzarella cheese slices over top. Return to oven and bake until cheese melts.

Chicken and Green Noodle Casserole

Cindy Wilkinson
Houston, TX
Drunkard's Path

Makes 8-10 servings

5-lb. stewing chicken
1 quart water
8-oz. pkg. green spinach noodles
4 Tbsp. butter
¼ cup flour
1 cup milk
1 cup chicken stock
1 pint sour cream
⅓-½ cup lemon juice
6-oz. jar mushroom pieces and juice
½ tsp. nutmeg
½ tsp. cayenne pepper
1 tsp. paprika
1 tsp. salt

¼ tsp. pepper
1 Tbsp. parsley flakes
½ cup toasted bread crumbs
½ cup grated Parmesan cheese

1. Cook chicken in water. Remove chicken and reserve stock. Cool and bone chicken, cutting into bite-sized pieces.

2. Cook noodles according to package directions. Drain.

3. Melt butter in a large saucepan. Stir in flour until bubbly. Gradually add milk and 1 cup chicken stock, stirring constantly until sauce thickens.

4. Remove sauce from heat and stir in sour cream, lemon juice, mushrooms, nutmeg, cayenne pepper, paprika, salt, pepper and parsley. Mix well.

5. Place drained noodles in greased 3-quart casserole dish. Layer with ½ of chicken, ½ of sauce, ½ of bread crumbs and ½ of Parmesan cheese. Repeat layers, ending with cheese.

6. Bake at 350° for 25 minutes or until hot and bubbly.

Aunt Doris's Noodle Surprise

Katherine A. Schwartz
Freeport, IL
Double Irish Chain

Makes 8-10 servings

1½ lbs. boneless pork roast
1 quart water
Salt and pepper to taste
16-oz. pkg. noodles
2 16-oz. cans cream-style corn
1 green pepper, diced
2 medium onions, chopped
1 cup sliced mushrooms
4-oz. jar pimentos, chopped
½ lb. Velveeta cheese, cubed
1 Tbsp. margarine

1. Simmer pork in water seasoned with salt and pepper for about 1 hour or until tender. Cool and cut into cubes.

2. Cook noodles according to package directions. Blanch in cold water. Put noodles, corn, green pepper, onions, mushrooms, pimentos, cheese and pork in large casserole dish. Dot with margarine.

3. Cover and bake at 325° for 1½ hours.

Cindy's Noodle Casserole

Lynne Fritz
Bel Air, MD
It's My Backyard, Too!

Makes 8 servings

½ lb. lean ground beef
2 tsp. sugar
2 tsp. salt
16-oz. can tomatoes, drained
8-oz. can tomato sauce
½ tsp. garlic powder
¼ tsp. black pepper
5-oz. pkg. egg noodles
1 cup sour cream
3-oz. pkg. cream cheese, softened
4 green onions, chopped
1 cup grated cheddar cheese

1. Brown ground beef. Drain excess fat. Add sugar, salt, tomatoes, tomato sauce, garlic powder and pepper. Simmer over low heat for 5-10 minutes.
2. Cook noodles according to package directions. Drain. Stir in sour cream, cream cheese and onions with tops.
3. Arrange noodle mixture and meat mixture in several alternate layers in 2-quart baking dish. Top with grated cheese.
4. Bake at 325° for 30-35 minutes.

❖

Pierogi

Charmaine Caesar
Lancaster, PA
Grandmother's Memories

Makes 24 pierogis

Dough:
4 cups white flour
8 eggs, beaten
¼ tsp. salt
4 Tbsp. water

Filling:
5 lbs. potatoes
16-oz. carton cottage cheese
½ tsp. salt
½ cup milk
4 Tbsp. butter

1. In a large bowl mix flour, eggs, salt and water to form dough. Work with floured hands until dough forms a ball and is no longer sticky.
2. To prepare filling peel and cube potatoes. Cook until softened. Drain well. Add cottage cheese, salt, milk and butter. Blend with electric mixer until smooth with no lumps.
3. Roll out dough to ¼-inch thickness. Use large round cookie cutter to cut out circles. Fill each circle with potato filling. Flip edges together and crimp with fingers to close tightly.
4. Drop into large kettle of boiling water. Cook for 2-3 minutes. Serve hot with fried onions and sour cream.

Note: To freeze, blanch with cold water after cooking. To re-heat, sauté in frying pan with butter.

Sharlene's Macaroni and Cheese

Irene Scheid
Woodhaven, NY
Memory Quilt

Makes 2-4 servings

4 ozs. elbow macaroni
1 quart boiling water
1 tsp. salt
1 Tbsp. butter
1 tsp. chopped onion
10¾-oz. can cream of mushroom soup
7-oz. can tuna
1 tsp. dry mustard
⅛ cup milk
¼ cup French dressing
¼ cup crushed potato chips

1. Cook macaroni in boiling salted water for 5-7 minutes. Drain. Turn into greased 1-quart casserole dish.
2. Melt butter in skillet. Sauté onion. Remove from heat and stir in soup, tuna, mustard, milk and dressing. Add soup mixture to macaroni and mix well. Top with crushed potato chips.
3. Bake at 375° for 25-30 minutes.

Pasta in a Pot

Vicki Long
Sterling, IL
Bear Paw

Makes 6-8 servings

2 lbs. ground beef
2 medium onions, chopped
8-oz. jar sliced
   mushrooms, drained
1 clove garlic, crushed
15-oz. jar spaghetti sauce
16-oz. can stewed tomatoes
8-oz. pkg. shell macaroni
8-oz. carton sour cream
1 lb. mozzarella cheese,
   grated

1. Brown ground beef
and onions in large skillet.
Drain excess fat. Add mushrooms, garlic, spaghetti
sauce and tomatoes. Sim-
mer 20 minutes.
2. Meanwhile, cook shell
macaroni according to di-
rections. Drain and rinse.
3. In a large greased casserole dish layer ½ of
shells, ½ of meat sauce, ½
of sour cream and ½ of
cheese. Repeat layers.
4. Cover and bake at 350°
for 35-45 minutes. Uncover
and bake 5 minutes longer.

Super Macaroni and Cheese

Pauline Morrison
St. Marys, ON
Signature Quilt

Makes 6 servings

2 cups uncooked macaroni
1 medium onion, chopped
6 cups boiling water
3 Tbsp. margarine, melted
2 Tbsp. flour
¼ tsp. salt
¼ tsp. pepper
1 cup sour cream
1¼ cups milk
2 cups grated cheddar
   cheese
Paprika

1. Cook macaroni and on-
ion in boiling water for 15
minutes. Drain through colander.
2. In large saucepan com-
bine margarine, flour and
salt and pepper, stirring until bubbly. Gradually stir in
¾ cup sour cream and 1¼
cups milk, stirring con-
stantly until thickened. Remove from heat and stir in
1½ cups cheese. Add maca-
roni and onion.
3. Turn into medium cas-
serole dish. Spread remaining sour cream and remaining cheese over top. Sprinkle with paprika.
4. Bake at 350° for 20-30
minutes or until hot and
bubbly.

Grandma's Macaroni and Cheese

Shirley Liby
Muncie, IN
At Loose Ends

Makes 8-10 servings

16-oz. can whole tomatoes
6 cups cooked macaroni
1 yellow onion, thinly
   sliced
¼ cup chopped green
   pepper
2 cups grated American
   cheese
2 Tbsp. butter
Milk
½ cup cracker crumbs

1. Drain and reserve the
juice from tomatoes.
2. Grease a 9" x 13" casserole dish and layer ingredients in following order: ½
macaroni, ½ yellow onion,
½ chopped green pepper,
½ tomatoes and ½ cheese.
Repeat all layers.
3. Top with dots of but-
ter. Pour tomato juice and
milk over ingredients until
liquid comes about half-
way up the sides of casserole dish. Top with cracker
crumbs.
4. Bake at 325-350° for 1
hour. Serve with a tossed
salad and garlic toast.

Vegetable Dishes

Zucchini with Mozzarella

Sarah Hadbavny
Edgewood, MD
Fishing

Makes 6 servings

1 medium onion, sliced
1 medium green pepper,
sliced
1 small garlic clove, chopped
2 Tbsp. cooking oil
16-oz. can whole tomatoes,
undrained
4 medium zucchini, sliced
¾ tsp. salt
½ tsp. oregano
¼ tsp. basil
8 ozs. mozzarella cheese,
shredded

1. Sauté onion, green pepper and garlic in oil until vegetables are almost tender. Add tomatoes, zucchini, salt and herbs. Cook until zucchini is tender.
2. Spoon into casserole dish and top with mozzarella cheese.
3. Bake at 350° for about 10 minutes or until cheese melts.

Zippy Zucchini

Linda Miles
Dumfries, VA
Watermelon Patch

Makes 6 servings

6 cloves garlic
2 Tbsp. olive oil
5 small zucchini, sliced
½ cup sliced mushrooms
Salt and pepper to taste
⅓ cup Parmesan cheese

1. Peel and press garlic. Sauté over low heat in olive oil until garlic is light golden, about 10 minutes.
2. Steam zucchini and mushrooms until tender-crisp, about 5 minutes. Place in serving dish. Pour garlic oil over vegetables.
3. Season with salt and pepper, top with cheese and serve.

Summer Vegetables and Cheese

Diana Huntress Deem
Bethesda, MD
Love in the Cabin

Makes 6 servings

1 small onion, thinly sliced
1-2 Tbsp. cooking oil
2 medium zucchini, sliced
2 medium yellow squash,
sliced
2-3 medium tomatoes,
diced
8 ozs. mozzarella cheese,
grated

1. Sauté onion with oil in large skillet or wok. Cook until clear.
2. Add zucchini and yellow squash and cook until just tender.
3. Add tomatoes and cheese and cook until cheese has just melted. Serve immediately.

Zucchini Corn Casserole

Katy J. Widger
Los Lunas, NM
Nikki's Ecology Quilt

Makes 8-10 servings

2 lbs. zucchini *or* yellow summer squash
1 large onion, chopped
2 Tbsp. butter *or* margarine
2 10-oz. pkgs. frozen corn
½ lb. processed cheese, cubed
4-oz. can chopped green chilies
Salt and pepper to taste

1. Cut squash into slices. Sauté squash and onion in butter until just tender.
2. Run hot water over frozen corn in a colander to thaw. Drain thoroughly. Add corn, cheese and chilies to squash and onions. Cook over low heat until cheese is melted, stirring constantly.
3. Season to taste. Pour into 2-quart casserole dish.
4. Bake, uncovered, at 350° for 30 minutes.

Zucchini Lasagna

Sue Gierhart
Voorhees, NJ
Friendship

Makes 6 servings

½ lb. ground meat
⅓ cup chopped onion
15-oz. can tomato sauce
½ tsp. salt
½ tsp. oregano
¼ tsp. basil
⅛ tsp. pepper
4 medium zucchini
8-oz. carton cottage cheese
1 egg
2 Tbsp. flour
¼ lb. mozzarella cheese, shredded

1. Brown ground meat and onion over medium heat in large skillet. Drain excess fat. Add tomato sauce, salt, oregano, basil and pepper and bring to a boil. Reduce heat to low and simmer for 5 minutes.
2. Slice zucchini lengthwise into ¼-inch thick slices.
3. In small bowl combine cottage cheese and egg.
4. Arrange ⅓ of zucchini in bottom of 8" x 12" baking dish. Sprinkle with 1 Tbsp. flour. Top with all of cottage cheese mixture and ⅓ of meat mixture. Repeat layers with remaining zucchini and flour. Sprinkle with mozzarella cheese and remaining meat mixture.
5. Bake at 375° for 40 minutes or until hot and bubbly. Let stand 10 minutes before serving.

Zucchini Sausage Skillet

Susan Knepp
New Paris, IN
Sampler

Makes 4 servings

1 lb. pork sausage
1 medium onion, chopped
3 small zucchini, sliced
1 cup tomato juice
¾ cup grated mozzarella *or* cheddar cheese

1. Brown sausage and onion in skillet. Drain off excess fat. Add zucchini and tomato juice and cook until tender, about 10 minutes. Stir occasionally.
2. Sprinkle with cheese and let it melt. Serve.

One of my favorite cooking memories revolves around helping my mother make doughnuts for Fassnacht Day. I have carried on the tradition with my own children, and they anticipate this day before Ash Wednesday as much as I did as a child.

—*Janice Way, Warrington, PA*

Zucchini Chicken Bake

Susan D. Fellin
Frenchtown, NJ

Makes 6 servings

4 ozs. uncooked spaghetti
4 slices bacon, chopped
½ cup chopped onion
1 clove garlic, minced
10¾-oz. can cream of
   mushroom soup
1 medium zucchini, sliced
½ cup milk
1 cup shredded mozzarella
   cheese
2 cups cubed, cooked
   chicken
¼ cup Parmesan cheese

1. Break spaghetti in half and cook according to package directions. Drain.

2. In medium saucepan cook bacon, onion and garlic until bacon is crisp. Drain excess fat. Add soup and blend well. Add zucchini and milk and cook on medium heat until zucchini is tender. Stir in mozzarella cheese.

3. Combine zucchini mixture, spaghetti and chicken in 2½-quart casserole dish. Sprinkle with Parmesan cheese.

4. Bake at 350° for 40 minutes.

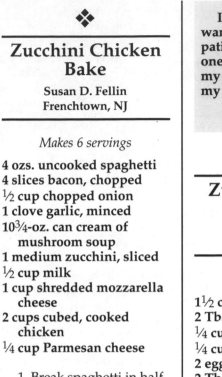

> In the mid-1980s my mother took up quilting. She wanted me to join her, but I told her I did not have the patience. She died with cancer soon after completing one lap-sized Rail Fence quilt. It is not perfect, but in my eyes and heart it is a warm and special memory of my mother. I have since taken up quilting myself.
>
> —*Nancy V. Schaub, Warminster, PA*

Zucchini Fritters

Kathi Stingle
Lederach, PA
Basket

Makes 4 servings

1½ cups grated zucchini
2 Tbsp. grated onion
¼ cup Parmesan cheese
¼ cup flour
2 eggs
2 Tbsp. mayonnaise
¼ tsp. oregano
Salt and pepper to taste
1 Tbsp. cooking oil

1. Combine all ingredients except cooking oil and mix well.

2. Heat oil in small skillet. Spoon 2 large tablespoons batter into skillet and flatten with spatula. Cook over medium heat until browned on both sides. Continue until batter has been used, adding more oil as needed.

3. Serve with tomato sauce and grated cheese.

Zucchini Patties

Mabel Rissler
Barnett, MO
*Boston Commons &
Broken Star*

Makes 4 servings

2 cups grated zucchini
1 egg, beaten
2 Tbsp. diced onion
4 Tbsp. cracker crumbs
Salt to taste
2 Tbsp. cooking oil
4 slices cheese

1. Combine all ingredients except oil and cheese and mix well. Divide batter into 4 patties.

2. Heat oil in skillet and fry patties on both sides until browned and heated through.

3. Top with slice of cheese. Let cheese melt and serve.

Summer Squash Casserole

Carole M. Mackie
Dahinda, IL
Prairie Flower
Jeanette Grant
Mountain Lake, MN
Double Wedding Ring

Makes 6-8 servings

6 cups sliced yellow
    summer squash
¼ cup chopped onion
10¾-oz. can cream of
    chicken soup
1 cup sour cream
1 cup shredded carrots
8-oz. pkg. herb-seasoned
    stuffing
½ cup margarine, melted

1. Cook summer squash
and onion in boiling water
for 5 minutes. Drain and set
aside.
2. Combine chicken soup
and sour cream. Stir in carrots. Fold in drained squash
and onion.
3. In a separate bowl
combine stuffing mix and
margarine. Spread ½ stuffing mix in bottom of 8" x
12" baking dish. Spoon
vegetable mixture on top.
Sprinkle with remaining
stuffing mix.
4. Bake at 350° for 25-30
minutes or until heated.

Checkerboard Cheese Bake

Martha J. Lewis
Carlisle, PA
Sampler

Makes 6 servings

3 medium yellow summer
    squash
6 Tbsp. butter *or* margarine
½ lb. fresh spinach
3 medium tomatoes, sliced
2 cups cottage cheese
1½ cups crumbled crackers
¼ tsp. oregano
¼ tsp. parsley
¼ tsp. sweet basil
¼ tsp. minced garlic
6 slices provolone cheese

1. Trim and thinly slice
summer squash. Sauté in 2
Tbsp. butter. Set aside.
2. Tear spinach into bite-
sized pieces and sauté in 2
Tbsp. butter. Set aside.
3. Sauté tomatoes in 2
Tbsp. butter. Set aside.
4. Combine cottage
cheese, crackers and herbs
in a small bowl.
5. Put squash into a 2-
quart baking dish. Add ½
cheese mixture, all of the
spinach, remaining cheese
mixture and tomato slices.
Top with provolone cheese
arranged in a checkerboard
fashion.
6. Bake at 375° for 30
minutes.

Squash Puffs

Norah Pledger
Bellville, TX
Strip-Pieced Cat

Makes 20-24 puffs

1 cup cooked squash
1 egg, beaten
⅓ cup flour
⅓ cup cornmeal
1 tsp. baking powder
½ tsp. salt *or* more
Dash pepper
1 medium onion, grated
1-2 cups cooking oil

1. Combine squash and
egg. Add all other ingredients except oil and mix until well blended.
2. Heat oil for deep fry-
ing.
3. Drop batter by level
tablespoonsful into hot oil.
Deep fry until golden
brown. Drain on paper towels.

Stuffed Acorn Squash

Philip S. Pipero
Brooklyn, NY

Makes 8 servings

4 acorn squash
1 lb. ground beef
1 cup chopped onion
1 cup tomato sauce
1 tsp. honey
½ tsp. cinnamon
Dash nutmeg
⅛ tsp. ground pepper
½ cup water
½ cup seedless raisins
1½ cups cooked rice

1. Cut squash in half and scoop out seeds and fiber. Place cut side down on greased roasting pan.
2. Bake at 375° for 40 minutes.
3. Cook beef and onion in a skillet. Drain well. Stir in tomato sauce, honey, cinnamon, nutmeg, pepper, water and raisins. Simmer 5 minutes, stirring occasionally. Remove from heat and stir in cooked rice.
4. Remove squash from oven and turn right side up. Fill each squash with meat mixture.
5. Bake 20-25 minutes longer or until squash is tender. Serve.

Microwave Acorn Squash

Sally A. Price
Reston, VA
Natalie's Memory Quilt

Makes 2 servings

1 whole acorn squash
⅛ tsp. nutmeg
1 tsp. lemon juice
1 Tbsp. margarine
2 tsp. brown sugar
¼ cup chopped pecans

1. Puncture acorn squash at several places on outside of shell.
2. Microwave whole squash on high for 1½ minutes.
3. Cut in half and discard seeds. Cover each half with plastic wrap.
4. Microwave on high for 10 minutes, rotating after 5 minutes.
5. Sprinkle centers with nutmeg and lemon juice. Add margarine, sugar and pecans. Cover immediately with plastic wrap and let stand for 5 minutes. Serve.

Crustless Spinach Pie

Helene Kusnitz
West Hempstead, NY
Flying Geese

Makes 6-8 servings

10-oz. pkg. frozen, chopped spinach
4 Tbsp. margarine, melted
3 Tbsp. flour
3 eggs, lightly beaten
½ tsp. salt
⅛ tsp. pepper
8-oz. carton cottage cheese
½ cup grated mozzarella cheese

1. Thaw and drain spinach.
2. Combine all ingredients and mix well. Spoon into a greased pie plate or quiche dish.
3. Bake at 350° for 30 minutes.

Spinach Casserole

Anne Guy
Florence, SC
Queen Anne Star

Makes 8 servings

2 10-oz. pkgs. frozen spinach
2 Tbsp. butter
2 Tbsp. flour
1 small onion, grated

1 tsp. dried dill weed
1 Tbsp. Worcestershire
  sauce
¾ cup milk
½ lb. sharp cheese, grated

1. Cook spinach according to directions. Drain.
2. Prepare a cheese sauce by melting butter in medium saucepan. Stir in flour until bubbly. Add onion, dill and Worcestershire sauce, stirring well. Gradually add milk, stirring constantly until thickened. Stir in cheese and mix until melted.
3. Combine spinach and cheese sauce in a casserole dish.
4. Bake at 350° for about 10 minutes or until heated through.

Spinach Artichoke Casserole

Dorothy M. VanDeest
Memphis, TN
The Bearish and Bullish Dow

Makes 4 servings

14-oz. can artichokes,
  drained
2 10-oz. pkgs. frozen
  spinach
8-oz. pkg. cream cheese
8 Tbsp. butter *or* margarine
½ cup Pepperidge Farm
  stuffing

1. Place artichokes in casserole dish.
2. Cook spinach according to directions and drain. Spoon over artichokes.
3. Cream together cream cheese and butter. Spread over spinach. Sprinkle with prepared stuffing.
4. Bake at 350° for 25 minutes.

Stuffed Cabbage Casserole

Dottie Doughty
Oklahoma City, OK
Alicia Swift
Sleepy Eye, MN
Ann Bateman
Arnprior, ON

Makes 6-8 servings

1 lb. ground beef
1 onion, chopped
½ cup uncooked rice
1 tsp. salt
½ cup water
1 medium head cabbage,
  chopped
10¾-oz. can tomato soup

1. Sauté ground beef and onion lightly. Do not brown beef. Drain excess fat. Remove from heat, add rice, salt and water and mix well.
2. Place ½ of cabbage into ungreased 9" x 13" baking dish. Cover with meat mixture. Put remaining cabbage over meat. Pour soup over all.
3. Cover and bake at 350° for 1½ hours.

Variation:
Delete ½ cup water. Dilute tomato soup with 1 can water before pouring over mixture.
Janice Yoskovich
Carmichaels, PA
Log Cabin

Cabbage and Noodles

Elizabeth Boyton
Gordonville, PA
Irish Chain

Makes 4 servings

8 ozs. egg noodles
¼ lb. butter
1 head cabbage, shredded
2 onions, chopped
Salt and pepper to taste

1. Cook and drain noodles according to package directions.
2. Melt butter in large skillet. Add cabbage and cook until soft. Add onions and continue cooking until cabbage is browned.
3. Stir in cooked noodles and season. Mix well and serve with bratwurst or ham loaf.

The quilt frame in our family is an heirloom. It was built by my great-grandfather about 1910 and used "hard" by my great-grandmother. She passed the frame to her daughter—my grandmother—who learned to enjoy quilting only after she had the frame. My mother borrowed the frame for six months and returned it to Grandmother who used it until her eyesight gave out. I inherited this family treasure, and today I almost always have a quilt in frame.

—*Jennifer L. Rhodes, Lancaster, PA*

Skillet Scalloped Corn

Jennifer Hall
Delta, PA
Heart and Home

Makes 6 servings

1 Tbsp. butter
½ cup dried bread crumbs
2 Tbsp. butter
¼ cup chopped green onions
2 Tbsp. flour
¼ tsp. dry mustard
¼ tsp. paprika
Dash pepper
¾ cup milk
1 egg, beaten
12-oz. can corn, drained

1. Melt 1 Tbsp. butter in medium skillet. Stir in bread crumbs and cook over medium heat until browned. Remove crumbs and set aside.

2. Melt 2 Tbsp. butter in same skillet. Add onions and cook until tender. Stir in flour, mustard, paprika and pepper. Cook until bubbly, stirring constantly.

3. Gradually add milk and egg. Cook until mixture comes to a boil and thickens, stirring constantly.

4. Stir in corn and cook until heated through. Remove to serving dish. Sprinkle with bread crumbs and serve.

Carrots with Dried Apricots

Julie McKenzie
Punxsutawney, PA
Teardrops and Tantrums

Makes 4-6 servings

1 medium onion, chopped
4 Tbsp. butter
1 lb. carrots, shredded
¼ lb. dried apricots, cut into strips
½ cup chicken broth *or* water
2 tsp. wine vinegar
Salt and pepper to taste

1. Sauté onion in butter until transparent. Add carrots and apricots and stir-fry for 2-3 minutes. Add broth or water. Cover and cook about 5 minutes.

2. Uncover and cook until liquid is gone.

3. Stir in vinegar, salt and pepper and serve.

Carrot Casserole

Joyce Parker
North Plainfield, NJ
Sampler

Makes 4-6 servings

2 cups sliced carrots
2 cups grated American cheese
8 Tbsp. margarine, melted
2 eggs, slightly beaten
¼ tsp. pepper
2 Tbsp. sugar

1. Cook carrots until softened. Drain and mash.

2. Combine all ingredients and spoon into ungreased casserole dish. Place dish in pan of water.

3. Bake at 350° for 45 minutes.

Fried Corn

Charlene Bement
Upland, CA
Whimsical Marbled Fish

Makes 4-6 servings

6 strips bacon
⅓ cup chopped onion
⅓ cup chopped bell pepper
16-oz. pkg. frozen corn
1 large tomato, skinned
  and diced
½ tsp. salt
Dash pepper
1 tsp. cumin

1. Fry, drain and crumble bacon. Reserve ¼ cup drippings.
2. Sauté onion and bell pepper in ¼ cup bacon drippings. Add corn, tomato, salt, pepper and cumin.
3. Cook over medium heat for about 10 minutes, stirring frequently.
4. Sprinkle bacon pieces over top and serve.

Corn Pudding

Ruby I. Cook
Newtown Square, PA
White on White

Makes 4-6 servings

2 eggs, beaten
¼ cup sugar
1 tsp. salt
⅛ tsp. pepper
2 Tbsp. butter, melted
½ cup milk
2 cups cut fresh corn

1. Mix all ingredients except corn until smooth. Add corn.
2. Spoon into greased casserole dish and place dish into pan of water.
3. Bake at 350° for 1 hour and 15 minutes.

Baked Corn

Rachel Pellman
Lancaster, PA
Panel for AIDS Quilt

Makes 8 servings

2 Tbsp. cornstarch
4 Tbsp. sugar
Salt and pepper to taste
4 eggs, slightly beaten
2 Tbsp. butter, melted
2 cups milk
1 quart cut, fresh *or* frozen
  corn

1. Stir together cornstarch, sugar, salt and pepper. Add eggs, butter, milk and corn. Mix well. Spoon into greased casserole dish.
2. Bake at 350° for 25 minutes. Stir and bake another 25 minutes or longer until browned and set.

Corn Filling Balls

Janet Yocum
Elizabethtown, PA
Dahlia

Makes 12 balls

1 cup cut, fresh corn
¾ cup water
3 eggs, beaten
1 Tbsp. minced onion
Salt and pepper to taste
10 ozs. soft bread crumbs
8 Tbsp. butter, melted

1. Cook corn in water while preparing other ingredients.
2. Combine eggs, onion, salt, pepper and soft bread crumbs. Mix well by hand. Add corn and mix well again. Shape mixture into balls.
3. Arrange corn balls in 9" x 13" baking pan. Pour melted butter over all.
4. Bake at 350° for 20 minutes.

Broccoli Corn Bake

Judy Mocho
Albuquerque, NM
Spool Charm

Makes 6 servings

10-oz. pkg. frozen,
  chopped broccoli
16-oz. can cream-style corn
½ cup cracker crumbs
1 egg, beaten
4 Tbsp. margarine, melted
1 Tbsp. onion flakes
1 tsp. salt
⅛ tsp. pepper

1. Thaw broccoli. Combine broccoli, corn, ¼ cup cracker crumbs, egg, 2 Tbsp. margarine, onion flakes, salt and pepper in a greased 2-quart casserole dish.
2. Mix remaining cracker crumbs with remaining margarine and sprinkle over casserole ingredients.
3. Bake, uncovered, at 350° for 45 minutes.

Broccoli Casserole

Barb Grauer
Owings Mills, MD
Log Cabin Star

Makes 6 servings

2 10-oz. pkgs. frozen
  broccoli
10¾-oz. can cream of
  mushroom soup
5-oz. can evaporated milk
½ lb. sharp cheddar cheese
2.8-oz. can French-style
  onions

1. Cook broccoli according to directions and drain well. Place in casserole dish.
2. Combine soup and milk and pour over broccoli.
3. Cut cheddar cheese into ½-inch cubes and spread over broccoli.
4. Bake, uncovered, at 350° for 55 minutes. Sprinkle onions over casserole dish and bake another 5 minutes.

Broccoli Cheese Bake

Lori Drohman
Rogue River, OR
Fan & Jacob's Ladder

Makes 8-10 servings

1 large head broccoli
10¾-oz. can cream of
  mushroom soup
½ cup milk
½ cup shredded cheese
¼ cup bread crumbs
1-2 Tbsp. butter *or*
  margarine

1. Cut broccoli flowerets and stems into pieces. Parboil and drain. Place in casserole dish.
2. Combine soup, milk and cheese. Pour over broccoli.
3. Top with bread crumbs and dot with butter.
4. Bake at 350° for 30 minutes.

> For years I have been going to Lancaster County, PA to admire the beautiful quilts. On Christmas Eve 1991 my husband took the family for a ride to Lancaster County. We kept stopping at all the shops and admiring quilts. Imagine my surprise when at one of the shops, he told me to choose the quilt of my dreams. I rode back to New Jersey with my Christmas present draped across my lap.
>
> —*Rhonda Burgoon, Collingswood, NJ*

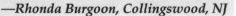

Asparagus with Lemon Sauce

Thelma Lowther
St. Marys, WV
Ohio Star & Tumbling Blocks

Makes 6 servings

10-oz. pkg. frozen asparagus spears
1 egg
1 pkg. artificial sweetener
½ tsp. cornstarch
1 Tbsp. low-calorie margarine
¼ cup lemon juice
2 tsp. grated lemon rind

1. Cook asparagus according to directions, omitting salt and margarine. Transfer to serving dish and keep warm.
2. Combine egg, sweetener and cornstarch, stirring to blend.
3. Melt margarine over low heat in small skillet. Add egg mixture and cook over medium heat until mixture thickens. Stir in lemon juice. Cook over medium heat until thick and bubbly.
4. Pour sauce over asparagus. Sprinkle with lemon rind and serve immediately.

Asparagus Casserole

Jean Shaner
York, PA
Whig Rose

Makes 4-6 servings

5 medium potatoes, thinly sliced
2 onions, diced
1¼ lbs. asparagus, diced
½ cup milk
¼ cup butter
Salt and pepper to taste
4 slices cheese

1. In a large casserole dish combine potatoes, onions and asparagus. Add milk. Dot with butter and salt and pepper to taste.
2. Cover and bake at 350° for 45-60 minutes.
3. Immediately before serving, lay cheese on top and let it melt slightly.

Lucy's Eggplant

Sara Harter Fredette
Williamsburg, MA
Teddy Bear's Cabin

Makes 4-6 servings

1 large eggplant
2 green peppers, diced
2 onions, diced
32-oz. jar spaghetti sauce

8 ozs. mozzarella cheese, shredded

1. Slice eggplant into ¼-inch slices. Parboil for 5 minutes. Drain and cool.
2. Put layer of eggplant into 1½-quart casserole dish. Follow with layer of green peppers, onions, spaghetti sauce and cheese. Repeat layers, ending with cheese.
3. Cover and bake at 350° for ½ hour. Uncover and bake at 400° for ½ hour.

Harvard Beets

Suzanne Oliva
N. Massapequa, NY

Makes 6-8 servings

3 cups cooked beets
½ cup sugar
1½ Tbsp. cornstarch
½ cup water
½ cup cider vinegar
2 Tbsp. butter

1. In a saucepan combine sugar, cornstarch, water and vinegar. Bring to a boil and boil 5 minutes.
2. Stir beets into mixture, cooking slowly and stirring occasionally until heated through. Add butter and continue cooking until butter has melted. Serve.

Spiced Green Beans

Elaine Untracht Pawelko
Monroe Township, NJ
Bride's Bouquet

Makes 6 servings

1 lb. fresh green beans
Water to cover
2 Tbsp. fresh lemon juice
1 clove garlic, minced
1 bay leaf
Dash allspice
Brown sugar to taste

1. Cut green beans and place in medium saucepan. Add water to cover and bring to boil. Cook for 5 minutes. Drain water.
2. Add all remaining ingredients to beans and cook 3 minutes longer.
3. Remove bay leaf and serve.

French Peas

Mary Elizabeth Bartlet
Schenectady, NY
Double Irish Chain

Makes 6-8 servings

2 10-oz. pkgs. frozen peas, thawed
Salt and pepper to taste
½ tsp. sugar
3 Tbsp. butter
1 lettuce leaf
⅔ cup thinly sliced radishes

1. Put peas in small baking dish. Sprinkle with salt, pepper and sugar. Dot with butter and cover with lettuce leaf.
2. Bake at 350° for 20-25 minutes or until heated through.
3. Remove lettuce and stir in radishes. Serve.

Sweet Tomato Pie

Mary Brubacker
Barnett, MO
Broken Star

Makes 6-8 servings

Crust:
8-oz. pkg. spaghetti
2 Tbsp. butter, melted
½ cup grated Parmesan cheese
1 egg, beaten

Filling:
1 lb. sweet Italian sausage
1 clove garlic, minced
1 small zucchini, chopped
½ cup chopped green onions and tops
4 large mushrooms, chopped
2 Tbsp. chopped fresh parsley
5 medium tomatoes, finely chopped
½ tsp. salt
¼ tsp. pepper
½-1 tsp. Italian seasoning
1 cup grated mozzarella cheese

1. To prepare crust cook and drain spaghetti according to package directions.
2. Combine spaghetti, butter, cheese and egg. Spread evenly into 10-inch pie plate.
3. To prepare filling remove sausage from casings and crumble into large skillet. Add garlic, zucchini, onions, mushrooms and parsley. Cook until sausage is

I grew up when our country was recovering slowly from the Great Depression. During the cold winter months in Colorado we slept in unheated bedrooms, but we always had warm quilts and comforters on our beds, thanks to our mother's hard work. I remember having so many covers on my bed that it was hard to turn over.

—*Betty Caudle, Colorado Springs, CO*

no longer pink.

4. Add tomatoes and seasonings and mix well. Simmer for 5 minutes, stirring occasionally. Stir in cheese until it melts.

5. Spread meat mixture evenly over spaghetti.

6. Bake at 350° for 25 minutes.

Tomato Gravy

Lillian McAninch
Leesburg, FL
My First Quilt

Makes 4-6 servings

1 small onion, chopped
1 small green pepper,
** chopped**
3 Tbsp. margarine *or* olive
** oil**
1 quart home-canned
** tomatoes**
1 tsp. salt
2 Tbsp. sugar
Dash pepper
2 Tbsp. flour
½ cup water

1. Sauté onion and green pepper in margarine until onion is transparent.

2. Add tomatoes, salt, sugar and pepper and bring to a slow boil.

3. In separate container combine flour and water into a smooth paste. Add to tomato mixture and continue cooking, stirring con-

stantly until thickened.

4. Serve with fish or rice.

Flossie Sultzaberger's Ratatouille

Flossie Sultzaberger
Mechanicsburg, PA
Nine Patch

Makes 10-12 servings

1½ lbs. zucchini
3 stalks celery
1 large green pepper
1 large eggplant
8 medium tomatoes
1 large onion
½ cup butter *or* margarine
3 cloves garlic, minced
1 Tbsp. oregano
1 Tbsp. basil
1 tsp. salt
4 Tbsp. grated Parmesan
** cheese**

1. Grease 9" x 13" baking dish. Slice zucchini and celery into dish.

2. Cut green pepper into large squares and cut eggplant into cubes. Add to dish.

3. Chop tomatoes into dish.

4. Cut onion into large squares. Sauté onion and garlic with butter 4-5 minutes. Add seasonings and sauté until onion is transparent. Pour mixture into casserole dish. Sprinkle

with cheese.

5. Bake at 350° for 25 minutes or until hot and bubbly.

Cindy Cooksey's Ratatouille

Cindy Cooksey
Irvine, CA
Albino Squid Races

Makes 6 servings

¾ cup chopped onion
2 cloves garlic, minced
⅓ cup olive oil
4 green peppers
2½ cups diced eggplant
3 cups zucchini, sliced
2 cups chopped tomatoes
Salt and pepper to taste

1. Sauté onion and garlic in olive oil until golden brown. Remove garlic.

2. Seed peppers and cut into bite-sized squares. Stir into onion and olive oil. Add all other ingredients.

3. Cover and simmer on very low heat 35-45 minutes. Serve either hot or cold.

Vegetables Fred

LuAnne S. Taylor
Canton, PA
Barnraising Log Cabin

Makes 8 servings

24-oz. pkg. frozen mixed
    vegetables
2 Tbsp. butter
½ tsp. salt
½ tsp. garlic salt
8 Tbsp. butter, melted
⅓ cup flour
¾ cup sour cream
¼ cup Parmesan cheese
½ cup bread crumbs

1. Cook vegetables according to package directions, adding 2 Tbsp. butter, salt and garlic salt.
2. To 8 Tbsp. melted butter add flour to make a paste. Stir into vegetables and cook until thickened, stirring constantly. Remove from heat and stir in sour cream and cheese.
3. Pour into greased casserole dish and cover with bread crumbs.
4. Bake at 350° for 30 minutes.

Vegetable Casserole

Kim Marlor
Owings Mills, MD
Fan

Makes 4-6 servings

16-oz. can French-style
    green beans
16-oz. can white corn
10¾-oz. can cream of
    celery soup
½ cup grated cheese
½ cup chopped celery
½ cup chopped onion
½ cup sour cream
8 Tbsp. margarine
1 stack Ritz crackers,
    crushed
¼-½ cup slivered almonds

1. Drain vegetables and mix with celery soup in 2-quart casserole dish. Add cheese, celery, onion and sour cream and mix well.
2. Melt margarine and stir in crushed crackers and almonds. Spread over vegetables.
3. Bake at 350° for 45 minutes.

Swiss Vegetable Medley

Sara M. Miller
Kalona, IA
Janice Yoskovich
Carmichaels, PA
Bonnie Grove
York, PA

Makes 6 servings

16-oz. pkg. frozen broccoli,
    carrots and cauliflower
    mixture
10¾-oz. can cream of
    mushroom soup
4 ozs. Swiss cheese,
    shredded
½ cup sour cream
¼ tsp. black pepper
4-oz. jar diced pimento,
    drained
2.8-oz. can French-style
    onions

1. Thaw and drain vegetable mixture.
2. In a large bowl combine vegetables, soup, ½ of cheese, sour cream, pepper, pimento and ½ of onions. Pour into shallow, 1-quart casserole dish.
3. Cover and bake at 350° for 30 minutes or until vegetables are done. Sprinkle remaining cheese and onions across top.
4. Bake, uncovered, 5 minutes longer or until onions are golden brown.

Sweet Potato Casserole

Jane L. Murphy
Malvern, PA
Doll Nine Patch

Makes 10-12 servings

Sweet Potato Mixture:
4 cups mashed, cooked
  sweet potatoes
½ cup white sugar
1 cup milk
1 egg, beaten
½ tsp. cinnamon
½ tsp. nutmeg

Topping:
¾ cup crushed cornflakes
¼ cup raisins
½ cup chopped nuts
½ cup brown sugar
4 Tbsp. margarine, melted

1. To prepare sweet potato mixture combine all ingredients. Place in greased 11" x 13" casserole dish.
2. Bake at 400° for 20 minutes.
3. To prepare topping combine all ingredients. Remove sweet potatoes from oven and spread with topping.
4. Return to oven and bake 10 minutes longer or until browned.

Caramel Sweet Potatoes

Geraldine A. Ebersole
Hershey, PA
Double Irish Chain

Makes 4-6 servings

4 medium sweet potatoes
3 Tbsp. butter
2 Tbsp. cornstarch
1 cup firmly packed brown
  sugar
1 cup water
¼ tsp. salt
½ tsp. nutmeg

1. Cook and peel potatoes and cut lengthwise. Place in greased, shallow baking dish.
2. Combine all remaining ingredients in a saucepan and cook slowly until thickened, stirring constantly. Pour sauce over potatoes.
3. Bake at 350° for 25-30 minutes, basting as needed.

Baked Potato Topping

Cora Nisly
Hutchinson, KS
Kansas Wheat Pattern

Makes 12-15 servings

3 lbs. ground beef
1 cup chopped green
  peppers
½ cup chopped onion
2 Tbsp. flour
3 cups milk
¾ lb. cheddar cheese,
  grated
¾ lb. American cheese,
  grated
½ tsp. red pepper
Salt and pepper to taste
¼ tsp. dry mustard

1. Brown ground beef with peppers and onion. Drain excess fat.
2. Stir in flour. Add milk and cook until thickened.
3. Add cheeses and seasonings and heat through. Serve with baked potatoes.

While I was at home with our three small children, I joined a group of women who invited an instructor to teach us how to make different quilt patterns. We always also brought our best recipes to share for lunch. I have gone back to full-time teaching, but the group still gets together, calling itself the Saylorsburg Quilt and Gourmet Society.

—*Maryellen Mross, Bartonsville, PA*

> My friend and I each have sons on our local school soccer team. One day they stood talking on the field. Kyle reached over and started pulling threads off my son Brian's clothing. He asked, "Does your mother quilt?" My son came home quite displeased with his decorated clothes. Kyle, not knowing that we knew each other, hurried home to his mother with the news that he had found a new quilting friend for her.
>
> —*Marilyn Mowry, Irving, TX*

Creamed Beef and Chicken-Topped Potatoes

Elaine Patton
West Middletown, PA
Dresden Plate

Makes 4 servings

4 large baking potatoes
Cooking oil
3 Tbsp. butter *or* margarine
¼ cup finely chopped onion
2 Tbsp. minced celery
2½-oz. jar sliced dried beef, finely chopped
3½ Tbsp. all-purpose flour
2 cups milk
½ cup cooked, diced chicken
1 tsp. lemon juice
1 tsp. Worcestershire sauce
¼ tsp. thyme
Dash pepper

1. Wash potatoes and rub with oil.
2. Bake at 400° for 1 hour or until soft.
3. Melt butter in medium saucepan. Sauté onion, celery and dried beef until on-ion is tender.
4. Gradually add milk and cook over medium heat until sauce thickens and bubbles, stirring constantly. Stir in remaining ingredients and continue cooking until mixture is thoroughly heated.
5. Split tops of potatoes lengthwise, fluff pulp and spoon topping over potatoes. Serve.

Beef in Potato Shells

Dorothy Kauffman
Millersburg, OH
Double Wedding Ring

Makes 6 servings

3 large potatoes
1 Tbsp. butter, melted
1 lb. ground beef
8-oz. jar pizza sauce
1 pkg. dry taco seasoning
½ cup shredded cheddar cheese
⅓ cup sour cream

1. Prepare whole pota-toes. Bake at 400° for 1 hour.
2. Cut each potato into lengthwise halves. Scoop out potato, leaving a ¼-inch shell. (Save potato pulp for mashed potatoes or potato pancakes.)
3. Brush outsides and in-sides of shells with butter. Place shells, cut side up, on ungreased baking sheet.
4. Bake at 400°, uncov-ered, until edges are crisp and brown, 15-20 minutes.
5. Meanwhile, brown ground beef. Drain excess fat. Add pizza sauce and taco seasoning and mix well. Spoon beef mixture into potato shells. Sprinkle with cheese. Heat just until cheese is melted. Immedi-ately before serving, top with sour cream.

Salmon-Stuffed Potatoes

Susan Harms
Wichita, KS
Sampler

Makes 4 servings

Potatoes:
4 large potatoes
7-oz. can salmon
Milk
2 Tbsp. butter
1 egg, beaten
3 Tbsp. Parmesan cheese
¼ tsp. salt

⅛ tsp. pepper
3 Tbsp. finely chopped
  onion

Cheese Sauce:
2 Tbsp. butter
2 Tbsp. flour
1 cup milk
½ tsp. salt
¼ tsp. dry mustard
¾ cup grated cheddar
  cheese

1. Bake potatoes at 400°
for 50 minutes or until tender. Cut in half lengthwise.
Scoop out potato pulp and
mash.

2. Drain and flake
salmon, reserving liquid.
Add milk to salmon liquid
to make ¼ cup.

3. Combine potato pulp,
milk liquid, butter, egg,
cheese and seasonings.
Fold in salmon flakes and
onion. Spoon mixture into
potato shells and arrange
on baking sheet.

4. Bake at 375° for 20
minutes or until filling is
lightly browned.

5. Prepare a cheese sauce
by melting butter in saucepan. Blend in flour and
cook until bubbly. Add
milk, salt and dry mustard.
Cook, stirring constantly
until thickened. Add cheese
and stir over low heat until
cheese melts.

6. Serve stuffed potatoes
with cheese sauce.

❖

Sweet and Sour New Potatoes

Barbara Neuhauser
Parkesburg, PA
Baby Quilt

Makes 6 servings

18 new potatoes
3 small onions, diced
3 Tbsp. butter
2 tsp. sugar
1 tsp. salt *or* less
2 Tbsp. flour
½ cup milk
1 cup sour cream
2 Tbsp. white vinegar

1. Boil potatoes in their
jackets.

2. Sauté onions in butter
until onions are transparent. Add sugar, salt and
flour and heat, stirring constantly. Slowly add milk
and cook until thickened,
stirring constantly.

3. Add sour cream and
vinegar and cook until slow
bubbles form.

4. Mix sauce with pota-
toes and serve.

❖

Make Ahead Potatoes

Edna Nisly
Partridge, KS
Encircled Tulips

Makes 12 servings

12 large potatoes
8-oz. pkg. cream cheese
8-oz. carton sour cream
1 tsp. salt
1 tsp. onion powder
½ tsp. black pepper
4 Tbsp. margarine, melted
Paprika

1. Peel and cube pota-
toes. Boil until softened.
Drain off all water.

2. Add all other ingredi-
ents except margarine and
paprika. Whip or mash un-
til fluffy. Add small
amount of milk if needed.

3. Place in large casserole
dish and refrigerate or
freeze until ready to use.

4. Immediately before
baking, drizzle melted margarine over top and sprinkle with paprika.

5. Bake at 350° for 1¼
hours.

Potato Filling

Frances Musser
Newmanstown, PA
Sweet Country

Makes 8 servings

2½-3 lbs. potatoes
2 cups water
1¾ cups milk
⅛ tsp. saffron
2 Tbsp. boiling water
½ cup chopped onion
1 cup chopped celery
¼ cup butter
½ loaf white bread, cubed
3 eggs, beaten
2 tsp. salt
⅛ tsp. pepper

1. Peel and cube potatoes. Cook in 2 cups water. Drain and mash with 1 cup milk. Set aside.
2. Soak saffron in boiling water. Set aside.
3. Sauté onion and celery in butter until soft. Set aside.
4. In a large bowl toss together bread, eggs, salt, pepper, ¾ cup milk and saffron. Add mashed potatoes and mix together with a large spoon until well blended.
5. Spoon into a 3-quart casserole dish.
6. Cover and bake at 350° for 1 hour or until heated through.

Katherine Lombard's Potato Casserole

Katherine S. Lombard
Deerfield, NH
Amish Center Square

Makes 10 servings

4 lbs. potatoes
½ cup butter *or* margarine
1 cup milk
3 large eggs, beaten
½ cup grated Parmesan cheese
½ cup chopped, fresh parsley
¼ cup chopped, fresh chives
1 tsp. salt
½ tsp. pepper

1. Peel and cube potatoes. Cook potatoes in water for about 30 minutes. Drain.
2. Add all remaining ingredients to drained potatoes and heat until smooth, stirring occasionally. Spoon into 3-quart baking dish.
3. Bake, uncovered, at 350° for 50 minutes or until puffed and browned.

Molly Wilson's Potato Casserole

Molly Wilson
Gonzales, TX
Marriage Quilt

Makes 8-10 servings

8-10 medium potatoes
10¾-oz. can cream of celery soup
10¾-oz. can cream of mushroom soup
1 cup grated cheddar cheese
Salt and pepper to taste

1. Peel and dice potatoes. Spread into 2-quart baking dish.
2. Combine soups and cheese. Pour over potatoes. Sprinkle with salt and pepper.
3. Cover and bake at 350° for about 45 minutes. Uncover and bake another 15 minutes.

Easy Roast Potatoes

Marjorie Mills
Bethesda, MD
Scrap Quilt

Makes 4 servings

4 medium potatoes
2½ Tbsp. cooking oil
½ tsp. black pepper
Salt

1. Cut unpeeled potatoes into 1-inch cubes, having a bit of skin on each piece. In a large bowl toss with oil and pepper.
2. Arrange potato cubes in single layer in a lightly greased shallow baking dish or roasting pan.
3. Bake at 350° for 50-60 minutes until crisp on outside and tender on inside. Season with salt.

Variation:
Cut potatoes into strips and arrange in baking dish. Sprinkle with salt, pepper, seasoned salt and garlic salt. Pour 8 Tbsp. butter, melted, over top and mix lightly. Cover tightly with aluminum foil. Bake at 400° for 1 hour.

Anna Musser
Manheim, PA
Lancaster Rose

Spicy Roasted Potatoes

Suzanne S. Nobrega
Duxbury, MA
Amish Nine Patch

Makes 4 servings

1½ tsp. dry mustard
1½ tsp. Dijon mustard
1 tsp. olive oil
1 clove garlic, minced
1 tsp. dried tarragon (optional)
¼ tsp. paprika
⅛ tsp. red pepper
2 large potatoes

1. In a medium bowl mix dry mustard, Dijon mustard, olive oil, garlic, tarragon, paprika and red pepper into a smooth paste.
2. Cut unpeeled potatoes into 1-inch chunks. Pat dry with paper towel and toss with mustard mixture until coated. Arrange potatoes in single layer on lightly greased baking pan.
3. Bake at 425° for 30-35 minutes or until chunks are tender.

Baked Potato Wedges

Sally A. Price
Reston, VA
Natalie's Memory Quilt

Makes 4 servings

4 large potatoes
8 Tbsp. margarine, melted
¼ cup ketchup
1 tsp. prepared mustard
½ tsp. paprika
¼ tsp. salt
¼ tsp. pepper

1. Wash potatoes and pat dry. Quarter each potato. Cut each quarter crosswise into ¼-inch slices, cutting to, but not through, bottom of potato to resemble a fan.
2. Place each potato wedge, skin side down, on large baking sheet. Set aside.
3. Combine all remaining ingredients and mix well. Brush tops and sides of potatoes with mixture.
4. Bake, uncovered, at 425° for 35-40 minutes.

Hash Brown Potatoes

Helen Gerber
Stoughton, WI
Spring Tulips
Janice Muller
Derwood, MD
Amish Roman Stripes

Makes 10-12 servings

32-oz. pkg. frozen hash brown potatoes, thawed
10¾-oz. can cream of chicken soup
1 cup sour cream
2 cups shredded cheddar cheese
4 Tbsp. margarine, melted
2 cups finely crushed cornflakes
4 Tbsp. margarine, melted

1. In a large bowl combine hash brown potatoes, chicken soup, sour cream, cheese and 4 Tbsp. margarine. Mix well and spread into a greased 9" x 13" baking pan.
2. Combine cornflakes and 4 Tbsp. melted margarine. Spread over potatoes.
3. Bake, uncovered, at 350° for 45-55 minutes or until hot and bubbly.

Variations:
Add 1 large onion, finely chopped, and 1 cup milk to the ingredients.
Ruth D. Mullen
Annapolis, MD
Nine Patch

Add 1 medium onion, diced, to the ingredients.
Mary Puskar
Baltimore, MD
Mitzi McGlynchey
Downingtown, PA
Dusty Graham
Hagerstown, MD
Arlene C. Kelly
Clarence, NY

Substitute cream of mushroom soup for cream of chicken soup and add 1 medium onion, chopped.
Julie Lynch Arnsberger
Gaithersburg, MD
Trip Around the World

Ham and Potato Casserole

Eleanor Larson
Glen Lyon, PA
Autograph & Basket
Mrs. Enos C. Yoder
Haven, KS
Plain Top with Wheat Pattern

Makes 4-6 servings

4 large potatoes
1 medium onion, grated
8 Tbsp. margarine, melted
3 eggs, slightly beaten
2 heaping Tbsp. flour
1 tsp. salt
½ tsp. pepper
1 cup milk
1 cup diced baked ham

1. Peel and grate potatoes. Combine all ingredients and spoon into well-greased 8" x 12" baking dish.
2. Bake at 350° for 1 hour until browned.

Scalloped Potatoes with Cornflakes

Ella G. Wenger
New Holland, PA
Country Bride & Country Lily

Makes 8-10 servings

10 medium potatoes
1 onion, sliced (optional)
4 slices bread, cubed
½ cup butter *or* margarine, melted
Salt and pepper to taste
¼ lb. cheddar cheese, grated
¾ cup milk
1 cup cornflakes, crushed

1. Boil potatoes until soft and slice them. Combine all ingredients except cornflakes in a bowl. Spread into a 9" x 13" baking dish.
2. Sprinkle cornflakes over top.
3. Bake at 350° for 1 hour.

❖

Potato Pancakes

Rebecca MeyerKorth
Wamego, KS
Jacob's Elevator

Makes 6 servings

6 medium potatoes
1 large onion
1 medium carrot
½ cup milk
1 egg white, lightly beaten
1 egg, lightly beaten
½ cup flour
Salt and pepper to taste
Cooking oil

1. Peel and grate potatoes and onion. Squeeze out excess liquid.
2. Peel and grate carrot.
3. Combine potatoes, onion, carrot, milk, egg white, egg, flour, salt and pepper and mix thoroughly.
4. In large skillet heat enough oil to cover bottom of pan with ¼ inch oil.
5. Using ¼-cup measure spoon batter into skillet. Fry each pancake until golden brown on both sides. Drain on paper towels, keep warm and serve.

❖

Old-Fashioned Kumle

Inga Paulsen
Stoughton, WI

Makes 4-6 servings

1 ham bone
Water to cover
4 cups grated raw potatoes
1 tsp. baking powder
1 tsp. salt
1 cup white flour
4 Tbsp. butter, melted

1. Cook ham bone in water until meat is done. Remove bone and keep broth hot.
2. Squeeze excess water from potatoes. Combine potatoes, baking powder, salt and flour. Work lightly into balls. Drop into broth.
3. Cover and cook slowly for 1 hour, stirring occasionally to keep kumle from sticking.
4. Dip in melted butter and serve.

❖

Curried Lima Bean Casserole

Alma C. Ranck
Paradise, PA
Trip Around the World

Makes 4 servings

20-oz. pkg. frozen baby lima beans
2 medium onions, chopped
1 bell pepper, diced
10¾-oz. can cream of mushroom soup
½ cup water
1 cup sour cream
1-1½ tsp. curry powder
⅓ cup seasoned bread crumbs
1 Tbsp. butter, melted
2 strips bacon

1. Cook lima beans as directed on package. Drain and reserve liquid.
2. In a saucepan combine onions, pepper, soup and ½ cup reserved liquid or water. Heat through.
3. Remove from heat and blend in sour cream and curry. Stir in lima beans. Turn mixture into a medium casserole dish.
4. Combine bread crumbs with melted butter. Fry, drain and crumble bacon. Mix bread crumbs and bacon together and sprinkle over lima bean mixture.
5. Bake, uncovered, at 350° for 25 minutes or until heated through.

Grandma's Beans

Celia LoPinto
San Francisco, CA
*Loma Prieta Meets the San
Francisco Pavement*

Makes 10 servings

**5 10-oz. pkgs. frozen lima
 beans**
½ cup brown sugar
8 wieners
12-oz. bottle chili sauce
12-oz. bottle pancake syrup
1 lb. sliced bacon

1. Cook lima beans according to package directions for 5 minutes only. Drain thoroughly and pour into flat roasting pan. Sprinkle with brown sugar.
2. Cut wieners into ½-inch slices and distribute through the beans. Pour chili sauce and pancake syrup evenly over beans. Completely cover ingredients with slices of bacon.
3. Bake, uncovered, at 400° for 1 hour. (Beans will turn a very dark color.)

Barbecue Bean Bake

Anna Barrow
Hatchville, MA
Sampler
Levina K. Stoltzfus
Loganton, PA
Sunshine and Shadow

Makes 20-24 servings

1 lb. ground beef
1 onion, chopped
½ cup ketchup
½ cup barbecue sauce
1 tsp. salt
4 Tbsp. prepared mustard
4 Tbsp. molasses
1 tsp. chili powder
¾ tsp. pepper
2 16-oz. cans kidney beans
**2 16-oz. cans pork and
 beans**
2 16-oz. cans butter beans
½ lb. bacon

1. Brown ground beef and onion. Drain excess fat. Stir in ketchup, barbecue sauce, salt, mustard, molasses, chili powder and pepper. Add beans and combine thoroughly. Pour into casserole dish.
2. Fry, drain and crumble bacon. Arrange over top of bean mixture.
3. Bake at 350° for 1 hour.

Montana Mountain Man Beans

Mary Brubacker
Barnett, MO
Broken Star

Makes 6-8 servings

1 lb. dry red beans
2½ cups water
⅓ lb. salt-dried pork
2 lbs. beef cubes
1 cup chopped onions
1 clove garlic, minced
6-oz. can tomato paste
4 tsp. chili powder
1 tsp. salt
1 tsp. cumin
1 tsp. red pepper
1 bay leaf

1. Soak and cook beans with water according to directions.
2. Brown pork and beef in skillet. Drain excess fat.
3. In large Dutch oven combine cooked beans and meats. Add all remaining ingredients and stir well.
4. Cover and simmer for 2 hours, adding hot water as needed.
5. Remove bay leaf and serve.

Three-Bean Casserole

Alicia Swift
Sleepy Eye, MN
Log Cabin
Judith Ann Govotsos
Monrovia, MD
Snowball Twist

Makes 8-10 servings

½ lb. bacon, diced
½ cup chopped onion
1 lb. ground beef
½ cup brown sugar
½ cup ketchup
2 Tbsp. prepared mustard
16-oz. can pork and beans
16-oz. can lima beans
16-oz. can kidney beans

1. Brown bacon and onion together. Drain excess fat. Add ground beef and brown. Pour into a casserole dish and stir in all remaining ingredients.
2. Bake at 325° for 40 minutes.

Jill's Baked Beans

Abbie Christie
Berkeley Heights, NJ
Bow Ties for Andy

Makes 4-6 servings

2 16-oz. cans baked beans
¾ cup brown sugar, packed

1 tsp. dry mustard
½ cup ketchup
6 slices bacon, chopped

1. Combine baked beans, brown sugar, mustard and ketchup. Pour into lightly greased baking dish. Arrange bacon pieces over top.
2. Bake, uncovered, at 325° for 2½ hours.

Baked Beans

Suzanne Bothell
Center, CO
Thread Spools

Makes 6-8 servings

2 cups dry pinto beans
4½ Tbsp. molasses
1½ Tbsp. cider vinegar
1½ tsp. dry mustard
⅓ cup brown sugar
1½ tsp. salt
¼ tsp. pepper
1 Tbsp. flour
½ cup water
3 slices bacon
1 medium onion, sliced

1. Soak and cook beans according to directions on package.
2. In separate dish combine all other ingredients except bacon and onion.
3. In 2-quart baking dish layer beans, bacon slices and onion slices. Pour molasses mixture over all.
4. Bake at 350° for 1

hour. Stir gently before serving.

Blackbeans and Rice

Robin Liberty
Bradenton, FL

Makes 6 servings

4 chicken breasts
3 5-oz. pkgs. yellow rice
2 16-oz. cans black beans
2 large onions, minced
2 Tbsp. red wine vinegar

1. Cook and bone chicken breasts. Cut chicken into cubes.
2. Prepare rice according to package directions. Add chicken pieces and mix well.
3. Meanwhile, cook black beans in a saucepan until heated through.
4. Spoon rice mixture and black beans into a serving dish and mix well. Sprinkle with onions and vinegar. Serve immediately.

Herbed Rice

E. Michaella Keener
Upper Darby, PA
Micki's Dream

Makes 4 servings

2 Tbsp. butter
1 clove garlic, minced
3 Tbsp. chopped onion
1 cup uncooked white rice
1 cup chicken broth
1 cup water
3 sprigs fresh parsley
1 sprig thyme, crushed
1 bay leaf

1. Melt butter in 2-quart saucepan. Add garlic and onion and sauté until garlic is golden.
2. Add rice and mix to coat. Add broth, water, parsley, thyme and bay leaf. Bring to a boil. Cover, lower heat and cook on low for 20 minutes or until liquid is absorbed.
3. Remove bay leaf and serve.

Skillet-Fried Rice

Candy Horton
Greenfield, OH
Cecil's Fan

Makes 12-15 servings

3 cups uncooked rice
6 Tbsp. cooking oil
5 eggs, beaten
6 Tbsp. soy sauce
¼ tsp. garlic powder
2 onions, chopped
2 cups sliced celery

1. Cook rice according to directions. Set aside.
2. Heat oil in large skillet. Pour in eggs. As eggs harden, cut up with 2 knives. Add soy sauce and garlic powder and stir-fry.
3. Add rice, onions and celery. Stir-fry over low heat 3-5 minutes until heated and well blended. Serve.

Rice Pilaf

Barbara Spicer
Gettysburg, PA
Endless Pyramids

Makes 12-15 servings

3 Tbsp. butter
2 onions, finely chopped
3 cups uncooked rice
1½ quarts chicken broth
Salt and pepper to taste

1. In a heavy casserole sauté onions in butter until softened, but not browned. Add rice and cook, stirring until rice appears transparent. Add broth and bring to a boil. Season.
2. Cover and bake at 350° for 20 minutes. Let stand 10 minutes. Stir to fluff and serve.

Variation:
Add an 8-oz. jar sliced mushrooms, drained, to onions in step 1.

F. Elaine Asper
Stroudsburg, PA
Duck and Ducklings

Lentil and Rice Curry

Celia LoPinto
San Francisco, CA
Loma Prieta Meets the San Francisco Pavement

Makes 5 servings

1½ cups lentils
3 cups water
Dash salt
2 cups uncooked brown rice
4 cups water
Dash salt
4 Tbsp. cooking oil
3 cups chopped onions
1 large bell pepper, chopped
1 small green apple, chopped

2 large cloves garlic,
   minced
2 Tbsp. curry powder
$\frac{1}{2}$ tsp. powdered cumin
$1\frac{1}{2}$ cups fresh *or* frozen
   peas
$\frac{1}{4}$ tsp. cayenne pepper
2 Tbsp. lemon juice
2 cups plain yogurt
1 small cucumber, chopped
2 Tbsp. minced fresh
   coriander
1 cup chutney
1 cup chopped peanuts
1 cup raisins

1. Combine lentils, 3
cups water and dash of salt
in a saucepan. Bring to a
boil, reduce heat, cover and
cook until lentils are tender,
about 25 minutes.

2. Meanwhile, combine
rice, 4 cups water and dash
of salt in another saucepan
and bring to a boil. Reduce
heat, cover and simmer until tender and all liquid is
absorbed, about 20-25 minutes.

3. Heat oil in large frying
pan and sauté onions, pepper, apple, garlic, curry and
cumin until vegetables are
soft. Add cooked lentils
and peas and mix well,
cooking about 5 minutes or
until peas are tender. Add
cayenne pepper and lemon
juice and heat through.

4. In a separate bowl
combine yogurt, cucumber
and coriander.

5. Serve lentil mixture
over rice with a dollop of
yogurt.

6. Put each condiment
(chutney, peanuts and raisins) in separate dish and
have guests serve them-
selves.

Mexican Rice

Judy McKee
Beatrice, NE

Makes 8 servings

3 Tbsp. bacon drippings
$\frac{2}{3}$ cup chopped onion
$1\frac{1}{2}$ cups uncooked rice
1 cup chopped green
   pepper
1 tsp. chili powder
$\frac{1}{2}$ cup ketchup
2 tsp. salt
1 cup tomato juice
3 cups water

1. In large saucepan
sauté onion in bacon drippings until onion is golden.
Add all other ingredients
and bring to a boil.

2. Reduce heat, cover
and simmer for 20 minutes
or until rice is tender. Serve.

❖❖
❖

Green Chili
Casserole

Carol Price
Los Lunas, NM
Double Wedding Ring

Makes 6-8 servings

12 corn tortillas
8 Tbsp. margarine, melted
2 4-oz. cans green chilies,
   chopped
$\frac{1}{2}$ lb. sharp cheese, grated
1 large onion, chopped
$10\frac{3}{4}$-oz. can cream of
   chicken soup
12-oz. can evaporated milk

1. Dip tortillas in melted
margarine. Tear into bite-
sized pieces and set aside.

2. Mix together all re-
maining ingredients. Fold
in tortilla pieces. Turn into
casserole dish.

3. Bake at 325° for about
1 hour.

Several years ago a large group of quilters made a bus
trip from Chicago to my community in Kalona, IA. We
served a salad and pie dinner at our home, including
twelve different kinds of homemade pie. After dinner
we spent time sharing our own rural quilting traditions
with the quilters from the city.

—*Sara M. Miller, Kalona, IA*

Cheese Soufflé

Agnes King
Atglen, PA

Makes 2-4 servings

¼ cup butter *or* margarine
3 Tbsp. flour
3 eggs, separated
1 cup milk
1 cup grated cheese
1 small onion, finely
    chopped
½ tsp. salt

1. Melt butter in a saucepan. Add flour and heat to bubbling, stirring constantly.
2. Beat egg yolks and stir into milk. Gradually add mixture to saucepan, stirring constantly until thickened. Add cheese and onion and heat through, stirring frequently.
3. Beat egg whites until soft peaks form. Fold into cheese mixture and spoon into casserole dish.
4. Bake at 350° for 25-30 minutes.

Cheese Onion Pie

Betty Stoltzfus
Honey Brook, PA

Makes 6 servings

4 cups thinly sliced onions
1 Tbsp. butter
2 cups grated cheese
3 eggs
⅔ cup milk
1 tsp. salt
¼ tsp. pepper
1 9" unbaked pie shell

1. Sauté onions in butter until onions are soft and golden brown.
2. In a pie shell with high, fluted edges spread alternate layers of onion and cheese, ending with cheese.
3. Combine eggs, milk, salt and pepper and beat lightly. Pour over onions and cheese.
4. Bake at 400° for 30 minutes.

Scalloped Pineapple

Elaine Patton
West Middletown, PA
Betsy Jevon, Pittsburgh, PA
Esther Lapp, Sterling, IL
Karen Moore, Fairfax, VA
Nancy V. Schaub
Warminster, PA

Makes 8 servings

3 eggs
1 cup white sugar
½ cup milk
8 Tbsp. butter, melted
20-oz. can crushed
    pineapple, drained
4-5 slices bread, cubed

1. Slightly beat eggs in bowl. Add sugar and mix well. Add milk, butter, pineapple and bread cubes and mix well.
2. Pour into greased 1½-quart casserole dish.
3. Cover and bake at 350° for 45 minutes.

Pineapple Casserole

Loutee H. Pardue
Florence, SC
Queen Anne Star
Vera E. Duncan
Sibley, MO
Fancy Nine Patch

Makes 4-6 servings

**10-oz. can pineapple
 tidbits, undrained**
**1 cup grated cheddar
 cheese**
3 Tbsp. flour
½ cup sugar
8 Tbsp. margarine, melted
**1 pkg. Ritz crackers, finely
 crushed**

1. Pour pineapple into greased 9-inch square baking dish.
2. In separate bowl combine cheese, flour and sugar. Sprinkle over pineapple.
3. Combine melted margarine and cracker crumbs. Sprinkle over cheese mixture.
4. Bake at 350° for about 25-30 minutes or until bubbly and brown.

Great-Grandma's Traditional Bread Stuffing

Terry Kessler
Bayside, NY
Great-Grandmother's Fan

Makes stuffing for 15-lb. bird

1 large loaf white bread
1 lb. sweet butter, melted
**1 medium onion, finely
 chopped**
1 cup celery, chopped
1 tsp. salt
¼ tsp. pepper
2 Tbsp. poultry seasoning
1 Tbsp. chopped parsley

1. Toast bread lightly in oven. Dice into medium pieces.
2. Melt butter in a large skillet. Add onion, celery, salt, pepper and poultry seasoning. Simmer until celery is tender.
3. Add parsley and pour over sliced toasted bread. Mix well and stuff lightly into bird cavity and neck.
4. Follow directions for roasting the bird.

Pies

French Apple Pie

Barbara F. Shie
Colorado Springs, CO
Pineapple

Makes 1 deep-dish 9" pie

6-8 cooking apples
1 tsp. cinnamon
**1 cup graham cracker
 crumbs**
½ cup flour
1 cup sugar
½ tsp. ground nutmeg
¼ tsp. ground ginger
**8 Tbsp. butter *or*
 margarine, melted**
1 9" unbaked pie shell

1. Peel, core and thinly slice apples.
2. Combine all dry ingredients.
3. Sprinkle 1 Tbsp. dry ingredients over bottom of deep-dish crust. Add layer of apple slices followed by layer of dry mixture. Continue alternating layers until apples are mounded in pie shell. Top with any remaining dry ingredients.
4. Carefully drizzle melted butter over all.
5. Bake at 350° for approximately 1 hour. Serve.

Applescotch Meringue Pie

LaVerne A. Olson
Willow Street, PA
Log Cabin Star

Makes 1 9" pie

Filling:
1 cup brown sugar
1 cup water
1½ tsp. vinegar
**6 large apples, pared and
 sliced**
3 Tbsp. butter
4 Tbsp. flour
½ tsp. salt
1 9" baked pie shell

Meringue:
2 egg whites
4 Tbsp. sugar
1 tsp. vanilla

1. Combine brown sugar, water and vinegar in a saucepan. Bring to a boil. Add apples and cook until tender. Remove apples from syrup and set aside.
2. Cream together butter and flour. Stir into hot syrup and cook until thickened and smooth, stirring constantly. Add salt and fold in apples. Cool. Turn into 9-inch baked pie shell.
3. To prepare meringue beat egg whites until stiff. Add sugar and vanilla and beat until just combined. Spread meringue over pie filling.
4. Bake at 350° for 9-10 minutes until meringue is lightly browned.

Sour Cream Apple Pie

Lee Ann Hazlett
Freeport, IL
Snowbound

Makes 1 9" pie

Filling:
6-8 apples
1¼ cups sugar
2 heaping Tbsp. flour
2 tsp. vanilla
2 eggs
¼ tsp. salt
⅔ cup sour cream
½ tsp. cinnamon
1 9" unbaked pie shell

Topping:
½ cup sugar
⅓ cup flour
1 tsp. cinnamon
4 Tbsp. butter
½ cup chopped nuts

1. Fill unbaked pie shell ¾ full with sliced apples.
2. Combine sugar, flour, vanilla, eggs, salt, sour cream and cinnamon and pour over apples.
3. Bake at 350° for 45-50 minutes.
4. To prepare topping combine all ingredients. Remove pie from oven and sprinkle topping ingredients over all. Return to oven and bake another 15 minutes.

Ambrosia Apple Pie

Jeannette R. Saunders
Albuquerque, NM
Friendship

Makes 1 9" pie

1½ cups quick-cooking oats
1½ cups water
½ tsp. salt
1¾ cups sugar
4 Tbsp. flour
4 large, tart apples
¼ cup water
½ tsp. cinnamon
1 Tbsp. butter
1 9" unbaked pie shell

1. In a saucepan cook oats, 1½ cups water and salt for 5 minutes. Press mixture through a sieve or run through food processor for several minutes. Reserve ½ cup of strained oat mixture.
2. Mix remaining oats with 1 cup sugar and flour. Pour into unbaked pie shell.
3. Pare and slice apples into a saucepan. Add ¼ cup water. Cover and cook apples over low heat for 10 minutes. Drain off all juice. Arrange apple slices over oatmeal mixture.
4. Combine ¾ cup sugar and cinnamon. Sprinkle over apples. Spread ½ cup strained oat mixture over top. Dot with butter.
5. Bake at 450° for 20 minutes or until done. Cool completely and serve with favorite cheese.

Swedish Apple Pie

Charlotte Shaffer
Ephrata, PA
Eight-Pointed Star

Makes 1 10" pie

2-3 cups sliced apples
1 tsp. nutmeg
1 tsp. cinnamon
½ tsp. sugar
1 cup sugar
1 cup flour
½ cup chopped nuts
8 Tbsp. butter, melted
1 egg
1 10" unbaked pastry shell

1. Fill pastry shell ¾ full with sliced apples.
2. Combine nutmeg, cinnamon and ½ tsp. sugar and sprinkle over apples.
3. In a mixing bowl combine 1 cup sugar, flour, nuts, melted butter and egg. Spread mixture over apples.
4. Bake at 350° for 40-45 minutes.

Naked Apple Pie

Rosalie W. Keegan
Enfield, CT
Amish Diamond

Makes 1 9" pie

1 egg
½ cup brown sugar
½ cup white sugar
1 tsp. vanilla
Pinch salt
½ cup flour
1 tsp. baking powder
2 medium apples, peeled and sliced
½ cup chopped pecans

1. Beat egg in medium bowl. Add sugars, vanilla, salt, flour and baking powder and mix well. Stir in apples and pecans.
2. Spread ingredients into greased 9-inch pie plate.
3. Bake at 350° for ½ hour. Serve with whipped cream or ice cream.

Rhubarb Apple Pie

Nancy George
De Pere, WI
Hearts and Strings

Makes 1 deep-dish 9" pie

3½ cups diced, tart apples
2 cups diced rhubarb
1 cup sugar
¼ tsp. salt
½ tsp. cinnamon
3 Tbsp. minute tapioca
2 Tbsp. butter
Pastry for 2-crust pie

1. Combine apples, rhubarb, sugar, salt, cinnamon and tapioca and mix well. Turn into pastry-lined 9-inch pie pan. Dot with butter. Cover with pastry top and seal edges.
2. Bake at 425° for 10-15 minutes. Reduce oven temperature to 375° and bake another 30-40 minutes.

Sour Cream Rhubarb Pie

Karen M. Rusten
Waseca, MN
Ocean Wave

Makes 1 deep-dish 9" pie

3 cups diced rhubarb
1 egg, slightly beaten
1½ cups sugar
Dash salt
3 Tbsp. tapioca
1 cup sour cream
1 9" unbaked pie shell

1. Arrange rhubarb in pie shell.
2. Blend together egg, sugar, salt, tapioca and sour cream. Pour over rhubarb.
3. Bake at 450° for 15 minutes. Reduce oven temperature to 350° and bake 35-45 minutes longer or until filling has set.

Strawberry Rhubarb Pie

Marilyn Maurstad
Beatrice, NE
Ohio Star Variation

Makes 1 9" pie

2 cups diced rhubarb
2 cups sliced strawberries
1¼ cups sugar
4 Tbsp. minute tapioca

My friends and I have a modern version of a quilting bee. Once a month we meet at one of our homes and spend the evening talking about our lives, stitching on our current projects and sharing snacks provided by the host. Our husbands call it the "hen club."

—Audrey Romonosky, Poughkeepsie, NY

¼ tsp. salt
1 Tbsp. butter
Pastry for 2-crust pie

1. Combine rhubarb and strawberries in large bowl.
2. Combine sugar, tapioca and salt in small bowl. Add to fruit and let stand while preparing pastry.
3. Spoon rhubarb mixture into pie shell. Dot with butter. Cover with top crust. Slit top and flute edges.
4. Bake at 400° for 40-45 minutes.

Rhubarb Custard Pie

Silva Beachy, Millersburg, OH
Jacqueline E. Deininger
Bethlehem, PA
Cecilia Stevens, Pittsburgh, PA

Makes 1 9" pie

2 cups finely chopped rhubarb
1¼ cups white sugar
1 rounded Tbsp. flour
½ cup cream
2 eggs
½ cup water
½ tsp. nutmeg
1 9" unbaked pie shell

1. Arrange rhubarb in unbaked pie shell.
2. Mix together sugar, flour, cream, eggs and water. Pour over rhubarb.

Sprinkle with nutmeg.
3. Bake at 400° for 10 minutes. Reduce oven temperature to 325° and bake another 35-40 minutes or until set.

Pink Lady Pie

Mrs. Crist H. Yoder
Hutchinson, KS

Makes 1 9" pie

2 cups diced rhubarb
1 cup sugar
½ cup water
3-oz. pkg. strawberry gelatin
1 Tbsp. lemon juice
2 cups whipped topping
1 9" baked pie shell

1. Cook rhubarb, sugar and water slowly until rhubarb is tender. Add dry gelatin and stir gently until dissolved. Let cool. Add lemon juice and cool to room temperature. Fold in whipped topping.
2. Spoon into baked pie shell and refrigerate to chill. Serve.

❖

Lettie's Pineapple Pie

Myrtle Mansfield
Alfred, ME
Log Cabin

Makes 1 9" pie

Crust:
2 cups graham cracker crumbs
½ cup sugar
8 Tbsp. margarine *or* butter

Filling:
2 small pkgs. instant vanilla pudding
20-oz. can crushed pineapple, undrained
1 pint sour cream

Topping:
½ pint whipping cream
1 tsp. vanilla

1. To prepare crust combine all ingredients and press into 9-inch pie pan.
2. Bake at 325° for 15 minutes. Cool.
3. To prepare filling combine all ingredients. Pour into cooled pie crust and refrigerate until filling sets.
4. To prepare topping combine cream and vanilla and whip until cream is spreadable. Immediately before serving, top filling with whipped cream.

Pineapple Cheese Pie

Maryalice DeLong
Elwood, IN
Eight-Pointed Star

Makes 1 9" pie

⅔ cup fine graham cracker
    crumbs
2 Tbsp. butter *or*
    margarine, softened
8-oz. pkg. lite cream
    cheese, softened
2 eggs *or* ½ cup egg
    substitute
¼ cup orange juice
¼ cup sugar
1 Tbsp. flour
1 Tbsp. vanilla
1 tsp. grated orange rind
Pinch salt (optional)
12-oz. can pineapple tidbits
1 tsp. unflavored gelatin

1. Combine graham cracker crumbs and butter. Mix well and press evenly into bottom of 9-inch pie pan.
2. Cream cream cheese. Add eggs and mix until smooth. Add orange juice, sugar, flour, vanilla, orange rind and salt. Mix until smooth. Pour into crumb crust.
3. Bake at 350° for 20-30 minutes or until filling is set. Chill.
4. To prepare topping drain pineapple juice into a saucepan. Soften gelatin in juice and warm gently until it dissolves. Chill until mixture begins to thicken.
5. Arrange pineapple tidbits over baked pie filling. Pour gelatin mixture over all. Chill for 1 hour or until firm. Serve.

Peach Pie

Anita Falk
Mountain Lake, MN
Double Irish Chain

Makes 1 9" pie

6-8 fresh peaches, sliced
½ cup cream
1 heaping Tbsp. flour
1 cup sugar
Pinch salt
1 tsp. cinnamon
1 9" unbaked pie shell

1. Arrange peach slices in pie shell.
2. Mix all remaining ingredients well and pour over peach slices.
3. Bake at 425° for 10 minutes. Reduce oven temperature to 375° and bake another 30-35 minutes.

Italian Peach Pie

Debbie Chisholm
Fallston, MD
Wreath of Roses

Makes 2 9" pies

Crust:
8-oz. pkg. cream cheese
8 Tbsp. butter
½ tsp. salt
2 cups flour

Filling:
2 cups crushed vanilla
    wafers
8-10 fresh peaches
1½ cups sugar
¾ tsp. cinnamon
⅓ cup butter, melted

1. Cream together cream cheese and butter. Add salt and work in flour. Divide dough and press into 2 9-inch pie pans.
2. Sprinkle with vanilla wafer crumbs.
3. Core, peel and slice peaches. Add sugar and cinnamon and mix well. Spoon over wafer crumbs in pie pans. Drizzle butter over peaches.
4. Bake at 350° for 45-60 minutes.

Here is a comment that is every dedicated quilter's nightmare. At the end of a long day of quilting one novice quilter says, "I did pretty good today because I did not stitch through the material one single time."

—Cora Nisly, Hutchinson, KS

Fresh Peach Pie

Trudi Cook
Newtown Square, PA
Amish Flower Garden

Makes 2 9-inch square pies

Crust:
3 cups flour
1 cup cooking oil
1 tsp. salt
¼ cup sugar
¼ cup milk

Filling:
2 cups water
1 cup sugar
6 Tbsp. cornstarch
4 Tbsp. light corn syrup
6-oz. pkg. peach gelatin
10-12 fresh peaches

1. To prepare crust combine all ingredients and mix well. Divide dough in half and press into 2 greased 9-inch square baking pans.
2. Bake at 400° for 10-15 minutes.
3. To prepare filling combine water, sugar, cornstarch and syrup in a saucepan. Bring to a boil and cook until thickened and clear, stirring constantly. Remove from heat and measure exactly 4 Tbsp. peach gelatin into mixture. Stir and cool slightly.
4. Core, peel and dice peaches. Fold into gelatin mixture. Divide mixture evenly between 2 baking dishes. Cool and serve.

Apricot Pie

Eleanor J. Ferreira
North Chelmsford, MA
Trip Around the World

Makes 1 9" pie

2 cups dried apricots
2 cups water
½ cup sugar
1½ Tbsp. cornstarch
Pinch salt
3 Tbsp. butter
Pastry for 2-crust pie

1. In a saucepan bring apricots and water to a boil. Cook for 10 minutes. Add sugar and cook another 5 minutes. Drain, reserving 1 cup of juice. Set apricots aside.
2. Pour 1 cup reserved apricot juice into saucepan and add cornstarch. Add salt and cook until mixture thickens, stirring frequently.
3. Arrange drained apricots in unbaked pie shell. Pour in thickened apricot juice. Dot with butter.
4. Cover with top crust. Slit top and flute edges.
5. Bake at 425° for 30 minutes.

Cranberry Pie

Elizabeth Haderer
East Quogue, NY
Grandmother's Fan

Makes 1 9" pie

2 cups sliced cranberries
1 cup seedless raisins
2 Tbsp. flour
1 cup sugar
⅛ tsp. salt
½ cup water
Pastry for 2-crust pie

1. Combine cranberries and raisins.
2. Combine flour, sugar and salt. Stir into cranberry and raisin mixture. Add water and mix well. Spoon into unbaked pie shell. Cover with top crust.
3. Bake at 425° for 10 minutes. Reduce oven temperature to 350° and bake another 25 minutes or until done.

Fresh Strawberry Pie

Julie Lynch Arnsberger
Gaithersburg, MD
Trip Around the World
Cindy Cooksey
Irvine, CA
Albino Squid Races

Makes 1 9" pie

6-oz. pkg. strawberry
  gelatin
1 cup sugar
1 Tbsp. cornstarch
2 cups boiling water
1 quart fresh strawberries
1 cup whipped topping
1 9" baked pie shell

1. Combine gelatin, sugar and cornstarch in saucepan. Gradually add boiling water and stir to dissolve. Bring to a boil. Remove from heat and cool at least 5 minutes.

2. Fold strawberries into gelatin mixture, reserving 5-6 berries for garnish. Pour into baked pie shell.

3. Refrigerate at least 4 hours to chill. Immediately before serving, top with whipped topping and garnish with whole strawberries.

> About a year ago my five-year-old twin grandsons wandered into my studio to examine the Baltimore Album squares I had hanging on my felt wall. One smartly commented, "That looks like a nice quilt you're making there, Gram." The other studied the wall a long time and said, "Gram, it needs more hearts!" So for him I have added several more squares with hearts in them.
>
> —Susan Orleman, Pittsburgh, PA

Creamy Cherry Pie

Brenda Stanfield
Costa Mesa, CA
Jacob's Fan

Makes 1 9" pie

16-oz. can cherry pie filling
½ tsp. almond extract
8-oz. pkg. cream cheese,
  softened
1 cup powdered sugar
1 cup heavy whipping
  cream
1 9" baked graham cracker
  crust

1. Combine pie filling and almond extract and set aside.

2. Cream together cream cheese and powdered sugar.

3. Whip cream. Fold into cream cheese mixture. Spoon into graham cracker crust. Spread cherry pie filling over all.

4. Chill and serve.

Frozen Summer Pie

Pat Higgins
Norman, OK
Sugar Loaf

Makes 1 9" pie

6-oz. can frozen orange
  juice concentrate
1 pint vanilla ice cream,
  softened
3½ cups whipped topping
6-oz. graham cracker
  crumb crust

1. In large bowl beat orange juice concentrate for 30 seconds. Blend in ice cream. Fold in whipped topping. If necessary, freeze until mixture will mound.

2. Spoon into prepared graham cracker crust. Freeze until firm, at least 4 hours.

3. Let stand at room temperature for 10 minutes before serving.

Lemon Meringue Pie

Blanche Cahill
Willow Grove, PA
Variegated Star

Makes 1 9" pie

Filling:
1½ cups sugar
1½ cups water
¼ tsp. salt
½ cup cornstarch
⅓ cup water
4 egg yolks, slightly beaten
½ cup lemon juice
3 Tbsp. butter
1 tsp. grated lemon rind
1 9" baked pie shell

Meringue:
4 egg whites
¼ tsp. salt
½ cup sugar

1. Combine sugar, 1½ cups water and salt in a saucepan. Heat to boiling.

2. Mix cornstarch with ⅓ cup water to make smooth paste. Gradually pour into boiling sugar mixture, stirring constantly. Cook until thickened and clear. Remove from heat.

3. Combine egg yolks and lemon juice. Stir into thickened mixture. Return to heat and cook, stirring constantly until mixture comes to a boil. Stir in butter and lemon rind. Remove from heat, cover and cool to lukewarm.

4. To prepare meringue add salt to egg whites and beat until fluffy. Gradually add sugar, beating until glossy peaks form. Stir 2 rounded Tbsp. meringue into lemon filling.

5. Pour lemon filling into baked pie shell. Spoon remaining meringue over top, swirling into peaks.

6. Bake at 325° for about 15-20 minutes or until meringue is lightly browned. Cool 1 hour before serving.

Raspberry Parfait Pie

Susan L. Schwarz
North Bethesda, MD
Paragon's Country Garden

Makes 1 9" pie

10-oz. pkg. frozen raspberries
3-oz. pkg. raspberry gelatin
1 pint vanilla ice cream
1 cup heavy cream
1 9" graham cracker pie shell

1. Thaw and drain juice from raspberries. Add hot water to make 1½ cups liquid. Set raspberries aside.

2. Dissolve gelatin in 1½ cups hot raspberry liquid. Stir well.

3. While still hot, add ice cream, stirring until ice cream melts.

4. Refrigerate until partially set. Fold in raspberries. Pour filling into pie shell. Refrigerate to chill thoroughly.

5. Immediately before serving, whip cream.

6. Top raspberry filling with whipped cream and serve.

Miss Jennie's Pumpkin Pie

Barbara G. Mann
Beatrice, NE
Double Irish Chain

Makes 1 8" pie

1 cup sugar
1 tsp. cinnamon
½ tsp. ginger
½ tsp. nutmeg
½ tsp. salt
2 Tbsp. flour
1 cup pumpkin
1 cup evaporated milk
2 eggs, well beaten
1 Tbsp. margarine, melted
1 8" unbaked pie shell

1. Combine sugar, spices and flour. Add all other ingredients and beat until smooth. Pour into unbaked pie shell.

2. Bake at 400° for 15 minutes. Reduce oven temperature to 350° and bake another 45 minutes or until knife blade comes out clean when inserted in center of pie.

Spicy Pumpkin Pie

Vicky Jo Bogart
Fargo, ND
Islamic Pinwheel

Makes 1 9" pie

2 eggs, slightly beaten
16-oz. can pumpkin
½ cup real maple syrup
½ tsp. salt
1-1½ tsp. cinnamon
¾ tsp. nutmeg
½ tsp. ginger
¼-½ tsp. ground cloves
1 tsp. pure vanilla
1 cup soy milk
1 9" unbaked pie shell

1. In a large bowl combine all ingredients in the order listed except pie shell. Mix well and pour into unbaked pie shell.
2. Bake at 425° for 15 minutes. Reduce oven temperature to 350° and bake another 40-50 minutes or until knife inserted in center comes out clean.

Note: This recipe was created to accommodate a low sugar, dairy-free diet.

Zucchini Pie

Mary Helen Wade
Sterling, IL
Family Star

Makes 1 9" pie

4 cups grated zucchini
¾ cup white sugar
2 Tbsp. lemon juice
1 tsp. cinnamon
1 cup flour
½ cup brown sugar
8 Tbsp. butter *or* margarine
1 9" unbaked pie shell

1. Combine zucchini, white sugar, lemon juice and cinnamon. Spoon into unbaked pie shell.
2. Combine flour, brown sugar and butter and mix until creamy. (Add more butter if needed.) Spread creamed mixture over zucchini mixture.
3. Bake at 400° for 1 hour.

Sweet Potato Pie

Mrs. Clarence E. Mitchell
Frederick, MD
Little Dutch Girl

Makes 3 9" pies

8 large sweet potatoes
1½ cups sugar
3 cups milk
2 tsp. nutmeg
1½ tsp. lemon extract
6 eggs
12 Tbsp. butter
3 9" unbaked pie shells

1. Boil sweet potatoes in jackets until tender. Peel and mash.
2. Add all remaining ingredients and mix well. Pour into unbaked pie shells.
3. Bake at 450° for 15 minutes. Reduce oven temperature to 350° and bake another 45 minutes.

German Sweet Chocolate Pie

Elaine Patton
West Middletown, PA
Dresden Plate

Makes 1 9" pie

4-oz. pkg. German sweet chocolate
¼ cup butter
12-oz. can evaporated milk
1¼ cups sugar
3 Tbsp. cornstarch
⅛ tsp. salt
2 eggs
1 tsp. vanilla
⅓ cup coconut
½ cup chopped pecans
1 9" unbaked pie shell

1. In a saucepan melt chocolate with butter over low heat, stirring until blended. Remove from heat

My family—six sons and four daughters—made a wall hanging-sized quilt for my parents 50th wedding anniversary. The quilting time spent with my one aunt and sisters brought up many fond memories of our childhood.

—*Rachel Pellman, Lancaster, PA*

and gradually blend in milk.

2. Combine sugar, corn-starch and salt in a bowl. Beat in eggs and vanilla. Gradually blend in choco-late mixture.

3. Pour filling into un-baked pie shell. Sprinkle with coconut and pecans.

4. Bake at 375° for 45 minutes or until browned and puffed.

Fudge Pie

Violette Denney
Carrollton, GA
1991 Sampler

Makes 1 9" pie

8 Tbsp. margarine
2 squares unsweetened
   chocolate
½ cup flour
1 cup sugar
Dash salt
3 eggs, beaten
1 cup chopped nuts
   (optional)

1. In double boiler melt together margarine and chocolate.

2. In a bowl combine flour, sugar, salt and eggs. Mix well. Add chocolate mixture and mix well. If de-sired, fold in nuts.

3. Pour into greased 9-inch pie plate.

4. Bake at 350° for 25-30 minutes.

Chocolate Prune Pie

Lois Landis
Sterling, IL
Dotted Swiss Nine Patch

Makes 1 9" pie

24 large marshmallows
½ cup milk
1 cup cooked prunes,
   chopped
¾ cup whipping cream
2 ozs. semi-sweet
   chocolate, shaved
1 9" baked pie shell

1. In a saucepan heat milk and marshmallows un-til melted. Cool and fold in chopped prunes.

2. Whip cream into soft peaks. Reserve ½ cup

whipped cream and 2 Tbsp. chocolate shavings. Fold re-maining whipped cream and chocolate into marsh-mallow mix. Pour into baked pie shell.

3. Chill in refrigerator. Top with reserved whipped cream and chocolate shav-ings and serve.

Walnut Pie

JoAnn Pelletier
Longmeadow, MA
6 Quilts in 14 days
Katie's Quilts
Millersburg, OH
Schoolhouse

Makes 1 9" pie

4 Tbsp. butter *or*
   margarine, melted
½ cup white sugar
½ cup brown sugar
¼ tsp. salt
3 eggs, beaten
½ cup evaporated milk
¼ cup light corn syrup
½ tsp. vanilla
1 cup chopped walnuts
1 9" unbaked pie shell

1. Combine butter, sug-ars and salt. Add eggs and mix well. Stir in milk, corn syrup, vanilla and walnuts. Pour into pie shell.

2. Bake at 400° for 25-30 minutes or until knife in-serted in center comes out clean.

Pecan Pie

Alana Robbins, Los Lunas, NM
Esther L. Lantz, Leola, PA
Marjorie Miller, Partridge, KS

Makes 1 9" pie

1 cup pecans
3 large eggs
¾ cup light *or* **dark corn syrup**
1 cup sugar *or* **less**
¼ cup butter *or* **margarine, melted**
1 tsp. vanilla
¼ tsp. salt
1 9" unbaked pie shell

1. Arrange pecans evenly in unbaked pie shell.
2. Combine all remaining ingredients and mix well. Pour over pecans.
3. Bake at 350° for 40-50 minutes.

Grapenut Pie

Phebe Hershberger
Goshen, IN

Makes 1 9" pie

½ cup grapenuts
½ cup warm water
3 eggs, well beaten
¾ cup sugar
1 cup dark corn syrup
Pinch salt
1 tsp. vanilla

3 Tbsp. butter, melted
1 9" unbaked pie shell

1. Combine grapenuts and warm water. Let stand until water is absorbed.
2. Combine beaten eggs with all other ingredients except pie shell. Fold in grapenuts. Spoon into pie shell.
3. Bake at 350° for 50 minutes.

Out of This World Pie

Sara M. Miller
Kalona, IA
Tulip Garden

Makes 1 9" pie

8 Tbsp. butter
1 cup sugar
3 eggs
¼ tsp. salt
½ tsp. vanilla
1 cup chopped nuts
1 cup raisins
1 9" unbaked pie shell

1. Cream together butter and sugar. Add eggs, salt and vanilla and beat well. Stir in nuts and raisins. Spoon into unbaked pie shell.
2. Bake at 350° for 40-60 minutes or until browned on top.

Raisin Crumb Pie

Minnie A. Stoltzfus
Lancaster, PA
Log Cabin

Makes 3 9" pies

1 lb. raisins
Water to cover
¾ cup sugar
1 Tbsp. flour *or* **cornstarch**
2 cups flour
1 cup sugar
½ cup shortening
2 tsp. baking powder
2 eggs, beaten
1 cup milk
3 9" unbaked pie shells

1. In a saucepan combine raisins, water to cover and ¾ cup sugar. Bring to a boil and boil slowly for 20 minutes. Add 1 Tbsp. flour to thicken. Stir well and set aside.
2. Mix together 2 cups flour, 1 cup sugar, shortening and baking powder until crumbly. Reserve ¾ cup crumbs.
3. To remaining crumbs add eggs and milk and mix well.
4. Divide raisin mixture evenly in pie shells. Spoon batter evenly over raisins. Top with reserved crumbs.
5. Bake at 350° for 40-45 minutes or until knife inserted in center comes out clean.

Toasted Coconut Cream Pie

Frances Musser
Newmanstown, PA
Sweet Country

Makes 1 10" pie

3-oz. pkg. instant vanilla pudding
8-oz. pkg. cream cheese, softened
½ cup powdered sugar
½ tsp. coconut flavoring
8-oz. container whipped topping
⅔ cup toasted coconut
1 10" baked pie shell

1. Prepare pudding according to package directions.
2. Combine cream cheese and powdered sugar and beat until smooth. Add flavoring, whipped topping and pudding and mix well.

Pour into baked pie shell.
3. To prepare toasted coconut spread in baking pan. Place under broiler for about 2 minutes. Watch carefully as this burns easily. Chill toasted coconut.
4. Spread coconut over pudding mixture and serve.

Coconut Custard Blender Pie

Mary Esther Yoder
Partridge, KS
Elsie Schlabach
Millersburg, OH
Sara Wolf, Washington, PA

Makes 1 10" pie

4 eggs
2 cups milk
½ cup flour
1 tsp. vanilla

About twenty years ago my grandmother pieced a scrap quilt using fabric from the clothes I had worn as a child. My mother told me about two sisters in rural Jackson County, Tennessee who did quilting for people. When they had quilted my top, I drove out to their home to pick it up. I had not previously negotiated a price (which was foolish). They began apologizing, saying they would have to charge me extra for the binding. They asked for $6.00. I gasped and offered to pay them more as I felt it was worth at least $75.00. Refusing to take the extra money, they explained to me that quilting was something they loved, not something they did to make money. Today these two industrious women are in their 90s and still quilting because they love it.

—*Jane L. Murphy, Malvern, PA*

1 cup sugar
6 Tbsp. butter
1 cup coconut

1. Blend all ingredients together on high speed in blender for 10 seconds.
2. Pour into greased and floured 10-inch pie pan.
3. Bake at 350° for 1 hour.

Custard Pie

Amanda Schlabach
Millersburg, OH
Lancaster Rose

Makes 1 9" pie

3 eggs
½ cup white sugar
⅛ tsp. salt
2 cups scalded milk
2 tsp. vanilla
1 Tbsp. butter, melted
⅛ tsp. nutmeg
1 9" unbaked pie shell

1. Beat eggs until light and foamy. Add sugar and salt and blend well. Add the scalded milk and vanilla.
2. Brush unbaked pie shell with melted butter. Pour custard into shell. Sprinkle lightly with nutmeg.
3. Bake at 450° for 10 minutes. Reduce oven temperature to 325° and bake another 25-30 minutes.

Caramel Whipped Cream Pie

Margaret Jarrett
Anderson, IN
Country Love

Makes 1 9" pie

1 cup light brown sugar
7 Tbsp. flour
1 Tbsp. cornstarch
¼ tsp. salt
2 eggs, beaten
2 cups milk
2 Tbsp. butter
1 tsp. vanilla
2 pints whipping cream
1 Heath bar, crushed
1 9" baked pie shell

1. Combine sugar, flour, cornstarch and salt in a saucepan.
2. In a bowl combine beaten eggs and milk. Add to dry ingredients and cook until thickened, stirring constantly.
3. Remove from heat and add butter and vanilla, beating until smooth. Let cool.
4. Beat whipping cream until peaks form. Stir ⅔ of whipped cream into cooled mixture. Pour into baked pie shell. Spread remaining cream over pie. Sprinkle crushed heath bar over top and refrigerate. (This pie should be prepared a day in advance.)

Brown Sugar Pie

Joyce Aigner
Bridgewater, VA
Scrap Quilt

Makes 2 9" pies

3 eggs, beaten
3 cups brown sugar
8 Tbsp. butter *or* margarine
1 cup milk
3 Tbsp. flour
2 9" unbaked pie shells

1. Mix eggs with brown sugar, butter and milk. Add flour and mix well. Pour into 2 unbaked pie shells.
2. Bake at 350° for approximately 1 hour or until knife inserted in center comes out clean.

Shoofly Pie

Naomi Lapp
New Holland, PA
Wedding Ring

Makes 1 9" pie

1 cup flour
⅔ cup brown sugar
1 Tbsp. shortening
1 egg
¾ cup molasses
¾ cup boiling water
1 tsp. baking soda

1. Mix together flour, brown sugar and shortening until crumbly. Reserve ½ cup crumbs. Arrange remaining crumbs across bottom of greased 9-inch pie pan.
2. In a bowl combine egg, molasses, boiling water and baking soda. Mix well and pour into pie pan. Cover with remaining crumbs.
3. Bake at 350° for 30 minutes.

Sour Cream Pie

Marjorie L. Benson
Yates City, IL
Ohio Star

Makes 1 9" pie

Pie:
1½ cups thick sour cream
1 cup powdered sugar
2 Tbsp. flour
2 egg yolks, well beaten
1 tsp. vanilla
½ cup seeded raisins
½ cup chopped nuts
1 9" baked pie shell

Meringue:
1 Tbsp. cornstarch
2 Tbsp. cold water
½ cup boiling water
3 egg whites
6 Tbsp. white sugar
Dash salt
1 tsp. vanilla

1. To prepare pie heat sour cream slowly. Add powdered sugar and continue heating slowly, stirring frequently.

2. Remove ½ cup creamed mixture and blend in flour. Pour into creamed mixture and heat, stirring frequently. Add egg yolks and bring to a boil. Remove from heat and stir in vanilla, raisins and nuts. Cool.

3. Pour into 9-inch pie shell.

4. To prepare meringue blend cornstarch and cold water in a saucepan. Add boiling water and cook, stirring until thickened and clear. Let stand until completely cooled.

5. Using electric mixer beat egg whites until foamy. Gradually add sugar and beat until stiff, but not dry. Add salt and vanilla and continue beating on low speed. Gradually add cornstarch mixture and beat on high speed until well mixed.

6. Spread meringue over pie filling.

7. Bake at 350° for several minutes until meringue is golden brown.

❖

Cheesecake Pie

**Joy Moir
Holtsville, NY
*Winter Cactus***

Makes 1 9" pie

**8-oz. pkg. cream cheese
½ cup sugar
2 eggs
1 cup sour cream
½ tsp. vanilla
1 9" unbaked graham cracker crust**

1. Cream together cream cheese and sugar. Add eggs, sour cream and vanilla. Spoon into graham cracker crust.

2. Bake at 350° for 40 minutes. Chill completely before serving.

❖

Blue Ribbon Pie Crust

**Sandy Brown
Connersville, IN
*Double Wedding Ring***

Makes 5 9" pie shells

**5 cups all-purpose flour
1¼ tsp. salt
1 tsp. baking powder
2½ cups shortening
1 tsp. vinegar
1 egg**

1. Combine flour, salt and baking powder. Cut in shortening until mixture has cornmeal texture.

2. In a 1-cup measure beat together vinegar and egg. Fill to 1 cup with cold water. Pour into flour mixture and work to mix. (Dough will be soft and sticky.)

3. Divide dough into 5 parts and roll out to ⅛-inch thickness. Put into lightly floured pie pans.

4. For pies requiring baked pie shells, press a piece of aluminum foil against the pie shell in pan.

5. Bake at 425° for 6 minutes. Remove aluminum foil and bake another 12 minutes. Cool completely.

Variation:

After dividing dough into 5 parts, wrap each ball separately in wax paper or plastic wrap and chill until ready to use. This recipe keeps 3-4 days in refrigerator and also freezes well. When ready to use, simply thaw and roll out, continuing with step 3.

**Jean H. Robinson
Cinnaminson, NJ
*Little School Girl***

Pie Crust

Joyce McFarland
Woodbridge, VA
Jackson Star

Makes 3 pastry shells

1 egg
1 tsp. vinegar
5 Tbsp. ice water
3 cups flour, sifted
1 tsp. salt
1⅓ cups shortening

1. Combine egg, vinegar and ice water and mix thoroughly.
2. Combine flour and salt. Cut in shortening until mixture resembles small peas. Add egg mixture and mix well to form a ball.
3. Divide dough into 3 parts. Roll out each ball onto well floured surface.
4. Place in pie pan and follow directions for making pie.

Pie Crust Mix

Florence H. Donavan
Lodi, CA
Mormor (Swedish for "Grandmother")

5 lbs. *or* 20 cups flour
2 Tbsp. salt
1½ lbs. lard
2 cups shortening

1. Mix all ingredients together until crumbly.
2. Store in tightly-covered container until needed. This should be refrigerated.
3. When ready to bake pies, combine 3 cups mix with ⅓ cup milk. This ratio will make enough dough for two 9-inch crusts.

Cakes

❖

Annabelle's Chocolate Sticky Cake

Karen Unternahrer
Shipshewana, IN
Early American Sampler

Makes 20-24 servings

Cake:
1 cup flour
2 tsp. baking powder
¼ tsp. salt
¾ cup sugar
2 Tbsp. cocoa
½ cup milk
2 Tbsp. margarine
1 tsp. vanilla
½ cup chopped nuts

Topping:
1 cup brown sugar
¼ cup cocoa
1¾ cups hot water

1. Combine all cake ingredients and spread into greased 9" x 13" baking pan.
2. Combine brown sugar and cocoa and sprinkle over cake batter. Pour hot water over batter.
3. Bake at 350° for 45 minutes. Serve immediately with vanilla ice cream.

❖

Moo's Chocolate Cake

Myrtle Mansfield
Alfred, ME
Log Cabin

Makes 8-10 servings

2 squares chocolate *or*
    3 Tbsp. cocoa
5 Tbsp. boiling water
8 Tbsp. butter
1½ cups sugar
3 eggs, separated
2 cups flour
½ cup milk
1 heaping tsp. baking
    powder
1 tsp. vanilla
1 tsp. cinnamon

1. If using chocolate squares, shred and dissolve in boiling water. If using cocoa, dissolve in boiling water.
2. Cream together butter and sugar. Add beaten egg yolks and chocolate. Add flour, alternating with milk. Mix well.
3. Beat egg whites until stiff. Fold into batter. Add baking powder, vanilla and cinnamon and mix lightly. Spoon into greased 9-inch square baking pan.
4. Bake at 350° for 40-60 minutes.
5. Frost with favorite fudge frosting.

One year our quilt guild of 130 members worked very hard on our raffle quilt, a beautiful Sampler of dusty blue, rose and light green calicoes. We drew the winning number at our annual show and anxiously awaited the appearance of the new owners. When they arrived carrying a large basket with two German Shepherd puppies, our hearts sank to the tiled floor. We did everything we could to impress them with how much this quilt meant to us. After promising to keep the bedroom door closed, they left with the quilt. We were surprised to receive several photos over the next few years showing the quilt in good condition.

—*Connee Sager, Tucson, AZ*

Surprise Chocolate Cake

Betty Richards
Rapid City, SD
Goose in the Pond

Makes 20-24 servings

Cake:
16 Tbsp. margarine, softened
4 Tbsp. cocoa
2 cups sugar
4 eggs
1½ cups flour
¼ tsp. salt
1 tsp. baking powder
1½ tsp. vanilla
1½ cups pecans (optional)
1 bag miniature marshmallows

Frosting:
4 Tbsp. margarine
½ cup evaporated milk
Dash salt
1-lb. box powdered sugar
½ cup cocoa
1 tsp. vanilla

1. To prepare cake combine margarine, cocoa, sugar, eggs (one at a time), flour, salt, baking powder, vanilla and pecans in mixing bowl. Spread mixture into greased 9" x 13" baking pan.
2. Bake at 350° for 30-40 minutes. Remove from oven and immediately pour marshmallows evenly over top.
3. To prepare frosting combine margarine, milk and salt in a saucepan and bring to a boil. Boil slowly for 1 minute.
4. Sift powdered sugar and stir in cocoa. Add to hot milk mixture. Add vanilla and beat until smooth. (If frosting seems too thick, add more milk.) While still hot, pour evenly over marshmallows. Cool and serve.

Stella's Chocolate Cake

Linda Roberta Pond
Los Alamos, NM
Not the Same Old Cat

Makes 20-24 servings

Cake:
2 cups flour
2 cups sugar
6 heaping Tbsp. cocoa
2 tsp. baking soda
Pinch salt
1 cup cooking oil
2 eggs
1 cup buttermilk
2 tsp. vanilla
1 cup boiling water

Frosting:
2 cups sugar
16 Tbsp. butter
6 tsp. cocoa
2 Tbsp. light corn syrup
½ cup cream
2 tsp. vanilla

1. To prepare cake sift dry ingredients together. Add all remaining ingredients and beat 1 minute. Spoon into greased and floured 9" x 13" baking pan.
2. Bake at 375° for 25 minutes or until done.
3. To prepare frosting combine all ingredients in large saucepan. Bring to a boil, stirring constantly. Boil 2½-3 minutes. Remove from heat and beat until frosting loses its sheen.
4. Pour over cake immediately.

Chocolate Deluxe Zucchini Cake

Arlene C. Kelly
Clarence, NY
Feathered Star Sampler
Bonnie Grove
York, PA

Makes 16-20 servings

3 squares unsweetened
  chocolate
3 cups flour
1½ tsp. baking soda
1½ tsp. baking powder
1 tsp. salt
¼ tsp. cinnamon
4 eggs
3 cups sugar
1½ cups cooking oil
1½ tsp. vanilla
½ tsp. almond extract
3 cups grated zucchini
½ cup sour cream
½ cup chopped nuts
  (optional)

1. Melt chocolate in microwave or double boiler. Cool.

2. Sift together flour, baking soda, baking powder, salt and cinnamon and set aside.

3. Beat eggs in large bowl until frothy. Gradually beat in sugar. Add oil, chocolate, vanilla and almond extract. Fold in dry ingredients.

4. Squeeze moisture from zucchini. Add zucchini to batter. Add sour cream and mix well. Pour into greased 10-inch tube pan.

5. Bake at 350° for 1-1¼ hours. (Cake will appear moist.) Let stand 20 minutes. Remove from pan and cool on rack. If desired, frost before serving.

Chocolate Zucchini Cake

Evi Wahl
Middletown, PA
Tri-Color Blue Baby Blocks

Makes 16-20 servings

Cake:
3 eggs
1½ cups sugar
1 tsp. vanilla
½ cup cooking oil
2 cups unsifted flour
⅓ cup cocoa
1 tsp. baking powder
1 tsp. baking soda
1 tsp. cinnamon
½ tsp. salt
¾ cup buttermilk
2 cups coarsely chopped
  zucchini

Glaze:
3 Tbsp. sugar
2 Tbsp. water
½ cup mint chips
1 Tbsp. marshmallow
  cream
½ tsp. hot water

1. In a large mixing bowl beat eggs on high until light and fluffy. Gradually beat in sugar and vanilla until thick and light in color. Gradually pour in oil and beat well.

2. In a separate bowl combine flour, cocoa, baking powder, baking soda, cinnamon and salt. Add to creamed batter alternately with buttermilk, beginning and ending with flour. Fold in zucchini. Pour into greased and floured 10-inch tube pan.

3. Bake at 350° for 50-55 minutes.

4. To prepare glaze combine sugar and 2 Tbsp. water in a saucepan and bring to a boil. Remove from heat and stir in mint chips until they have melted. Stir in marshmallow cream, adding hot water if needed.

5. Pour glaze over warm cake and serve.

Chocolate Sauerkraut Cake

Evelyn M. Becker
Paradise, PA
Double Irish Chain

Makes 20-24 servings

½ cup shortening
1¼ cups sugar
2 eggs
⅛ tsp. salt
1 tsp. vanilla
¼ cup cocoa
2 cups flour
1 tsp. baking powder
1 tsp. baking soda
1 cup water
8 ozs. sauerkraut

1. Cream shortening. Add sugar and eggs and beat well. Add salt and vanilla and beat until blended.
2. Sift together cocoa, flour, baking powder and baking soda. Add dry ingredients to batter, alternating with water. Blend well.
3. Wash and drain sauerkraut. Chop into fine pieces. Add sauerkraut to batter and mix well. Pour batter into a greased and floured 9" x 13" baking pan.
4. Bake at 350° for 35-45 minutes or until done.

Mary's Glossy Chocolate Icing

Gerry Fix
Hagerstown, MD

Makes 1 cup icing

½ cup white sugar
2 Tbsp. cornstarch
1 oz. unsweetened chocolate
Dash salt
½ cup boiling water
1½ Tbsp. margarine *or* butter
½ tsp. vanilla

1. Mix sugar and cornstarch together in a saucepan. Add chocolate, salt and boiling water. Cook on medium heat, stirring constantly until it thickens.
2. Remove from heat and add margarine and vanilla. Mix well. Spread on favorite chocolate cake while still hot. This is a glossy, semisweet icing.

Chocolate Mint Cake

Janet Groff
Stevens, PA
Country Love

Makes 20-24 servings

Cake:
2 cups flour
2 cups sugar
1 tsp. baking powder
2 tsp. baking soda
¼ tsp. salt
½ cup cocoa
½ cup cooking oil
1 cup strong liquid coffee
1 cup milk
1 tsp. vanilla
2 eggs

Mint Frosting:
2 cups powdered sugar
½ cup soft butter *or* margarine
3 Tbsp. creme de menthe syrup

Glaze:
6-oz. pkg. chocolate chips
6 Tbsp. butter *or* margarine

1. To prepare cake batter sift all dry ingredients together. Add remaining in-

I have a quilting sister with whom I share recipes, quilting patterns and day-to-day experiences. Though she lives in Saudi Arabia, we have developed an ongoing, amazing and wondrous kinship where we occasionally find ourselves unintentionally working on the same quilting pattern at the same time.

—*Lorraine Moore Lear, Del City, OK*

gredients and beat 2 minutes. Pour into a 9" x 13" baking pan.

2. Bake at 350° for 40-45 minutes or until wooden pick inserted in center comes out clean. Cool on wire rack.

3. To prepare mint frosting beat all ingredients until light and fluffy. Spread frosting on cooled cake.

4. To prepare glaze melt chocolate chips and butter together. Cool slightly and spread over mint frosting layer.

5. Chill in refrigerator 10-15 minutes. Remove and store at room temperature.

Variation:
Substitute 1 cup buttermilk for the milk and omit the mint frosting layer.
Lucille Brubacker
Barnett, MO
Country Love

Heavenly Hash Cake

Judy Miller
Hutchinson, KS
Star of the East

Makes 20-24 servings

Cake:
16 Tbsp. margarine
2 cups sugar *or* less
4 eggs
1½ cups flour

4 Tbsp. cocoa
1 cup miniature marshmallows

Frosting:
8 Tbsp. margarine
1-lb. box powdered sugar
4 Tbsp. cocoa
8 Tbsp. evaporated milk
½ cup coconut
½ cup chopped pecans *or* walnuts

1. To prepare cake cream together margarine and sugar. Add eggs, one at a time. Stir in flour and cocoa and mix well. Spoon batter into greased 9" x 13" baking pan.

2. Bake at 350° for 30 minutes.

3. To prepare frosting combine all ingredients except coconut and pecans and beat well. Fold in coconut and pecans.

4. When finished, remove cake from oven and immediately sprinkle top with miniature marshmallows. Spread frosting over cake while still hot. Cool and serve.

Variation:
Add 1 tsp. vanilla and 1 cup chopped pecans to this cake batter. Delete coconut from the frosting. I call this Mississippi Mud Cake.
Jackie Clegg
Rapid City, SD
My Little Garden

Wacky Cake

Denise S. Rominger
Cranbury, NJ
Crazy Patch

Makes 20-24 servings

3 cups flour
2 cups sugar
⅔ cup cocoa
2 tsp. baking soda
1 tsp. salt
¾ cup cooking oil
2 tsp. vinegar
1 tsp. vanilla
2 cups cold water
Powdered sugar

1. Combine all ingredients except powdered sugar in large mixing bowl and beat well (3 minutes at high speed with mixer). Pour batter into 2 greased layer cake pans.

2. Bake at 375° for 30 minutes.

3. When cooled, dust lightly with powdered sugar and serve.

Variation:
Add 2 Tbsp. instant coffee to ingredients. Substitute favorite chocolate frosting for powdered sugar.
Evelyn Becker
Paradise, PA
Double Irish Chain

Upside Down German Chocolate Cake

Julie McKenzie
Punxsutawney, PA
Teardrops and Tantrums

Makes 20-24 servings

1½ cups coconut
1½ cups pecans
1 box German chocolate
   cake mix
8-oz. pkg. cream cheese,
   softened
8 Tbsp. margarine, melted
3½ cups powdered sugar

1. Sprinkle coconut and pecans into bottom of greased and floured 9" x 13" baking pan.
2. Prepare cake mix according to directions. Pour batter over coconut and pecans.
3. Combine cream cheese, margarine and powdered sugar and mix until smooth. Drop by large spoonsful onto cake batter.
4. Bake at 350° for 45-50 minutes.

Ho Ho Cake

Donna Hardy
Washington, DC
Kaleido Crosses

Makes 20-24 servings

1 box chocolate cake mix
5 Tbsp. flour
1¼ cups milk
1 cup white sugar
½ cup shortening
16 Tbsp. margarine
1 egg
1 tsp. vanilla
3 Tbsp. cocoa
2 Tbsp. hot water
1½ cups powdered sugar

1. Prepare cake mix according to directions. Spoon into greased 9" x 13" baking pan and bake according to directions.
2. In a saucepan combine flour and milk. Cook, stirring constantly until thickened. Let cool.
3. Cream together white sugar, shortening and 8 Tbsp. margarine. Add flour and milk mixture and beat until mixture looks like whipped cream. Spread over cake and refrigerate overnight.
4. Melt remaining 8 Tbsp. margarine and let cool. Combine margarine, egg, vanilla, cocoa, water and powdered sugar and mix well. Pour over cooled cake with topping and refrigerate. Serve.

Mrs. Sharak's Chocolate Cake

M. Jeanne Osborne
Sanford, ME
Gwen's Tulips

Makes 20-24 servings

4 squares chocolate
6 Tbsp. butter, softened
2 cups sugar
2 eggs, lightly beaten
2 cups flour
2 tsp. baking soda
2 cups water
4 tsp. vanilla

1. Melt chocolate in double boiler.
2. Cream together butter and sugar. Add eggs and mix well. Blend in melted chocolate.
3. Sift together flour and baking soda. Add to batter, alternating with water. Beat well and add vanilla. Pour batter into greased 9"x 13" baking pan.
4. Bake at 350° for 45-50 minutes.

Scotch Cake

Rosalie W. Keegan
Enfield, CT
Amish Diamond
Lynne Fritz
Bel Air, MD
Farmer's Window

Makes 20-24 servings

Cake:
2 cups sugar
2 cups flour
4 Tbsp. cocoa
16 Tbsp. margarine
1 cup water
2 eggs, lightly beaten
1/2 cup buttermilk
1 tsp. baking soda
1 tsp. cinnamon
1 tsp. vanilla

Frosting:
8 Tbsp. margarine
4 Tbsp. cocoa
6 Tbsp. milk
2 cups powdered sugar
1 tsp. vanilla
1 cup chopped nuts
    (optional)

1. To prepare cake sift together sugar and flour and set aside.
2. In a saucepan bring cocoa, margarine and water to a boil. Pour over sugar and flour and mix thoroughly. Add eggs, buttermilk, baking soda, cinnamon and vanilla and mix. Pour onto greased and floured 11" x 17" baking sheet.
3. Bake at 350° for 20-25

minutes. Do not overbake.
4. To prepare frosting bring margarine, cocoa and milk to a boil. Stir in powdered sugar, vanilla and nuts. Pour frosting over hot cake. (The frosting partially sinks into this very rich, very chocolate cake.)

Grandma's Fudge Cake

Joan Ranck
Christiana, PA
Bow Tie Doll Crib Quilt

Makes 20-24 servings

2 1/4 cups white sugar
3/4 cup butter
1 1/2 tsp. vanilla
3 eggs
3 squares unsweetened
    chocolate, melted
3 cups flour
1 1/2 tsp. baking soda
1 1/2 tsp. baking powder
3/4 tsp. salt
1 1/2 cups ice water

1. To prepare cake cream together sugar, butter and vanilla. Add eggs and beat well. Blend in melted chocolate.
2. Combine all dry ingredients and add to batter, alternating with ice water. Pour onto greased 11" x 17" baking sheet.
3. Bake at 350° for 35 minutes or longer.

4. Sprinkle with powdered sugar or spread with favorite chocolate frosting. Serve.

Hot Fudge Pudding Cake

Naomi Stoltzfus
Leola, PA
Four Sisters

Makes 8-10 servings

1 cup flour
3/4 cup white sugar
1/4 tsp. salt
2 tsp. baking powder
2 Tbsp. cocoa
1/2 cup milk
2 Tbsp. shortening, melted
1/2 cup chopped nuts
    (optional)
1 cup brown sugar
1/4 cup cocoa
1 3/4 cups hot water

1. Measure flour, white sugar, salt, baking powder and 2 Tbsp. cocoa into a bowl. Blend in milk and shortening. Add nuts. Pour into ungreased 9-inch square cake pan.
2. Combine brown sugar and 1/4 cup cocoa. Spread evenly over batter. Pour hot water directly over batter.
3. Bake at 350° for 40-45 minutes. Serve either hot or cold with milk or ice cream.

Rhonda-lee's VCR Cake

Rhonda-lee Schmidt
Scranton, PA
Donnie's Christmas Sampler

Makes 20-24 servings

Cake:
2¼ cups all-purpose flour
½ cup unsweetened cocoa
1½ tsp. baking soda
1 tsp. salt
½ cup shortening
1 cup sugar
1 tsp. vanilla
3 eggs, separated
1⅓ cups cold water
¾ cup sugar
½-1 cup raspberry jam

Frosting:
1 cup shortening
1½ tsp. vanilla
4½ cups powdered sugar, sifted
3-4 Tbsp. milk
½ cup coconut

1. To prepare cake combine flour, cocoa, baking soda and salt and set aside.
2. In a large bowl beat shortening until creamy. Add 1 cup sugar and vanilla and beat until fluffy. Add egg yolks, one at a time, and beat for about 1 minute after each addition.
3. Add dry ingredients to batter, alternating with water and beating on low speed until just combined.
4. In a separate bowl beat egg whites until soft peaks form. Gradually add ¾ cup sugar, beating until stiff peaks form. Fold into cake batter and combine well. Pour into 2 greased and floured round layer pans.
5. Bake at 350° for 30-35 minutes or until cake tests done. Cool on wire rack.
6. To prepare frosting beat shortening and vanilla until creamy. Gradually add sugar, alternating with milk, and beat until creamy.
7. When cake has cooled, spread raspberry jam over bottom layer. Place second layer on top and frost. Top with shredded coconut.

Light Fluffy Frosting

Sharon Honegger
Hawthorne, NY
Miniature Tulip Applique Quilt

Makes 2 cups frosting

1 cup milk
2-3 squares unsweetened chocolate
¼ cup flour
⅓ cup milk
16 Tbsp. butter
1 cup sugar
1 tsp. vanilla

1. Put 1 cup milk and chocolate squares in top of double boiler over boiling water.
2. In small bowl combine flour and ⅓ cup milk and mix until smooth.
3. When milk in double boiler is hot, add flour and milk mixture and cook until smooth and thick, stirring constantly. Remove mixture to a bowl. Cover contents with plastic wrap to prevent skin from forming and refrigerate.
4. Cream butter. Add sugar and vanilla and beat until smooth.
5. When refrigerated chocolate mixture has cooled, add creamed mixture and mix well. Frost cake of choice and serve.

Fudgy Icing

Marsha Sands
Ocean City, MD
Window of Miracles

Makes enough for 1 cake

8 Tbsp. butter
3 Tbsp. cocoa
4-5 Tbsp. milk
2 cups powdered sugar
1 tsp. vanilla

1. Combine all ingredients and mix well.
2. Frost favorite chocolate cake and serve.

Jacquelyn Kreitzer's Peanut Butter Cake

Jacquelyn Kreitzer
Mechanicsburg, PA
Lap Sampler

Makes 20-24 servings

Cake:
¾ cup butter, softened
¾ cup creamy peanut butter
2 cups brown sugar, packed
3 eggs
2 cups flour
1 Tbsp. baking powder
½ tsp. salt
1 cup milk
1 tsp. vanilla
½ cup chopped peanuts

Rich Chocolate Frosting:
1 cup semi-sweet chocolate morsels
½ cup half-and-half
1 cup butter *or* margarine
2½ cups sifted, powdered sugar

1. Cream together butter and peanut butter. Gradually add sugar, beating well at medium speed with mixer. Add eggs, one at a time, beating well after each addition.
2. Combine flour, baking powder and salt. Add to creamed mixture alternately with milk, beginning and ending with flour mixture. Mix well after each addition. Add vanilla.
3. Spoon into greased and floured 9" x 13" baking pan.
4. Bake at 350° for 45-50 minutes. Cool before frosting.
5. To prepare frosting combine chocolate, half-and-half and butter in double boiler. Heat until melted and smooth. Blend in sugar. Set pan in ice and beat at medium speed with mixer until frosting holds its shape.
6. Frost cake liberally with rich chocolate frosting and sprinkle with peanuts. Serve.

Sara Wilson's Peanut Butter Cake

Sara Wilson
Clinton, MO
Burgundy and Mauve Sampler

Makes 20 servings

Cake:
16 Tbsp. margarine
1 cup water
1 cup peanut butter
2 cups flour
2 cups sugar *or less*
1 tsp. baking soda
½ tsp. salt
½ cup milk + 1 tsp. vinegar
2 eggs
1 tsp. vanilla

Frosting:
8 Tbsp. margarine
6 Tbsp. milk
½ cup peanut butter
1 lb. powdered sugar
1 tsp. vanilla

1. To prepare cake melt margarine in saucepan. Add water and peanut butter. Bring to a boil, stirring frequently.
2. Combine flour, sugar, baking soda and salt in large mixing bowl. Pour peanut butter mixture over dry ingredients. Add milk, eggs and vanilla and mix well. Spread onto 12" x 17" baking pan.
3. Bake at 350° for 15-20 minutes.
4. To prepare frosting combine margarine, milk and peanut butter in a saucepan and bring to a boil. Add powdered sugar and vanilla and mix well. Pour frosting over hot cake. Cool and serve.

White Frosting

Deb Koelsch
Lancaster, PA
Clown

Makes about 4 cups frosting

1 cup milk
4 heaping tsp. flour
8 Tbsp. margarine
½ cup shortening
1 tsp. vanilla
1 cup white sugar

1. Cook milk and flour until pasty, stirring constantly. Cool ½ hour in refrigerator.
2. Cream together all remaining ingredients. Add milk and flour mixture and beat until fluffy.
3. Tastes great with peanut butter cake.

Peanut Butter and Jelly Cake

Deb Koelsch
Lancaster, PA
Clown

Makes 1 2-layer cake

2½ cups flour
⅔ cup white sugar
4 tsp. baking powder
½ tsp salt
1 cup brown sugar, packed

⅓ cup shortening
1 cup peanut butter
1½ cups milk
3 eggs
1 tsp. vanilla
1 cup peanut butter
½ cup strawberry jelly

1. Sift together flour, white sugar, baking powder and salt. Add brown sugar, shortening, 1 cup peanut butter and milk and beat 2 minutes. Add eggs and vanilla and beat another 2 minutes.
2. Spoon into 2 greased and floured 9-inch round layer pans.
3. Bake at 375° for 30-35 minutes. Cool.
4. Spread 1 cup peanut butter and jelly between layers. Frost with white frosting and serve.

Oatmeal Chocolate Chip Cake

Betty Caudle
Colorado Springs, CO
Kathleen Martin, Batavia, NY
Joan Lemmler
Albuquerque, NM

Makes 20-24 servings

1¾ cups boiling water
1 cup uncooked oatmeal
1 cup brown sugar, lightly packed
1 cup white sugar
8 Tbsp. margarine
2 large eggs
1¾ cups unsifted flour
1 tsp. baking soda
½ tsp. salt
1 Tbsp. cocoa
12-oz. pkg. chocolate chips
¾ cup chopped walnuts

1. Pour boiling water over oatmeal in large bowl. Let stand at room temperature for 10 minutes. Add sugars and margarine and stir until margarine has melted. Add eggs and mix well.
2. Sift together flour, baking soda, salt and cocoa. Add flour mixture to batter and mix well. Fold in ½ of

Presently I am putting together a memory quilt with fabric from the dresses and aprons worn by my mother. A woman from the "corset and housedress era," she was also a wonderful cook. As I stitch, I remember the many delightful dinners our family enjoyed together.

—*Margaret Morris, Middle Village, NY*

chocolate chips.

3. Pour batter into greased and floured 9" x 13" baking pan. Sprinkle with remaining chocolate chips and walnuts.

4. Bake at 350° for about 40 minutes.

Moist Oatmeal Cake

**Mrs. Enos C. Yoder
Haven, KS**
Plain Top Wheat Pattern
**Debbie Chisholm
Fallston, MD**
Wreath of Roses

Makes 20-24 servings

Cake:
1 cup uncooked oatmeal
8 Tbsp. butter *or* margarine
1½ cups boiling water
1 cup white sugar
1 cup brown sugar
2 eggs
1½ cups flour
1 tsp. baking soda
½ tsp. cinnamon
½ tsp. nutmeg

Topping:
6 Tbsp. butter *or* margarine, melted
⅓ cup cream *or* milk
1 cup coconut
½ cup nuts
½ cup brown sugar

1. Mix oatmeal, butter and boiling water in sauce-pan and let stand for 20 minutes. Add sugars and eggs. Beat well. Add all remaining cake ingredients. Beat well.

2. Spoon into greased and floured 9" x 13" baking pan.

3. Bake at 350° for 30 minutes.

4. To prepare topping combine all ingredients and mix well. Spread over hot cake immediately. Place under broiler 1-2 minutes until topping is brown and bubbly. Cool and serve.

Carrot Cake

**Philip S. Pipero
Brooklyn, NY**

Makes 10 servings

2 cups flour
2 tsp. baking powder
1½ tsp. baking soda
½ tsp. salt
2 tsp. ground cinnamon
2 cups sugar
1½ cups cooking oil
4 eggs
2 cups finely chopped carrots
8-oz. can crushed pineapple, drained
½ cup chopped nuts
4 ozs. flaked coconut

1. Sift together flour, baking powder, baking soda, salt and cinnamon. Add sugar, oil and eggs and mix well. Add carrots, pineapple, nuts and coconut and blend thoroughly.

2. Pour into greased and floured 9-inch tube pan.

3. Bake at 350° for 35-40 minutes. Remove from oven and cool several minutes in pan. Turn onto rack and cool thoroughly. Frost top and sides if desired.

Variation:
Omit nuts and coconut. Add 1 tsp. vanilla.
**Carolee Kidd
Albuquerque, NM**
Sunrise and Sunset

Cream Cheese Frosting

**Barbara Deuitch
Lake Ridge, VA**
Flight 159

Makes enough to frost 1 9"x 13" cake

8-oz. pkg. cream cheese
8 Tbsp. butter
3 cups powdered sugar
2 Tbsp. orange juice

1. Cream together cream cheese and butter.

2. Add sugar and enough orange juice to make frosting spreadable, beating at high speed until well mixed.

3. Use to frost favorite cake.

Our Great Dane puppy loves to chase cats. Recently, I made a baby quilt with a large appliqued cat in the center. After I had the quilt in the frame, I stood back to admire my handiwork and along comes our puppy. He jumped up and landed in the middle of the framed quilt, knocking everything down and tearing the edges. My husband comfortingly assured me I should not be upset because the cat must have looked real!

—*Eileen Plementos, Williams Lake, BC*

Shoofly Cake

Barbara Deuitch
Lake Ridge, VA
Flight 159

Makes 20-24 servings

1 lb. brown sugar
½ lb. butter
4 cups flour
2 cups molasses
2 cups boiling water
2 tsp. baking soda
1 tsp. salt

1. Mix brown sugar, butter and flour until crumbly. Reserve 2 cups crumbs.
2. Arrange remaining crumbs on bottom of 9" x 13" baking pan and press down.
3. Mix well all remaining ingredients and pour mixture over crumbs. Top with reserved crumbs.
4. Bake at 350° for 45 minutes.

Easy Pineapple Cake

Kathryn Stoltzfus
Sarasota, FL
Miriam Stoltzfus
Ronks, PA
Giant Dahlia

Makes 20-24 servings

Cake:
2 cups sugar
2 cups unsifted flour
2 tsp. baking soda
2 eggs
¼ tsp. salt
1 tsp. vanilla
20-oz. can crushed
    pineapple, undrained
1 cup chopped walnuts

Frosting:
8 Tbsp. margarine
1½ cups powdered sugar
8-oz. pkg. cream cheese
1 tsp. vanilla

1. In a large bowl combine all cake ingredients and mix thoroughly. Pour into a greased 9" x 13" baking pan.
2. Bake at 350° for 40-45 minutes.

3. To prepare frosting cream together all ingredients. Frost cake while it is still hot.

Note: This cake freezes well and is actually best when served several days after it is made.

Marjory Garman
Florence, SC
Tree of Life

Hummingbird Cake

Marian Brubacker
Barnett, MO
Country Love

Makes 20-24 servings

Cake:
3 cups flour
2 cups sugar
1 tsp. baking soda
1 tsp. salt
1 tsp. cinnamon
3 eggs, beaten
1 cup cooking oil
1½ tsp. vanilla
8-oz. can crushed
    pineapple, undrained
1 cup chopped pecans *or*
    walnuts
2 cups diced bananas

Frosting:
8-oz. pkg. cream cheese
2 cups powdered sugar
1 tsp. vanilla
½ cup pecans

1. To prepare cake combine all dry ingredients in a large bowl. Add eggs and oil and stir until moist. Do not beat. Stir in vanilla, pineapple, pecans and bananas. Spoon into greased 9" x 13" baking pan.

2. Bake at 350° for 25-30 minutes. Cool.

3. To prepare frosting cream together cream cheese, powdered sugar and vanilla. Fold in pecans.

4. When cake has cooled, frost and serve.

Orange Pineapple Cake

Ruth Day
Sturgis, SD
Double Jacob's Ladder

Makes 20-24 servings

11-oz. can mandarin oranges
1 box yellow cake mix
2 eggs
⅓ cup cooking oil
1 large pkg. instant vanilla pudding
8-oz. can crushed pineapple
9-oz. carton whipped topping

1. Combine undrained oranges, cake mix, eggs and cooking oil and beat at least 3 minutes. Pour into greased 9" x 13" baking pan.

2. Bake according to cake mix directions. Cool.

3. Combine pudding and pineapple with juice and mix well. Fold in whipped topping. Spread on cooled cake.

4. Refrigerate until ready to serve.

Variation:
Delete mandarin oranges from cake. For topping add 8-oz. pkg. cream cheese and 1½ cups milk to 20-oz. can drained pineapple and pudding. Sprinkle ¼ cup chopped walnuts and ¼ cup maraschino cherries over frosting on cake.

Cindy Krestynick
Glen Lyon, PA
Nine Patch

Dump Cake

Barbara L. McGinnis
Ocean City, NJ
Rosy Log Cabin
Carol Sucevic
Hopwood, PA
Jungle Strike

Makes 20-24 servings

16-oz. can cherry pie filling
16-oz. can crushed pineapple, undrained
1 box white cake mix
8 Tbsp. margarine, cut into bits
8-oz. container whipped topping

1. Spread cherry filling over bottom of greased 9" x 13" baking pan. Spread pineapple over cherries. Sprinkle cake mix evenly over all and top with bits of margarine. Do not stir.

2. Bake at 300° for 40 minutes.

3. Serve with whipped topping.

Variation:
Sprinkle ½ cup chopped pecans over cake mix. Melt margarine and pour evenly over batter. Sprinkle with another ½ cup chopped pecans. Continue with step 2.

Grace Sabala
Boise, ID
Sunbonnet Sue

Lemon Pudding Cake

Jeanette E. Barthold
Bethlehem, PA
Baby Quilt

Makes 8-10 servings

¾ cup sugar
Dash salt
3 Tbsp. butter *or*
   margarine, melted
¼ cup sifted flour
1 tsp. grated lemon rind
¼ cup lemon juice
3 eggs, separated
1½ cups milk

1. Cream together sugar, salt and butter. Stir in flour, lemon rind and juice.
2. In a separate bowl beat egg yolks with a fork. Add milk and mix well. Stir into batter.
3. In a separate bowl beat egg whites until stiff. Fold into batter. Pour into greased 8-inch square baking pan.
4. Place baking pan in a larger pan of warm water.
5. Bake at 350° for 40 minutes. Serve.

Pistachio Marble Cake

Mildred Kennel
Atglen, PA
Sailboat
Rhonda Burgoon
Collingswood, NJ
Field of Dreams

Makes 16-20 servings

1 yellow cake mix
1 small pkg. instant
   pistachio pudding
4 eggs
1 cup water
½ cup cooking oil
½ tsp. almond extract
¼ cup chocolate syrup
Powdered sugar (optional)

1. Combine cake mix, pudding mix, eggs, water, oil and almond extract in large mixing bowl. Beat with electric mixer at medium speed for 2 minutes.
2. Measure 1½ cups batter into another bowl. Stir chocolate syrup into it. Spoon batters alternately into greased and floured 10-inch bundt or tube pan. Zigzag spatula through batter to create marbled effect.
3. Bake at 350° for 50 minutes. Cool 15 minutes, remove from pan and finish cooling on rack.
4. Sprinkle with powdered sugar if desired.

Walnut Glory Cake

Ella G. Wenger
New Holland, PA
Country Bride & Country Lily

Makes 16-20 servings

¾ cup flour
1 tsp. salt
2 tsp. cinnamon
9 eggs, separated
1½ cups sugar
2 tsp. vanilla
2 cups finely chopped
   walnuts

1. Sift flour with salt and cinnamon. Set aside.
2. In a large mixing bowl beat egg whites until soft peaks form. Gradually add ¾ cup sugar and continue beating until very stiff.
3. In separate bowl combine egg yolks, ¾ cup sugar and vanilla. Beat until thick. Stir in dry ingredients. Gently fold this batter into egg whites. Fold in walnuts and spoon into 10-inch tube pan.
4. Bake at 350° for 55-60 minutes. This cake resembles angel food cake.

Date Cake

Irma Harder
Mountain Lake, MN
Double Wedding Ring

Makes 20-24 servings

Cake:
8-oz. pkg. dates
1 cup hot water
¼ cup shortening, softened
1 cup white sugar
1 egg
1 tsp. vanilla
1⅔ cups flour
1 tsp. baking soda
½ tsp. salt
1 Tbsp. cocoa
½ cup chopped nuts

Topping:
½ cup semi-sweet
   chocolate chips
2 Tbsp. white sugar
½ cup finely chopped nuts

1. Pour hot water over dates. Set aside.
2. Combine shortening, sugar, egg and vanilla in mixing bowl and beat 5 minutes on high speed.
3. In separate bowl stir together flour, baking soda, salt and cocoa. Add to sugar mixture in four additions, alternating with dates and mixing on low speed. Begin and end with dry ingredients. Blend until smooth and fold in nuts. Spoon into greased and floured 9" x 13" baking pan.
3. To prepare topping combine all ingredients.

Sprinkle topping over cake batter.
4. Bake at 350° for 30-35 minutes.

Queen Elizabeth Cake

Kaye Schnell
Falmouth, MA
Baltimore Album

Makes 20-24 servings

Cake:
1 large ripe banana
1 cup chopped dates
¾ cup boiling water
1 tsp. baking soda
½ cup butter *or* margarine
¾ cup white sugar
1 egg
1½ cups flour
1 tsp. baking powder
½ tsp. salt
½ cup chopped nuts
1 tsp. vanilla

Topping:
5 Tbsp. brown sugar
3 Tbsp. sweet cream
3 Tbsp. butter *or* margarine
¾ cup slivered almonds
¾ cup coconut

1. To prepare cake mash banana and add to dates. Combine water and baking soda and pour over dates and banana. Let cool.
2. Cream together butter, sugar and egg and beat well.
3. Sift together dry ingredients and add to creamed mixture. Add date and banana mixture and beat fairly well. Fold in nuts and vanilla and spoon into greased and floured 9" x 13" baking pan.
4. Bake at 350° for about 30-35 minutes.
5. To prepare topping combine all ingredients in a saucepan and cook about 3 minutes, stirring constantly.
6. Pour topping over hot cake. Return to oven for about 5 minutes to brown topping.

My kitchen and sewing room are at opposite ends of my house. One day I was cooking beans in my pressure cooker. Suddenly, I smelled burned beans. As I raced into the kitchen, the safety plug blew on the cooker. I got there just in time to keep the beans from flying all over the kitchen. I have learned not to use the pressure cooker and quilt at the same time.

—*Kelly Wagoner, Albuquerque, NM*

Grandma's Fresh Coconut Cake

Joyce Swinney
Mooresville, IN
Carrousel Horses

Makes 12 servings

Cake:
16 Tbsp. butter
2 cups sugar
2 tsp. vanilla
1¼ cups fresh coconut milk
3 cups cake flour
3 tsp. baking powder
⅛ tsp. salt
1 cup finely grated coconut
4 egg whites, stiffly beaten

Frosting:
1½ cups sugar *or* less
2 egg whites
5 Tbsp. water
3 tsp. white corn syrup
Pinch salt
1 tsp. vanilla

1. To prepare cake batter cream together butter and sugar until very fluffy. Set aside.
2. Combine vanilla and coconut milk. Set aside.
3. Combine flour, baking powder and salt. Add dry ingredients to creamed mixture, alternating with coconut milk. Begin and end with flour and beat well after each addition. Add grated coconut and beat well. Gently fold in stiffly beaten egg whites. Pour into 3 greased and floured 8-inch round layer pans.

4. Bake at 325° for 35-40 minutes.
5. To prepare frosting combine all ingredients except vanilla in double boiler. Heat, beating at high speed until fluffy, about 5-7 minutes. Stir in vanilla and remove from heat.
6. Spread frosting evenly between layers and over outside of cooled cake. Generously sprinkle outside with extra coconut.

Note: This cake is best when made with fresh coconuts. I buy coconuts when the local grocer gets a new shipment so they will be fresher and have more milk. I grate the coconut meat in a food processor and freeze it for future use. Coconut milk may also be frozen.

❖

Italian Cream Cake

Roseann Wilson
Albuquerque, NM
Friendship

Makes 20-24 servings

Cake:
2 cups sugar
8 Tbsp. margarine
½ cup shortening
5 eggs, separated
1 cup buttermilk
1 tsp. baking soda
2 cups flour
1 tsp. vanilla
1 cup chopped pecans

1 cup grated coconut

Frosting:
8-oz. pkg. cream cheese
1 tsp. vanilla
8 Tbsp. margarine
1-lb. box powdered sugar

1. Cream together sugar, margarine and shortening. Add egg yolks and mix well.
2. Combine buttermilk and baking soda. Add flour to creamed mixture, alternating with buttermilk. Stir in vanilla, pecans and coconut.
3. Beat egg whites to stiff peaks and fold into cake batter. Spoon into greased and floured 9" x 13" baking pan.
4. Bake at 325° for about 35-40 minutes.
5. To prepare frosting cream together cream cheese, vanilla and margarine. Add powdered sugar until spreading consistency. When cake has cooled, frost.

❖

Poor Man's Cake

Cindy Krestynick
Glen Lyon, PA
Nine Patch

Makes 20-24 servings

1 cup raisins
1 cup sugar
1 cup margarine

2 tsp. ground cloves
½ tsp. salt
½ tsp. nutmeg
2 cups water
4 cups flour
1 tsp. baking powder
1 tsp. baking soda

1. In a saucepan combine raisins, sugar, margarine, cloves, salt, nutmeg and water and cook about 3 minutes. Let cool.

2. Add all remaining ingredients and mix well. Pour into greased and floured 9" x 13" baking pan.

3. Bake at 350° for 25 minutes or until done. Frost as desired.

❖

Gingerbread Spice Cake

Fannie M. Beiler
New Holland, PA
Teddy Bear Pillows

Makes 20-24 servings

3 eggs
2 cups brown sugar
¾ cup lard
1 cup sour milk
2-2½ cups flour
1 tsp. baking soda
1 tsp. cinnamon
1 tsp. nutmeg
1 tsp. ground cloves
1 tsp. ginger

1. Beat eggs and brown sugar together. Mix in lard.

Add milk and mix well.

2. Sift together flour, baking soda and spices. Add to batter, stirring until well blended. Pour into greased 9" x 13" baking dish or 3 8-inch round layer pans.

3. Bake at 375° for 35 minutes or until cake tests done. Cool and spread with favorite frosting.

Note: Add a bit of water or milk to batter if it seems too stiff.

❖

Cinnamon Cake

Ruth D. Mullen
Annapolis, MD
Nine Patch

Makes 16-20 servings

Cake:
2 cups white sugar
8 Tbsp. butter
1 egg

3 cups flour
2 tsp. baking powder
¼ tsp. salt
1½ cups milk
1½ tsp. vanilla

Topping:
3 Tbsp. sugar
3 tsp. cinnamon

1. To prepare cake cream together sugar and butter. Add egg and mix well.

2. Sift together dry ingredients. Add to creamed mixture, alternating with milk. Add vanilla and mix well. Spoon batter into 3 8-inch greased cake pans.

3. To prepare topping combine sugar and cinnamon. Spread evenly over cake batter.

4. Bake at 350° for 25-30 minutes. Remove cakes from pans and cool. Serve.

Note: Do not substitute margarine for butter. Butter is the secret to this cake.

In 1986 we relocated from Georgia to Pennsylvania three days before my daughter began her senior year in high school. Her adjustments were difficult and continued into the next year when she went away to college. I knew how much she missed her friends. So I made my first quilt using her old T-shirts with their various designs and sayings. The quilt included blocks from her schools, family vacations, concerts she had attended with friends in Georgia and even the college logos of her parents' alma maters. Her reaction on Christmas morning told me I had given the perfect gift. It is a moment I will never forget.

—F. Elaine Asper, Stroudsburg, PA

Carry Away Cake

Joyce Swinney
Mooresville, IN
Dresden Hearts

Makes 16-20 servings

Cake:
1 cup honey graham
cracker crumbs
½ cup white sugar
1 cup brown sugar
1 tsp. salt
1 tsp. baking powder
1 tsp. baking soda
3 eggs
½ tsp. cinnamon
½ tsp. nutmeg
16 Tbsp. butter *or*
margarine, softened
1 cup orange juice
1 Tbsp. grated orange rind
2 cups flour
1 cup chopped nuts

Topping:
2 Tbsp. brown sugar
1 Tbsp. butter
5 Tbsp. milk
¾ cup powdered sugar
¼-⅓ cup chopped nuts

1. Combine all cake ingredients except nuts in large mixing bowl. Mix on low speed to blend and beat 3 minutes on medium speed. Fold in nuts.
2. Spoon cake batter into greased and floured 10-inch tube pan.
3. Bake at 350° for 45-50 minutes or until cake tester comes out clean. Cool in pan 15 minutes. Invert onto serving plate and cool completely.
4. To prepare topping combine brown sugar, butter and milk in small saucepan and heat until melted. Remove from heat and add powdered sugar. Blend until smooth.
5. Drizzle topping over cooled cake. Sprinkle with nuts and serve.

❖

Tomato Soup Cake

Deb Koelsch
Lancaster, PA
Handy Andy

Makes 8-10 servings

1½ Tbsp. butter
1 cup sugar
1 egg
1 tsp. baking soda
10¾-oz. can tomato soup
1½ cups flour
½ tsp. baking powder
½ tsp. ground cloves
1 tsp. cinnamon
1 tsp. nutmeg

1. Cream together butter and sugar. Add egg.
2. Add baking soda to tomato soup, stirring until it foams. Stir into creamed mixture.
3. Sift together all dry ingredients. Combine creamed mixture and dry mixture. Pour into 2 round, greased and floured cake pans.
4. Bake at 350° for 30 minutes.
5. Ice with a fluffy white frosting and serve.

❖

Easy Apple Cake

Audrey Romonosky
Poughkeepsie, NY
Double Irish Chain

Makes 6 servings

½ cup flour
½ cup sugar
1 tsp. baking powder
1 tsp. cinnamon
⅛ tsp. salt
¼ tsp. nutmeg
2-3 medium apples
¼ cup raisins
1 egg, slightly beaten
1 tsp. vanilla

1. Combine flour, sugar, baking powder, cinnamon, salt and nutmeg in medium bowl. Mix well.
2. Peel, core and chop apples. Add apples and raisins to dry mixture, stirring lightly to coat.
3. Combine egg and vanilla in a small bowl. Add to apple and raisin mixture, stirring until dry ingredients are moistened. Spoon mixture into greased 9-inch pie plate.
4. Bake at 350° for 30 minutes or until lightly browned.

Cinnamon Apple Cake

**Blanche Cahill
Willow Grove, PA
*Variegated Star***

Makes 20-24 servings

**5 medium apples
¾ cup sugar
16 Tbsp. margarine *or*
    butter
3 cups flour
1 cup milk
2 tsp. cinnamon
1 tsp. baking powder
1 tsp. salt
2 tsp. vanilla
3 large eggs
¾ cup chopped pecans
3 Tbsp. apple jelly**

1. Peel and dice 3 apples. Core and slice remaining apples into rings, cut rings in half.
2. In large bowl with mixer on high speed beat sugar and butter until light and fluffy. Reduce speed to low and add flour, milk, cinnamon, baking powder, salt, vanilla and eggs. Beat until just blended. Increase speed to medium and beat 3 minutes.
3. With rubber spatula gently fold in pecans and diced apples. Spread batter evenly into greased and floured 9" x 13" baking pan. Arrange apple ring slices on top of batter.
4. In small saucepan over medium heat melt apple jelly. With pastry brush spread jelly over apple slices.
5. Bake at 350° for 45-50 minutes until cake tester comes out clean. Cool on wire rack or serve immediately.

❖

Raw Apple Cake

**Elsie Long, Sterling, IL
Barbara Forrester Landis,
Lititz, PA
Linda Miles, Dumfries, VA**

Makes 20-24 servings

**Cake:
2 eggs
4 cups diced apples
½ cup cooking oil
2 cups sugar
½ tsp. salt
2 tsp. baking soda
2 tsp. cinnamon
2 tsp. vanilla
2 cups flour
2 cups nuts, large pieces**

**Frosting:
4 Tbsp. butter *or* margarine
8-oz. pkg. cream cheese
2 tsp. vanilla
1½ cups powdered sugar**

1. Combine all cake ingredients and mix well. Spoon into lightly greased 9" x 13" baking pan.
2. Bake at 350° for 1 hour or until done. Cool.
3. To prepare frosting cream together all ingredients. Frost cake after it has cooled. Serve.

❖

Apple Chunk Cake

**Doris Perkins
Mashpee, MA
*Card Trick***

Makes 16-20 servings

**2 cups peeled, cubed
    apples
1 cup molasses
2 eggs, beaten
1 cup sugar
1 cup melted shortening
1 cup milk
4 cups sifted flour
2 tsp. baking soda
1 tsp. salt
1 tsp. cinnamon
1 tsp. ground cloves
1 Tbsp. vanilla
1 Tbsp. lemon extract
1 cup raisins *or* walnuts**

1. Combine apples and molasses in a saucepan. Bring to a boil and cook 5 minutes on medium heat. Cool slightly. Add all remaining ingredients and mix well. Divide ingredients into 2 9-inch greased loaf pans.
2. Bake at 350° for 45-50 minutes. Slice and serve.

Fresh Apple Cake

Mary Saunders
Albuquerque, NM
Trip Around the World

Makes 20-24 servings

Cake:
4 cups thinly sliced apples
2 cups sugar
2 cups flour
1½ tsp. cinnamon
1 tsp. salt
2 eggs
¾ cup cooking oil
1 tsp. vanilla
1 cup chopped nuts

Sauce:
1 cup sugar
8 Tbsp. butter
½ cup cream *or* evaporated
  milk
1 tsp. vanilla

1. To prepare cake batter stir together apples and sugar in a large bowl. Add dry ingredients and stir well.

2. In a separate bowl beat eggs, oil and vanilla. Stir this mixture into the apple mixture. Blend until thoroughly moistened. Fold in nuts. Pour into well-greased 9" x 13" baking pan.

3. Bake at 350° for 50 minutes or until toothpick inserted in center comes out clean.

4. To prepare sauce put all ingredients into a saucepan and bring to a boil over medium-high heat, stirring constantly. Cook for 3 minutes.

5. Serve warm sauce over fresh apple cake. (This sauce is also good with ice cream.)

Old-Fashioned Applesauce Cake

Jeanette E. Barthold
Bethlehem, PA
Baby Quilt

Makes 16-20 servings

1¾ cups coarsely chopped
  walnuts
1¾ cups raisins
3½ cups sifted flour
2 tsp. baking soda
¼ tsp. salt
1½ tsp. cinnamon
1 tsp. ground cloves
1 tsp. ginger
¼ tsp. nutmeg
1 cup butter
2 cups sugar
2 large eggs
2 cups applesauce

1. Dredge nuts and raisins in ¼ cup flour. Set aside.

2. Sift together remaining flour, baking soda, salt and spices. Set aside.

3. Cream butter until light and fluffy. Gradually add sugar. Beat in eggs, one at a time. Add dry ingredients, alternating with applesauce and beginning and ending with dry ingredients. Fold in nuts and raisins. Spoon batter into well-greased and floured 9-inch tube pan.

4. Bake at 350° for 1 hour and 25 minutes or until cake feels springy and has pulled away from sides. Invert and cool.

5. Cut into small slices and serve.

Jewish Apple Cake

Connie Weaver
Bethlehem, PA
Log Cabin

Makes 20-24 servings

6-7 medium apples
2 tsp. cinnamon
5 Tbsp. sugar
1 cup butter
2 cups sugar
3 cups unsifted flour
½ cup orange juice
4 eggs
3 tsp. baking powder
2½ tsp. vanilla

1. Peel, quarter and cut apples into slices. Mix with cinnamon and 5 Tbsp. sugar. Set aside.

2. Cream together butter and 2 cups sugar. Add ½ of flour, ½ of juice, 2 eggs, baking powder and vanilla. Mix well. Add remaining ingredients and mix well. Fold in apples. Spoon into

greased 9" x 13" baking pan.

3. Bake at 350° for 50 minutes or until toothpick inserted in center comes out clean. Cool and serve.

Blueberry Crumb Cake

Eleanor J. Ferreira
North Chelmsford, MA
Trip Around the World
Elizabeth Haderer
East Quogue, NY
Grandmother's Fan

Makes 8-10 servings

Cake:
2 cups sifted flour
2 tsp. baking powder
½ tsp. salt
4 Tbsp. butter *or* margarine
¾ cup sugar
1 egg, beaten
½ cup milk
2 cups blueberries

Crumb Topping:
½ cup sugar
¼ cup flour
½ tsp. cinnamon
4 Tbsp. butter *or* margarine

1. Sift together flour, baking powder and salt. Set aside.

2. Cream butter and gradually beat in sugar. Add egg and milk and beat until smooth. Add dry ingredients.

3. Dust blueberries

lightly with flour. Fold into batter. Spread into greased and floured 9-inch square baking pan.

4. To prepare topping mix together sugar, flour and cinnamon. Cut in butter and mix into coarse crumbs.

5. Sprinkle crumb mixture over cake batter.

6. Bake at 375° for 40-45 minutes.

Blueberry Dump Cake

Ruth D. Mullen
Annapolis, MD
Nine Patch

Makes 12-16 servings

2 pints fresh blueberries
¾ cup sugar
1 box white cake mix
1 cup chopped nuts
8 Tbsp. margarine, melted

1. Pour berries into 9" x 13" baking pan. Sprinkle sugar, dry cake mix and nuts over berries. Pour melted margarine over entire mixture.

2. Bake at 325° for 1 hour. Serve.

Fresh Peach Cake

Eunice B. Heyman
Baltimore, MD
Joanne's Anniversary Quilt

Makes 12-16 servings

1 cup butter
2 cups sugar
4 eggs
2 cups flour
2 tsp. baking powder
¼ cup sour cream
2 tsp. vanilla
6-8 fresh peaches, peeled and sliced
1 tsp. cinnamon
1 tsp. sugar

1. Cream butter and sugar until light and fluffy. Add eggs, one at a time.

2. Sift together dry ingredients and add to batter, alternating with sour cream and vanilla. Mix well, but do not beat. Spoon batter into greased and floured 9" x 13" baking pan.

3. Top with sliced peaches and sprinkle with cinnamon and sugar.

4. Bake at 350° for 45-50 minutes.

Rhubarb Cake

Fannie M. Beiler
New Holland, PA
Teddy Bear Pillows

Makes 20-24 servings

Cake:
½ cup margarine
½ cup brown sugar
1 egg
1 cup milk
2 cups flour
½ tsp. salt
1 tsp. baking soda
2 cups diced rhubarb

Topping:
½ cup white sugar
1 tsp. cinnamon
½ cup chopped nuts

1. Cream together margarine and brown sugar. Add egg and milk.
2. Sift together flour, salt and baking soda. Add to batter and stir until moistened. Fold in rhubarb. Spoon into greased 9" x 13" baking pan.
3. Combine all topping ingredients and sprinkle over cake batter.
4. Bake at 350° for 35-40 minutes.

Mom's Lazy Daisy Cake

Mrs. Paul Gray
Beatrice, NE

Makes 8-10 servings

Cake:
½ cup milk
1 Tbsp. butter
2 eggs
1 cup sugar
1 cup flour
1 tsp. baking powder
½ tsp. salt
1 tsp. vanilla

Frosting:
⅔ cup brown sugar
⅓ cup butter, melted
2 Tbsp. heavy cream
½ cup coconut
½ cup chopped nuts

1. In a saucepan combine milk and butter and heat. Do not boil.
2. Beat eggs until light. Add sugar and beat vigorously.
3. Sift together flour, baking powder and salt. Stir into egg mixture and add vanilla. Add milk mixture, stirring carefully. Pour into a 9-inch square baking pan.

4. Bake at 350° for 30-35 minutes.
5. To prepare frosting heat sugar, butter and cream in a saucepan, stirring until creamy. Pour over warm cake. Sprinkle with coconut and nuts.
6. Place cake under broiler for 5 minutes to caramelize frosting.

Ice Cream Layer Cake

Naomi Lapp
New Holland, PA

Makes 10-12 servings

2 eggs, separated
½ cup sugar
1¼ cups flour
1 cup sugar
½ cup cocoa
¾ tsp. baking soda
½ tsp. salt
½ cup cooking oil
1 cup sour milk
1 quart ice cream

1. In a medium bowl beat egg whites until foamy. Add ½ cup sugar and beat until stiff. Set aside.
2. Combine remaining dry ingredients in another bowl. Add oil, sour milk and egg yolks and beat until smooth. Gently fold in egg whites. Spoon into 3 8-inch round, greased cake pans.

When our daughter was expecting a baby, I put together a Little Lamb baby quilt. She surprised everyone, including her doctor, and gave birth to twin daughters. Needless to say, I quickly went to work on the second Little Lamb baby quilt.

—Elsie Long, Sterling, IL

3. Bake at 350° for 15-20 minutes. Cool slightly, remove cakes from pans and cool completely.

4. Immediately before serving, spread ice cream between each layer.

Gaynelle's Poppy Seed Cake

Katie Reed
Floresville, TX
Feather Medallion

Makes 16-20 servings

Cake:
3 cups flour
1½ tsp. salt
1½ tsp. baking powder
2¼ cups sugar
1⅛ cups cooking oil
1½ cups milk
3 eggs, beaten
1½ tsp. vanilla
1½ tsp. almond extract
2 Tbsp. poppy seed

Glaze:
1 cup powdered sugar
¼ cup fresh orange juice
½ tsp. vanilla
½ tsp. almond extract

1. To prepare cake combine flour, salt, baking powder and sugar in a large bowl. Stir in oil, milk, eggs, vanilla and almond extract and mix until smooth. Add poppy seed.

Pour into lightly greased 10-inch tube pan.

2. Bake at 350° for 1 hour. Cool in pan for 20 minutes. Remove from pan and glaze.

3. To prepare glaze mix all ingredients until smooth. Pour over warm cake. Serve.

Poppy Seed Cake

Rosaria V. Strachan
Old Greenwich, CT
Nine Patch

Makes 16-20 servings

Cake:
16 Tbsp. butter
8-oz. pkg. cream cheese
1½ cups sugar
1½ tsp. vanilla
4 eggs
2½ cups flour
1½ tsp. baking powder
½ cup raisins
1 cup finely chopped walnuts

Filling:
¼ cup poppy seeds
¼ cup sugar
1 tsp. lemon rind
¼ tsp. vanilla

1. In large bowl cream together butter and cream cheese until light and fluffy. Add sugar and vanilla and beat 5 minutes. Add eggs, one at a time,

beating after each addition.

2. Sift together flour and baking powder. Add to creamed mixture. Fold in raisins and walnuts. Spoon ½ of batter into greased 10-cup bundt pan.

3. To prepare filling combine all ingredients. Sprinkle batter with filling mix and top with remaining batter. Using a knife, swirl to spread filling throughout.

4. Bake at 325° for 65-70 minutes, checking occasionally.

I was a homemaker with time on my hands when I began piecing quilts. My mother had taught me to sew so I began with a simple Log Cabin quilt. A friend from Massachusetts sent me a photograph of a Sampler and asked whether I would be willing to piece one for her. After checking numerous quilt books for the many different patterns, I finally completed it. I felt as though I should have about a thousand dollars for it! At the time that would have been an unheard of price. However, I'm glad I took on the challenge as piecing Samplers has become my personal quilt specialty.

—*Naomi Lapp, New Holland, PA*

Banana Nut Bundt Cake

Elsie F. Porter
Baltimore, MD
Nine Patch Star

Makes 16-20 servings

1 cup margarine, softened
2 cups sugar
4 eggs
4 cups all-purpose flour
2 tsp. baking soda
½ tsp. salt (optional)
6 large, ripe bananas, mashed
1 cup chopped nuts
2 tsp. vanilla

1. Cream together margarine and sugar. Add eggs, one at a time, beating after each addition.
2. Sift together flour, baking soda and salt. Stir into creamed mixture until just blended. Fold in bananas, nuts and vanilla. Spoon into 10-cup greased and floured bundt pan.
3. Bake at 350° for about

Seven-Up Cake

Barbara F. Shie
Colorado Springs, CO
Lois Niebauer
Pedricktown, NJ
Barbara Y. Spicer
Gettysburg, PA

Makes 10-15 servings

24 Tbsp. margarine
3 cups sugar
5 eggs
3 cups flour
1 Tbsp. lemon extract
1 Tbsp. vanilla extract
¾ cup 7-Up
Powdered sugar

1. Cream together margarine and sugar. Add eggs, one at a time, beating well

1 hour and 20 minutes. Cool 10 minutes in pan. Remove from pan and cool completely. Store in covered container.

after each addition. Add flour and extracts and beat well. Gently fold in 7-Up. Pour into well-greased 10-cup bundt pan.
2. Bake at 325° for 1-1¼ hours.
3. Dust with powdered sugar and serve.

Variation:

Cream an 8-oz. pkg. cream cheese with margarine and sugar. Delete lemon extract, vanilla extract and 7-up. Use 2 tsp. vanilla and blend 1 pkg. dry whipped topping into batter. Proceed according to directions.

Melissa Myers
Indian Head, MD
Bow Tie

Sour Cream Cake

Ann Harrison
Garland, TX
Marilyn Wallace
Alfred, ME
Ann Sunday McDowell
Newtown, PA

Makes 16-20 servings

16 Tbsp. butter or margarine
3 cups sugar
6 eggs
½ pint sour cream
3 cups cake flour
¼ tsp. baking soda
1 tsp. vanilla

I learned to quilt when I was 13 years old. My mother usually had a quilt in the frame during the winter months. I pieced several for myself and really enjoyed quilting. After I married and our children were growing up, I had little time to think about quilts.

My mother pieced quilt tops for each of her grandchildren, and when our grandchildren were growing up, I decided to follow her example. That meant getting nine quilts made. Then with the help of our daughter I made three quilted bedspreads of plain material; one for her and one for our two daughters-in-law.

Now that the great-grandchildren have come along, I make quilted pillows. They are very pleased with their pillows, and I have no more responsibility for making quilts, unless I decide to make a spread for myself.

—Phoebe Hershberger, Goshen, IN

1. Cream butter and add sugar ¼ cup at a time. Beat until light. Add eggs, one at a time, beating after each addition. Add sour cream and mix.

2. Sift together flour and baking soda. Add to creamed mixture. Stir in vanilla and beat 2 minutes. Spoon into greased and floured 10-cup bundt pan.

3. Bake at 325° for 1 hour and 20 minutes. Cool in pan for 20 minutes. Remove from pan and cool completely.

Rich Pound Cake

Joan T. Schneider
Seaford, NY
Baby Animal Quilt

Makes 16-20 servings

16 Tbsp. margarine
2 cups sugar
4 eggs, separated
3 cups flour
3 tsp. baking powder
½ tsp. salt
1 cup milk

1. Cream together margarine, sugar and egg yolks.

2. Sift together flour, baking powder and salt. Add flour mixture to creamed mixture, alternating with milk.

3. Beat egg whites until stiff. Carefully fold into batter. Put into greased 10-inch bundt pan.

4. Bake at 350° for 1 hour.

Lemon Sauce for Pound Cake

Melinda Moritz
Flourtown, PA
Sampler

Makes 3 cups sauce

4 eggs, beaten
2 cups sugar
8 Tbsp. butter
1 Tbsp. grated lemon rind
½ cup lemon juice

1. Combine all ingredients in saucepan. Cook over medium heat, stirring constantly until mixture is thick and bubbly, about 10 minutes.

2. Chill and serve with pound cake.

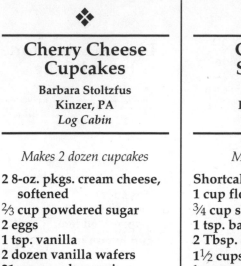

Cherry Cheese Cupcakes

Barbara Stoltzfus
Kinzer, PA
Log Cabin

Makes 2 dozen cupcakes

2 8-oz. pkgs. cream cheese, softened
2/3 cup powdered sugar
2 eggs
1 tsp. vanilla
2 dozen vanilla wafers
21-oz. can cherry pie filling.

1. Cream together cream cheese, sugar, eggs and vanilla. Mix well.
2. Place 1 vanilla wafer in bottom of each greased muffin tin. Fill 3/4 full with cheese mixture.
3. Bake at 350° for 20 minutes. When cooled, place 1 tsp. pie filling on each cupcake. Refrigerate and serve.

Cranberry Shortcake

Betsy Jevon
Pittsburgh, PA
Gift of Stars

Makes 8 servings

Shortcake:
1 cup flour
3/4 cup sugar
1 tsp. baking powder
2 Tbsp. shortening
1 1/2 cups fresh cranberries
1/2 cup milk
Hot Butter Sauce:
1/2 cup butter *or* margarine
1/2 cup brown sugar
1/2 cup heavy cream
1/2 tsp. vanilla

1. To prepare shortcake sift together flour, sugar and baking powder. Cut in shortening. Carefully fold in cranberrries. Add milk and mix lightly. Spoon into greased 8-inch square baking pan.
2. Bake at 375° for 30 minutes.
3. To prepare butter sauce melt butter. Stir in brown sugar until it dissolves. Add cream and vanilla and heat slowly. Do not bring to a boil.
4. Serve hot shortcake with hot butter sauce.

Chocolate-Speckled Sponge Cake

Sharon Honegger
Hawthorne, NY
Miniature Tulip Applique

Makes 10-12 servings

1 1/2 cups flour
1/2 tsp. baking powder
1/4 tsp. salt
6 eggs, separated
1 1/3 cups sugar
1/2 cup cold water
1 square unsweetened chocolate
2/3 cup ground walnuts
1 tsp. vanilla

1. Sift together flour, baking powder and salt.
2. Beat together egg yolks and sugar until thick and lemon colored. Add water. Gently fold in sifted, dry ingredients until well mixed.
3. Coarsely grate chocolate. Fold chocolate and walnuts into batter.
4. Beat egg whites, add vanilla and beat until stiff but not dry. Gently fold into batter until evenly blended. Spoon into 2 9-inch round pans, lined with waxed paper.
5. Bake at 375° for 25 minutes. Remove from pan immediately and cool on racks.
6. Serve with whipped topping.

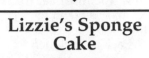

Lizzie's Sponge Cake

Fanny Stoltzfus
Rebersburg, PA
Sunshine and Shadow

Makes 8-10 servings

1¼ cups cake flour
1 cup sugar
½ tsp. baking powder
6 medium eggs, separated, and at room temperature
½ tsp. salt
1 tsp. cream of tartar
½ cup sugar
¼ cup cold water
1 tsp. vanilla *or* lemon extract

1. Sift together flour, 1 cup sugar and baking powder. Set aside.
2. Beat 6 egg whites, salt and cream of tartar until soft peaks form. Gradually add ½ cup sugar, beating until stiff peaks form. Set aside.
3. Combine 4 egg yolks, cold water and extract. Blend with dry ingredients, beating at medium speed for 1 minute.
4. Gently fold ¼ of batter at a time into stiffly beaten egg whites. Do not stir. Spoon into ungreased 10-inch tube pan. Cut gently through batter to remove air pockets.
5. Bake at 350° for 40-50 minutes. Invert immediately and let cool in pan at least 1 hour.

Cream-Filled Cupcakes

Sherry Sommers
Millersburg, OH
Lady's Fan

Makes 24-30 cupcakes

1 box chocolate cake mix
8-oz. pkg. cream cheese, softened
⅓ cup sugar
1 egg
⅛ tsp. salt
6-oz. pkg. chocolate chips

1. Prepare cake mix according to directions, but do not bake. Set aside.
2. In a separate bowl cream together cream cheese and sugar. Add egg and salt and mix well. Fold in chocolate chips.
3. Fill paper-lined muffin tins ½ full with batter. Drop 1 rounded teaspoon cream filling on each cupcake.
4. Bake at 350° for 25 minutes.

German Fruitcake

Evi Wahl
Middletown, PA
Tri-Color Blue Baby Block

Makes 15-20 servings

1 lb. fresh sausage
2 cups very hot water
2 cups sugar
2 tsp. baking soda
2 tsp. vinegar
1 tsp. nutmeg
1 tsp. ground cloves
1 tsp. cinnamon
1 tsp. salt
1 lb. raisins
1 lb. currants (optional)
1 lb. candied fruit
3½-4 cups all-purpose flour
1 lb. walnuts, coarsely chopped

1. Place sausage in a large bowl and pour hot water over sausage, stirring until sausage breaks apart.
2. Add sugar, soda and vinegar and mix well. Add all remaining ingredients and mix well. Pour into one large tube pan or 2 medium-sized loaf pans.
3. Bake at 375° for 30 minutes. Cover and bake another 30 minutes or until done.

Notes: Before baking, decorate top with candied fruit, nuts or cherries. Do not store in closed container. The best way to store fruitcake is to wrap it in cheesecloth. It may also be frozen.

My poor fingers were so sore after working on my first quilting project. I could not understand how the other women could work so quickly and have such tiny, neat stitches. My teacher finally came over and checked my quilting thread. I had been appliqueing with a spool of carpet thread!

—*Linda Miles, Dumfries, VA*

Fruit Cake

Doris L. Orthmann
Wantage, NJ
*Sunbonnet Sue & Kissing
Cousin*

Makes many servings

1½ cups liquid coffee
15-oz. box raisins
1½ tsp. baking soda
¾ cup cooking oil
2 cups sugar
3 eggs
3 cups flour
¼ tsp. baking powder
2 tsp. salt
1 tsp. cinnamon
1 tsp. allspice
½ tsp. ground cloves
½ tsp. mace
8 ozs. walnuts, chopped
1 jar maraschino cherries,
    undrained
1 lb. mixed fruit

1. Boil raisins in coffee. (Use leftover coffee.) Add baking soda and let stand until cool.
2. Cream together oil, sugar and eggs. Add flour, baking powder, spices and nuts, adding cherry juice and coffee to make mixing easier. Fold in cherries, raisins and mixed fruit. Spoon into 4-5 small greased and floured loaf pans.
3. Bake at 325° for about 1 hour and 20 minutes. Cake is done when it springs back to a light touch. When completely cooled, wrap in aluminum foil.

Unbaked Fruitcake

L.W. Weaver
Ephrata, PA
Country Love

Makes 24 small servings

16 Tbsp. margarine
1½ lbs. marshmallows
1 lb. graham crackers,
    finely crushed
1 lb. dates, chopped
½ cup sliced maraschino
    cherries
¾ cup chopped pecans
¾ cup chopped walnuts
1½ cups raisins

1. In a saucepan melt margarine and marshmallows together.
2. Combine all remaining ingredients. Pour marshmallow mixture over fruit mixture and blend together.
3. Pack in an 8-inch square baking pan. Chill before serving. Sliced thinly, this makes a delicious snack.

Cookies and Bars

❖

Peanut Butter Cookies

Carolyn Callis
Houston, TX
Ohio Star

Makes 4-5 dozen cookies

4 Tbsp. butter
½ cup brown sugar
½ cup white sugar
1 egg
1 cup flour
1 tsp. baking soda
½ cup peanut butter

1. Cream together butter and sugars. Add egg and mix lightly.
2. Combine flour and baking soda. Add to creamed mixture and mix well. Add peanut butter and mix well. Roll into small balls.
3. Arrange on greased cookie sheet and press down with fork dipped in cold water.
4. Bake at 350° for 10-12 minutes or until brown.

❖

Peanut Butter Blossoms

Delores Scheel
West Fargo, ND
Lone Star
Sara Ann Miller
Fredericksburg, OH
Plain Light Gray

Makes 4 dozen cookies

1⅓ cups flour
1 tsp. baking soda
1 tsp. salt
½ cup shortening
½ cup creamy peanut butter
½ cup white sugar
½ cup brown sugar
1 egg, unbeaten
2 Tbsp. milk
1 tsp. vanilla
½ cup white sugar
1 pkg. chocolate candy kisses

1. Sift together flour, baking soda and salt.
2. Cream together shortening, peanut butter, ½ cup white sugar and brown sugar. Add egg, milk and vanilla and mix well. Add dry ingredients and mix thoroughly. Chill.
3. Using teaspoon, shape into balls. Roll balls in ½ cup white sugar and place on ungreased baking sheet.
4. Bake at 375° for 8 minutes. Remove from oven and press 1 chocolate candy kiss on each cookie, pressing down until cookie cracks around edges.
5. Bake another 3-5 minutes.

We live in a large, modern home in rural Oklahoma. My living room almost always has one large and several small quilts in frames. Recently, a guest was admiring our home and upon entering the living room commented, "Oh, what a nice touch." My husband quickly informed the person that it was much more than a "nice touch."

—*Alix Botsford, Seminole, OK*

Soft Oatmeal Cookies

Mary Lou Mahar
Williamsfield, IL
Lone Star

Makes 4-5 dozen cookies

1 cup raisins
1 cup water
¾ cup soft margarine
1½ cups white sugar
2 eggs
1 tsp. vanilla
2½ cups flour
½ tsp. baking powder
1 tsp. baking soda
1 tsp. salt
1 tsp. cinnamon
½ tsp. ground cloves
2 cups rolled oats
½ cup chopped nuts

1. Simmer raisins and water over low heat until raisins are plump, about 20-30 minutes. Drain liquid into measuring cup. Add water to make ½ cup. Set aside.
2. Cream together margarine, sugar, eggs and vanilla. Stir in raisin liquid.
3. Blend together flour, baking powder, baking soda, salt, cinnamon and cloves. Add to creamed mixture and mix well. Fold in oats, nuts and raisins.
4. Drop by teaspoonful onto greased cookie sheet.
5. Bake at 400° for 8-10 minutes.

Peanut Butter Balls

Jean Turner
Williams Lake, BC
Sashiko-Style Wall Hanging

Makes 2 dozen cookies

1 cup powdered sugar
1 cup peanut butter
1 cup finely chopped dates
1 cup finely chopped walnuts
½ cup white sugar
1 Tbsp. water
1 cup coconut

1. Combine powdered sugar, peanut butter, dates and walnuts and mix well. Roll into 1-inch balls.
2. Combine white sugar and water. Dip balls in sugar and water solution and roll in coconut. Store in airtight container.

Old-Fashioned German Oatmeal Cookies

Laura Barrus Bishop
Boerne, TX
Log Cabin

Makes 5-6 dozen cookies

1 cup shortening
1 cup brown sugar
1 cup white sugar
2 eggs, beaten
2 Tbsp. water
1½ cups flour
1 tsp. salt
1 tsp. baking soda
2 tsp. cinnamon
1 tsp. nutmeg
1 tsp. ground cloves
3 cups oats
2 cups raisins

1. Cream together shortening and sugars. Stir in eggs and water. Add dry ingredients and raisins and mix well.
2. Drop by teaspoonful onto ungreased cookie sheet.
3. Bake at 375° for 10-15 minutes.

Oatmeal Raisin Cookies

Catherine Wenzel
Center Moriches, NY
Crazy Cats

Makes 3 dozen cookies

3 cups quick-cooking oats
1¼ cups all-purpose flour
½ tsp. baking soda
¾ tsp. salt
¾ cup butter, softened
1 cup dark brown sugar, packed
½ cup white sugar
1 egg
¼ cup milk
1 tsp. vanilla
1 cup raisins

1. In a large bowl combine oats, flour, baking soda and salt.
2. In another bowl cream together butter, sugars, egg, milk and vanilla. Fold in dry ingredients. (Do not overmix.) Fold in raisins.
3. Drop by tablespoonsful onto greased cookie sheets about 2 inches apart.
4. Bake at 350° for 12 minutes or until cookies are golden brown. Remove cookies to wire rack to cool.

Oatmeal Chocolate Chip Cookies

Fannie M. Beiler
New Holland, PA
Lois Stoltzfus, Honey Brook, PA
Sarah S. King, Gordonville, PA
Judy Steiner Buller, Beatrice, NE
Vicki Long, Sterling, IL

Makes 5-6 dozen cookies

1 cup shortening
¾ cup brown sugar
¾ cup white sugar
2 eggs
1 tsp. hot water
1 tsp. vanilla
1½ cups flour
1 tsp. baking soda
1 tsp. salt
2 cups quick-cooking oats
12-oz. pkg. chocolate chips
1 cup chopped nuts

1. Cream together shortening and sugars. Add eggs, water and vanilla.
2. Sift together flour, baking soda and salt. Add to creamed mixture and mix well. Fold in oats, chocolate chips and nuts. Chill dough in refrigerator.
3. Drop onto ungreased cookie sheets.
4. Bake at 350° for 10-15 minutes.

Chocolate Oatmeal Cookies

Cindy Cooksey
Irvine, CA
Albino Squid Races

Makes 3 dozen cookies

3 ozs. unsweetened chocolate
⅔ cup soft butter *or* margarine
1 cup brown sugar, packed
1 egg
1 tsp. vanilla
1 cup all-purpose flour
½ tsp. salt
½ tsp. baking powder
¼ cup milk
2 cups rolled oats
1 cup semi-sweet chocolate chips

1. Melt chocolate in double boiler. Cool slightly.
2. Cream together shortening, sugar, egg and vanilla. Blend in cooled chocolate.
3. Combine flour, salt and baking powder. Add to creamed mixture. Stir in milk, oats and chocolate chips.
4. Drop by teaspoonsful onto ungreased cookie sheet.
5. Bake at 350° for about 12 minutes.

No-Bake Chocolate Oatmeal Cookies

LuAnne S. Taylor
Canton, PA
Log Cabin Barnraising
Anna Oberholtzer
Lititz, PA
Dahlia

Makes 3-4 dozen cookies

2 cups sugar
4 Tbsp. cocoa
8 Tbsp. butter
½ cup milk
Pinch salt
½ cup peanut butter
1 tsp. vanilla
3 cups oatmeal
½ cup chopped nuts

1. Combine sugar, cocoa, butter, milk and salt in large saucepan. Bring to a boil. Boil for 30 seconds, stirring constantly. Cool.
2. Add peanut butter to cooled mixture and mix well. Add vanilla, oatmeal and nuts and mix well.
3. Drop by teaspoonful onto cookie sheets or waxed paper. Chill and serve.

Banana Oatmeal Cookies

Lydia Brubacker
Barnett, MO
Appliqued Butterfly

Makes about 4 dozen cookies

1 cup white sugar
¾ cup shortening
1 egg
1½ cups all-purpose flour
½ tsp. salt
1 tsp. cinnamon
½ tsp. baking soda
¼ tsp. nutmeg
1¾ cups oatmeal
1 cup mashed ripe bananas
½ cup chopped nuts *or* raisins

1. Cream together sugar, shortening and egg. Add all other ingredients and mix well.
2. Drop by rounded teaspoonsful onto ungreased cookie sheet.
3. Bake at 400° for about 10 minutes or until light brown.

Grandma's Molasses Cookies

Verda Wilsman
Pittsburgh, PA
Flying Geese

Makes 6 dozen cookies

1 cup shortening
1 cup white sugar
1 cup molasses
5 cups flour
1 Tbsp. ginger
1 Tbsp. cinnamon
1 tsp. salt
1 Tbsp. baking soda
½ cup warm water

1. Cream together shortening, sugar and molasses. Add flour and spices and mix well.
2. Dissolve baking soda in water and add to batter, mixing well.
3. Roll out to ½-inch thickness onto floured waxed paper. Using 2¼-inch cookie cutter, cut out cookies. Arrange on greased cookie sheet.
4. Bake at 350° for 15 minutes.
5. Transfer from cookie sheet to tin container while cookies are still warm, arranging in layers between waxed paper. (This will keep cookies soft.)

> **When my son got married on April 2, 1992, I made a reversible quilt for him and his new bride. I attached a label to the quilt reminding them, "This quilt is like your marriage; always remember there are two sides to everything."**
>
> —*Molly Wilson, Gonzales, TX*

Molasses Cookies

Naomi Lapp
New Holland, PA
Double Wedding Ring
Marcia S. Myer
Manheim, PA
Dresden Plate

Makes 10 dozen cookies

2 cups light brown sugar
2 cups Brer Rabbit molasses
1½ cups shortening
7 cups flour
2 Tbsp. baking soda
½ tsp. ginger
1½ cups sour milk
1 egg, beaten

1. Cream together sugar, molasses and shortening.
2. In separate bowl combine flour, baking soda and ginger. Add to batter, alternating with sour milk. Chill.
3. Roll into balls by tablespoonsful. Arrange on greased cookie sheet and brush tops with beaten egg.
4. Bake at 350° for 12-15 minutes.

Molasses Ginger Cookies

Linda Glaros
Lodi, CA
Verna Keim
Millersburg, OH
Star Spin

Makes 3-4 dozen cookies

8 Tbsp. butter
1 cup white sugar
1 egg
¼ cup molasses
1 tsp. baking soda
2 cups flour
½ tsp. ground cloves
½ tsp. ginger
½ tsp. salt
1 tsp. cinnamon
½ cup white sugar

1. Cream together butter, 1 cup sugar, egg and molasses. Add all other ingredients except ½ cup sugar and mix well. Chill in refrigerator.
2. Form into walnut-sized balls and roll in sugar. Arrange on greased cookie sheet.
3. Bake at 350° for 8-10 minutes.

Note: Watch carefully to avoid baking cookies too long as they will become hard.

Variation:
We like these very spicy. Change to 2 tsp. baking soda, 2 tsp. ground cloves, 2 tsp. ginger and 2 tsp. cinnamon. Omit salt.

Laura Barrus Bishop
Boerne, TX
Log Cabin

Laura Bishop's Sugar Cookies

Laura Barrus Bishop
Boerne, TX
Log Cabin

Makes 4 dozen cookies

¾ cup margarine *or* butter
1¼ cups sugar
1 egg
2 tsp. vanilla
2½ cups flour
½ tsp. salt

1. Cream together margarine, sugar and egg at high speed. Stir in vanilla. Add flour and salt and mix well. Chill dough overnight.
2. Roll out dough onto lightly floured surface to ¼-inch thickness. Cut with cookie cutter and arrange on lightly greased baking sheets.
3. Bake at 350° for 12 minutes.

Note: Substitute either lemon or almond extract for vanilla.

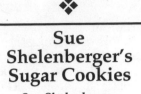

Sue Shelenberger's Sugar Cookies

Sue Shelenberger
Conneaut, OH
Ohio Star Challenge

Makes 7 dozen cookies

16 Tbsp. margarine
1 cup cooking oil
1 cup white sugar
1 cup powdered sugar
1 tsp. vanilla
1 tsp. almond extract
2 eggs
4½ cups flour
1 tsp. baking soda
1 tsp. cream of tartar
1 cup white sugar

1. Cream margarine. Add oil, 1 cup white sugar, powdered sugar, vanilla, almond extract and eggs and blend together. Add flour, baking soda and cream of tartar and mix well. Refrigerate overnight.
2. Roll dough into balls and dip into 1 cup sugar. Arrange on lightly greased baking sheets.
3. Bake at 350° for 8-10 minutes.

It was the week of my fiftieth birthday and I was feeling particularly self-centered when I received a phone call reminding me that I was expected at the local quilt shop to teach a class. I flew to the shop and discovered a surprise party. Each student had put aside her own project to make and present me with a Friendship quilt block in my favorite colors. The evening ended with a dessert named and made in my honor.

—*Katherine A. Schwartz, Freeport, IL*

Inez Dillon's Sugar Cookies

Inez E. Dillon
Tucson, AZ
Seven Sisters

Makes 5-6 dozen cookies

3 cups sifted flour
1 tsp. salt
1 tsp. baking soda
1 tsp. baking powder
½ cup shortening
½ cup butter
2 eggs
1½ cups sugar
1½ tsp. vanilla
½ tsp. almond extract
2 Tbsp. sugar *or* caraway seeds

1. Sift together flour, salt, baking soda and baking powder. Sift two more times. Cut shortening and butter into dry ingredients.
2. Beat eggs lightly and add 1½ cups sugar gradually, beating constantly. Combine 2 mixtures. Add vanilla and almond extracts.
3. Roll out dough onto lightly floured surface.

Sprinkle with sugar or caraway seeds and roll into dough. Cut with cookie cutter and arrange on lightly greased baking sheet.
4. Bake at 375° for about 6 minutes.

Sugar Jumbles

Janis Landefeld
Baltimore, MD
Antique Nine Patch

Makes about 3 dozen cookies

½ cup shortening
½ cup butter *or* margarine, softened
1 cup sugar
2 eggs
2 tsp. vanilla
2¼ cups flour
½ tsp. baking soda
1 tsp. salt

1. Cream together shortening, butter and sugar. Add eggs and vanilla and mix thoroughly.
2. Sift together flour, baking soda and salt and add

to creamed mixture. Mix well.

3. Drop by rounded teaspoonful about 2 inches apart onto lightly greased baking sheet.

4. Bake at 375° for about 8-10 minutes until delicately browned. (Cookies should still be soft.) Cool slightly before removing from cookie sheet.

❖

Brown Sugar Drop Cookies

Frances Musser
Newmanstown, PA
Sweet Country

Makes 5 dozen cookies

1 cup white sugar
1 cup brown sugar
1 cup margarine
3 eggs
2 cups flour
½ tsp. salt
¾ tsp. baking soda
2 Tbsp. hot water
1 cup chocolate chips
2 cups oatmeal
2 cups cornflakes
1 cup shredded coconut
½ cup chopped nuts
1 tsp. vanilla

1. Cream together sugars and margarine. Add eggs and beat well.

2. Sift flour and salt. Combine with creamed mixture.

3. Dissolve baking soda in hot water. Add to batter.

4. Stir in all remaining ingredients. Drop by teaspoonful onto lightly greased baking sheet.

5. Bake at 350° for about 12 minutes.

❖

Mellowy Moments Tea Cookies

Ann Bateman
Arnprior, ON
Doreen Copeland
Florence, SC
Celtic Wall Hanging

Makes 5 dozen cookies

1 cup butter
1½ cups brown sugar
1 egg
1 tsp. vanilla
2 cups flour
1 tsp. baking soda
Pinch salt

1. Cream together butter and brown sugar. Add egg and vanilla and mix well.

2. Sift together flour, baking soda and salt. Add to creamed mixture and mix well.

3. Drop by teaspoonful onto greased baking sheet. Flatten slightly with fork.

4. Bake at 350° for 8-10 minutes or until cookies are light brown.

Chocolate Chip Cookies

Gail Garber
Rio Rancho, NM
New Century Star Sampler

Makes 3-4 dozen cookies

¾ cup shortening
½ cup white sugar
¼ cup brown sugar
1 egg
1 tsp. vanilla
1½-2 cups flour
¾ tsp. salt
½ tsp. baking soda
6-oz. pkg. chocolate chips
½ cup chopped nuts (optional)

1. Cream together ½ cup shortening, sugars, egg and vanilla until very light and fluffy. Add ¼ cup shortening and mix well.

2. Mix in 1 cup flour, salt and baking soda. Add remaining flour, a little at a time, until dough is no longer wet and sticky. Fold in chocolate chips and nuts.

3. Drop by heaping teaspoonful onto greased cookie sheet. (Roll each cookie into a round ball to make perfectly round cookies.)

4. Bake at 350° for 10-15 minutes.

Buttermilk Chocolate Chip Cookies

Susan D. Fellin
Frenchtown, NJ

Makes about 8 dozen cookies

1 cup shortening
1 cup white sugar
1 cup brown sugar, packed
2 eggs
1½ tsp. vanilla
3 cups sifted flour
1 tsp. baking soda
½ cup buttermilk
6-oz. pkg. semi-sweet
    chocolate chips
1 cup chopped pecans

1. Cream together shortening and sugars until light and fluffy. Beat in eggs, one at a time. Blend in vanilla.
2. Sift together flour and baking soda. Add to creamed mixture, alternating with buttermilk and mix well. Fold in chocolate chips and pecans.
3. Drop by teaspoonful onto greased cookie sheets about 2 inches apart.
4. Bake at 350° for 12-15 minutes or until done. Remove from sheets and cool on wire rack.

> When I am quilting, I find it very difficult to break away to prepare a meal. It seems the quilt has a little voice which keeps begging, "Just a few more stitches," while the meat slowly burns and the vegetables simmer to dry.
>
> —*Charmaine Keith, Marion, KS*

Baby Ruth Cookies

Debra Jane Jackson
Rancho Cucamonga, CA

Makes 2-3 dozen cookies

8 Tbsp. butter
¾ cup sugar
1 egg
1⅓ cups flour
½ tsp. salt
½ tsp. baking soda
½ tsp. vanilla
1-2 Baby Ruth candy bars

1. Cream together butter and sugar until smooth. Beat in egg. Add all remaining ingredients except candy bars and mix well.
2. Cut candy bars into tiny pieces. Fold into cookie dough.
3. Chill dough. Drop by teaspoonful onto greased cookie sheet.
4. Bake at 375° for 10-12 minutes.

Chocolate Drops

Edna Neff Schloton
Eastchester, NY
Mrs. MacGregor's Garden

Makes 4-5 dozen cookies

14-oz. can condensed milk
4 ozs. unsweetened
    chocolate, chopped
4-oz. pkg. semi-sweet
    chocolate chips
1½ cups flaked coconut
1 cup chopped nuts
2 tsp. vanilla

1. Pour milk, chocolate and chocolate chips into double boiler. Melt over medium heat, stirring until blended. Remove from heat. Stir in coconut, nuts and vanilla and mix well.
2. Drop by heaping teaspoonful onto lightly greased cookie sheets about 1 inch apart.
3. Bake at 350° for 10 minutes. Cool about 10 minutes before removing from cookie sheets.

Pumpkin Chocolate Chip Cookies

Stephanie Braskey
Pottstown, PA
Applique Album Blocks
Judy Sharer
Port Matilda, PA
Brook's & Codey's Baby Quilts

Makes 5 dozen cookies

1 cup cooked pumpkin
1 cup white sugar
½ cup shortening *or*
  cooking oil
1 egg, beaten
2 cups flour
2 tsp. baking powder
1 tsp. cinnamon
1 tsp. salt
1 tsp. baking soda
1 tsp. milk
1 cup chocolate chips
½ cup chopped nuts
1 tsp. vanilla

1. Combine pumpkin, sugar, shortening and egg.
2. In separate bowl combine flour, baking powder, cinnamon and salt. Stir into pumpkin mixture.
3. Dissolve baking soda in milk and stir into batter. Mix well. Add chocolate chips, nuts and vanilla and mix well.
4. Drop by teaspoonsful onto lightly greased cookie sheets.
5. Bake at 375° for 10-12 minutes.

Pinwheels

Janice Way
Warrington, PA
Amish Diamond

Makes 4 dozen cookies

2 cups sifted flour
4 tsp. baking powder
½ tsp. salt
½ tsp. cream of tartar
2 tsp. sugar
½ cup shortening
⅔ cup milk
2-3 Tbsp. butter *or*
  margarine, melted
2 Tbsp. sugar
1 tsp. cinnamon
Raisins (optional)

1. Sift together flour, baking powder, salt, cream of tartar and 2 tsp. sugar. Cut in shortening until mixture resembles coarse crumbs. Add milk and stir until dough follows fork around bowl.
2. Turn out onto lightly floured surface. Knead gently for ½ minute. Roll out dough to ¼-inch thickness.
3. Spread with melted butter. Sprinkle with 2 Tbsp. sugar, cinnamon and raisins. Roll up and seal edges. Cut into ½-inch slices. Arrange, cut side down, on greased baking sheet.
4. Bake at 450° for 12-15 minutes.

Raisin Ice Box Cookies

Ethel Rush
Avella, PA
Star Flower

Makes 4-5 dozen cookies

Dough:
¾ cup shortening
2 cups brown sugar
3 eggs
1 tsp. vanilla
4½ cups flour
1 tsp. baking soda
1 tsp. baking powder

Filling:
2 cups raisins
½ cup chopped walnuts
½ cup sugar
½ cup water

1. Cream together shortening and sugar. Add eggs and vanilla and beat well. Add dry ingredients and mix well. Chill dough.
2. Roll out dough onto lightly floured surface.
3. To prepare filling combine all ingredients. Spread over rolled out dough. Roll up and chill or freeze. Slice and arrange on baking sheets.
4. Bake at 400° for 10-12 minutes or until light brown.

Ice Box Cookies

Marion Matson
Comfrey, MN
Amish Baskets

Makes 4-5 dozen cookies

½ **cup butter**
½ **cup margarine**
½ **cup white sugar**
½ **cup brown sugar**
1 egg
2½ **cups flour**
½ **tsp. baking soda**
¼ **tsp. salt**
½ **cup finely chopped**
  walnuts

1. Cream together butter, margarine and sugars. Add egg and beat well.
2. Sift together flour, baking soda and salt. Add to creamed mixture. Fold in walnuts. Shape batter into a long roll. Wrap in waxed paper and put into a plastic bag. Freeze several hours or overnight.
3. Remove from freezer and cut frozen roll into ⅛-inch slices. Arrange on ungreased cookie sheets.
4. Bake at 350° for 12-15 minutes.

Rich Cookies

Kathryn M. Geissinger
Ephrata, PA
Philadelphia Pavement

Makes 12-14 dozen cookies

2 lbs. light brown sugar
16 Tbsp. butter *or* lard
5 eggs
2 cups sour cream
2 tsp. baking soda
2 tsp. cream of tartar
2 tsp. vanilla
10-12 cups flour
5 egg whites, beaten
1 cup colored sugar

1. Cream together sugar and butter until fluffy. Add eggs, one at a time, beating after each addition.
2. Combine sour cream, baking soda, cream of tartar and vanilla. Add to creamed mixture, alternating with flour and beating well.
3. After adding 9 cups flour, add only enough remaining flour so dough is no longer sticky when punched with a finger.
4. Chill dough overnight.
5. Remove portion of dough from bowl and return remaining dough to refrigerator. Roll dough onto lightly floured board. Cut out cookies with round cookie cutter. Arrange on baking sheets. Repeat with remaining dough.
6. Brush tops with beaten egg white. Sprinkle with colored sugar.
7. Bake at 375° for 10-12 minutes or until cookies are light golden brown.

Sour Cream Cookies

Kathleen D. Martin
Batavia, NY
Grandmother's Flower Garden

Makes 5 dozen cookies

½ **cup shortening**
1½ **cups sugar**
2 eggs, well beaten
3½ **cups flour**
½ **tsp. salt**
½ **tsp. baking soda**
2 tsp. baking powder
1 cup thick sour cream
1 tsp. lemon *or* vanilla
  extract

1. Cream together shortening and sugar. Add eggs and beat well.
2. Sift together flour, salt, baking soda and baking powder. Add to creamed mixture, alternating with sour cream. Add flavoring and mix well.
3. Drop by teaspoonful onto greased baking sheets.
4. Bake at 400° for 10-15 minutes.
5. If desired, frost before serving.

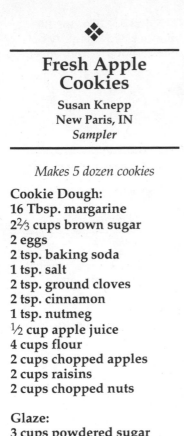

Fresh Apple Cookies

Susan Knepp
New Paris, IN
Sampler

Makes 5 dozen cookies

Cookie Dough:
16 Tbsp. margarine
2²/₃ cups brown sugar
2 eggs
2 tsp. baking soda
1 tsp. salt
2 tsp. ground cloves
2 tsp. cinnamon
1 tsp. nutmeg
½ cup apple juice
4 cups flour
2 cups chopped apples
2 cups raisins
2 cups chopped nuts

Glaze:
3 cups powdered sugar
5 Tbsp. apple juice
¼ tsp. salt
½ tsp. vanilla
2 Tbsp. margarine

1. Cream together margarine, brown sugar and eggs. Add baking soda, spices and apple juice and mix well. Gradually add flour, mixing well after each addition. Fold in apples, raisins and nuts.
2. Drop by heaping teaspoonsful onto lightly greased cookie sheet.
3. Bake at 375° for 10-12 minutes.
4. To prepare glaze combine all ingredients and

beat until smooth.
5. With a knife spread warm cookies with glaze. Freeze between layers of waxed paper in plastic container.

Applesauce Raisin Cookies

Betty Cook & Thelma Thomas
Winter Haven, FL

Makes 5 dozen cookies

8 Tbsp. margarine
1 egg
1 cup white sugar
1¾ cups flour
½ tsp. baking powder
1 tsp. baking soda
½ tsp. salt
1 tsp. cinnamon
½ tsp. ground cloves
½ tsp. nutmeg
1 cup raisins
1 cup oats
1 cup applesauce

1. Cream together margarine, egg and sugar. Add all other ingredients and mix well.
2. Drop by teaspoonsful onto greased cookie sheet.
3. Bake at 375° for 15 minutes.

Lemon Bon Bons

Alice Walker
Winter Haven, FL

Cookie Dough:
6 Tbsp. butter *or* margarine
⅓ cup powdered sugar
¼ cup cornstarch
1¼ cups sifted flour

Frosting:
1 cup powdered sugar
1 tsp. butter
2 Tbsp. lemon juice
1 drop yellow food coloring
½ cup finely chopped pecans

1. To prepare dough cream together butter and powdered sugar until fluffy.
2. Sift together cornstarch and flour and add to batter, beating until well mixed. Refrigerate at least 1 hour.
3. Shape batter into walnut-sized balls. Arrange on lightly greased cookie sheet.
4. Bake at 350° for 15 minutes or until light brown. Cool before frosting.
5. To prepare frosting combine all ingredients except pecans and mix well. Spread frosting over cookies. Dip top of each cookie in finely chopped pecans.

On Christmas Eve we love using our antique pink and white Irish Chain quilt, covered with a thin sheet of clear plastic, as a tablecloth. With the silverware shining, the candles glowing and the crystal sparkling, our family sits down to a traditional dinner of Chicken Divan with all the trimmings.

—*Mitzi McGlynchey, Downingtown, PA*

Just Delicious Cookies

Mrs. Melvin A. Yoder
Hutchinson, KS
Broken Star

Makes about 100 cookies

1 cup white sugar
1 cup brown sugar
1 cup soft margarine
1 cup cooking oil
2 eggs
1 tsp. vanilla
½ tsp. butter extract
3½ cups flour
1 tsp. cream of tartar
1 tsp. baking soda
1 tsp. salt
1 cup oatmeal
1 cup coconut
1 cup chopped pecans
3 cups Rice Krispies

1. Combine all ingredients, adding to bowl in order listed. Mix well.
2. Shape into balls and arrange on cookie sheet. Dip fork or drinking glass into white sugar and flatten each cookie.
3. Bake at 350° for 10-12 minutes.

Everything Cookies

Sarah Hadbavny
Edgewood, MD
Fishing

Makes 2-3 dozen cookies

½ cup white sugar
½ cup brown sugar
½ cup butter
1 egg
1 tsp. vanilla
½ tsp. baking soda
½ tsp. cinnamon
¼ tsp. salt
1½ cups uncooked oatmeal
¾ cup flour
½ cup raisins
½ cup chopped, dried apricots
½ cup chopped nuts
½ cup chocolate chips
½ cup coconut (optional)

1. Cream together sugars, butter, egg and vanilla. Add baking soda, cinnamon, salt, oatmeal and flour and mix well. Fold in raisins, apricots, nuts, chocolate chips and coconut.
2. Drop onto ungreased cookie sheet.

3. Bake at 375° for 10 minutes. Cool slightly before removing from sheet.

Walneto's Cookies

Charmaine Caesar
Lancaster, PA
Grandmother's Memories

Makes 3 dozen cookies

2¾ cups sifted flour
1 tsp. baking soda
1 tsp. salt
1 cup shortening, softened
¾ cup white sugar
¾ cup brown sugar
1 tsp. vanilla
½ tsp. water
2 eggs, beaten
1 cup chopped walnuts

1. Combine flour, baking soda and salt.
2. Cream together shortening, sugars and vanilla. Add water and eggs and mix well. Add walnuts and dry ingredients and mix well.
3. Drop by teaspoonful onto greased baking sheet.
4. Bake at 350° for 10-12 minutes.

Note: To keep cookies from spreading use cooled baking sheet each time. Makes a nice chewy cookie.

Nut Snowballs

Barb Grauer
Owings Mills, MD
Log Cabin Star

Makes 4 dozen cookies

1 cup butter *or* margarine
¼ cup powdered sugar
1 tsp. vanilla
⅛ tsp. almond extract
2 cups sifted flour
1 cup chopped walnuts
1 cup powdered sugar

1. Cream together butter and ¼ cup powdered sugar until light and fluffy. Add flavorings and mix well. Stir in flour and nuts and mix well.

2. Form dough into small balls. Arrange on ungreased baking sheet.

3. Bake at 350° for 15-20 minutes. While cookies are still warm, roll in powdered sugar.

Hungarian Walnut Cookies

Berta Stegmeier
Silver Spring, MD
Friends and Food

Makes 12 dozen small cookies

Dough:
2 8-oz. pkgs. cream cheese
16 Tbsp. butter
5 cups flour
2 cups sugar

Walnut Filling:
1 lb. ground walnuts
1 tsp. vanilla
½-¾ cup strawberry jam
1 cup powdered sugar

1. Combine all dough ingredients by hand until dough is smooth. Divide into 4 balls.

2. Roll out each ball to ⅛-inch thickness. Cut into 2 ½-inch squares with knife.

3. To prepare filling combine all ingredients except powdered sugar to make a thick paste.

4. Drop ½ tsp. walnut filling onto corner of each cookie square. Roll cookie square to opposite corner. Arrange on baking sheet.

5. Bake at 350° for 9 minutes. Sprinkle with powdered sugar and serve.

Maple Pecan Cookies

Frances Musser
Newmanstown, PA
Sweet Country

Makes 5-6 dozen cookies

2⅔ cups brown sugar
1 cup margarine
2 eggs
1 tsp. maple flavoring
4 cups flour
1 tsp. baking soda
1 tsp. baking powder
½ tsp. salt
1 cup shredded coconut
1 cup chopped pecans

1. Cream together sugar and margarine. Add eggs and flavoring.

2. Sift together flour, baking soda, baking powder and salt. Add to creamed mixture.

3. Fold in coconut and pecans. Form dough into a roll approximately 2 inches in diameter. Wrap with waxed paper and chill overnight.

4. Cut into ½-inch slices and arrange on cookie sheets.

5. Bake at 350° for 10-12 minutes.

I do custom quilting. Several years ago a gentleman brought me two quilt tops. After his wife died, he discovered that she had saved his neckties for 50 years. Using the neckties, he designed quilt blocks, piecing them all by hand. He chose to make the entire quilt with silk and brought me silk thread for the quilting. He had done beautiful work and gave the two quilts to his son and daughter as Christmas gifts.

—Erma Landis, Sterling, IL

Honey Crunch Cookies

Audrey L. Kneer
Williamsfield, IL
Snowball & Nine Patch

Makes 3 dozen cookies

2½ cups sifted flour
2 tsp. baking powder
½ tsp. salt
1 cup margarine *or* butter
1 cup honey
2 eggs
1 cup shredded coconut
1 cup butterscotch chips
4 cups Rice Krispies

1. Sift together flour, baking powder and salt.
2. Cream margarine. Add honey slowly and mix well. Add eggs, one at a time, and mix well. Gradually add dry ingredients. Fold in coconut, butterscotch chips and Rice Krispies.
3. Drop by tablespoonsful onto lightly greased baking sheet.
4. Bake at 350° for about 12 minutes.

Dishpan Cookies

Peggy Hamilton, Hillsboro, OH
Vera E. Duncan, Sibley, MO
Robin Schrock
Millersburg, OH

Makes 12-14 dozen cookies

2 cups white sugar
2 cups brown sugar
2 cups cooking oil
4 eggs
2 tsp. vanilla
4 cups flour
2 tsp. baking soda
1 tsp. salt
1½ cups quick oats
4 cups cornflakes
1 cup raisins *or* chocolate chips

1. Cream together sugars and oil. Add eggs and vanilla and mix well.
2. Combine flour, baking soda and salt. Add to creamed ingredients and mix well. Add all remaining ingredients and mix well.
3. Drop by teaspoonsful onto greased baking sheet.
4. Bake at 350° for 8-10 minutes.

Macaroons

Betty Ann Sheganoski
Bayonne, NJ
Schoolhouse

Makes 3-4 dozen cookies

6 Tbsp. water
½ Tbsp. light corn syrup
Pinch salt
1¾ cups + 2 Tbsp. sugar
1 lb. unsweetened coconut
7 large eggs

1. Line baking sheets with parchment paper. Set aside.
2. In a saucepan bring water, corn syrup and salt to a boil. Add sugar and stir to dissolve. Pour into mixing bowl and add coconut, stirring until well blended.
3. Separate eggs. Add egg whites to cookie mixture and mix well. (Save yolks for future use.)
4. Spoon batter into pastry bag and pipe into 1-inch mounds about ½ inch apart on baking sheets.
5. Bake at 325° in lower third of oven for 20-25 minutes or until light golden color. Cool on wire racks before removing from baking sheet.

Note: Unsweetened coconut may be purchased in health food stores.

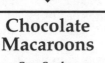

Chocolate Macaroons

Sue Seeley
Black Forest, CO
Flying Geese

Makes 2 dozen cookies

14-oz. can sweeteened condensed milk
3 squares unsweetened chocolate
¼ tsp. salt
8 ozs. coconut
1 tsp. vanilla

1. Combine condensed milk, chocolate and salt in top of double boiler. Cook, stirring frequently, until chocolate melts and mixture thickens. Remove from heat.
2. Stir in coconut and vanilla and mix well.
3. Drop by rounded tablespoonsful about 1 inch apart onto generously greased cookie sheet.
4. Bake at 350° for 10-12 minutes. Cool on wire rack and store in airtight container.

Little Debbie Cookies

Elizabeth Chupp
Arthur, IL
Whirling Star
Lucille Z. Brubacker
Barnett, MO
Country Love

Makes about 3-4 dozen cookies

Cookie Dough:
1 cup margarine
3 cups brown sugar
4 eggs
2 tsp. cinnamon
1½ tsp. nutmeg
1 tsp. baking soda
3 cups flour
3 cups uncooked oatmeal

Filling:
2 egg whites
2 tsp. vanilla
4 Tbsp. milk
4 cups powdered sugar
1 cup shortening

1. To prepare cookie dough cream together margarine, sugar, eggs, cinnamon and nutmeg. Add all remaining ingredients and mix well.
2. Drop by teaspoonful onto greased cookie sheet and flatten.
3. Bake at 350° for 10-12 minutes. Do not overbake.
4. To prepare filling beat egg whites. Add vanilla, milk and 2 cups powdered sugar and beat thoroughly. Add remaining sugar and shortening and mix well.

5. Spread filling over one cookie and top with another one, making a sandwich.

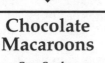

African Sesame Crisps

Marcia S. Myer
Manheim, PA
Dresden Plate

Makes 2-3 dozen cookies

1 cup sesame seeds
½ cup grated coconut
2 cups flour
1 tsp. baking powder
½ tsp. salt
½ tsp. baking soda
¾ cup butter *or* margarine
1 cup brown sugar
1 egg
1 tsp. vanilla

1. Toast sesame seeds and coconut at 350° for 10 minutes, stirring every few minutes.
2. Sift together flour, baking powder, salt and baking soda.
3. Cream together butter, sugar, egg and vanilla. Add dry ingredients, sesame seeds and coconut and mix well.
4. Drop by teaspoonsful onto ungreased cookie sheet. Flatten with spoon.
5. Bake at 350° for 10-12 minutes.

Pumpkin Whoopie Pies

Lydia Brubacker
Barnett, MO
Appliqued Butterfly

Makes 2 dozen cookies

Cookie Dough:
2 cups brown sugar
1 cup cooking oil
1½ cups pumpkin
2 eggs
3 cups flour
1 tsp. salt
1 tsp. baking powder
1 tsp. baking soda
1 tsp. vanilla
1½ Tbsp. cinnamon
½ Tbsp. ginger
½ Tbsp. ground cloves

Filling:
3 cups shortening
4 cups powdered sugar
1 Tbsp. milk
4 egg whites, beaten
4 Tbsp. flour
2 Tbsp. vanilla

1. Cream together brown sugar and oil. Add pumpkin and eggs and mix well.
2. Combine all remaining ingredients and mix into creamed mixture. Drop by large tablespoonsful onto greased baking sheet.
3. Bake at 350° for 10-12 minutes.
4. To prepare filling combine all ingredients and mix well.
5. Make whoopie pies by spreading filling on flat side of one cookie and making a sandwich with another cookie. Store in airtight container.

Cookie Pops

Cheryl Bartel
Hillsboro, KS
Traditional Sampler

Makes 10 cookie pops

½ cup sugar
½ cup brown sugar, firmly packed
½ cup margarine *or* butter, softened
½ cup peanut butter
1 tsp. vanilla
1 egg
1½ cups flour
½ tsp. baking powder
½ tsp. baking soda
¼ tsp. salt
10 wooden popsickle sticks
10 large Milky Way candy bars

1. In large bowl cream together sugars, margarine, peanut butter, vanilla and egg. Add flour, baking powder, baking soda and salt and mix well.
2. Securely insert wooden stick lengthwise into candy bar. Shape ⅓ cup dough smoothly around each candy bar, making sure bar is completely covered. Arrange about 4 inches apart on un-greased cookie sheets.
3. Bake at 375° for 14-16 minutes or until golden brown. Cool 10 minutes. Remove from baking sheets and cool completely.

Note: These cookie pops are huge. For birthday treats put plastic bag over the cookie and tie with a ribbon.

Candy Cane Cookies

Marion Nanopoulos
Oxford, PA
Bermuda Triangles

Makes 2 dozen 5-inch cookies

1 cup shortening
1 cup sugar
1 egg
1½ tsp. flavoring*
1 tsp. vanilla
2½ cups flour
1 tsp. salt
1-2 drops red food coloring

*Use choice of any of following flavorings: rum, lemon, peppermint or walnut

1. Cream together shortening, sugar, egg, flavoring and vanilla and mix well.
2. Sift together flour and salt. Stir into creamed mixture and mix well. Add enough flour to make a stiff dough.

3. Divide dough in half and add red food coloring to ½ of dough. Let other half white.

4. Roll 1 tsp. red dough into pencil-thick log. Roll 1 tsp. white dough into pencil-thick log. Twist 2 logs together and bend top over to form candy cane. Repeat with remaining dough. Arrange on ungreased baking sheet.

5. Bake at 375° for 9 minutes. Cool slightly before removing from baking sheets. Cookies are fragile but delicious.

Snickerdoodles

**Connie Weaver, Bethlehem, PA
Nancy V. Schaub,
Warminster, PA
Jo Ellen Rousey, Anderson, IN**

Makes 6 dozen cookies

½ **cup margarine**
½ **cup butter**
1½ **cups sugar**
2 eggs
2¾ **cups flour**
2 tsp. cream of tartar
1 tsp. baking soda
¼ **tsp. salt**
2 Tbsp. sugar
2 tsp. cinnamon

1. Cream together margarine, butter, 1½ cups sugar and eggs.
2. Combine flour, cream of tartar, baking soda and

salt. Stir into creamed mixture and mix well. Shape dough into 1-inch balls.

3. Combine 2 Tbsp. sugar and cinnamon. Roll dough balls into sugar and cinnamon mixture. Arrange 2 inches apart on ungreased baking sheet.

4. Bake at 400° for 8-10 minutes.

Prize Mincemeat Cookies

**Bonnie McCulley
Winter Haven, FL**

Makes 6-7 dozen cookies

1½ **cups sugar**
1 cup shortening
3 eggs
3 cups unsifted flour
1 tsp. baking soda
½ **tsp. salt**
**9-oz. can condensed
    mincemeat, crumbled**

1. In large bowl cream together sugar and shortening until fluffy. Beat in eggs.
2. In separate bowl sift together dry ingredients. Add to creamed ingredients and mix well. Stir in mincemeat.
3. Drop by rounded teaspoonsful onto greased baking sheet, about 2 inches apart.
4. Bake at 375° for 8-10 minutes or until lightly brown.

❖

Potato Chip Cookies

**Carol M. Mifflin
Houston, TX**
Scrap Pastel Basket
**Evelyn M. Becker
Paradise, PA**
Double Irish Chain

Makes 3-4 dozen cookies

16 Tbsp. butter
¾ **cup sugar**
1½ **cups flour**
1 tsp. vanilla
1 cup crushed potato chips
1 cup chopped pecans
Powdered sugar

1. Cream together butter and sugar. Gradually add flour and mix well. Add vanilla and potato chips and mix well. Fold in nuts.
2. Drop onto ungreased cookie sheets and flatten with bottom of a drinking glass which has been dipped in sugar.
3. Bake at 350° for 8-10 minutes.

While I work for weeks and sometimes months on my latest quilt, my husband patiently watches the progress and frequently says, "I can't wait until you are finished so we can use that cover up." The first night after we have used the new quilt, he usually wakes up with the following comment, "That's the best night's sleep I have had in months."

—*Rose Hankins, Stevensville, MD*

Lebkuchen

Merlie Vidette
Duxbury, MA
Trip Around the World

Makes 5-6 dozen cookies

Cookie Dough:
2¾ cups flour
1 cup brown sugar
¼ tsp. baking soda
5 Tbsp. honey
½ tsp. cinnamon
½ tsp. ground cloves
½ tsp. allspice
2 eggs
Grated rind of ½ lemon

Frosting:
1 egg white
Powdered sugar

1. Combine all cookie dough ingredients by hand in large bowl. Dough will be moist and slightly sticky.
2. Roll out dough, a little at a time, to ⅛-inch thickness. Cut into shapes with cookie cutter. Arrange on greased baking sheets.
3. Bake at 350° for approximately 8-10 minutes. Let cool.

4. To prepare frosting beat egg white with enough powdered sugar to make of spreading consistency.
5. Spread cooled cookies with frosting and let dry. Store in airtight container.

Note: These cookies soften with age and increase in flavor. They have no fat and will not turn rancid.

Cranberry Bar Cookies

Irma H. Schoen
Windsor, CT
Hobby Horse

Makes 3 dozen bars

8 Tbsp. butter, softened
1½ cups sugar
1½ cups flour
2 eggs, beaten
1 cup chopped nuts
1½ cups fresh cranberries

1. Cream together butter and sugar. Add flour and eggs and mix well.

2. Fold in nuts and cranberries. Spoon into greased and floured 9" x 13" baking pan.
3. Bake at 350° for 35-40 minutes. Cool and refrigerate.
4. Cut into bars before serving.

Cranberry Chews

Mary Wheatley
Mashpee, MA
Round the Twist

Makes 64 small bars

2⅓ cups all-purpose flour
1 cup brown sugar, packed
1 tsp. ground cinnamon
½ tsp. ground nutmeg
¼ tsp. ground cloves
½ tsp. salt
1 cup cold margarine, cut up
1½ cups quick oats
16-oz. can whole berry cranberry sauce
½ cup orange marmalade
1 tsp. vanilla
1 cup chopped walnuts

1. Combine 2 cups flour, brown sugar, spices and salt. Cut in margarine with pastry blender until mixture resembles coarse crumbs. Stir in oats. Reserve 1½ cups mixture.
2. Firmly press remaining mixture over bottom of greased 10" x 15" jelly roll pan.

3. Bake at 350° for 15 minutes. Cool 10 minutes before filling.

4. In medium bowl stir together cranberry sauce, marmalade and vanilla. Add remaining⅓ cup flour, 1 Tbsp. at a time, blending well after each addition. Spread evenly over cooled crust.

5. Add nuts to reserved 1½ cups crumb mixture. Sprinkle over cranberry filling.

6. Bake another 30 minutes or until lightly browned. Cool in pan on rack. Cut into 64 bars, cutting 8 strips each way.

❖

Raspberry Almond Bars

Suzanne S. Nobrega
Duxbury, MA
Amish Nine Patch

Makes 24 bars

1 cup all-purpose flour
¾ cup quick oats
½ cup white sugar
8 Tbsp. butter *or* margarine, softened
½ tsp. almond extract
½ cup red raspberry preserves
⅓ cup sliced almonds

1. Combine flour, oats and sugar in large bowl. Cut in butter until mixture resembles coarse crumbs. Stir in extract until blended. Reserve 1 cup crumbs.

2. Press remaining crumbs into foil-lined and greased 8-inch square baking pan. Spread preserves over crust to about ½ inch from the edges.

3. Combine almonds with reserved crumbs. Sprinkle evenly over preserves and press down gently.

4. Bake at 350° for 25-30 minutes or until edges are golden. Cool in pan and lift foil by edges to remove large bar. Cut into smaller bars and serve.

❖

Apple Pastry Squares

Susan Orleman
Pittsburgh, PA
Island Stars

Makes 24 squares

Pastry:
2 cups flour
½ tsp. salt
⅔ cup shortening
2 egg yolks
1 Tbsp. lemon juice
¼ cup cold water

Filling:
¼ cup brown sugar, firmly packed
2 Tbsp. cornstarch
1 cup water

1 Tbsp. lemon juice
4 cups thinly sliced apples
1 tsp. cinnamon
1 tsp. nutmeg

Glaze:
1 cup powdered sugar
½ tsp. vanilla
2 Tbsp. butter
2 Tbsp. milk

1. To prepare pastry combine flour and salt. With a pastry blender cut in shortening until mixture is crumbly. Blend in egg yolks, lemon juice and water. Divide dough in half. Reserve ½ of dough.

2. Roll remaining ½ of dough out to fit bottom and halfway up sides of 9" x 13" baking pan.

3. To prepare filling combine brown sugar, cornstarch, water and lemon juice in a saucepan, mixing until smooth. Add apples and heat to a rolling boil, stirring constantly. Lower heat and simmer 5 minutes, stirring occasionally to prevent scorching.

4. Spread apple mixture over pastry. Sprinkle with cinnamon and nutmeg.

5. Roll out reserved dough to fit top of pan. Fold down sides and seal. Cut slashes in top to allow steam to escape.

6. Bake at 400° for 30-40 minutes.

7. In a medium bowl combine all glaze ingredients and beat until smooth. Drizzle over warm pastry. Slice into squares and serve.

Danish Pastry Apple Bars

Sara Wilson
Clinton, MO
Sampler

Makes 20-24 bars

2½ cups sifted flour
1 tsp. salt
½ cup shortening
½ cup margarine
1 egg, separated
Milk
1 cup cornflakes
8-10 apples
½ cup white sugar
1 tsp. cinnamon
1 cup powdered sugar
3-4 Tbsp. milk

1. Combine flour and salt. Cut in shortening and margarine.
2. In measuring cup beat egg yolk. Add enough milk to make ⅔ cup and mix well. Pour egg mixture into flour mixture and mix well.
3. Roll out ½ of dough into bottom of 9" x 13" baking pan. Sprinkle with cornflakes.
4. Peel and slice apples and layer over cornflakes.
5. Combine white sugar and cinnamon and sprinkle over apples.
6. Roll out remaining dough and place over top. Seal edges and cut slits in top.
7. Beat egg white until frothy. Brush top of crust with egg white.

> Many years ago, I attended a quilting bee at my grandmother's home. We were stitching away savoring the odor of pork, sauerkraut and dumplings when we suddenly smelled burned sauerkraut. My aunt was terribly embarrassed because she had been quilt watching instead of pot watching. That pan never did get clean.
>
> —*Jean Harris Robinson, Cinnaminson, NJ*

8. Bake at 350° for 45 minutes.
9. Combine powdered sugar and milk and drizzle over warm cake. Cut into bars and serve.

Pineapple Coconut Bars

Elizabeth Boyton
Gordonville, PA
Irish Chain

Makes 10 bars

Crust:
1¼ cups flour
¼ cup sugar
½ cup shortening

Topping:
20-oz. can crushed
  pineapple, drained
1 Tbsp. soft butter
½ cup sugar
1 egg
1½ cups coconut

1. To prepare crust combine flour and sugar and cut in shortening. Pat into 10-inch square baking pan.
2. Bake at 350° for 15 minutes.
3. Remove from oven and spread pineapple over top.
4. Cream together butter, sugar and egg. Fold in coconut and spread over pineapple layer.
5. Bake at 325° for another 25-30 minutes.

Rhubarb Bars

Ruth Liebelt
Rapid City, SD
Americana
Kathleen Leach
Mooresville, IN
Tree of Life

Makes 20-24 bars

2 Tbsp. cornstarch
¼ cup water
3 cups chopped rhubarb
1½ cups sugar
1 Tbsp. butter
1 tsp. vanilla
1½ cups uncooked oatmeal
1 cup margarine
1½ cups flour

1 cup brown sugar
½ tsp. baking soda
½ cup chopped nuts

1. Dissolve cornstarch in water. Add rhubarb and sugar and cook until thickened. Add butter and vanilla and mix well. Cool slightly.

2. Combine oats, margarine, flour, brown sugar, baking soda and nuts and blend until crumbly. Reserve ¼ of mixture.

3. Press remaining mixture into lightly greased 9" x 13" baking pan. Pour in rhubarb mixture. Sprinkle top with reserved crumbs.

4. Bake at 375° for 30-35 minutes. Cut into bars and serve.

❖

Banana Bars

Linda Baker
Arnold, MD
Tree of Life

Makes 36 bars

Batter:
½ cup pecans
2 cups flour
2 tsp. baking powder
⅛ tsp. cinnamon
2-3 bananas
¼ cup shortening, room
   temperature
1 cup sugar
2 eggs
1 tsp. vanilla

Glaze:
½ lb. powdered sugar
1 tsp. rum extract
Water *or* orange juice

1. In a food processor chop pecans. Set aside in small bowl.

2. Combine flour, baking powder and cinnamon in food processor. Set aside in bowl.

3. Process bananas. Measure out 1 cup bananas. Freeze any remaining bananas for future use.

4. Cream together shortening and sugar in processor. Add eggs, vanilla and bananas and mix thoroughly. Add dry ingredients and mix until just combined. Add pecans. Spread batter onto greased jelly roll pan.

3. Bake at 350° for 20-25 minutes.

4. To prepare glaze combine powdered sugar, rum extract and enough water to make pouring consistency. Glaze cake while still warm. Cut into small bars and serve.

❖

Frosty Lemon Bars

Marilyn Wallace, Alfred, ME
Fanny E. Hymes
Clarksville, MD
Karen Moore, Fairfax, VA

Makes 20-24 bars

Crust:
2¼ cups flour
½ cup powdered sugar
16 Tbsp. margarine, melted

Filling:
4 eggs
¼ cup lemon juice
2 cups white sugar
¼ cup flour
1 tsp. baking powder

1. To prepare crust combine flour and powdered sugar. Add margarine and mix well, working by hand. Press into 9" x 13" baking pan.

2. Bake at 350° for 15 minutes.

3. To prepare filling beat eggs well with fork. Add lemon juice and mix well.

4. Combine all dry ingredients and add to egg mixture, beating thoroughly. Pour over crust.

5. Bake at 350° for 25 minutes. Cool and sprinkle with powdered sugar. Cut into squares and serve.

Lemon Bars

Donna Hardy
Washington, DC
Kaleido Crosses

Makes 20-24 bars

3 eggs
⅓ cup margarine
1 box lemon cake mix
1 cup white sugar
½ tsp. baking powder
¼ tsp. salt
¼ cup lemon juice

1. Mix together 1 egg, margarine and dry cake mix until crumbly. Reserve 1 cup. Press remaining mixture into ungreased 9" x 13" baking pan.
2. Bake at 350° for 15 minutes.
3. Beat 2 eggs, sugar, baking powder, salt and lemon juice until light and foamy. Pour over hot crust. Sprinkle with reserved crust mixture.
4. Bake at 350° for 15 minutes or until light brown.
5. Sprinkle with powdered sugar, cool and cut into bars.

Lemon Butter Chews

Suellen Fletcher
Noblesville, IN
Double Irish Chain
Carole M. Mackie
Dahinda, IL
Prairie Flower

Makes 20-24 bars

1 box lemon cake mix
1 egg
8 Tbsp. butter, melted
8-oz. pkg. cream cheese
2 eggs
2 cups powdered sugar

1. Combine cake mix, 1 egg and butter. Spoon into ungreased 9" x 13" baking pan.
2. Combine cream cheese, 2 eggs and powdered sugar and beat at least 3 minutes or until smooth. Spread over cake batter.
3. Bake at 350° for 45 minutes. Cool and slice into squares before serving.

Variation:
Substitute 21-oz. can pumpkin pie filling for cream cheese layer. Bake at 350° for 50-55 minutes or until pumpkin sets. Serve with whipped topping.
Helen L. Anderson
Titusville, IN
Stacked Bricks

Grandma Wells's Date Nut Bars

Marsha Sands
Ocean City, MD
Window of Miracles

Makes 20-24 bars

¾ cup butter
1½ cups sugar
½ tsp. baking soda
1 cup buttermilk
3 cups flour
1 tsp. baking powder
1½ cups whole dates, chopped
1 cup chopped walnuts
Powdered sugar

1. Cream together butter and sugar.
2. Stir together baking soda and buttermilk. Add to creamed mixture and beat well.
3. Sift together flour and baking powder. Stir into creamed mixture. Fold in dates and walnuts. Spoon into greased 9" x 13" baking pan.
4. Bake at 325° for 25 minutes or until lightly browned. Cool slightly, cut into squares and dredge in powdered sugar.

Date Squares

Sally Bradley
Arnprior, ON
Sampler

Makes 20-24 squares

1¼ **cups flour**
½ **tsp. salt**
1 **tsp. baking soda**
1¼ **cups rolled oats**
1 **cup brown sugar**
8 **Tbsp. butter**
½ **lb. dates**
1½ **cups boiling water**

1. Sift together flour, salt and baking soda. Add oats and brown sugar and mix well. Cut in butter.

2. Spread ¾ of mixture into greased 9" x 13" baking pan.

3. Chop dates and add to boiling water in saucepan. Simmer until thickened. Spread mixture over crust. Spread remaining crust mixture over top of dates.

4. Bake at 350° for 20 minutes.

Sour Cream Raisin Bars

Susie Braun, Rapid City, SD
Adella Halsey, Wymore, NE
Marian Brubacker
Barnett, MO

Makes 20-24 bars

Crust:
1 **cup brown sugar**
1 **cup butter**
1 **tsp. baking soda**
1¾ **cups uncooked oatmeal**
1¾ **cups flour**

Filling:
2 **cups raisins**
Water to cover
3 **egg yolks, beaten**
1½ **cups sour cream**
1 **cup sugar**
2 **Tbsp. cornstarch**

1. To prepare crust cream together brown sugar and butter. Add baking soda, oats and flour and mix well. Press ½ of mixture into 9" x 13" baking pan.

2. Bake at 350° for 7 minutes.

3. To prepare filling simmer raisins in water to cover until raisins are softened. Drain and cool.

4. In a heavy saucepan combine egg yolks, sour cream, sugar and cornstarch and cook over medium-high heat until it begins to thicken, stirring constantly. Remove from heat and stir in raisins. Pour over baked crust. Sprinkle remaining ½ of crust mixture over top.

5. Bake at 350° for 15-20 minutes. Cool and refrigerate until ready to serve.

❖

Raisin Bars

Anna Stoltzfus
Honey Brook, PA
Bird and State

Makes 36 bars

5 **cups raisins**
1½ **cups water**
6 **tsp. lemon juice**
4 **tsp. clear gel**
1 **cup margarine**
1 **cup brown sugar**
2 **cups flour**
1 **tsp. salt** *or* less
1 **tsp. baking soda**
2 **cups rolled oats**

1. In a saucepan combine raisins, water, lemon juice and clear gel and cook over low heat until clear gel has dissolved. Cool.

2. In a mixing bowl cream together margarine and sugar. Add all remaining ingredients and mix until crumbly. Firmly press ½ crumb mixture into greased 9" x 13" baking pan. Spread with cooled filling and cover with remaining crumbs.

3. Bake at 400° for 25-30 minutes. Cut into small bars while still warm. Serve.

Old-Fashioned Raisin Bars

Debra M. Zeida
Waquoit, MA
Pennsylvania Bride

Makes 24 bars

1 cup seedless raisins
1 cup water
½ cup cooking oil
1 cup sugar
1 egg, lightly beaten
1¾ cups sifted flour
¼ tsp. salt
1 tsp. baking soda
1 tsp. cinnamon
½ tsp. nutmeg
½ tsp. allspice
½ tsp. ground cloves

1. Combine raisins and water in a saucepan. Bring to a boil and remove from heat. Stir in cooking oil and cool to lukewarm. Stir in sugar and egg.
2. Sift together all remaining ingredients and beat into raisin mixture. Pour into 9" x 13" baking pan.
3. Bake at 375° for 20 minutes or until done.
4. When cooled, cut into bars and serve.

Cherry Cheesecake Bars

Frani Shaffer
West Caln, PA
Rose of Sharon
Janet Hallard
Watchung, NJ
Friendship

Makes 12-16 bars

Crust:
6 Tbsp. butter
½ cup light brown sugar, packed
1 cup flour
¾ cup toasted almonds
1 cup cherry preserves

Cheese Filling:
8 Tbsp. sugar
8-oz. pkg. cream cheese, softened
1 egg
2 Tbsp. milk
½ tsp. almond extract

1. To prepare crust cream together butter and brown sugar. Blend in flour and almonds until mixture is crumbly. Reserve ½ cup crumbs. Press remaining crumbs into 8-inch square baking pan.
2. Bake at 350° for 12-15 minutes or until crust is golden. Cool slightly. Spread preserves over crust.
3. To prepare filling cream together sugar and cream cheese. Blend in egg, milk and almond extract. Spread filling over preserves. Sprinkle with re-

served crumbs.
4. Return to oven and bake 20 minutes longer. Cool.
5. Cut into bars and store in refrigerator.

Viennese Walnut Bars

Pamela R. Kerschner
Stevensville, MD
Bunny Trail

Makes 20-24 bars

Pastry:
8 Tbsp. butter, softened
3-oz. pkg. cream cheese, softened
¼ cup sugar
1¼ cups all-purpose flour
1 cup chopped walnuts
6-oz. pkg. semi-sweet chocolate chips

Topping:
1 cup all-purpose flour
¼ tsp. baking powder
¼ tsp. salt
1½ cups light brown sugar, packed
4 Tbsp. butter, softened
2 large eggs
1 tsp. instant coffee
1 Tbsp. hot water
½ cup chopped walnuts

1. To prepare pastry cream together butter, cream cheese and sugar. Gradually beat in flour. Press evenly into bottom of

greased 9" x 13" baking pan. Sprinkle with walnuts and chocolate chips.

2. To prepare topping sift together flour, baking powder and salt.

3. Cream together brown sugar, butter and eggs in medium bowl.

4. Dissolve coffee in hot water and add to creamed mixture. Gradually add flour mixture. Spoon over crust, spreading gently to cover. Sprinkle with walnuts.

5. Bake at 350° for 30 minutes or until lightly browned. Cool on wire rack. Cut into bars and serve.

Lee's Granola Bars

Berta Stegmeier
Silver Spring, MD
Friends and Food

Makes 24 bars

2 cups uncooked oatmeal
3 cups granola
½ cup chopped nuts
⅓ cup raisins
¼ cup cooking oil
¼ cup light corn syrup
⅓ cup honey
2 tsp. cinnamon

1. Combine all ingredients in order listed. Press into greased 10" x 15" baking pan. Flatten mixture into pan using a rolling pin.

2. Bake at 325° for 18 minutes. After baking, flatten mixture again using rolling pin. Cool and cut into bars.

Oatmeal Jumble Bars

LaVerne H. Olson
Willow Street, PA
Log Cabin Star

Makes 20-24 bars

3 cups uncooked oatmeal
1½ cups flour
1 cup brown sugar
1 cup margarine, melted
¾ tsp. salt
½ tsp. baking soda
10-12-oz. jar preserves

1. In large bowl combine all ingredients except preserves and mix well. Reserve 1 cup mixture. Press remaining mixture into greased 9" x 13" baking pan.

2. Spread preserves over crumb crust to within ½ inch of the edge. Sprinkle with reserved crumbs.

3. Bake at 350° for 25-30 minutes.

Crunchy Bars

Barbara Stoltzfus
Kinzer, PA
Log Cabin

Makes 12-16 bars

4 cups uncooked oatmeal
1 cup whole wheat flour
1½ cups chopped nuts
1 cup honey
1 tsp. vanilla
1 tsp. salt
¾ cup butter *or* margarine

1. Combine all ingredients and mix well. Press into well-greased 9-inch square baking pan.

2. Bake at 425° for 10-12 minutes or until golden brown. Cool and cut into bars.

❖

Chocolate Layer Bars

Betty Nalewajka
Winter Haven, FL

Makes 20-24 bars

1½ cups graham cracker
  crumbs
¼ cup sugar
4 Tbsp. margarine, melted
8-oz. pkg. cream cheese,
  softened
½ cup sugar
1 egg
¾ cup coconut
¾ cup chopped nuts
6-oz. pkg. semi-sweet
  chocolate chips

1. Combine graham
cracker crumbs, ¼ cup
sugar and margarine. Press
into bottom of 9" x 13" baking pan.
2. Bake at 325° for 10
minutes.
3. Cream together cream
cheese, ½ cup sugar and
egg. Spread over crust.
Sprinkle with coconut, nuts
and chocolate chips. Press
lightly into surface.
4. Bake at 350° for 25-30
minutes or until lightly
browned. Cool and cut into
bars.

I am a member of a small quilting guild called
Grapevine Quilters. I have found that quilters are very
sharing people. We share quilt patterns. We share ideas.
We share recipes. And we share stories about our lives
as we sit together working on our various projects.

—*Laura Heller, Delanco, NJ*

Seven-Layer Bars

Martha Smith
Galt, CA
Fanny E. Hymes
Clarksville, MD
Sampler

Makes 20-24 bars

8 Tbsp. margarine
1 cup graham cracker
  crumbs
1 cup coconut
6-oz. pkg. butterscotch
  chips
6-oz. pkg. chocolate chips
14-oz. can condensed milk
1 cup chopped nuts

1. Melt margarine in 9" x
13" baking pan. Add re-
maining ingredients in order listed. Do not mix together. After adding nuts,
press down thoroughly
with spoon.
2. Bake at 350° for 30-40
minutes. While still warm,
cut into 2-inch squares and
cool before removing from
pan.

❖

Coconut Toffee Squares

Vera E. Duncan
Sibley, MO
Grandma's Fan
Lydia Brubacker
Barnett, MO
Appliqued Butterfly

Makes 20-24 squares

1½ cups flour
1 tsp. baking powder
¼ tsp. salt
1½ tsp. cinnamon
½ cup shortening
1 cup brown sugar
1 egg
1 cup coconut
12-oz. pkg. chocolate chips

1. Sift together flour, baking powder, salt and cinnamon. Set aside.
2. Cream together short-
ening and sugar. Beat in
egg and dry ingredients
and mix well. Fold in coconut and chocolate chips
and blend well. Press into
ungreased 9" x 13" baking
pan.
3. Bake at 375° for 15
minutes. When cooled, cut
into squares.

Buttermilk Cinnamon Bars

Susan D. Fellin
Frenchtown, NJ

Makes 20-24 bars

Crumb Mixture:
2 cups flour
1¼ cups white sugar
¼ cup brown sugar
8 Tbsp. margarine, softened
½ cup chopped nuts
1 tsp. baking soda
1 tsp. cinnamon
¾ tsp. salt
1 cup buttermilk
1 tsp. vanilla
1 egg

Frosting:
2 cups powdered sugar
3-4 Tbsp. milk *or* light cream
¼ tsp. vanilla

1. In a large bowl combine flour, sugars and margarine and mix at low speed until crumbly. Press 2 cups mixture into ungreased 9" x 13" baking pan.
2. To remaining crumb mix add nuts, baking soda, cinnamon, salt, buttermilk, vanilla and egg and blend well. Pour evenly over crumb crust.
3. Bake at 350° for 20-25 minutes or until done. Cool 20 minutes.
4. To prepare frosting blend all ingredients until smooth. Spread over cooled cake. Cut into bars and serve.

Marble Brownies

Geraldine A. Ebersole
Hershey, PA
Double Irish Chain

Makes 20-24 servings

Brownies:
1 cup shortening, softened
2 cups sugar
4 eggs
1½ cups sifted flour
1 tsp. baking powder
1 tsp. salt *or* less
1 tsp. vanilla
2 ozs. unsweetened chocolate, melted

Frosting:
1 oz. unsweetened chocolate
2 Tbsp. margarine
4 Tbsp. milk
2 cups sifted, powdered sugar
½ cup chopped nuts

1. Cream together shortening, sugar and eggs and blend thoroughly.
2. Sift together flour, baking powder and salt and stir into creamed mixture. Divide batter into 2 bowls.
3. To ½ of batter add vanilla and mix well.
4. To ½ of batter add melted chocolate and mix well. Spoon 2 batters into greased 9" x 13" baking pan in checkerboard fashion. Swirl slightly with spatula.
5. Bake at 350° for 35 minutes. Cool.
6. To prepare frosting melt together chocolate and margarine. Add milk and powdered sugar and beat well. Spread over brownies and sprinkle with nuts. Cut and serve.

Saucepan Brownies

Vicki Long
Sterling, IL
Bear Paw

Makes 12-16 brownies

8 Tbsp. margarine
2 squares unsweetened chocolate
1 cup sugar
1 cup broken pecans
½ cup flour
1 tsp. baking powder
1 tsp. vanilla
2 eggs

1. In a double boiler melt margarine and chocolate. Remove from heat. Add all ingredients except eggs and beat well. Add eggs and beat well.
2. Pour into greased 9-inch square baking pan.
3. Bake at 350° for 30 minutes.

My husband's family comes to our home each summer for a family reunion. Many of us happen to love sewing, and one year I proposed that we do a quilt each year. Each summer we choose a name and that person becomes the owner of the next summer's quilt. She chooses the fabric and brings it washed, ironed and cut into 18" x 22" pieces. Every "sewing" person takes home a packet, completes the square and mails it to the recipient of the quilt who puts it together and brings it for quilting at the reunion. So far we have done only samplers, but I have heard that my sister-in-law wants an applique quilt. That should be a challenge!

—*Barbara A. Nolan, Pleasant Valley, NY*

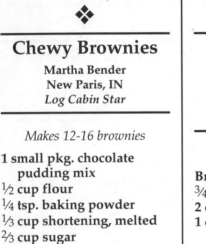

Chewy Brownies

Martha Bender
New Paris, IN
Log Cabin Star

Makes 12-16 brownies

1 small pkg. chocolate
   pudding mix
½ cup flour
¼ tsp. baking powder
⅓ cup shortening, melted
⅔ cup sugar
2 eggs
1 tsp. vanilla
½ cup chopped walnuts

1. Mix dry pudding with flour and baking powder.
2. Blend together melted shortening and sugar and mix well. Beat in eggs, one at a time. Blend in vanilla and pudding mixture. Fold in nuts. Spoon into 8-inch square baking pan.
3. Bake at 350° for 35 minutes. Cool and cut into bars.

Meriruth's Brownies

Katie Reed
Floresville, TX
Feather Medallion

Makes 12-16 brownies

Brownies:
¾ cup cocoa
2 cups sugar
1 cup butter *or* margarine,
   melted
4 eggs
1 tsp. vanilla
1¼ cups flour
¼ tsp. salt
1 cup chopped walnuts
   (optional)

Frosting:
2 cups powdered sugar,
   sifted
¼ cup cocoa
3 Tbsp. butter *or*
   margarine, melted
1 tsp. vanilla
2 Tbsp. half-and-half
½ cup chopped walnuts

1. To prepare brownies stir cocoa and sugar together. Add melted butter and mix well. Add eggs and vanilla and stir again. Add flour and salt and mix until smooth. If desired, fold in walnuts.
2. Scrape mixture into greased 8-inch square baking pan and spread into an even layer.
3. Bake at 350° for about 40-50 minutes. Cool, frost and serve.
4. To prepare frosting combine powdered sugar and cocoa. Add melted butter, vanilla and half-and-half and stir until smooth. Fold in walnuts and spread over brownies.

Brownies

Donna Lantgen
Rapid City, SD
Dresden Plate

Makes 20-24 brownies

Brownies:
½ cup margarine
1 cup sugar
4 eggs
16-oz. can chocolate syrup
1 cup + 1 heaping Tbsp. flour

Frosting:
1½ cups powdered sugar
6 Tbsp. milk
6 Tbsp. margarine
½ cup chocolate chips

1. To prepare brownies cream together margarine, sugar and eggs. Add chocolate syrup and flour and mix well. Spread into greased 9" x 13" baking pan.

2. Bake at 350° for 25 minutes.

3. To prepare frosting combine powdered sugar, milk and margarine in a saucepan and bring to a boil. Boil for 30 seconds. Remove from heat, add chocolate chips and beat thoroughly. Spread over brownies.

❖

Deep-Dish Brownies

Mary Lou Kirtland
Berkeley Heights, NJ
Blackford's Beauty

Makes 36 small brownies

¾ **cup butter, melted**
1½ **cups sugar**
1½ **tsp. vanilla**
3 **eggs**
½ **cup flour**
½ **cup cocoa**
½ **tsp. baking powder**
½ **tsp. salt**
1 **cup peanut butter chips**

1. Cream together butter, sugar and vanilla. Add eggs and mix well. Add all dry ingredients and beat thoroughly. Fold in peanut butter chips. Spoon into

lightly greased 9" x 13" baking pan.

2. Bake at 350° for 40-45 minutes until brownies begin to pull away from pan. Cool before cutting. Do not overbake.

❖

Peppermint Brownies

Marilyn Wallace
Alfred, ME
Myrtle's Log Cabin
Sherry Bradley
Albuquerque, NM
Teddy Bear Log Cabin

Makes 24 small brownies

Brownies:
2 **squares unsweetened chocolate**
½ **cup margarine**
2 **eggs**
1 **cup sugar**
½ **cup chopped nuts**
½ **cup flour**
1 **tsp. vanilla**

Frosting:
4 **Tbsp. soft margarine**
2 **cups powdered sugar**
½ **tsp. milk**
2 **Tbsp. sour cream**
½ **tsp. peppermint extract**
Drop green food coloring

Glaze:
2 **squares unsweetened chocolate**
2 **Tbsp. margarine**

1. To prepare brownies melt chocolate and margarine together.

2. Combine all other ingredients and add to chocolate mixture. Mix thoroughly. Pour into 8-inch square baking pan.

3. Bake at 350° for 20-25 minutes. Cool.

4. To prepare frosting combine all ingredients and mix well. Spread over cooled brownies and let stand until frosting sets.

5. To prepare glaze melt chocolate and margarine together. Drizzle over frosting and tilt pan to spread thinly. Cut into bars and serve.

Recently my quilt group put together a quilt which I designed showing my family's favorite foods. There are 25 patches showing everything from Hungarian Begli to a bunch of ripe yellow bananas. Each quilter in the group appliqued two patches onto a red and white checkered tablecloth background fabric. This delightful "Friends and Foods" quilt hangs in my kitchen and is a feast for the eyes.

—*Berta Stegmeier, Silver Spring, MD*

Carole's Oatmeal Brownies

Carole M. Mackie
Dahinda, IL
Prairie Flower

Makes 20-24 servings

Brownies:
1¼ cups boiling water
1 cup quick oats
8 Tbsp. margarine
1 cup sugar
2 eggs
1⅓ cups flour
1 tsp. baking soda
½ tsp. nutmeg
1 cup brown sugar
½ tsp. salt
½ tsp. cinnamon
½ cup chopped nuts

Frosting:
8 Tbsp. margarine
1 cup brown sugar
Pinch salt
4 Tbsp. milk
2½ cups powdered sugar, sifted
½ tsp. vanilla
1 cup coconut

1. To prepare brownies pour boiling water over oats and margarine in a large bowl. Cover and let stand for 20 minutes. Add all remaining ingredients and beat until smooth. Pour batter into greased jelly roll pan.

2. Bake at 350° for 30-35 minutes.

3. To prepare frosting melt margarine in a saucepan. Stir in brown sugar and salt. Cook 2 minutes over low heat, stirring constantly. Add milk, stirring until mixture comes to a boil.

4. Remove from heat and gradually stir in powdered sugar and vanilla and mix well. (If mixture seems too thick, thin with milk.) Fold in coconut.

5. Spread frosting over hot brownies and serve.

Desserts and Candies

Punch Bowl Trifle

Joan Coale Klosek
Ellicott City, MD
Progressive Quilt
Fanny E. Hymes
Clarksville, MD
Sampler

Makes 12-16 servings

1 pound cake
1 small pkg. instant vanilla
  pudding
21-oz. can cherry pie filling
20-oz. can pineapple sauce
  or crushed pineapple
12-oz. carton whipped
  topping
1 small jar maraschino
  cherries, drained
Crushed walnuts (optional)

1. Cut cake in half. Cut
½ of cake into small cubes
and line bottom of glass
punch bowl.
2. Prepare pudding ac-
cording to directions. Pour
½ of pudding over cake
cubes. Pour ½ of pie filling
over pudding. Pour ½ of
pineapple over pie filling.

Top with ½ of whipped
topping. Repeat layers, beginning with remaining ½
of cake.
3. Garnish with mara-
schino cherries and sprinkle with nuts if desired. Refrigerate at least 4 hours to
set. Serve.

Chocolate Pudding Dessert

Esther Lapp
Sterling, IL
Bear Paw

Makes 6-8 servings

1 cup sugar *or* less
2 Tbsp. cocoa
2 tsp. flour
¾ cup hot water
1 tsp. vanilla
Pinch salt
1 cup flour
2 Tbsp. cocoa
¾ cup sugar *or* less
2 tsp. baking powder
2 Tbsp. cooking oil *or*

melted margarine
⅔ cup milk
¼ cup chopped nuts *or*
  chopped dates

1. In a saucepan combine
1 cup sugar, 2 Tbsp. cocoa,
2 tsp. flour and hot water.
Bring to a boil and cook for
1 minute. Add vanilla and
salt and cool slightly.
2. In a bowl combine 1
cup flour, 2 Tbsp. cocoa, ¾
cup sugar, baking powder,
oil and milk. Pour into
greased 9-inch square baking pan. Sprinkle with nuts
or dates. Pour hot syrup
over batter.
3. Bake at 350° for 25-30
minutes or until baked
through.
4. Serve with ice cream
or whipped topping.

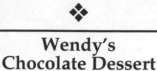

Wendy's Chocolate Dessert

Ann Judge
Queenstown, MD
Sampler

Makes 10-15 servings

1 cup flour
8 Tbsp. butter
1½ cups pecans
8-oz. pkg. cream cheese, softened
1½ cups powdered sugar
8-oz. carton whipped topping
3 cups cold milk
2 large pkgs. instant chocolate pudding

1. Mix flour and butter. Add 1¼ cups pecans and press into bottom of 9" x 13" baking dish.
2. Bake at 350° for 15 minutes. Cool.
3. Cream together cream cheese, sugar and 1 cup whipped topping. Spread over cooled crust.
4. Mix milk with pudding. Spread over cream cheese mixture. Let set until firm. Spread remaining whipped topping over pudding. Sprinkle with ¼ cup pecans. Refrigerate until ready to serve.

Moon Dessert

Joyce Shackelford
Green Bay, WI
Sampler

Makes 15-20 servings

1 cup water
8 Tbsp. butter
1 cup flour
4 eggs
1 large pkg. instant vanilla pudding
2¾ cups milk
8-oz. pkg. cream cheese, softened
12-oz. carton whipped topping
8-oz. can chocolate syrup

1. In a saucepan bring water and butter to a rapid boil. Add flour and remove from heat. Add eggs, one at a time. Spread batter onto 10" x 15" jelly roll pan.
2. Bake at 350° for 20 minutes. Cool.
3. Mix pudding and milk. Add cream cheese and mix well. Spread over cooled crust. Top with whipped topping. Drizzle with chocolate syrup and serve.

Party Dessert

Blanche Cahill
Willow Grove, PA
Variegated Star

Makes 8-10 servings

4 squares unsweetened chocolate
¾ cup sugar
⅓ cup milk
6 eggs, separated
1½ cups unsalted butter
1½ cups powdered sugar
⅛ tsp. salt
1½ tsp. vanilla
3 dozen lady fingers, split
¾ cup heavy cream

1. Melt chocolate in top of double boiler.
2. Combine sugar, milk and egg yolks. Add to chocolate and cook until smooth, stirring constantly. Cool.
3. Cream butter well. Add ¾ cup powdered sugar and cream thoroughly. Stir in cooled chocolate mixture and mix well.
4. In separate bowl beat egg whites with salt until stiff, gradually adding ¾ cup powdered sugar. Fold into chocolate mixture. Add vanilla.
5. Line sides and bottom of 9-inch springform pan with lady fingers. Fill with chocolate mixture. Chill in refrigerator overnight.
6. Whip cream until soft peaks form.
7. Top lady fingers and

> I well remember my first quilting experience with my grandmother Florence Stauffer. I was newly married and desperately wanted my stitches to be even. I pulled the needle through on the bottom and back through to the top each time. She graciously complimented my even stitches, then showed me how to guide my needle underneath with my opposite hand to accomplish even stitches on both the top and bottom.
>
> —*Jul Hoober, New Holland, PA*

chocolate mixture with whipped cream and serve.

Fantasy Dessert

**Cynda Leininger
Mechanicsburg, PA**

Makes 12-15 servings

First Layer:
1 cup vanilla cookies, crushed
½ cup finely chopped walnuts
8 Tbsp. butter, softened

Second Layer:
8-oz. pkg. cream cheese
1 cup whipped topping
1 cup powdered sugar

Third Layer:
2 small pkgs. instant chocolate pudding
3 cups milk

Fourth Layer:
16-oz. carton whipped topping
½ cup chopped nuts

1. To prepare first layer mix all ingredients and pat into 9" x 13" baking pan.
2. Bake at 350° for 8-9 minutes.
3. To prepare second layer mix all ingredients thoroughly and spread over first layer in pan.
4. To prepare third layer beat ingredients until thickened and spread over second layer in pan.
5. Top with whipped topping and chopped nuts. Refrigerate overnight before serving.

Dirt Pudding

**Sue Graziadio, White Mills, PA
Joyce Niemann
Fruitland Park, FL
Irma H. Schoen, Windsor, CT**

Makes 10-12 servings

8-oz. pkg. cream cheese
4 Tbsp. butter
1 cup powdered sugar
2 small pkgs. instant vanilla pudding
3½ cups milk
12-oz. carton whipped topping
20-oz. pkg. Oreo cookies

1. Cream together cream cheese and butter. Add powdered sugar and mix well.
2. In separate bowl combine pudding and milk. Stir in whipped topping. Combine creamed mixture and pudding mixture.
3. Blend Oreo cookies in blender until fine.
4. In a new sterilized flower pot alternate layers of cookie crumbs and pudding mixture. End with cookie mixture.
5. Decorate with silk flower or candy worms. Serve with a plastic shovel.

Rice Pudding with Lemon Sauce

Mary Pat Sloan
Downingtown, PA
Log Cabin

Makes 10 servings

Pudding:
3 cups milk
1½ Tbsp. butter *or* margarine
⅓ cup white sugar
3 eggs
2 cups uncooked rice
⅛ tsp. salt
½ tsp. vanilla
⅛ tsp. nutmeg
¼ cup raisins

Lemon Sauce:
½ cup white sugar
2 Tbsp. cornstarch
1 cup water
4 Tbsp. butter
3 Tbsp. lemon juice
1 tsp. grated lemon rind

1. To prepare pudding scald milk. Add butter and sugar. Set aside to cool.
2. Lightly beat eggs. Slowly pour milk mixture into eggs. Stir in rice, salt, vanilla, nutmeg and raisins.
3. Pour into greased baking dish. Set into pan of hot water.
4. Bake at 325° for 45-60 minutes.
5. To prepare lemon sauce combine sugar and cornstarch in a saucepan. Add water and heat mixture, stirring constantly un-til it comes to a boil. Reduce heat and simmer for 3 minutes.
6. Remove from heat, stir in butter, lemon juice and rind. Chill. Pour over rice pudding and serve.

Honey Comb Pudding

Judy Sharer
Port Matilda, PA
Codey's & Brook's Baby Quilts

Makes 6-8 servings

8 Tbsp. butter *or* margarine, softened
½ cup sugar
½ cup sour milk
½ cup flour
½ cup molasses
4 eggs, well beaten
1 tsp. baking soda
¼ cup hot water
1 cup whipped topping

1. Mix together butter, sugar, sour milk, flour and molasses. Stir in eggs.
2. Dissolve baking soda in hot water. Add to pudding mixture and stir until blended. Pour into 1½-quart baking dish.
3. Bake at 350° for 30 minutes or until center springs back when touched.
4. Cool and serve with whipped topping.

Graham Cracker Pudding

Ruth Ann Hoover
New Holland, PA
White on White

Makes 6-8 servings

2 egg yolks
½ cup sugar
⅔ cup milk
1 pkg. unflavored gelatin
½ cup cold water
2 egg whites, beaten
2 cups whipped topping
1 tsp. vanilla
14 graham crackers, crushed
3 Tbsp. butter, melted

1. In a saucepan beat egg yolks. Add sugar and milk and cook until slightly thickened.
2. Dissolve gelatin in cold water. Pour hot mixture over gelatin and stir until smooth. Chill for 20-30 minutes.
3. Beat egg whites until soft peaks form. Fold into chilled gelatin mixture. Fold whipped topping into mixture. Add vanilla.
4. Combine crushed graham crackers with melted butter. Reserve ½ cup crumbs.
5. Arrange graham cracker crumbs across bottom of 8-inch square baking dish. Pour pudding mixture over crackers. Top with reserved crumbs and serve.

Cracker Pudding

Betty Stoltzfus
Honey Brook, PA

Makes 6-8 servings

1 quart milk
⅔ cup sugar
2 eggs, separated
2 cups broken saltines
1 cup grated coconut
1 tsp. vanilla

1. Heat milk and stir in sugar.
2. Beat egg yolks until frothy and add to hot milk. Stir in crackers and coconut and cook until thickened. Remove from heat.
3. Beat egg whites until stiff. Fold into pudding mixture along with vanilla. Cool.
4. Pour into serving dish.

Date Pudding

Alma Miller
Partridge, KS
Lovers' Hearts

Makes 10-12 servings

1 cup sugar
Pinch salt
2 cups boiling water
¾ cup chopped dates
1¾ cups sifted flour
1 tsp. baking powder
½ tsp. baking soda

1 cup milk
¾ cup chopped nuts
3 cups whipping cream

1. Pour sugar, salt and boiling water over dates in a 9" x 13" baking pan. Mix well.
2. Sift together flour, baking powder and baking soda. Add milk and blend well. Mix well with date mixture in baking pan. Fold in nuts.
3. Bake at 325° for 40 minutes or until done.
4. Whip whipping cream until soft peaks form.
5. To serve cut date mixture into small squares and layer alternately with whipped cream in large serving bowl.

Banana Pudding

Ann Harrison
Garland, TX
Strawberry Patch

Makes 10-12 servings

1 large pkg. instant vanilla
pudding
1 small box vanilla wafers
5-6 bananas
8-oz. carton whipped
topping
14-oz. can condensed milk

1. Prepare vanilla pudding according to package directions.

2. In bottom of 9" x 13" baking pan arrange vanilla wafers in layers. Top with slices of bananas.
3. Combine whipped topping, condensed milk and pudding and mix well. Pour over bananas.
4. Refrigerate for 1 hour and serve.

Variations:

Add 8-oz. carton sour cream to ingredients in step 3. Arrange 2-3 layers of ingredients in large serving bowl. Top with whipped topping, refrigerate 24 hours and serve.
Jeanette Grant
Mountain Lake, MN
Double Wedding Ring

Arrange ingredients in 2-3 layers in large serving bowl. Top with whipped topping and ½ cup chopped nuts.
Maureen Csikasz
Wakefield, MA
Trip Around the World

Creamy Rice Pudding

Elizabeth Boyton
Gordonville, PA
Irish Chain
Agnes Little
Ringtown, PA
Double Wedding Ring

Makes 8-10 servings

2 quarts whole milk
½ cup + 1 Tbsp. uncooked rice
¾ cup raisins
2 eggs
1 cup sugar
1½ tsp. vanilla
Cinnamon

1. In a large saucepan scald 1½ quarts milk. Add rice and raisins. Cover and cook slowly, approximately 20 minutes.
2. While rice cooks, beat together eggs, sugar, vanilla and remaining milk. Add to cooked rice mixture and continue cooking until mixture thickens, approximately 1 hour.
3. Remove from heat and let stand for 15 minutes.
4. Pour into serving bowl and sprinkle with cinnamon.

> Crazy quilts have always reminded me of minestrone. You add bits and pieces of wonderful vegetables to the soup, providing a rich color and texture. For a beautiful crazy quilt you need bits and pieces of wonderful fabric to achieve a richness in color and texture.
>
> —*Frances D. Bents, Annapolis, MD*

Caramel Pudding

Kathryn M. Geissinger
Ephrata, PA
Philadelphia Pavement

Makes 2-4 servings

2 Tbsp. butter *or* margarine
½ cup brown sugar
1 cup milk
1 Tbsp. cornstarch
1 egg, beaten
1 Tbsp. cold water
1 tsp. vanilla
Pinch salt
2 bananas, sliced
½ cup chopped nuts

1. Cook butter and sugar together over medium heat until smooth and bubbly.
2. In a medium bowl combine milk, cornstarch and egg, beating until smooth.
3. Carefully add cold water to butter and sugar mixture. Gradually add milk mixture, stirring constantly over medium heat until mixture thickens and begins to boil.
4. Remove from heat and stir in vanilla and salt. Cool slightly and pour into serving dish.
5. Top with sliced ba-nanas and chopped nuts and serve.

Butterscotch Pudding

Elsie Miller
Winesburg, OH
Lone Star

Makes 10-12 servings

First Layer:
1 cup flour
8 Tbsp. margarine
½ cup finely chopped nuts

Second Layer:
1 cup white sugar
8-oz. pkg. cream cheese, softened
1 cup whipped topping

Third Layer:
2 large pkgs. instant butterscotch pudding
½ cup chopped nuts

1. To prepare first layer combine all ingredients until crumbly. Press into an 8" x 12" baking pan.
2. Bake at 350° for 8-10 minutes or until slightly browned.
3. To prepare second layer cream together sugar and cream cheese. Fold in whipped topping. Spread over cooled first layer.
4. To prepare third layer mix pudding according to directions. Spread over

cream cheese mixture and let pudding set in refrigerator.

5. Sprinkle with nuts and serve.

❖

Cinnamon Cake Pudding

Mary Ellen Esh
Gordonville, PA
Giant Dahlia

Makes 12-15 servings

Sauce:
3 cups brown sugar *or* **less**
2¼ cups water
6 Tbsp. butter
⅛ tsp. salt

Cake:
1 cup white sugar *or* **less**
2 Tbsp. butter
1⅔ cups flour
2 tsp. baking powder
2 tsp. cinnamon
½ tsp. salt
1 cup milk

1. To prepare sauce combine brown sugar, water, butter and salt in a saucepan. Bring to a boil, stirring occasionally. Set aside.

2. To prepare cake cream together white sugar and butter. In a separate bowl combine flour, baking powder, cinnamon and salt. Add dry ingredients to creamed mixture, alternating with milk.

3. Spoon into 9" x 13" baking pan. Pour sauce over cake batter.

4. Bake at 325° for 45 minutes. Chill at least 2 hours in refrigerator. Serve with whipped cream or ice cream.

❖

Coconut Crunch Dessert

Sara Wilson
Clinton, MO

Makes 10-12 servings

8 Tbsp. margarine, melted
1 cup sugar
1 cup flour
1 cup coconut
1 cup chopped pecans
2 small pkgs. instant butter pecan pudding
3 cups milk
8-oz. carton whipped topping

1. Mix together margarine, sugar, flour, coconut and pecans until crumbly. Spread onto cookie sheet.

2. Bake at 350° for 30-40 minutes, stirring frequently. Remove from oven and reserve 2 cups crumbs for topping.

3. Spread remaining crumbs into 9" x 13" baking pan.

4. Prepare pudding with milk and chill until set. Fold in whipped topping.

Spread pudding mixture over cooled crumbs. Top with reserved topping.

5. Freeze. Refrigerate to soften slightly before serving.

❖

Brown Sugar Tapioca

Martha Bender
New Paris, IN
Log Cabin Star

Makes 6-8 servings

3 Tbsp. minute tapioca
1 cup brown sugar
⅛ tsp. salt
2 cups water
¾ tsp. vanilla
1 cup whipped topping

1. In a saucepan combine tapioca, brown sugar, salt and water. Bring to a boil and stir until tapioca appears clear. Remove from heat and stir in vanilla.

2. Cool and serve with whipped topping.

Lemon Lush Dessert

Dorothy Shank
Sterling, IL
Sunbonnet Sue & Overall Bill

Makes 12-15 servings

8 Tbsp. margarine
1¼ cups flour
¾ cup chopped pecans
8-oz. pkg. cream cheese, softened
1 cup powdered sugar
8-oz. carton whipped topping
2 large pkgs. instant lemon pudding
3 cups milk

1. Cream together margarine, flour and pecans. Press into 9" x 13" baking pan.
2. Bake at 350° for 15 minutes. Remove from oven and cool.
3. Cream together cream cheese and powdered sugar. Fold in ½ of whipped topping. Spread over cooled crust.
4. Prepare pudding with milk according to package directions. Spread over cream cheese layer. Top with remaining whipped topping and serve.

❖

Lemon Sponge Pudding

Agnes M. King
Atglen, PA

Makes 4-6 servings

1 cup sugar
2 Tbsp. flour
1 Tbsp. margarine
2 eggs, separated
1 cup milk
Juice of 2 lemons

1. Cream together sugar, flour and margarine.
2. Beat yolks and add to creamed mixture. Add milk and juice of lemons.
3. Beat egg whites until soft peaks form. Fold into pudding. Spoon into 8-inch square baking dish.
4. Bake at 350° for 35-40 minutes. Cool and serve.

❖

Peach Crumb Pudding

Jeannette R. Saunders
Albuquerque, NM
Friendship

Makes 6-8 servings

Filling:
5 ripe peaches
½ cup sugar
3 Tbsp. flour

Crust:
½ cup sugar
1 cup flour
8 Tbsp. butter

1. To prepare filling peel and slice peaches.
2. Combine sugar and flour and mix gently with peaches. Arrange peaches in greased 9-inch square baking dish.
3. To prepare crust mix sugar and flour. With a pastry blender cut in butter until crumbly.
4. Spread crumbs over peach filling.
5. Bake at 350° for about 1 hour or until peaches are tender and crumbs are browned.
6. Serve with whipped topping or thick unwhipped cream.

❖

Peaches and Pudding Crisp

Kelly Bailey
Mechanicsburg, PA
Pineapple Log Cabin

Makes 4 servings

Pudding:
2-3 cups drained, canned peaches
¼ cup peach syrup
1 small pkg. instant vanilla pudding
¼ cup brown sugar

Topping:
½ cup flour
¾ cup uncooked oatmeal
¼ cup brown sugar
½ cup margarine, melted
½ tsp. salt
1 tsp. cinnamon
Reserved instant vanilla
   pudding

1. To prepare pudding combine peaches, syrup, 1 Tbsp. dry pudding mix and brown sugar in ungreased 8-inch square baking dish. Reserve remaining pudding mix.
2. Combine all topping ingredients until well blended and crumbly. Sprinkle over peach mixture.
3. Bake at 350° for 45-50 minutes or until bubbly.
4. Serve with ice cream.

Peach Melba Mold

Delores Scheel
Fargo, ND
All in Red Cross-Stitch Quilt

Makes 8-10 servings

16-oz. can sliced peaches
2 Tbsp. lemon juice
3-oz. pkg. lemon gelatin
1 cup hot water
2 tsp. milk
2 Tbsp. mayonnaise
3-oz. pkg. cream cheese,
   softened
2 Tbsp. finely chopped

pecans
10-oz. pkg. frozen red
   raspberries
2 Tbsp. lemon juice
3-oz. pkg. raspberry gelatin
1 cup hot water

1. Drain peaches, reserving syrup. Combine syrup with 2 Tbsp. lemon juice and add enough cold water to make 1 cup. Set aside.
2. Dissolve lemon gelatin in 1 cup hot water. Add syrup mixture and mix well. Chill until partially set. Fold in peaches and pour into 6½-cup ring mold. Chill until almost set.
3. Combine milk, mayonnaise and cream cheese. Fold in pecans and spread over peach gelatin.
4. Thaw and drain raspberries, reserving syrup. Combine syrup with 2 Tbsp. lemon juice and add enough cold water to make 1 cup. Set aside.
5. Dissolve raspberry gelatin in 1 cup hot water. Add syrup mixture and mix well. Chill until partially set. Fold in raspberries and pour over cheese layer. Chill until firm.
6. Unmold and serve.

Three-Layer Strawberry Pretzel Charm

L. Jean Moore
Anderson, IN
Family Sampler
Carol M. Mifflin
Houston, TX
Scrap Pastel Basket

Makes 12-15 servings

3 Tbsp. sugar
3 cups coarsely crushed
   pretzels
12 Tbsp. margarine, melted
8-oz. pkg. cream cheese,
   softened
8-oz. carton whipped
   topping
2 cups miniature
   marshmallows
2 cups powdered sugar,
   sifted
6-oz. pkg. strawberry
   gelatin
2½ cups boiling water
16-oz. pkg. frozen
   strawberries

1. Combine sugar, pretzels and margarine. Press into 9" x 13" baking pan.
2. Bake at 350° for 15 minutes. Cool.
3. Combine cream cheese, whipped topping, marshmallows and powdered sugar. Spread over pretzel crust and chill.
4. Dissolve gelatin in boiling water. Stir in frozen strawberries and pour over cream cheese mixture. Refrigerate and chill until set.

Twenty-Four-Hour Strawberry Dessert

Jane Talso
Albuquerque, NM
Balloon Quilt

Makes 4-6 servings

2 cups fresh strawberries,
   sliced
2 Tbsp. brown sugar
1 cup miniature
   marshmallows
1 cup sour cream
Dash salt
4-6 whole strawberries

1. Sprinkle 2 cups strawberries with sugar. Let stand 10 minutes.

2. Fold marshmallows and sour cream into strawberries. Add salt and mix gently. Place in covered container and refrigerate overnight.

3. To serve spoon into individual dishes and garnish with a whole strawberry.

Frozen Strawberry Dessert

Alma Miller
Partridge, KS
Lovers' Hearts

Makes 12-15 servings

Crust:
2 cups flour
1 cup chopped nuts
½ cup brown sugar
¾ cup margarine

Filling:
1½ pints strawberries
1 cup strawberry gelatin
¾ cup sugar
8-oz. pkg. cream cheese
1 quart whipping cream

1. Combine all crust ingredients and mix well. Press into 9" x 13" baking pan.

2. Bake at 350° for 15-20 minutes. Cool.

3. To prepare filling bring ½ of strawberries to a boil in a saucepan. Dissolve gelatin in cooked strawberries. Fold in remaining berries and cool.

4. Cream together sugar and cream cheese and mix with strawberry gelatin mixture. Chill until slightly congealed.

5. Whip cream and fold into mixture. Pour over cooled crust.

6. Freeze before serving.

Cherry Delight

Mildred E. Houser
St. Marys, WV
Maple Leaf

Makes 10-15 servings

2½ cups graham cracker
   crumbs
½ cup melted butter
4 cups whipped topping
¾ cup sugar
1 tsp. vanilla
8-oz. pkg. cream cheese,
   softened
21-oz. can cherry pie filling

1. Combine graham cracker crumbs and melted butter. Press into 9" x 13" baking pan.

2. Combine whipped topping, sugar and vanilla. Add cream cheese and whip until stiffened. Spread into graham cracker crust.

3. Spoon cherry pie filling over cream cheese mixture. Chill for 24 hours before serving.

The summer I turned 14, I kept house for my recently widowed grandfather in the Finger Lakes region of New York. At the end of the summer my parents arrived from Massachusetts to take me home. For the occasion I decided to make a spice cake. I doubled the amount of raisins and nuts, assuming twice as many would be twice as good. In my rush I also tried to frost it before it was cool. The cake was much too soggy and sweet to eat. I remember that as the day I learned to follow recipes.

—*Sara Harter Fredette, Williamsburg, MA*

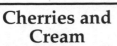

Cherries and Cream

Donna A. Lessmann
Commack, NY
Wall Grouping I

Makes 4 servings

1 cup light sour cream
1 Tbsp. sugar
21-oz. can cherry pie filling
1 tsp. lemon juice
Fresh mint leaves
(optional)

1. Beat sour cream and sugar in small bowl. Set aside.
2. Reserve 4 cherries from pie filling. Set aside.
3. Combine remaining cherry pie filling with lemon juice.
4. Alternate layers of cherry pie filling with cream mixture in four parfait glasses, ending with pie filling.
5. Dollop with cream mixture. Garnish with cherry and fresh mint. Serve.

Blueberry Crunch

Georgianna Verbrugge
Houston, TX
Scrap Basket

Makes 20-24 small servings

15-oz. can crushed
pineapple, undrained
16-oz. pkg. frozen
blueberries
¾ cup white sugar
1 box yellow cake mix
12 Tbsp. margarine, melted
¼ cup white sugar
1 cup chopped nuts
½ cup flaked coconut

1. In a greased 9" x 13" baking pan arrange ingredients in following order: pineapple and juice, blueberries, ¾ cup sugar, dry cake mix, melted margarine, ¼ cup sugar, chopped nuts and coconut.
2. Bake at 325° for 1 hour. Serve either warm or cold.

Crumb-Topped Rhubarb

Rosalyn J. Clem
Silver Spring, MD
Game Quilt

Makes 8-10 servings

3 cups fresh, diced rhubarb
1 Tbsp. flour
½ cup white sugar
1 tsp. cinnamon
⅛ tsp. salt
1 Tbsp. water
6 Tbsp. butter
6 Tbsp. flour
½ cup brown sugar,
packed
½ cup quick-cooking oats

1. Combine rhubarb, 1 Tbsp. flour, white sugar, cinnamon, salt and water in a 9-inch square baking dish.
2. Cream together butter, flour and brown sugar. Stir in oats and sprinkle over rhubarb mixture in baking dish.
3. Bake at 350° for 40 minutes or until rhubarb is tender and top is brown.

Rhubarb Pastry

Patti Boston
Coshocton, OH
Flywheel

Makes 8-10 servings

Crust:
8 Tbsp. butter, softened
1 Tbsp. sugar
1 egg yolk
1 cup flour
¼ tsp. salt
½ tsp. vanilla

Filling:
2 cups fresh, diced rhubarb
2 Tbsp. butter
4 Tbsp. flour
1½ cups sugar
2 eggs, beaten
1 cup heavy cream

1. Mix together all crust ingredients and pat into 9-inch square baking pan.
2. Spread diced rhubarb over crust.
3. Combine all remaining filling ingredients and pour over rhubarb.
4. Bake at 350° for 1 hour or until set.

Saucy Yogurt Delight

Debbie Chisholm
Fallston, MD
Wreath of Roses

Makes 8 small servings

6-oz. pkg. sugar-free raspberry gelatin
2 cups boiling water
½ cup chilled applesauce
½ tsp. cinnamon
1 cup vanilla yogurt

1. Dissolve gelatin in boiling water. Reserve 1½ cups of this mixture. Chill remaining gelatin until slightly thickened.
2. Add applesauce and cinnamon to reserved 1½ cups gelatin. Pour into 8 small dessert dishes. Chill until set but not firm.
3. Blend yogurt into slightly thickened gelatin from step 1. Spoon yogurt mixture over gelatin in dessert dishes.
4. Chill about 3 hours or until set. Serve.

Cranberry Apple Goodie

Lois Stoltzfus
Honey Brook, PA
Dresden Plate

Makes 8 servings

Batter:
½ cup sugar
1 Tbsp. flour
⅛ tsp. salt
1 tsp. cinnamon
4 cups sliced apples
⅓ cup fresh *or* frozen cranberries

Topping:
1 cup uncooked oatmeal
½ cup brown sugar
½ cup flour
⅛ tsp. baking soda
⅛ tsp. baking powder
4 Tbsp. butter, melted

1. To prepare batter combine sugar, flour, salt and cinnamon. Stir into sliced apples and cranberries and spoon into baking dish.
2. To prepare topping combine all dry ingredients. Stir in butter. Spread crumb topping over apple mixture.
3. Bake at 375° for 35-40 minutes. Serve with ice cream or milk.

For years I thought quilts were beautiful and wished I had one. In 1986 while at the Grange Fair in Centre Hall, Pennsylvania, I purchased a chance for a gorgeous white on white quilted by one of the local women's groups. I won! Owning one quilt made me wish for more. I signed up for quilting classes and have become an avid quilter.

—Cyndie Marrara, Port Matilda, PA

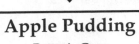

Apple Pudding

Betty A. Gray
Ellicott City, MD
Miniature Sunbonnet Sue

Makes 6 servings

1 cup flour
1 cup sugar
1 tsp. baking powder
1 egg, well beaten
4 large apples
2 Tbsp. sugar
1 tsp. cinnamon
1 tsp. nutmeg
2 Tbsp. butter
¼ cup water

1. Sift together flour, 1 cup sugar and baking powder. Add egg.
2. Slice apples into greased baking dish. Cover with flour mixture.
3. Combine 2 Tbsp. sugar, cinnamon and nutmeg. Sprinkle over flour mixture. Dot with butter and sprinkle with water.
4. Bake at 350° for 40 minutes.

Apple Crisp for Quilters

M. Jeanne Osborne
Sanford, ME
Gwen's Tulips

Makes 4 servings

4 tart apples
6 Tbsp. flour
6 Tbsp. rolled oats
½ cup light brown sugar
½ tsp. cinnamon
¼ tsp. mace
6 Tbsp. light margarine
Light whipped topping

1. Peel, core and cut apples into wedges. Arrange in greased baking dish.
2. In a bowl combine all dry ingredients. Cut in margarine and mix until crumbly. Spread over apples in baking dish.
3. Bake at 375° for 30 minutes. Serve with a light whipped topping.

Jody's Apple Walnut Crisp

Janis Landefeld
Baltimore, MD
Antique Nine Patch

Makes 6 servings

4-5 tart apples
1 Tbsp. lemon juice
½ cup flour
½ cup brown sugar, firmly packed
¼ tsp. salt
¼ tsp. nutmeg
½ tsp. cinnamon
4 Tbsp. butter *or* margarine
½ cup chopped walnuts

1. Pare, core and thinly slice apples to measure 4 cups. Arrange in greased 8-inch square baking pan. Sprinkle with lemon juice.
2. Combine flour, sugar, salt, nutmeg and cinnamon. Work in butter until crumbly and add walnuts. Sprinkle crumb mixture evenly over apples.
3. Bake at 375° for 35-45 minutes or until topping is brown and apples are tender.
4. Serve warm with cream, whipped topping or ice cream.

I have a most unusual opportunity and experience whenever I visit my daughter who owns the Osage County Quilt Factory in Overbrook, Kansas. The Quilt Factory is located in a 110-year-old former church building.

Visiting family members have the unique honor of spending the night in a place called the upper room, formerly a Sunday School classroom on the upper level of the church. Today it is equipped with all the amenities of a posh hotel. But no hotel can offer me what the upper room does. I awaken in the wee hours of the morning and go shopping in a wonderful quilt and fabric store in my nightgown and slippers and all by myself. What a thrill to run my hands over 2000 bolts of beautiful quilt fabric!

—*Cleda Cox, Estes Park, CO*

Apple Goodie

Mrs. Paul Gray
Beatrice, NE

Makes 8-10 servings

3 cups sliced apples
1 cup white sugar *or* less
1 rounded Tbsp. flour
⅛ tsp. salt
1 tsp. cinnamon
¼ tsp. baking soda
¼ tsp. baking powder
¾ cup uncooked oatmeal
¾ cup flour
¾ cup brown sugar *or* less
⅓ cup melted butter

1. Combine apples, white sugar, 1 rounded Tbsp. flour, salt and cinnamon. Spoon into greased 9-inch square baking dish.
2. Combine baking soda, baking powder, oats, flour, brown sugar and melted butter and mix well. Pat over top of apple mixture.
3. Bake at 375° for 30-40 minutes.

Apple Strudel

Peggy Smith
Hamlin, KY
Evening View Through the Window

Makes 10-12 servings

Crust:
½ cup sifted flour
¼ cup sugar
¼ tsp. salt
8 Tbsp. margarine
1 egg yolk
2 Tbsp. milk
1 tsp. lemon juice

Filling:
¼ cup fine dry bread crumbs
¼ cup chopped nuts
3 Tbsp. margarine, melted
2 medium apples, sliced
2 tsp. lemon juice
⅓ cup sugar
1 tsp. cinnamon
¼ cup raisins

Topping:
1 egg white, slightly beaten

1. To prepare crust sift together flour, sugar and salt. Cut in margarine.
2. In separate bowl blend together egg yolk, milk and lemon juice. Stir into flour mixture and form into a ball. Place on an 18-inch long piece of waxed paper. Flatten slightly and top with another piece of waxed paper. Roll out into 8" x 13" rectangle. Remove waxed paper and turn onto large baking sheet.
3. To prepare filling combine bread crumbs, nuts and margarine. Sprinkle over center third of dough.
4. Combine remaining filling ingredients and toss gently. Place apple mixture over crumb mixture. Fold one side of dough over apples. Brush lightly with beaten egg white. Fold other side of dough up and seal both ends. Brush top with egg white.
5. Bake at 400° for 30 minutes. Loosen from pan with knife.
6. Cool, slice and serve.

Apple Dumplings Supreme

Ruth Meyer
Linn, KS
Cat Walk

Makes 6 servings

Pastry:
2¼ cups sifted flour
¾ tsp. salt
¾ cup shortening
5 Tbsp. cold water

Apples:
6 medium tart apples
½ cup sugar
1½ tsp. cinnamon
2 Tbsp. butter

Syrup:
1 cup sugar
2 cups water
4 Tbsp. butter
¼ tsp. cinnamon

1. To prepare pastry sift together flour and salt. Cut in shortening. Add cold water and form into ball. Roll dough out into large rectangle and cut into 6 equal squares.

2. Peel and core apples. Place whole apple in center of each square.

3. Combine ½ cup sugar and 1½ tsp. cinnamon and feel cavity of each apple with this mixture. Dot with butter.

4. With water moisten 4 points of each pastry square and bring opposite points up over apple, overlapping them. Seal well. Arrange about 2 inches apart in 9" x 13" baking pan.

5. To prepare syrup combine all ingredients in a saucepan. Bring to a boil and boil for 3 minutes. Pour hot syrup over apples.

5. Bake at 425° for 40-45 minutes.

Apple Roll-Ups

Joanne Spatz
Lebanon, PA
The Chief

Makes 12 servings

Pastry:
1 egg, beaten
8-oz. carton sour cream
2 cups flour
2 Tbsp. white sugar
2 tsp. baking powder
¼ tsp. baking soda
¼ tsp. salt

Filling:
4 cups sliced apples
¼ cup sugar
½ tsp. cinnamon
¼ tsp. nutmeg

Lemon Sauce:
1½ cups water
1¼ cups brown sugar, packed
2 Tbsp. cornstarch
2 Tbsp. lemon juice
2 Tbsp. butter

1. To prepare pastry combine egg and sour cream.

2. Mix together flour, sugar, baking powder, baking soda and salt. Add to sour cream mixture and mix well. On lightly floured surface roll dough into a 12-inch square.

3. Spread sliced apples onto dough. Combine sugar, cinnamon and nutmeg and sprinkle over apples. Carefully roll up dough, jelly roll style. Cut into 12 1-inch slices.

4. Place slices, cut side down, in greased 9" x 13" baking pan.

5. Combine all lemon sauce ingredients except butter in a saucepan. Bring to a boil, stirring frequently. Pour lemon sauce over apple roll-ups and dot with butter.

6. Bake, uncovered, at 350° for 35-45 minutes until golden brown.

Baked Apple Chunks

Trudy Kutter
Corfu, NY
Cake Stand

Makes 4-5 servings

4-5 medium apples
2 Tbsp. sugar
¼ tsp. cinnamon
⅛ tsp. nutmeg
1-2 Tbsp. margarine
2 Tbsp. water

1. Core and peel apples and cut into thick chunks. Arrange in 8-inch square baking dish.
2. Combine sugar, cinnamon and nutmeg. Sprinkle over apples. Dot with margarine and sprinkle with water.
3. Bake at 350° for 20-25 minutes or until apples are soft but not mushy.
4. Serve warm with vanilla ice cream.

Pineapple Sheets

Susan Melton
Olney, MD

Makes 10 servings

Crust:
4 cups sifted flour
1 tsp. salt
1⅓ cups + 4 Tbsp. shortening
½ cup ice cold milk

Filling:
2 20-oz. cans crushed pineapple
1 egg
1 Tbsp. cornstarch
1 cup sugar

Frosting:
8-oz. pkg. cream cheese
2 Tbsp. milk
2½ cups powdered sugar
1 tsp. vanilla

1. To prepare crust combine flour and salt. With pastry blender cut in shortening. Sprinkle with milk, mixing with fork until moistened. Gather dough into 4 equal balls. Chill.
2. Roll each piece dough into 14-inch round. Place 2 pieces dough on 2 12-inch pizza pans with edges slightly lifted to prevent overflow.
3. To prepare filling drain pineapple thoroughly. Combine all ingredients and mix well. Pour ½ of mixture onto each pizza pan. Cover with re-

maining pieces dough and pinch edges to seal closed.
4. Bake at 350° for 25 minutes. Cool completely.
5. To prepare frosting cream all ingredients together until thoroughly mixed. Frost each of the cooled pineapple sheets and serve.

Sweet Noodle Kugel

Mary Jane Pozarycki
Neptune City, NJ
Fancy Nine Patch

Makes 12-15 servings

16-oz. pkg. wide egg noodles
3 large apples
24-oz. carton cottage cheese
8-oz. can crushed pineapple, undrained
1¼ cups raisins
1 Tbsp. cinnamon
¾ cup sugar
2 Tbsp. butter *or* margarine, melted

1. Cook noodles according to package directions. Drain and rinse.
2. Core, peel and slice apples. Reserve 10-12 slices apples for garnish.
3. In large mixing bowl combine apples, cottage cheese, pineapple and raisins.
4. In small bowl combine

cinnamon and sugar.

5. In a greased 9" x 13" baking dish arrange ⅓ of noodles, ½ of cottage cheese mixture and ⅓ of sugar mixture. Repeat layers.

6. Top with remaining ⅓ of noodles. Brush with melted butter. Sprinkle with remaining ⅓ of sugar mixture. Arrange 10-12 apple slices over top.

7. Cover and bake at 325° for 1 hour. Serve immediately.

Luckshen Kugel

Joy Moir
Holtsville, NY
Winter Cactus

Makes 12-15 dessert servings

½ lb. egg noodles
4 Tbsp. butter *or* margarine
½ cup sugar
3-oz. pkg. cream cheese
4 eggs, beaten
1 cup cottage cheese
1 cup sour cream
Cinnamon

1. Cook noodles according to package directions. Drain and rinse.

2. Cream together butter and sugar. Add cream cheese and cream well. Add eggs, cottage cheese and sour cream. Blend well. Fold in drained noodles.

3. Spoon mixture into greased 9" x 13" baking pan. Sprinkle liberally with cinnamon.

4. Bake at 350° for 1 hour.

Note: This dish may be served hot or cold, as a main dish or side dish or as a dessert with fruit.

Cookie Salad

Alicia Swift
Sleepy, MN
Log Cabin

Makes 6 servings

1 cup buttermilk
8-oz. carton whipped topping
1 large pkg. instant vanilla pudding
15-oz. can pineapple chunks, drained
11-oz. can mandarin oranges, drained
½ pkg. fudge cookies

1. In a bowl combine buttermilk, whipped topping and dry pudding mix. Mix well. Add well drained pineapple chunks and mandarin oranges.

2. Break cookies into bite-sized pieces.

3. Immediately before serving, stir broken cookies into pudding mixture.

❖

Kathy's Buster Bar Dessert

Katherine A. Schwartz
Freeport, IL
Double Irish Chain
Carol Jacobs
Freeport, IL
Irish Chain with Hearts

Makes 10-12 servings

8 Tbsp. butter
2 cups powdered sugar
⅔ cup chocolate chips
1½ cups evaporated milk
1 tsp. vanilla
1 lb. Oreo cookies, crushed
8 Tbsp. butter, melted
½ gallon ice cream
1½ cups dry roasted peanuts

1. In a saucepan combine 8 Tbsp. butter, powdered sugar, chocolate chips and milk. Bring to a boil and cook for 8 minutes. Remove from heat and stir in vanilla. Cool.

2. Mix crushed cookies and 8 Tbsp. melted butter together. Press into 9" x 13" baking pan. Cool.

3. Soften ice cream and spread over cookie crust. Sprinkle with peanuts. Pour cooled chocolate mixture over top and freeze.

4. Remove from freezer and soften for 10-15 minutes before serving.

271

Ice Cream Cake Dessert

Hazel Lightcap Propst
Oxford, PA
Amish Sunshine and Shadow

Makes 8-10 servings

1 cup flour
¼ cup quick oats
¼ cup brown sugar
8 Tbsp. butter
½ cup chopped walnuts
½ gallon ice cream, softened
8-oz. can chocolate syrup

1. Combine flour, oats and brown sugar. Cut in butter and add walnuts. Crumble into 9" x 13" baking pan.
2. Bake at 400° for 15 minutes. (Watch carefully to be sure it does not burn.) Cool and crumble.
3. Arrange ⅔ of crumbs in 9-inch square baking pan. Spoon softened ice cream over crumbs. Drizzle with chocolate syrup. Top with remaining crumbs. Freeze before serving.

Through the years our quilt club, the Arnprior Lionettes, has sponsored heritage quilt auctions. I have often been amazed at the women who bring in beautiful quilts and ask for only a few hundred dollars. One year the first place quilt was a Boston Commons. The quilter herself refused to put a reserve bid on it. Since I was chair of the committee, I put the bid on. Probably because the quilt had won first place, bidders were scared off and no one bid on the quilt. I felt terrible contacting the woman with the news, especially because I did not have the money to come up with the reserve bid. When my husband returned the quilt to her, she talked him into buying it for me for Christmas. He bought it, but insisted on making monthly installments up to the reserve price because he too felt it was worth much more than she thought. That Christmas I had a wonderful surprise.

—*Sheilagh Poole, Arnprior, ON*

❖

Ice Cream Delight

Marjorie Miller
Conneaut Lake, PA
Wedding Ring Variation

Makes 10-12 servings

8 Tbsp. butter, melted
⅔ cup brown sugar
½ cup chopped nuts
2 cups crushed Rice Chex
1 cup coconut
½ gallon ice cream, softened

1. Combine melted butter and brown sugar. Stir in nuts, Rice Chex and coconut until coated. Press into 9" x 13" baking pan, reserving ½ cup of mixture.
2. Spread softened ice cream over crumbs in baking pan. Sprinkle with remaining crumbs. Freeze.

3. Remove from freezer and let stand about 15 minutes before serving.

❖

Florida Dessert

Anna Barrow
Hatchville, MA
Sampler

Makes 12-15 servings

8 Tbsp. butter
1 cup brown sugar
2½ cups Rice Krispies
½ cup chopped nuts
1 cup coconut
½ gallon ice cream, softened

1. In a saucepan bring butter and sugar to a boil, stirring constantly.

2. In a bowl combine Rice Krispies, nuts and coconut. Pour butter sauce over Rice Krispies mixture and mix well. Press ½ of mixture into bottom of greased 9" x 13" baking dish.

3. Spread ice cream over Rice Krispies. Top with remaining ½ of Rice Krispies mixture.

4. Freeze before serving.

Easy Vanilla Ice Cream

**Louise Stackhouse
Benton, PA**
Log Cabin Lone Star

Makes ½ gallon ice cream

**4 eggs
12-oz. can evaporated milk
14-oz. can condensed milk
1 quart whole milk
1½ cups sugar *or less*
1-2 tsp. vanilla**

1. In a large bowl combine all ingredients until completely creamy.

2. Pour into ice cream freezer and follow directions for making ice cream.

Butter Pecan Ice Cream

**Donna Miller
Partridge, KS**
Star Spin

Makes 1 gallon ice cream

**2-3 eggs
½ cup brown sugar
½ cup dark corn syrup
4 cups whole milk
3 cups cream
2 small pkgs. instant
   vanilla pudding
1 tsp. salt
1 tsp. vanilla
3 Tbsp. butter
1 cup chopped pecans
¼ cup brown sugar**

1. Beat eggs and add ½ cup brown sugar and syrup. Mix well. Add milk, cream, pudding, salt and vanilla. Mix until smooth. Pour pudding mixture into ice cream freezer and follow directions for making ice cream.

2. Melt butter and add pecans and ¼ cup brown sugar. Spread on baking sheet.

3. Toast in oven at 300° for 20 minutes, stirring occasionally.

4. Add pecans to ice cream mixture after it has started to harden. Continue freezing until ice cream is ready to serve.

Fruit Pizza

**Elizabeth J. Yoder
Millersburg, OH**
Log Cabin
**Lola Kennel
Strang, NE**
*Broken Star & Appliqued
Roses*

Makes 10-12 servings

**¾ cup sugar
8 Tbsp. margarine
1 egg, beaten
1½ cups flour
1 tsp. baking powder
¼ tsp. salt
8-oz. pkg. cream cheese,
   softened
¼ cup sugar
½ tsp. vanilla
1 cup whipped topping
Assortment of fruit pieces**

1. Cream together ¾ cup sugar, margarine and egg. Blend in flour, baking powder and salt. Pat mixture into ungreased 14-inch pizza pan.

2. Bake at 375° for 10-12 minutes or until lightly browned. Cool.

3. Cream together cream cheese, ¼ cup sugar and vanilla. Fold in whipped topping. Spread mixture over cooled crust.

4. Arrange an assortment of fruit pieces over cream cheese mixture. Glaze with an orange sauce and serve immediately.

Fruit Pizza Variation

Mary Pat Sloan
Downingtown, PA
Log Cabin

Makes 10-12 servings

Crust:
¾ cup butter *or* margarine, softened
½ cup powdered sugar
1½ cups flour

Filling:
10-oz. pkg. Hershey's vanilla milk chips
¼ cup cream
8-oz. pkg. cream cheese, softened
Assortment of fruit pieces

Topping:
¼ cup sugar
1 Tbsp. cornstarch
½ cup pineapple juice
½ tsp. lemon juice

1. Cream together butter and powdered sugar. Blend in flour. Press mixture onto bottom and sides of 12-inch round pizza pan.
2. Bake at 300° for 20 minutes until lightly browned. Cool completely.
3. To prepare filling melt chips in cream in a saucepan. Beat in cream cheese until smooth. Spread over cooled crust. Chill.
4. To prepare topping combine sugar and cornstarch in a saucepan. Stir in juices and cook, stirring constantly until thickened. Cool.
5. Slice and arrange an assortment of fruits over chilled cream cheese mixture. Pour cooled topping over fruit and serve immediately.

Orange Sauce

Susan Alexander
Baltimore, MD
Nine Patch

Makes 1 cup sauce

½ cup sugar
Dash salt
1 Tbsp. cornstarch
½ cup orange juice
2 Tbsp. lemon juice
¼ cup water

1. In a small saucepan mix sugar, salt and cornstarch. Gradually add orange juice, lemon juice and water. Cook over medium heat, stirring constantly until thickened and boiling. Boil and stir 1 minute.
2. Remove from heat. Cool and spoon over fruit pizza.

Mandarin Orange Sauce

Anita Falk
Mountain Lake, MN
Double Irish Chain

Makes 1½ cups sauce

11-oz. can mandarin oranges
Water
2 Tbsp. cornstarch
1 Tbsp. lemon juice
½ cup sugar

1. Drain juice from oranges. Use mandarin oranges as one of fruits on fruit pizza. Add enough water to juice to make 1 cup.
2. Combine all ingredients in saucepan and cook until clear and thickened, stirring frequently. Cool completely.
3. Pour over fruit on fruit pizza. Serve.

> I belong to a satellite group of the Quilters' Guild of North Dakota called Designing Quilters. We are all both fabric-holics and chocolate-holics. Our meetings always feature quilts and chocolate.
>
> —*Vicky Jo Bogart, Fargo, ND*

Fresh Fruit Salad

Sue Graziadio
White Mills, PA
Michael's Star

Makes 4 servings

Any fresh fruits in season
2 Tbsp. lemon juice
2 Tbsp. lime juice
2 Tbsp. orange juice
⅓ cup water
⅔ cup sugar

1. Cut enough fruit into chunks to fill a medium serving bowl.
2. Mix lemon juice, lime juice, orange juice, water and sugar. Pour over fruit and toss lightly. Serve.

Fruit Slush

Karen Unternahrer
Shipshewana, IN
Early American Sampler Quilt

Makes about 8 quarts

5 cups sugar
12 cups warm water
3 12-oz. cans frozen orange juice
4 15-oz. cans crushed pineapple
6 lbs. bananas, sliced

1. Dissolve sugar in warm water. Add all remaining ingredients and mix lightly. Freeze. (I prefer freezing in quart containers which is just enough to serve my family.)
2. One hour before serving, remove from freezer. Immediately before serving, chop up with a spoon and mix together.
3. Great served as part of a breakfast bar, a side dish with spicy foods or as a dessert with brownies.

Variation:

Follow directions as given, but use the following smaller amounts: 2 cups sugar, 3 cups water, 6-oz. can frozen orange juice, 20-oz. can crushed pineapple and 5 bananas.
Debra Kennel Jaberg
Strang, NE

Frozen Grape Salad

Julie McKenzie
Punxsutawney, PA
Teardrops and Tantrums

Makes 10-12 servings

2 3-oz. pkgs. cream cheese, softened
2 Tbsp. mayonnaise
2 Tbsp. pineapple syrup
2 cups miniature marshmallows
20-oz. can pineapple tidbits, drained
1 cup heavy cream, whipped
2 cups red grapes, halved and seeded
½-1 cup nuts (optional)

1. Blend together cream cheese and mayonnaise. Beat in pineapple syrup from canned pineapple. Fold in marshmallows and pineapple tidbits. Fold in whipped cream and grapes. Add nuts if desired.
2. Spoon into container and freeze.
3. Remove from freezer 1-2 hours before serving.

Note: Salad should be served frozen, but soft enough to scoop out of bowl.

I belong to St. James Lutheran Church in Pleasantville, Pennsylvania. About five years ago our pastor was a young, single woman. She decided to get married and planned to move to Harrisburg. Even though only two of us had ever made a quilt, the congregation decided to make a quilt as a combination going-away and wedding gift. We planned to surprise her, but because she was constantly visiting people, it became increasingly difficult. We told her about the quilt and she joined in the fun. We had several potluck suppers and lunches with lots of laughter and joy as we worked together on what became for all of us a labor of love.

—Theresa Leppert, Schellsburg, PA

Alix Botsford's Cheesecake

Alix Botsford
Seminole, OK
Double Wedding Ring

Makes 10-12 servings

Crust:
1 cup graham cracker crumbs
¼ cup oat bran
4 Tbsp. sugar
4 Tbsp. margarine

Filling:
4 8-oz. pkgs. lowfat cream cheese, softened
1 cup sugar
4 Tbsp. unbleached flour
1 tsp. vanilla
1½ cups yogurt
4 jumbo eggs

Topping:
1 cup sour cream
2 Tbsp. sugar
1 tsp. vanilla
1 quart strawberries

1. To prepare crust combine graham crumbs, oat bran and sugar. Melt margarine and pour into crumb mixture. Mix well. Press into 10-inch springform pan.

2. Bake at 325° for 10 minutes. Remove from oven and reduce temperature to 250°.

3. To prepare filling combine cream cheese, sugar, flour, vanilla and yogurt. Mix well. Add one egg at a time, mixing well after each addition. Pour filling into hot crust.

4. Bake at 250° for 1½ hours or until firm in center. Cake will also pull away from pan sides when done.

5. To prepare topping combine sour cream, sugar and vanilla. Spread over cheesecake and continue baking for 10 more minutes. Loosen cake from rim of pan. Cool before removing rim of pan.

6. Garnish with fresh sliced strawberries and serve.

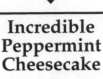

Incredible Peppermint Cheesecake

Susan Thomson
Houston, TX
Ohio Star

Makes 10-12 servings

1½ cups crushed Oreos
4 Tbsp. butter *or* margarine, melted
¼ cup sugar
2 8-oz. pkgs. cream cheese
14-oz. can sweetened condensed milk
1 cup crushed peppermint candy
½ cup mini chocolate chips
1 pint heavy cream

1. Combine cookies, butter and sugar. Press into 9-inch springform pan or 9" x 13" baking pan. Set aside.

2. Beat cream cheese until fluffy. Add condensed milk gradually. Stir in candy and chocolate chips.

3. Beat cream until stiff. Fold into batter. Pour over cookie crust. Cover and freeze.

4. To serve let stand for a few minutes. (Remove sides of springform pan). Garnish with additional crushed peppermint if desired.

Velvet Cheesecake

Terry Kessler
Bayside, NY
Great-Grandmother's Fan

Makes 10-12 servings

1 lb. ricotta cheese
2 8-oz. pkgs. cream cheese
1 lb. sour cream
1½ cups sugar
4 eggs
1 Tbsp. vanilla
3 Tbsp. cornstarch
3 Tbsp. flour
8 Tbsp. butter, melted

1. Cream together ricotta cheese, cream cheese, sour cream and sugar. Add eggs, one at a time. Add vanilla and mix well.
2. While mixer is still going, sprinkle cornstarch and flour around sides of bowl. Mix in melted butter. (Batter should be thin.) Pour into greased 9-inch springform pan.
3. Bake at 325° for 1 hour. Turn off oven and let cheesecake set for 2 hours. Remove from oven and chill before taking out of pan.

Jean Reistle's Cheesecake

Jean Reistle
Mickleton, NJ
Oh My Stars!

Makes 20-24 servings

5 8-oz. pkgs. cream cheese, softened
5 eggs
2 Tbsp. fresh lemon juice
1 tsp. vanilla
1¼ cups sugar
2 Tbsp. melted butter
1 pint light cream
1 tsp. cinnamon
1 tsp. nutmeg

1. Cream cream cheese and add all remaining ingredients except cinnamon and nutmeg, one at a time, in order listed. Beat for 40 minutes at slowest speed. Pour into 2 ungreased 10-inch springform pans.
2. Sprinkle cinnamon and nutmeg over top. Place springform pans in larger pans and pour boiling water around them.
3. Bake at 350° for 1 hour. Let stand for 5 hours at room temperature, cover with aluminum foil and refrigerate overnight.
4. Remove sides of springform pans and serve.

Adelle Ward's Cheesecake

Adelle Ward
Scotia, NY
Double Nine Patch

Makes 10-12 servings

Crust:
1¾ cups graham cracker crumbs
¼ cup sugar
¼ cup finely chopped walnuts
½ tsp. cinnamon
½ cup melted butter

Filling:
2 8-oz. pkgs. cream cheese
3 eggs
3 cups sour cream
1 cup sugar
2 tsp. vanilla

1. Combine all crust ingredients and pat into bottom of 10-inch springform pan.
2. To prepare filling cream cream cheese and add eggs one at a time. Add sour cream, sugar and vanilla. Pour over crust.
3. Bake at 325° for 1¼-1½ hours or until knife comes out clean. Cool slowly.

Cheese Blintzes

Pat Garrow
Lodi, CA
Irish Chain
Rose M. Hoffman
Schuylkill Haven, PA
Schuylkill Haven Community Quilt

Makes 15-20 blintzes

1 loaf white bread, crusts removed
8-oz. pkg. cream cheese
2 egg yolks
½ cup sugar
¾ cup melted butter
1 cup sugar
3-4 tsp. cinnamon

1. Roll out bread slices until thin.
2. Cream together cream cheese, egg yolks and sugar. Spread mixture over each slice bread. Roll up as for jelly roll.
3. Combine sugar and cinnamon.
4. Dip each roll into melted butter; then into sugar and cinnamon mixture. Arrange on baking sheet, seam side down, and freeze. After frozen, remove to plastic bags for storage.

5. Bake, as needed, at 400° for 15-20 minutes or until crisp.

❖

Blueberry Cheesecake

Ada Miller
Sugarcreek, OH
Log Cabin Broken Star

Makes 12-15 small servings

24 graham crackers
¾ cup sugar
¼ cup butter, melted
2 eggs
8-oz. pkg. cream cheese
21-oz. can blueberry pie filling
2-3 cups whipped topping

1. Crush graham crackers. Reserve ½ cup. Add ¼ cup sugar and melted butter. Press into 9" x 13" baking dish.
2. In a bowl beat eggs until fluffy. Add cream cheese and ½ cup sugar. Beat well and pour over graham cracker crust.
3. Bake at 350° for 15 minutes. Let cool thoroughly.
4. Spread blueberry filling over cooled crust. Top with whipped topping and serve.

❖

Viennese Chocolate Torte

Merlie Vidette
Duxbury, MA
Trip Around the World

Makes 8-10 servings

Torte:
5-oz. pkg. semi-sweet chocolate chips
7 medium eggs, separated
¾ cup sugar
1½ cups walnuts, ground
1 handful plain bread crumbs

Frosting:
3 level Tbsp. powdered sugar
1 Tbsp. butter
3 Tbsp. boiling water
4 ozs. sweet chocolate

1. Melt chocolate chips in double boiler.
2. Beat egg yolks and sugar until thick and lemon colored. Add chocolate and mix well.
3. Beat egg whites until stiff peaks form. Mix chocolate batter into egg whites by spoonsful, alternating with ground nuts and bread crumbs. Pour into

greased and floured spring-form pan.

4. Bake at 350° for 40-45 minutes or until no longer sticky.

5. To prepare frosting combine sugar, butter and water and stir until mixture appears clear.

6. Melt chocolate in double boiler. Add to sugar mixture and stir until smooth. Pour over cake and serve.

Note: The longer you stir the frosting, the thicker it becomes. Cake may also be served with whipped topping.

Easy Sticky Buns

Stephanie Braskey
Pottstown, PA
Applique Album Blocks

Makes 6-8 servings

1 pkg. unbaked frozen rolls
8 Tbsp. butter *or*
 margarine, melted
4-oz. pkg. non-instant
 vanilla pudding
½ cup brown sugar
½ cup chopped pecans

1. Arrange rolls in well-greased bundt pan. Pour melted butter over rolls.

2. Combine dry pudding mix, brown sugar and pecans. Sprinkle over rolls. Cover with waxed paper

and a cloth and let stand overnight.

3. Bake at 350° for 30 minutes.

Jelly Roll

Theresa Leppert
Schellsburg, PA
Grandmother's Flower Garden

Makes 10 servings

3 eggs
1 cup white sugar
⅓ cup water
1 tsp. vanilla
¾ cup all-purpose flour
1 tsp. baking powder
¼ tsp. salt
⅔ cup jelly *or* jam
4-6 Tbsp. powdered sugar

1. Line 10" x 15" jelly roll pan with aluminum foil or waxed paper. Grease foil or paper.

2. In medium bowl beat eggs. Gradually beat in sugar. Blend in water and vanilla. Gradually add flour, baking powder and salt, beating until batter is just smooth. Pour into jelly roll pan, spreading batter to corners.

3. Bake at 375° for 12-15 minutes or until toothpick inserted in center comes out clean. Loosen cake from edges of pan. Invert onto lint-free towel which has been sprinkled with pow-

dered sugar. Carefully remove foil or paper and trim off any stiff edges.

4. While still hot, roll up cake and towel from narrow end. Cool on rack. Unroll cake and remove towel.

5. Beat jelly slightly with fork to soften. Spread over cake. Roll up cake, sprinkle with powdered sugar, slice and serve.

Date Nut Torte

Jeanne Allen
Los Alamos, NM
Scrap-a-holic

Makes 6-8 servings

4 eggs
1 cup sugar
1 cup dry bread crumbs
1 tsp. baking powder
2 cups pitted dates,
 chopped
1 cup coarsely chopped
 nuts

1. Beat eggs until thick and lemon colored. Gradually add sugar. Stir in bread crumbs and baking powder. Fold in dates and nuts. Spread into greased 8-inch square baking pan.

2. Bake at 350° for 35 minutes.

3. Cool and serve with ice cream or whipped topping.

Pumpkin Cake Roll

Sally Thorpe
Roanoke Rapids, NC
Neon Fish
Karen Summers
Mine Run, VA
Double Wedding Ring

Makes 8-10 servings

Cake:
3 eggs
1 cup white sugar
⅔ cup canned pumpkin
1 tsp. lemon juice
¾ cup flour
1 tsp. baking powder
2 tsp. cinnamon
1 tsp. ginger
½ tsp. nutmeg
½ tsp. salt
1 cup finely chopped
    walnuts
2 Tbsp. powdered sugar

Filling:
1 cup powdered sugar
8-oz. pkg. cream cheese
4 Tbsp. butter *or* margarine
½ tsp. vanilla

1. Beat eggs on high speed for 2-3 minutes. Gradually add sugar, pumpkin and lemon juice.
2. In separate bowl combine flour, baking powder, cinnamon, ginger, nutmeg and salt. Stir into pumpkin mixture and mix well.
3. Line 10" x 15" jelly roll pan with waxed paper. Grease waxed paper and spread pumpkin mixture over paper. Top with walnuts.
4. Bake at 375° for 15 minutes.
5. Turn out onto lint-free towel. Sprinkle with powdered sugar and roll up with towel. Cool completely.
6. To prepare filling combine all ingredients and beat until smooth.
7. Unroll cake and spread with filling. Roll up without towel, wrap securely in plastic wrap or aluminum foil and refrigerate to chill.

When I think of quilting today, I always return to my earliest memories of hiding underneath my grandmother's quilting frame in a small clapboard house in the wooded hills of Kentucky. The frame was built from spare planks nailed at the corners and hung from the ceiling by ropes. Several times a week my mother, grandmother and her friends would gather in her front room for a "bee." I would sit underneath at my mother's feet, watching the needles dart in and out of the muslin with rhythmic precision. It was always the quilters' hands that most fascinated me. How did they manage to hold the needle so delicately and guide it with such purpose? My favorite part of those quilting days was poking my hand into the quilt from underneath amid the stern warnings of my mother and the giggles of my friends.

—Laura Barrus Bishop, Boerne, TX

Raisin Scones

Eleanor J. Ferreira
North Chelmsford, MA
Trip Around the World
Marcia S. Myer
Manheim, PA
Dresden Plate

Makes 12 scones

2 cups flour
2 Tbsp. sugar
2 tsp. baking powder
½ tsp. baking soda
½ tsp. salt
½ tsp. nutmeg
8 Tbsp. butter
1 cup raisins
¾ cup buttermilk
1 egg white, lightly beaten
1-2 tsp. sugar

1. In large bowl combine flour, sugar, baking powder, baking soda, salt and nutmeg. Cut in butter until

mixture resembles coarse crumbs. Fold in raisins. With a fork mix in buttermilk. Knead dough in bowl for about 2 minutes.

2. On floured surface roll dough into large ½-inch thick round. With a sharp knife cut dough into 12 3-inch triangles. Space apart on greased baking sheet or pizza pan. Brush tops with egg white. Sprinkle with sugar.

3. Bake at 425° for 12-15 minutes or until nicely browned.

Danish Pastry Puffs

Joyce Niemann
Fruitland Park, FL
Lap Sampler

Makes 12 servings

Pastry Puffs:
16 Tbsp. butter *or* **margarine**
2 cups flour
2 Tbsp. ice water
1 cup water
1 tsp. almond extract
3 eggs

Frosting:
2 cups powdered sugar
Milk
½ cup chopped nuts

1. To prepare puffs cut 8 Tbsp. butter into 1 cup

flour with pastry blender until mixture resembles coarse meal. Sprinkle ice water, 1 Tbsp. at a time, evenly over surface. Stir with a fork until dry ingredients are moistened.

2. Divide dough in half. Pat each half into 3" x 12" rectangle on lightly greased baking sheet. Set pastry aside.

3. Place remaining 8 Tbsp. butter and 1 cup water in saucepan. Bring to a boil. Stir in almond extract. Reduce heat to low and add remaining 1 cup flour, stirring vigorously until mixture leaves sides of pan and forms a smooth ball. Remove from heat and cool slightly.

4. Add eggs, one at a time, and beat with spoon after each addition. Beat until batter is smooth. Spread evenly over pastry rectangles.

5. Bake at 350° for 55-60 minutes until golden.

6. To prepare frosting combine powdered sugar with milk until spreading consistency. (Do not use too much milk.) Spread pastry puffs with frosting and sprinkle with chopped nuts.

Creamy Chocolate Fudge

Jane L. Murphy
Malvern, PA
Miniature Nine Patch
Janice Muller
Derwood, MD
Amish Roman Stripes

Makes 9" x 13" pan

3 4-oz. bars German chocolate
12-oz. pkg. semi-sweet chocolate chips
7-oz. jar marshmallow cream
12-oz. can evaporated milk
4½ cups sugar *or* **less**
2 Tbsp. butter
1 Tbsp. vanilla
2 cups walnuts

1. Break up chocolate bars. Mix together bars, chocolate chips and marshmallow cream. Set aside.

2. In a 2-quart saucepan combine evaporated milk, sugar and butter. Bring to a boil and boil 6 minutes on medium heat.

3. Pour hot mixture over chocolate marshmallow mixture. Mix until smooth and creamy. Add vanilla and walnuts. Pour into greased 9" x 13" baking pan.

4. Let stand at room temperature for 24 hours before serving.

Peanut Butter Fudge

Nancy Wall
Duncansville, PA
Miniature Trip Around the World

Makes 9-inch square pan

16 Tbsp. margarine
4 Tbsp. cocoa
1 tsp. vanilla
1 cup peanut butter
3 cups powdered sugar

1. Melt margarine. Add cocoa and vanilla. Turn burner off and let pan on warm burner. (For gas stove, turn to very low simmer.) Add peanut butter and stir to smooth consistency. Add sugar and continue stirring until well mixed and smooth.
2. Press fudge mixture into greased 9-inch square baking dish. Refrigerate approximately ½ hour to cool. Cut into 36 pieces and serve.

Marshmallow Cream Fudge

Jo Ellen Rousey
Anderson, IN
Counted Cross-Stitch Quilt

Makes 9-inch square pan

3 cups sugar
1 cup evaporated milk
6 Tbsp. butter *or* margarine
7-oz. jar marshmallow cream
1 cup chopped nuts (optional)
12-oz. pkg. chocolate chips

1. In a saucepan bring sugar, milk and butter to a boil. Cook to medium soft ball stage (236°), stirring frequently.
2. Remove from heat. Immediately add marshmallow cream, nuts and chocolate chips. Stir until melted. Pour into greased 9-inch square baking pan.
3. Let cool and cut into squares.

Butterfudge Fingers

Esther L. Lantz
Leola, PA
Irish Chain

Makes 9" x 13" pan

Layer 1:
4 ozs. unsweetened chocolate
⅔ cup butter
2 cups sugar
4 eggs
1½ cups sifted flour
1 tsp. baking powder
1 tsp. salt
1 cup chopped nuts

Layer 2:
½ cup butter, melted
4 cups powdered sugar
4 Tbsp. cream *or* milk
2 tsp. vanilla

Layer 3:
2 ozs. unsweetened chocolate
2 Tbsp. butter

1. To prepare layer one melt chocolate and butter in double boiler. Remove from heat and beat in sugar and eggs.
2. Sift together dry ingredients. Add to chocolate mixture and mix well. Fold in nuts and spread into greased 9" x 13" baking pan.
3. Bake at 350° for 30-35 minutes. Cool slightly.
4. To prepare layer two combine all ingredients and mix until smooth. Spread

> Quilts and quiltings became a part of my life when I was very young. I have many fond memories of gathering with all the aunts and cousins at Grandma's house and playing around the quilt. Grandma made quilts for all of her children and some of her grandchildren. My mother made three quilts for each of her 15 children. I have continued the tradition, making quilts and comforters for my own children.
>
> —*Mary Esther Yoder, Partridge, KS*

evenly over layer one. Cool completely.

5. To prepare layer three melt chocolate and butter in double boiler. Pour over layer two. Chill and serve.

Microwave Fudge

Joan Lemmler
Albuquerque, NM
Bearry Agee

Makes 8-inch square pan

1 lb. powdered sugar
⅓ cup cocoa
8 Tbsp. margarine
¼ cup milk
1 tsp. vanilla
1 cup chopped nuts

1. In a microwave-safe bowl combine powdered sugar, cocoa, margarine and milk. Do *not* stir.

2. Microwave on high for 2 minutes and 45 seconds. Beat until smooth with a hand mixer.

3. Fold in vanilla and nuts. Turn into greased 8-inch square baking pan. Chill and serve.

Caramels

Darlene S. Rosenberry
Fayetteville, PA
Swan

Makes 5-6 dozen caramels

2 cups white sugar
1 cup brown sugar
1 cup light corn syrup
1 cup heavy cream
1 cup milk
16 Tbsp. butter
1¼ Tbsp. vanilla

1. In a saucepan combine all ingredients except vanilla. Cook slowly to firm ball stage (248°), stirring frequently.

2. Remove from heat and add vanilla. Pour into greased 9-inch square baking pan. Cool.

3. When firm, cut into squares and wrap individually in waxed paper.

Butterscotch Candy

Jean Reistle
Mickleton, NJ
Oh My Stars!

Makes 2-3 dozen candies

2 6-oz. pkgs. butterscotch bits
2 cups Chinese noodles
2 cups peanuts

1. Melt butterscotch bits in double boiler. Add noodles and peanuts. Stir until well coated.

2. Drop by rounded teaspoonsful onto baking sheet and let harden.

3. Place in covered tin and store for use.

English Toffee

Joyce Parker
North Plainfield, NJ
Friendship

Makes 2 dozen candies

1 cup sugar
16 Tbsp. butter
¼ cup water
1 tsp. vanilla
6-oz. pkg. chocolate chips
½ cup finely chopped walnuts

1. In a saucepan combine sugar, butter and water. Over medium heat bring to hard crack stage (300°), stirring occasionally. (This takes about 30 minutes.)

2. Remove from heat and stir in vanilla. Pour onto ungreased baking sheet while still hot. Sprinkle with chocolate chips, spreading after they have melted. Sprinkle with chopped walnuts.

3. Cool completely and break into jagged pieces.

My grandmother, Lily Caldwell, was a delightful cook and talented quilter. At the age of 16, she rode a buckboard into Oklahoma territory in hopes of staking a homestead for her family. Her horses were not fast enough and the family instead settled on some land in Kansas.

—*Marge Jarrett, Gaithersburg, MD*

Pralines

Evelyn Horne
Macon, GA
Christmas Sampler

Makes 1-2 dozen pralines

1 cup buttermilk
2 cups sugar
1 tsp. baking soda
1 tsp. vanilla
1 Tbsp. butter *or* margarine
2 cups pecan halves

1. In a 2-quart saucepan combine buttermilk, sugar and baking soda. Bring to a boil. Boil until mixture forms a soft ball, stirring frequently. Remove from heat.
2. Add vanilla, butter and pecans. Beat until mixture becomes smooth and glossy. Quickly, drop by rounded teaspoonful onto waxed paper.

Note: If mixture becomes too hard, simply reheat.

Old-Fashioned Easter Eggs

Anona M. Teel
Bangor, PA
Tulip

Makes 2-3 dozen eggs

1 medium potato, peeled
1 Tbsp. butter
1 lb. powdered sugar
18-oz. jar peanut butter
12-oz. pkg. chocolate chips

1. Boil potato until mushy. Drain and mash with butter until smooth. Add sugar and mix well. Add peanut butter and mix well.
2. Shape mixture into eggs and arrange on waxed paper-lined baking sheet. Let stand overnight or until firm.
3. Melt chocolate in double boiler. Coat peanut butter eggs with chocolate. Set aside in cool place until chocolate hardens.

Chocolate Acorns

Mary Ann Potenta
Neshanic Station, NJ
Katelyn's Amish Bars

Makes 4-5 dozen acorn candies

1 cup butter
⅔ cup sugar
3 egg yolks
1 tsp. almond extract
2½ cups flour
2-3 drops green food coloring
8-oz. pkg. chocolate chips

1. Cream together butter and sugar. Add egg yolks and almond extract and mix well. Add flour and food coloring and mix until well blended.
2. Pinch off small balls and roll into acorn shape in palms of hands. Arrange on greased and floured baking sheets at least 2 inches apart.
3. Bake at 375° about 10 minutes until sheen disappears and acorn candies are solid. Remove from pan and cool.
4. Meanwhile, melt chocolate chips in double boiler. Dip wide end of each acorn cookie into melted chocolate. Arrange on waxed paper and set aside in cool place until chocolate hardens.

Breakfast Foods

Salmon Quiche

Brenda J. Marshall
St. Marys, ON
*Christmas in the Corners
Charm Quilt*

Makes 6 servings

1 cup shredded cheddar
cheese
2 Tbsp. chopped onion
2 7-oz. cans salmon
3 eggs
1 cup milk
¼ tsp. basil
¼ tsp. tarragon
¼ tsp. oregano
¼ tsp. parsley

1. Grease an 8-inch pie
plate. Sprinkle cheese and
onion on bottom.
2. Drain salmon and
flake over cheese and onion.
3. Mix together eggs and
milk and pour evenly over
all. Sprinkle with seasonings and herbs.
4. Bake at 350-375° for 50
minutes or until set. Serve
hot.

Spinach and Cheese Pie

Rebecca Eldredge
Honolulu, HI
Kohala Beauty

Makes 6 servings

12-oz. carton cottage cheese
2 cups grated cheddar
cheese
3 eggs
2 Tbsp. flour
10-oz. pkg. frozen spinach
1 9" unbaked pastry shell

1. Combine cottage
cheese, cheddar cheese,
eggs and flour in large
bowl.
2. Thaw spinach and
drain thoroughly. Fold into
cheese mixture. Spoon into
unbaked pie shell.
3. Bake at 400-425° for 40-
60 minutes until top is
puffy and lightly browned.

Chicken and Spinach Quiche

Norah Pledger
Bellville, TX
Strip-Pieced Cat

Makes 6 servings

1 cup chopped, cooked
chicken
1 cup shredded Swiss
cheese
½ cup cooked, chopped
spinach, drained
¼ cup chopped onion
2 eggs, lightly beaten
¾ cup mayonnaise
¾ cup milk
⅛ tsp. pepper
1 9" unbaked pastry shell

1. In a large bowl mix
chicken, cheese, spinach
and onion. Spoon mixture
into pastry shell.
2. Stir together eggs,
milk, mayonnaise and pep-
per until smooth. Pour over
chicken mixture.
3. Bake at 350° for 45-50
minutes.

Best Ever Broccoli Quiche

Jane L. Murphy
Malvern, PA
Nine Patch

Makes 6 servings

3 eggs, beaten
⅔ cup chicken broth
½ cup heavy cream *or* evaporated milk
½ tsp. salt
¼ tsp. Tabasco
¼ cup Parmesan cheese
2 cups chopped, fresh broccoli
1 cup grated Swiss cheese
¼ cup sliced scallions
1 9" unbaked pastry shell

1. In a bowl beat eggs with broth, cream, salt and Tabasco. Set aside.
2. Prick bottom and sides of pastry shell and bake at 450° for 5 minutes. Remove from oven.
3. Sprinkle pastry shell with ½ of Parmesan cheese. Scatter ½ of broccoli, ½ of Swiss cheese and ½ of scallions into shell. Repeat broccoli, Swiss cheese and scallion layers. Pour egg mixture over these ingredients and sprinkle with remaining Parmesan cheese.
4. Bake at 450° for 10 minutes. Reduce oven temperature to 325° and bake 25 minutes longer or until knife inserted in center comes out clean.

Broccoli Quiche

Ella Miller
Fredericksburg, OH
Crystalis

Makes 6 servings

2 cups fresh broccoli, chopped
½ cup diced, cooked ham
½ cup chopped green pepper
⅓ cup chopped onion
1 cup shredded cheddar cheese
1 cup milk
½ cup Bisquick
3 eggs
¼ tsp. salt
¼ tsp. pepper

1. Steam broccoli until crisp tender. Arrange in lightly greased 9-inch pie plate. Sprinkle with ham, green pepper, onion and cheese.
2. In a blender or food processor combine milk, Bisquick, eggs, salt and pepper. Blend until smooth. Pour over broccoli mixture.
3. Bake at 375° for 25 minutes or until set and lightly browned. Let stand about 5 minutes before serving.

Quick Quiche

Sybil Turner
Bellville, TX
Tennessee Album

Makes 6 servings

¼ cup margarine, melted
2 4-oz. cans whole green chilies
2 cups grated sharp cheddar cheese
2 cups grated Monterey Jack cheese
3 eggs, beaten
2 cups milk
1 cup Bisquick
½ tsp. salt

1. Melt margarine in a large casserole dish. Layer green chilies over margarine. Sprinkle cheeses over chilies.
2. In a separate bowl beat eggs and milk together. Set aside.
3. Combine Bisquick and salt and stir into milk mixture. Pour over cheese and chili mixture.
4. Bake at 350° for 35 minutes. Let stand 10 minutes before cutting to serve.

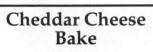

Cheddar Cheese Bake

Merlie Vidette
Duxbury, MA
Trip Around the World

Makes 6 servings

12 slices white bread
3 Tbsp. butter, melted
1 lb. cheddar cheese, shredded
½ lb. mushrooms, sliced
⅓ cup minced green pepper
4 eggs
3 cups milk
½ tsp. salt
½ tsp. paprika
Dash pepper

1. Trim crust from bread and brush each piece with butter. Arrange 6 slices bread in a greased 9" x 13" baking pan. Top with ½ of cheese and ½ of mushrooms. Repeat layers. Sprinkle with green pepper.
2. In large bowl combine eggs, milk and seasonings and beat well. Pour over bread layers in baking pan. Cover and refrigerate until ready to bake.
3. Bake, uncovered, at 350° for 40-50 minutes or until knife inserted in center comes out clean.

Egg Soufflé Casserole

Linda Roberta Pond
Los Alamos, NM
Not the Same Old Cat
Priscilla M. Wade
Voorhees, NJ
Bear Paw & Triple Rail Fence

Makes 6-8 servings

1 loaf French bread, cubed
1 lb. sausage
8 Tbsp. margarine
4 cups milk
12 eggs, beaten
2½-3 cups grated cheddar cheese
1½ tsp. dry mustard
1 tsp. salt
Pepper to taste

1. Brown sausage in skillet. Drain all excess fat.
2. Melt margarine in 9" x 13" pan. Arrange cubed bread over margarine. Spread browned sausage on top.
3. Beat all other ingredients together and pour over top. Refrigerate overnight.
4. Bake at 350° for 45 minutes.

Variation:
Substitute 1 10¾-oz. can cream of mushroom soup for 1 cup milk.

Shan D. Lear
Middleton, MA
Nine Patch & Hearts

Egg and Potato Bake

Karen Unternahrer
Shipshewana, IN
Early American Sampler Quilt

Makes 4-6 servings

3 medium potatoes
3 hard-boiled eggs, sliced
2 Tbsp. butter
2 Tbsp. flour
1 cup milk
1 tsp. salt
¼ tsp. pepper
1 tsp. Worcestershire sauce
1 cup grated cheese
¼ lb. fresh mushrooms, sliced
¼-½ cup wheat germ

1. Cook potatoes and slice thinly.
2. Meanwhile, prepare a cheese sauce by melting butter in a saucepan. Stir in flour. Slowly add milk, salt, pepper, Worcestershire sauce and cheese, stirring constantly until thickened.
3. In greased casserole dish arrange ½ potatoes, ½ eggs and ½ cheese sauce. Repeat. Top with mushrooms and wheat germ.
4. Bake at 350° for 20-25 minutes.

Overnight Breakfast Casserole

Bonita Ensenberger
Albuquerque, NM
Jessica's Nine Patch

Makes 6 servings

1 lb. lean bulk sausage
6 slices white bread, cubed
2 Tbsp. butter, melted
1½ cups shredded cheese
5 eggs, beaten
2 cups half-and-half
1 tsp. salt
1 tsp. dry mustard

1. Brown sausage and drain excess fat.
2. Toss bread cubes with melted butter and arrange in greased 9" x 13" baking pan. Top evenly with sausage and cheese.
3. Combine all remaining ingredients and mix well. Pour over casserole dish and chill overnight.
4. Bake at 350° for 40-50 minutes. Serve.

Bacon and Egg Sauce

Naomi Stoltzfus
Leola, PA
Four Sisters

Makes 6 servings

6 slices bacon
1 medium onion, chopped
10¾-oz. can cream of mushroom soup
½ cup milk
5 hard-boiled eggs, sliced
2 cups shredded cheddar cheese
Salt and pepper to taste

1. Fry, drain and crumble bacon. Reserve 2 Tbsp. bacon drippings.
2. Sauté onion in bacon drippings. Add soup and milk and stir well. Gently stir in eggs and cheese and adjust seasoning.
3. Spoon into 9-inch square baking dish. Top with crumbled bacon.
4. Bake at 350° for 20 minutes.
5. Serve on toast or English muffins.

Mustard Eggs

Marlene Fonken
Upland, CA
Crazy Patch

Makes 6 servings

4 Tbsp. margarine
3 Tbsp. minced onion
⅓ cup + 2 tsp. flour
1½ cups chicken broth
1½ cups milk
1½ tsp. lemon juice
1 Tbsp. prepared mustard
½ tsp. Worcestershire sauce
Salt and pepper to taste
12 hard-boiled eggs
Paprika

1. Melt margarine. Add onion and cook until tender but not browned. Add flour and cook until bubbly.
2. Gradually add chicken broth and milk and heat, stirring constantly until thickened and smooth. Add lemon juice, mustard, Worcestershire sauce, salt and pepper and heat through.
3. Peel and slice eggs.
4. Spread thin layer of sauce into bottom of 9" x 13" baking pan. Fan eggs evenly over sauce. Pour remaining sauce over eggs. Sprinkle with paprika. Serve immediately.

I belong to a group called **Swamp Fox Quilters** in Florence, SC. The past year we spent many wonderful hours together organizing and working on a Friendship quilt as a surprise gift.

—*Marjory Garman, Florence, SC*

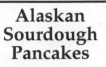

Alaskan Sourdough Pancakes

Anna Musser
Manheim, PA
Lancaster Rose

Makes 6 pancakes

1 pkg. yeast
2 cups flour
2 cups warm water
1-2 eggs
1 tsp. baking soda
1 tsp. salt
1 Tbsp. sugar
2 Tbsp. shortening, melted

1. In a glass mixing bowl combine yeast, flour and warm water. Beat well with plastic or wooden spoon and set in warm place for 8 hours or overnight.
2. Add all remaining ingredients and beat again with plastic or wooden spoon.
3. Spoon desired amounts of batter into pancake shapes in oiled skillet. Fry on both sides. Serve with syrup.

Note: Do NOT use metal bowl or metal spoon for this batter.

Sweet Milk Pancakes

Irene Dewar
Pickering, ON
Barns

Makes 12 pancakes

2 cups flour
4 tsp. baking powder
1 tsp. salt
4 Tbsp. sugar
2 eggs
2 cups milk
4 Tbsp. cooking oil

1. Stir together flour, baking powder, salt and sugar in large mixing bowl.
2. In another bowl beat eggs well. Add milk and oil and beat well.
3. Make a well in dry ingredients and gradually stir in liquid ingredients, mixing until smooth.
4. Heat skillet on high with 1-2 Tbsp. cooking oil. Spoon batter into skillet to form 4-inch pancakes. Brown on both sides. Serve with syrup or jam.

French Pancakes

Sandra Church
New York, NY
Log Cabin

Makes 6 pancakes

6 eggs
1/4 tsp. salt
1 cup milk
1/2 cup flour
1 Tbsp. sugar
Margarine
6-8 Tbsp. black raspberry jam
Powdered sugar
Cinnamon

1. Beat eggs. Add salt, milk, flour and sugar and beat well.
2. Heat skillet on medium-high. Put dab margarine in hot pan. Spoon in 2 Tbsp. batter and shake gently to distribute pancake evenly. Cook on both sides.
3. Flip pancake from pan. Spread line of jam down center. Roll up like jelly roll. Sprinkle with powdered sugar and cinnamon and serve. Continue with remaining batter.

Whole Wheat Pancakes

Emma Troyer
Partridge, KS
Crib Quilt
Cathy Mazur
Williams Lake, BC
Bear Paw

Makes 16-20 small pancakes

2 cups whole wheat flour
2 Tbsp. brown sugar
2 tsp. baking powder
1 tsp. baking soda
1 tsp. salt
2 eggs
2 cups buttermilk
4 Tbsp. margarine, melted

1. Combine flour, brown sugar, baking powder, baking soda and salt. Add eggs, buttermilk and margarine and beat well.
2. Spoon batter by tablespoonful into hot, oiled skillet. Brown on both sides. Serve.

Note: Substitute 2 cups whole milk mixed with 2 Tbsp. vinegar for buttermilk.

In the spring of 1991 I was midway into quilting an Amish-style quilt for my youngest daughter. Unfortunately, I became quite ill and struggled for several months, narrowly avoiding surgery. My strength slowly began coming back, and I returned to the quilt. With its brilliant colors, the quilt always cheered me, and quilting became a time of healing for me. Today I am very healthy and remember with great fondness how that quilt helped me through a difficult period in my life.

—*Suzanne S. Nobrega, Duxbury, MA*

Sour Cream Pancakes

Charlene Bement
Upland, CA
Whimsical Marbled Fish

Makes 8-10 small pancakes

½ tsp. baking soda
1 cup sour cream
2 eggs, separated
2 Tbsp. sugar
1 tsp. salt
½ cup sifted flour

1. Stir baking soda into sour cream. Set aside.
2. Beat egg whites until soft peaks form. Set aside.
3. Combine egg yolks, sugar and salt and beat well. Add sour cream and flour and beat thoroughly. Fold in egg whites.
4. Spoon batter into hot, oiled skillet by tablespoonsful. Brown each pancake on both sides. Serve.

Finnish Pancakes

JoAnn Pelletier
Longmeadow, MA
6 quilts in 14 days

Makes 4 servings

2 Tbsp. butter
2 cups milk
4 large eggs
2-2½ Tbsp. sugar
½ tsp. salt
½ cup flour

1. Melt butter in 9" x 13" baking pan.
2. Combine milk and eggs and beat lightly. Add sugar, salt and flour. Pour into baking pan.
3. Bake at 400° for 20-25 minutes.
4. Serve with maple syrup, jelly or butter.

Baked Pancake

Mary Saunders
Albuquerque, NM
Trip Around the World

Makes 4-6 servings

3 eggs
½ cup all-purpose flour
½ tsp. salt
½ cup milk
2 Tbsp. butter *or* margarine
Powdered sugar
4-6 lemon wedges

1. In a medium bowl beat eggs until very light.
2. Add flour, salt and milk and beat well.
3. Rub bottom and side of a 10-inch cast-iron or heavy skillet with butter. Pour all of batter into skillet.
4. Bake at 450° for 15 minutes. Reduce heat to 350° and bake 5 minutes longer or until set.
5. Remove from skillet, dust with powdered sugar, slice into wedges and serve immediately with lemon.

Baked Apple Pancake

Rhonda-lee Schmidt
Scranton, PA
Donnie's Christmas Sampler

Makes 6-8 servings

3 apples
4 Tbsp. butter
1 cup flour
1 cup milk
6 eggs
1 tsp. vanilla
½ tsp. salt
¼ tsp. nutmeg
Powdered sugar

1. Turn oven to 450° and place cast-iron skillet in oven while preparing ingredients.
2. Cut apples into thin wedges.
3. In a heavy skillet melt 2 Tbsp. butter and sauté apples.
4. Place flour, milk, eggs, vanilla, salt and nutmeg in blender in the order given. Blend until well mixed.
5. Remove skillet from oven and melt remaining 2 Tbsp. butter. Quickly arrange sautéed apples in skillet and pour batter over apples.
6. Place in 450° oven and bake 15 minutes. Reduce oven temperature to 375° and bake 10 minutes longer.
7. Sprinkle with powdered sugar, slice into wedges and serve with maple syrup.

Waffles

Christine H. Weaver
Reinholds, PA
Applique Table Runner

Makes 6-8 waffles

1 cup sugar
4 Tbsp. margarine
2 large eggs
1¼ cups milk
2½ cups flour
2½ tsp. baking powder
1 tsp. vanilla
½ tsp. salt
⅓ cup melted butter *or* cooking oil

1. Cream together sugar, margarine and eggs. Add all remaining ingredients except butter and blend well. Pour melted butter over batter and do not mix.
2. Dip batter onto heated waffle iron and follow directions for making waffles.
3. Serve with syrup or choice of topping.

Note: Sandwich ice cream between waffles for a wonderful dessert.

Brenda Marshall's Belgian Waffles

Brenda J. Marshall
St. Marys, ON
*Christmas in the Corners
Charm Quilt*

Makes 18 waffles

2 eggs, separated
2 cups milk
2 cups all-purpose flour
1 Tbsp. baking powder
1/2 tsp. salt
1/3 cup cooking oil

1. Beat egg whites until stiff. Set aside.
2. Combine all remaining ingredients and mix until smooth. Gently fold egg whites into batter.
3. Pour 1/2 cup batter onto hot waffle iron. Bake 2 1/2-3 minutes.
4. Serve with favorite topping.

Bonita Ensenberger's Belgian Waffles

Bonita Ensenberger
Albuquerque, NM
Jessica's Nine Patch

Makes 12 waffles

2 eggs, separated
2 1/4 cups flour
1/2 tsp. salt
2 Tbsp. sugar
2 1/4 tsp. fast-acting yeast
1 1/2 cups warm water
4 Tbsp. butter *or* margarine, melted
1 tsp. vanilla

1. Beat egg whites until soft peaks form. Set aside.
2. In medium bowl combine flour, salt, sugar and yeast. Add water, butter, vanilla and egg yolks and beat well. Fold in egg whites. Let rise 15 minutes.
3. Pour 1/2 cup batter onto hot waffle iron. Bake to desired doneness, approximately 1 1/2 minutes. Repeat with remaining batter.
4. Serve with syrup, hot applesauce or fruits and whipped topping.

Syrup for Pancakes and Waffles

Emma Troyer
Partridge, KS
Crib Quilt

Makes 1 pint syrup

1 cup white sugar
2 heaping Tbsp. brown sugar
2 heaping Tbsp. flour
1 cup water
1/2 tsp. maple flavoring
1/4 tsp. salt

1. In a saucepan combine all ingredients and bring to a boil. Cook for several minutes, stirring constantly.
2. Serve hot with pancakes or waffles.
3. Store in refrigerator and reheat before serving again.

One of my cats loves quilts. She usually sits near me when I am working, finding a way to lie on some part of the new quilt.

—*Irma H. Schoen, Windsor, CT*

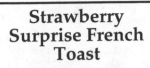

Strawberry Surprise French Toast

Sandra Fulton Day
Oxford, PA
Pineapple Log Cabin

Makes 4 servings

4 1-inch slices French bread
3 Tbsp. strawberry jam
2 eggs
½ cup skim milk
1 Tbsp. shortening

1. Make a pocket in each slice bread, cutting almost in half lengthwise.
2. Fill each pocket with about 2 tsp. strawberry jam. Lay flat in square baking pan.
3. In small bowl beat together eggs and milk. Pour over bread slices, coating each slice evenly.
4. Melt shortening on griddle. Fry bread slices on both sides until golden brown. Serve.

Stuffed French Toast

Sandi Monterastelli
Ontario, CA
Lover's Knot

Makes 6 servings

8 slices white bread
2 8-oz. pkgs. cream cheese
12 eggs, beaten
⅓ cup maple syrup
2 cups milk
2 cups stewed apples
Cinnamon

1. Cut crusts from bread and cube. Arrange ½ of bread cubes across bottom of 9" x 13" baking pan. Cube cream cheese and place on bread. Cover with remaining bread.
2. Beat together eggs, syrup and milk. Pour over bread and cheese. Spread apples over top. Sprinkle with cinnamon and refrigerate overnight.
3. Bake at 375° for 45 minutes.

Oven French Toast

Stephanie Braskey
Pottstown, PA
Applique Album Blocks

Makes 4-6 servings

4-oz. loaf French bread
6 large eggs
1½ cups milk
1½ cups half-and-half
1 tsp. vanilla
⅛ tsp. nutmeg
½ tsp. cinnamon
6 Tbsp. butter, softened
1 cup light brown sugar, packed
2 Tbsp. dark corn syrup
1 cup coarsely chopped pecans

1. Cut bread into 1-inch thick slices. Fill heavily greased 9-inch square baking pan to the top with French bread slices.
2. In a bowl combine eggs, milk, half-and-half, vanilla, nutmeg and cinnamon. Pour mixture over bread slices. Cover and refrigerate overnight.
3. Combine butter, brown sugar and corn syrup and mix well. Stir in pecans. Spread evenly over bread.
4. Bake at 350° for 40 minutes until puffy and golden. Let stand 5 minutes before serving.

Fond memories take me back to my childhood when my mother and I would go to my grandmother's house for a quilting bee. We children played under the quilt and listened to the chatter of the quilters. The best part was tea time and Grandma's marvelous ginger cookies.

—*Pauline Morrison, St. Marys, ON*

Breakfast Soup

Sue Starr
Mechanicsburg, PA
Round Tablecloth

Makes 4-6 servings

2 cups milk
1 cup cream of potato soup
½ cup minced, smoked beef
½ cup shredded sharp cheese
2-3 pieces bread

1. In a saucepan gradually stir milk into soup. Add beef and cheese. Cook and stir until mixture is heated through, about 5 minutes.
2. Toast bread and cut each piece into 2 triangles.
3. Pour soup into individual serving bowls and top with a triangle of toast. Serve.

Baked Oatmeal

Jennifer Hall
Delta, PA
Heart and Home

Makes 4-6 servings

½ cup cooking oil
1 cup honey
2 eggs
3 cups uncooked oatmeal

2 tsp. baking powder
1 cup milk
1 cup chopped nuts, raisins *or* apples

1. Combine oil, honey and eggs. Add all remaining ingredients and mix well.
2. Pour into greased 8-inch square baking pan.
3. Bake at 350° for 30 minutes. Serve hot with milk.

Granola Mix

Adella Halsey
Wymore, NE
Blazing Star Christmas Quilt

Makes many servings

7 cups rolled oats
2½ cups whole wheat flour
½ cup sesame seed
1 cup flaked coconut
½ cup chopped almonds
1 cup wheat germ
¾ cup cooking oil
1 tsp. salt
½ cup brown sugar
½ cup honey
½ cup water
1½ tsp. vanilla
1½ tsp. maple flavoring
1 cup chopped dates
1 cup raisins

1. Combine oats, flour, sesame seed, coconut, almonds and wheat germ.
2. In a blender combine oil, salt, brown sugar, honey, water, vanilla and maple flavoring. Blend until mixture is liquid.
3. Pour over oats mixture and add dates and raisins. Mix well.
4. Store in airtight container at least 24 hours before serving.

❖

Granola

Donna Miller
Partridge, KS
Star Spin

Makes 20-24 servings

2 cups brown sugar
6 cups uncooked oatmeal
2 cups wheat flour
1 cup wheat germ
2 cups coconut
1½ cups sunflower seeds
1 cup cooking oil
1 cup water
2 Tbsp. vanilla
1 tsp. salt

1. Combine brown sugar, oatmeal, wheat flour, wheat germ, coconut and sunflower seeds. Add oil, water, vanilla and salt and mix well. Arrange on two 10" x 15" baking pans.
2. Bake at 275° for 1 hour, stirring every 15 minutes. Bake longer for crunchier cereal.

❖

Lowfat Granola

Christine H. Weaver
Reinholds, PA
Applique Table Runner

Makes 8 servings

1 egg
2 tsp. baking powder
1 cup skim milk
1 cup brown sugar
2 cups uncooked oatmeal
½ cup bran
¾ cup cornmeal
1 tsp. salt

1. Mix all ingredients together. Spread thinly on baking sheet.
2. Bake at 325° until browned. Crumble and bake at 300° for 50 minutes or until cereal is crisp, stirring occasionally.

❖

Cranberry Coffee Cake

Janet S. Gillespie
Gilbertsville, KY
Log Cabin Schoolhouse

Makes 15-20 servings

Cake:
¾ cup margarine, softened
1½ cups sugar
3 eggs, room temperature
1½ tsp. almond extract
3 cups all-purpose flour

1½ tsp. baking powder
1½ tsp. baking soda
¾ tsp. salt
1½ cups sour cream
16-oz. can whole berry cranberry sauce
½ cup chopped walnuts

Glaze:
¾ cup powdered sugar
1 Tbsp. water
½ tsp. almond extract

1. In a large bowl cream together margarine and sugar until light. Add eggs, one at a time, beating well after each addition. Beat in extract.
2. Sift together flour, baking powder, baking soda and salt. Add to creamed mixture, alternating with sour cream and beating well after each addition.
3. Spoon ⅓ of batter into greased and floured 9" x 13" baking pan. Crumble ⅓ of cranberry sauce over batter. Repeat layers 2 more times, ending with cranberry sauce. Sprinkle with walnuts.
4. Bake at 350° for 45-60 or until cake tests done. Cool in pan 5 minutes. Remove from pan and finish cooling on wire rack.
5. To prepare glaze combine all ingredients and beat until smooth. Drizzle glaze over cake and serve.

❖

Blueberry Coffee Cake

Vivian Angstadt
Mertztown, PA
Dahlia

Makes 10-15 servings

Cake:
¾ cup sugar
¼ cup shortening
1 egg
½ cup milk
2 cups flour
2 tsp. baking powder
½ tsp. salt
2 cups blueberries

Topping:
½ cup sugar
⅓ cup flour
½ tsp. cinnamon
¼ cup softened butter

1. Cream together sugar, shortening and egg. Add milk, flour, baking powder and salt and mix well. Fold in blueberries. Pour into greased 8" x 12" baking pan.
2. Combine all ingredients for topping. Sprinkle over batter.
3. Bake at 375° for 40-45 minutes.

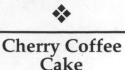

Cherry Coffee Cake

Robin Schrock
Millersburg, OH
Triple Irish Chain

Makes 12-15 servings

Cake:
16 Tbsp. margarine
1½ cups sugar
4 eggs
1 tsp. vanilla
3 cups flour
1½ tsp. baking powder
½ tsp. salt
21-oz. can cherry pie filling

Glaze:
1½ cups powdered sugar
½ tsp. vanilla
2 Tbsp. melted butter
3 Tbsp. warm milk

1. Cream margarine and sugar. Add eggs one at a time, beating well after each addition. Add vanilla.
2. Sift together flour, baking powder and salt. Add to creamed mixture. Spread ⅔ of batter into greased 10" x 15" jelly roll pan. Cover with cherry pie filling and spoon remaining ⅓ of batter over top.
3. Bake at 350° for 30-40 minutes.
4. To prepare glaze combine all ingredients, adding enough milk to make thin consistency. Drizzle over warm cake and serve.

Crumb Coffee Cake

Irene P. Dietlin
New Hartford, CT
Cupid's Nine Patch

Makes 8-10 servings

1½ cups sifted flour
1 cup sugar
½ cup butter *or* margarine
1 tsp. baking soda
½ cup sour milk
1 egg, beaten
1 tsp. cinnamon

1. Mix together flour, sugar and butter until crumbly. Reserve ¾ cup crumbs for topping.
2. Add baking soda, milk and egg to remaining crumbs and mix well. Spoon into greased and floured 8-inch square pan.
3. Add cinnamon to ¾ cup crumbs and sprinkle over batter.
4. Bake at 350° for 30-35 minutes. Cool in pan about 15 minutes before serving.

Very Best Coffee Cake

Cheryl Bartel
Hillsboro, KS
Traditional Sampler

Makes 15-20 servings

Cake:
¾ cup sugar
8 Tbsp. margarine *or* butter, softened
1 tsp. vanilla
3 eggs
2 cups flour
1 tsp. baking powder
1 tsp. baking soda
¼ tsp. salt
1 cup sour cream

Streusel Filling:
1¼ cups firmly packed brown sugar
1 cup chopped walnuts
2 tsp. cinnamon
3 Tbsp. margarine *or* butter, melted

1. In large bowl cream together sugar and margarine. Add vanilla and eggs and mix well.
2. Combine flour, baking powder, baking soda and salt. Add flour mixture to creamed mixture, alternating with sour cream. Begin and end with flour mixture.
3. In small bowl combine all filling ingredients and mix well.
4. Spread ½ of batter into greased and floured 10-inch tube pan. Sprinkle with ½ of filling. Repeat layers.

5. Bake at 350° for 35-40 minutes or until toothpick inserted in center comes out clean. Cool upright in pan for 15 minutes. Invert onto large plate or cookie sheet. Invert again onto serving plate and serve with streusel side up.

Jo's Coffee Cake

Carol Jacobs
Freeport, IL
Irish Chain with Hearts

Makes 12 servings

Cake:
16 Tbsp. margarine
1 cup sugar
2 eggs
1 tsp. vanilla
2 cups flour
2 tsp. baking powder
½ tsp. salt
21-oz. can peach pie filling

Topping:
2 Tbsp. margarine
¼ cup brown sugar
½ cup flour

1. To prepare cake cream together margarine and sugar. Add eggs and beat thoroughly. Add vanilla.
2. Sift dry ingredients together. Add to creamed mixture and blend thoroughly. Spread ½ of batter into greased and floured 9" x 13" baking pan. Spread pie filling over top and cover with remaining batter.
3. Mix topping ingredients until crumbly and sprinkle over top.
4. Bake at 350° for approximately 40 minutes.

My grandmother taught me to quilt when I was about 12 years old. While she was very poor, she had a wonderful sense of humor and never wasted a bit of fabric. What she could not put into a quilt, she would cut into narrow strips, sew the ends together and crochet into rag rugs. Today I am 72 years old and I still make Crazy Patch quilts and crocheted rugs. My sense of humor could be improved.

—*Betty Krueger, Rogue River, OR*

Overnight Coffee Cake

Priscilla M. Wade
Voorhees, NJ
Bear Paw & Triple Rail Fence

Makes 10-15 servings

¾ cup margarine, softened
1 cup sugar
2 eggs
8 ozs. sour cream
2 cups flour
1 tsp. baking soda
1 tsp. baking powder
½ tsp. salt
1 tsp. nutmeg
¾ cup brown sugar
½ cup chopped walnuts
1 tsp. cinnamon

1. Cream together margarine and sugar until light and fluffy. Add eggs and sour cream, mixing well.
2. Combine flour, baking soda, baking powder, salt and nutmeg. Fold dry ingredients into batter and mix well. Pour into greased and floured 9" x 13" baking pan.
3. Combine brown sugar, walnuts and cinnamon. Sprinkle over batter. Cover and refrigerate overnight.
4. Bake, uncovered, at 350° for 35-40 minutes or until cake tests done.

Quick Coffee Cake

Sue Dieringer-Boyer
Walkersville, MD
Stage Quilts for Quilters
Ruth Ann Hoover
New Holland, PA
White on White

Makes 20-24 small servings

Cake:
1 box yellow cake mix
1 small pkg. instant
  butterscotch pudding
1 small pkg. instant vanilla
  pudding
1 cup water
½ cup cooking oil
4 eggs

Topping:
¾ cup brown sugar,
  packed
1 cup chopped nuts
1 tsp. cinnamon

1. Combine cake mix and puddings. Set aside.
2. Combine water, oil and eggs. Thoroughly mix into dry ingredients. Set aside.
3. Combine all topping ingredients.
4. Pour ½ of batter into greased and floured 9" x 13" baking pan. Sprinkle with ½ of topping. Repeat layers.
5. Bake at 350° for 55 minutes or until cake tests done. Cool at least 30 minutes before serving.

Variation:
Slice 2 large apples and add a layer of apples each time in step 4. Bake at 350° for 1 hour.
Kim Marlor
Owings Mills, MD
Fan

Featherweight Breakfast Cake

Anne Guy
Florence, SC
Queen Anne Star

Makes 6-8 servings

4 Tbsp. shortening
1 egg
½ cup milk
1 cup flour
½ cup sugar
3 tsp. baking powder
½ tsp. salt
2 Tbsp. sugar
½ tsp. cinnamon

1. Melt shortening. Cool slightly and mix with egg and milk.
2. Sift flour, ½ cup sugar, baking powder and salt several times. Stir into liquid mixture and mix well. Pour into greased 8-inch square baking pan.
2. Combine 2 Tbsp. sugar and cinnamon and sprinkle over batter.
3. Bake at 375° for 12-15 minutes. Serve hot.

Beverages

Lemonade

Kathryn M. Geissinger
Ephrata, PA
Philadelphia Pavement

Makes 2 quarts lemonade

3 lemons
½ cup sugar
Cold water
Sugar to taste

1. Cut lemons into thin slices. Put lemon slices into a large flat-bottomed container. Add ½ cup sugar. With a masher pound sugar and lemons until sugar is dissolved and mixture is quite juicy.
2. Add cold water to make 2 quarts. Add sugar to your taste. Serve.

Orange Grapefruit Drink

Juanita Marner
Shipshewana, IN
Giant Dahlia

Makes 1 gallon drink

46-oz. can unsweetened grapefruit juice
1⅓ cups instant orange mix
2 Tbsp. lemon juice
Water and ice to make 1 gallon

1. Combine all ingredients and mix well.
2. Serve.

Pink Cherry Sodas

Joyce Niemann
Fruitland Park, FL
Lap Sampler

Makes 6 servings

1 pkg. unsweetened cherry Kool Aid
1 cup sugar *or* less
2 cups milk
1 quart vanilla ice cream
1 quart carbonated water

1. Combine Kool Aid and sugar. Add milk and mix well.
2. Fill 6 tall drinking glasses ½ full with mixture. Add 2-3 scoops ice cream. Fill glass with carbonated water.
3. Serve on a hot summer day.

I was introduced to quilting by my grandparents. Grandmother did custom quilting for people in the Chicago area in the 1940s. Grandfather always traced the quilting patterns for her. I think they must have spent many evenings together tracing and quilting.

—*Susan G. Sneer, Mountain Lake, MN*

Ginger Peach Fizz

Sandra Fulton Day
Oxford, PA
Pineapple Log Cabin

Makes 3-4 servings

12-oz. can Sprite
¼ tsp. powdered ginger
1½ cups peeled, sliced
peaches
2 Tbsp. lemon juice
2 Tbsp. sugar
6-8 ice cubes

1. Combine all ingredients except ice in blender. Blend until smooth.
2. Add ice cubes and blend again until smooth.
3. Serve.

Iced Tea

Joan Ranck
Christiana, PA
Bow Tie Doll Crib Quilt

Makes 2½ gallons tea

2 quarts water
24 individual cup-sized tea
bags
3 cups sugar
3 lemons, sliced
2 gallons water

1. Bring 2 quarts water to a boil. Place tea bags in boiling water and let steep about 20 minutes. Remove tea bags.
2. Add sugar, lemons and 2 gallons water. Stir well and refrigerate.
3. After 2 hours, remove lemons and serve with ice.

Quick Iced Tea

Lois J. Cassidy
Willow Street, PA
The Last Shall Be First

Makes 2 quarts tea

¼ cup instant tea mix
⅓ cup lemon juice
½ cup sugar
Enough water to make 2
quarts

1. Combine all ingredients and mix well.
2. Serve with ice.

Tea and Fruit Punch with Mint

Jane S. Lippincott
Wynnewood, PA
Flowers on Yellow

Makes 2-3 quarts punch

2 cups boiling water
2 Tbsp. black tea leaves
½ cup sugar
½ cup lemon juice
1 cup orange juice
1 lemon, sliced
1 orange, sliced
¾ cup sliced strawberries
6 sprigs mint
4 cups ice cubes

1. Pour boiling water over tea leaves. Cover and let steep 5 minutes. Strain through sieve into bowl. Add sugar, lemon juice and orange juice and stir to dissolve.
2. In a punch bowl combine lemon slices, orange slices, strawberries, mint and ice cubes. Pour tea mixture over fruit.
3. Stir well and serve.

Red Burgundy Punch

Erma Landis
Sterling, IL
Dresden Plate

Makes 1½ gallons punch

Lemonade ice ring
8 cups cranberry juice
2 cups grape juice
6-oz. can orange pineapple
concentrate
6-oz. can lemonade
concentrate
2 6-oz. cans water
2 quarts gingerale

1. Make a lemonade ice ring by freezing a round

container of lemonade, approximately 6 inches in diameter.

2. In a punch bowl combine all remaining ingredients and mix well.

3. Add frozen lemonade ring and serve.

Nutritious Fruit Punch

Evelyn M. Becker
Paradise, PA
Double Irish Chain

Makes 2 gallons punch

1 quart canned peaches
  with juice
1 banana
3 lemons
1 lemon rind, grated
1½ cups sugar
46-oz. can pineapple juice
12-oz. can frozen orange
  juice
Water

1. Mix peaches and banana in a blender.

2. Juice lemons and grate rind of one lemon.

3. In a large container combine all ingredients and add enough water to make 2 gallons. Mix well. Chill and serve.

Mountain Berry Punch

Marjorie Miller
Partridge, KS
Crib Quilt

Makes 2½ quarts punch

½ cup sugar
1 pkg. Mountain Berry
  Kool Aid
1 quart milk
1 pint ice cream, softened
16-oz. bottle Mountain
  Dew

1. Mix sugar and Kool Aid in punch bowl. Pour milk over mixture and stir to dissolve.

2. Add ice cream by scoops and mix lightly.

3. Pour Mountain Dew over all and serve.

No Name Punch

Dottie Doughty
Oklahoma City, OK
Stars of a New Decade

Makes 1½-2 gallons punch

2 pkgs. raspberry *or* cherry
  Kool Aid
1 cup sugar
1 quart apple juice
1 quart gingerale
1 quart strawberry soda
Ice

1. Combine Kool Aid, sugar and apple juice. Refrigerate until serving time

2. Fill punch bowl ¼-½ full of ice. Add Kool Aid mixture, gingerale and soda and mix well.

3. Serve.

Orange Punch

Anna Tompkins
Greenfield, OH
Card Trick

Makes 1½ gallons punch

1 pkg. orange Kool Aid
1 cup sugar
32-oz. can orange drink
6-oz. can orange juice
  concentrate
16-oz. can orange soda
11-oz. can mandarin
  oranges

1. Fill 3 ice cube trays with a mixture of Kool Aid, sugar and water. Freeze.

2. Combine all remaining ingredients and mix well.

3. Before serving, pour into punch bowl and add orange ice cubes.

Banana Crush

Mary Helen Wade
Sterling, IL
Printed Peony Wall Hanging

Makes 2½ gallons punch

3 cups water
2 cups sugar
1½ cups orange juice
¼ cup lemon juice
46-oz. can pineapple juice
3 bananas, mashed
3 quarts gingerale *or* 7-Up

1. In a saucepan combine water and sugar and cook into syrup. Remove from heat and stir in orange juice, lemon juice, pineapple juice and bananas. Freeze mixture.
2. When ready to serve, place mixture in punch bowl, let thaw and pour in gingerale.
3. Or you may chop off small pieces of mixture, enough to fill glasses ½ full. Fill glasses with gingerale and serve.

Russian Tea

Sara Ann Stoltzfus
Spring Mills, PA
Wedding Ring

Makes 1½ quarts concentrate

1 quart water
1 tsp. whole cloves
1-2 sticks cinnamon, broken
5 individual cup-sized tea bags
2½-3 cups sugar
⅓ cup lemon juice
6-oz. can orange juice concentrate

1. In a saucepan combine water, cloves and cinnamon and bring to a boil. Remove from heat, add tea bags and steep for 10 minutes.
2. Remove tea bags and strain liquid to remove cloves and cinnamon.
3. Add sugar, lemon juice and orange concentrate to tea and mix well. Store in refrigerator.
4. To serve mix 1 part concentrate with 3 parts water. Serve hot or iced.

Wassail Punch

Gerry Fix
Hagerstown, MD
Nine Patch

Makes 5 quarts punch

2 quarts hot orange spice tea
1 quart cranberry juice
1 quart apple juice
2 cups orange juice
12 whole cloves
3 cinnamon sticks
1 cup white sugar
1 orange, sliced (optional)
1 lemon, sliced (optional)

1. Combine all ingredients except orange and lemon slices. Bring to a boil and let simmer at least 20-30 minutes. Remove spices before serving.
2. Pour into punch bowl and serve warm. If desired, float orange and lemon slices in punch.

> **For as long as I can remember my grandmother, Anna Oberholtzer, has been quilting. As a graduation gift each of her grandchildren has been given the opportunity to choose the material and pattern for his or her own quilt. Today when my family goes to sleep we are covered with Grandma's special handiwork and love.**
>
> —*Tina Snyder, Manheim, PA*

Old Country Store Percolator Punch

The Old Country Store
Intercourse, PA
Sandy Brown
Connersville, IN
Double Wedding Ring

Makes many small servings

1 cup brown sugar, packed
4½ tsp. whole cloves
3 whole cinnamon sticks
½ tsp. salt
9 cups cranberry juice
9 cups unsweetened
pineapple juice
4½ cups water

1. In a large coffee maker (at least 30-cup) layer brown sugar, cloves, cinnamon and salt in the basket where coffee grounds would go.
2. Pour all liquids into the coffee maker and percolate.
3. Serve on a cold winter day.

Note: During the month of December The Old Country Store in Intercourse, PA spices up its atmosphere and pleases its customers by serving this delightful hot punch.

Hot Cranberry Punch

Jane Talso
Albuquerque, NM
1992 Balloon Quilt

Makes 1 gallon punch

6 cups cranberry juice
2 cups orange juice
2 Tbsp. lemon juice
2 cups sugar
3 cinnamon sticks
1 tsp. cloves
2 quarts water

1. In a large saucepan combine all ingredients except water and bring to a boil. Simmer 1-2 minutes and add water. Heat to simmer.
2. Remove cloves and serve hot.

Hot Chocolate Mix

Gertrude W. Byler
Smicksburg, PA
Glimmering Star

Makes many servings

9 cups instant dry milk
2½ cups powdered sugar
1 cup coffee creamer
2 lbs. powdered chocolate
mix
1 tsp. salt

1. Mix all ingredients thoroughly and store in tightly covered container.
2. To serve put ¼ cup mix into a cup and fill with hot water. Mix well.

Condiments

French Dressing

Frances Musser
Newmanstown, PA
Sweet Country
Mary Esther Yoder
Partridge, KS
Double Irish Chain

Makes 1 cup dressing

⅓ cup ketchup
½ cup white sugar
1 tsp. salt
⅓ tsp. pepper
½ cup cooking oil
1 small onion, minced
6 Tbsp. lemon juice

1. Put all ingredients into blender and mix until smooth.
2. Serve with your favorite salad greens.

> **My husband frequently brings fabric home from his business trips. One year I decided to make a Double Wedding Ring wall hanging with the pieces. For us, each piece of fabric in the finished product has a story of its own.**
>
> —*Alana Robbins, Los Lunas, NM*

Kaye Schnell's Homemade Salad Dressing

Kaye Schnell
Falmouth, MA
Baltimore Album

Makes 1½ cups dressing

5-oz. can evaporated milk
½ cup cooking oil
¼ cup chili sauce
3 Tbsp. lemon juice
1 tsp. sugar, rounded
1 tsp. salt
1 tsp. dry mustard
¼ tsp. pepper

1. Measure all ingredients into a jar and shake well.
2. Dressing will keep in refrigerator for a few weeks.

Lydia Weaver's Homemade Salad Dressing

Lydia H. Weaver
New Holland, PA
Hagerstown Feather

Makes 1 quart dressing

2 cups mayonnaise
¼ cup vinegar
2 tsp. dry mustard
4 tsp. water
1½ cups sugar
½ cup ketchup
½ tsp. salt
½ cup cooking oil

1. Combine all ingredients and beat well. Store in glass jar.
2. Dressing will keep in refrigerator for a few weeks.

Salad Dressing

Fannie M. Beiler
New Holland, PA
Teddy Bear Pillows

Makes 1 quart dressing

4 eggs
2 cups sugar
1-2 tsp. dry mustard
2 Tbsp. margarine
½ cup vinegar
1 tsp. salt (optional)
1 pint mayonnaise

1. Combine all ingredients except mayonnaise in a saucepan or double boiler and cook until thickened. Remove from heat and cool.
2. Add mayonnaise and mix well. This dressing keeps up to 2 months when refrigerated.

Thousand Island Dressing

Frances Musser
Newmanstown, PA
Sweet Country

Makes 2 cups dressing

1 cup mayonnaise
3 Tbsp. vinegar
¼ tsp. garlic powder
1 tsp. prepared mustard
¼ tsp. paprika
¼ tsp. Worcestershire

sauce
3 Tbsp. cooking oil
½ cup white sugar
3 Tbsp. ketchup
¼ tsp. salt
1 Tbsp. sweet pickle relish

1. Put all ingredients except pickle relish into blender and mix until smooth.
2. Stir in pickle relish and serve with your favorite salad greens.

Mary Ellen's Spinach Salad Dressing

Jane L. Murphy
Malvern, PA
Miniature Nine Patch

Makes 1 pint dressing

2 cups olive oil
1 tsp. dry mustard
1 tsp. salt
1 small onion, quartered
⅔ cup apple vinegar
1¼ cups sugar *or* less

1. Combine oil, mustard, salt and onion in blender or food processor. Add vinegar and sugar and blend well.
2. Keeps well. Good on spinach or lettuce salad.

Dijon Vinaigrette

Ann Stutts
Grants Pass, OR
Flight

Makes 1¼ cups dressing

4 Tbsp. Dijon mustard
3 Tbsp. red wine vinegar
1 Tbsp. white wine vinegar
¼ tsp. salt
1-2 cloves garlic
½ tsp. basil
⅛ tsp. black pepper
2 drops Tabasco
1 Tbsp. grated onion
12 Tbsp. safflower oil

1. Combine mustard and vinegars in blender. Add salt, garlic, basil, black pepper, Tabasco and onion and blend well.
2. With blender running add oil, 1 Tbsp. at a time. Chill.
3. Dressing will keep several weeks in refrigerator.

Marinade for Poultry

Denise S. Rominger
Cranbury, NJ
Crazy Patch

Makes 1 cup marinade

¾ **cup bottled Italian**
 dressing
2 Tbsp. soy sauce
1 tsp. sesame oil
¼ **tsp. garlic powder**
Pinch fresh ground black
 pepper

1. Combine all ingredients and mix well. Pour over chicken pieces in shallow dish.
2. Marinade for several hours or overnight in refrigerator, turning occasionally. Use leftover marinade to baste during baking or grilling.

Ginny's Mustard

Laura Heller
Delanco, NJ
This Old House

Makes 2 cups mustard

¾ **cup dry mustard**
¾ **cup distilled white**
 vinegar
½ **cup honey**
2 egg yolks

1. In small bowl combine mustard and vinegar. Cover and let stand at room temperature overnight.
2. Mix all 4 ingredients in a saucepan. Cook over low heat, stirring until thickened (about 7 minutes). Cool.
3. Mustard will keep in refrigerator for 2 weeks.

❖

Ketchup

Alma Miller
Partridge, KS
Lovers' Hearts

Makes about 16 pints ketchup

8 quarts tomato juice
3 cups chopped onion
3½ cups vinegar
½ **cup + 1½ Tbsp. salt**
5 cups sugar
1¾ tsp. ground cloves
1¾ tsp. red pepper
1¾ tsp. ginger
3½ tsp. cinnamon
2⅓ cups clear gel
Red food coloring

1. Spoon chopped onion with 2 cups tomato juice into blender. Blend well.
2. In large canning kettle combine 7 quarts tomato juice, blended onions, vinegar, salt, sugar, cloves, red pepper, ginger and cinnamon. Bring to a boil and simmer for 30-45 minutes.
3. Combine clear gel

with remaining 2 cups tomato juice. Stir into tomato mixture and bring to a boil, stirring constantly.
4. Return to blender to make ketchup smooth and desired consistency.
5. Pour into sterilized glass pint jars. Seal with canning lids which have been sterilized in boiling water.
6. Bring water in canner to a rolling boil. Process jars in hot water bath for 10 minutes. Remove from water and set aside to seal. When jars have sealed, store in cold cellar until ready to use.

Note: It is important to use proper canning equipment and procedures for steps 5 and 6. Canners may be purchased in many kitchen supply stores.

❖

Arlene Wengerd's Salsa

Arlene Wengerd
Dundee, OH
Broken Star

Makes 8 pints salsa

3 quarts thick tomato juice
6 onions, chopped
2 cloves garlic, chopped
4 cups chopped green
 peppers
½ **cup chopped jalapeño**
 peppers with seeds

1 quart chopped tomatoes, peeled
12-oz. can tomato paste
1 Tbsp. salt
1 Tbsp. vinegar
3 Tbsp. white sugar

1. Pour 1 cup of tomato juice into blender. Add onions, garlic, and peppers and blend well.
2. Combine all ingredients in large kettle. Simmer for 2-3 hours, stirring frequently.
3. Fill sterilized glass pint jars with scalding salsa. Quickly put on canning lids with seal, which have been sterilized in boiling water. Store in cold cellar until ready to use.

Note: Keep sauce, jars and lids scalding hot until all jars have been filled in order for seal to work.

Barbara Spicer's Salsa

Barbara Y. Spicer
Gettysburg, PA
Endless Pyramids

Makes 1 quart salsa

5 jalapeño peppers, seeded and chopped
4 tomatoes, diced
1 small onion, chopped
⅓ cucumber, diced
1 clove garlic, crushed
1 tsp. dried oregano

Juice of ½ lime
1 Tbsp. olive oil
Salt to taste

1. Mix all ingredients together.
2. Chill and serve with tortilla chips.

Pizza Sauce

Fannie M. Beiler
New Holland, PA
Teddy Bear Pillows

Makes 7 pints pizza sauce

3 large onions, diced
4 Tbsp. cooking oil
2 Tbsp. garlic salt
2 tsp. salt
3 quarts tomato juice
2 tsp. sugar
2 Tbsp. oregano
2 Tbsp. chili powder
Dash pepper
Clear gel

1. Brown onions in oil. Add both salts and all remaining ingredients except clear gel. Bring to a boil and simmer 20 minutes.
2. Thicken with clear gel. Pour hot sauce into sterilized pint jars. Seal with canning lids which have been sterilized in boiling water.

Note: To ensure that jars will seal keep sauce, jars and lids scalding hot until all jars have been filled.

❖

Barbecue Sauce

Lois J. Cassidy
Willow Street, PA
The Last Shall Be First

Makes 2½ cups sauce

1 medium onion, chopped
2 Tbsp. cooking oil
2 Tbsp. vinegar
2 Tbsp. brown sugar
1 cup ketchup
3 Tbsp. Worcestershire sauce
½ tsp. dry mustard
½ cup water
Salt and pepper to taste

1. Brown onion in oil. Add remaining ingredients and bring to a boil. Simmer 30 minutes.
2. Sauce keeps in refrigerator for about a month.

Kimpel's Favorite Barbecue Sauce

Emilie Kimpel
Arcadia, MI
Mauve on Mauve

Makes 2½ cups sauce

1 cup ketchup
1 cup water
1 Tbsp. flour
3 Tbsp. tarragon vinegar
Dash garlic salt
1 Tbsp. Worcestershire
  sauce
¼ tsp. oregano
⅛ tsp. marjoram
⅛ tsp. thyme
1 small onion (optional)

1. Combine all ingredients in a blender and mix well.
2. Use as a marinade for most any meat, especially chicken or pork.

Coney Sauce for Hot Dogs

Marjory Garman
Florence, SC
Tree of Life

Makes 2½ cups thick sauce

1 lb. lean ground beef
½ cup ketchup
1 tsp. dry mustard
½ tsp. sugar
Salt and pepper to taste
Dash Tabasco (optional)

1. In a saucepan brown ground beef very slowly, stirring frequently. Pour off all excess fat.
2. Add ketchup, mustard and sugar and heat through.
3. Add seasonings and heat through again.
4. Serve hot with hot dogs.

Onion Relish

Dorothy Dyer
Lee's Summit, MO
Lover's Heart

Makes 2 cups relish

4 large onions
1 Tbsp. coarse salt
1 jalapeño pepper, seeded
  and julienned
¼ cup pitted and sliced
  olives
¼ cup olive oil
¼ cup red wine vinegar
Fresh ground white pepper
  to taste
Salt to taste

1. Peel and cut onions in half vertically. Place onions, cut side down, on a board and thinly slice into half rings. Place in stainless steel bowl, sprinkle with salt and mix thoroughly. Let stand for 1 hour at room temperature.
2. Transfer onions to colander, rinse under cold running water and drain well. Return onion rings to stainless steel bowl. Add hot pepper, olives and oil and toss well. Add vinegar and toss.
3. Correct seasoning to taste with salt and pepper. Store in refrigerator in tightly closed container.

Several years ago my husband and I visited Kalona, Iowa. Of course, we had to stop at Kalona Kountry Kreations Quilt Shop. In about half an hour I found all of the fabric I needed for a Sunshine and Shadow quilt ranging from light peach to eggplant. When the quilt was completed, it won the Better Homes and Gardens Nebraska Award for traditional quilting.

—Carol A. Findling, Beatrice, NE

Sweet Pickle Relish

Elsie F. Porter
Baltimore, MD
Nine Patch Star

Makes 20 pints relish

**5 quarts shredded
cucumbers**
1 quart chopped onions
**1 quart chopped sweet
peppers**
1 pint thinly sliced celery
Non-iodized salt
4 cups sugar
6 cups vinegar
1 tsp. dry mustard
**5 Tbsp. mixed pickling
spices**

1. Shred and chop vegetables into a large stainless steel or enameled container (no aluminum). Sprinkle with non-iodized salt. When all are chopped, stir and taste. Add more salt if needed. Let stand 2 hours.
2. In large kettle combine sugar, vinegar and mustard. Tie pickling spices in clean white cloth and add to mixture. Bring to a boil and add chopped vegetables. Bring again to boil, stirring often. Lower heat and simmer for 20 minutes, stirring occasionally.
3. Spoon hot relish into sterilized jars. Cover with canning lids which have been sterilized in hot water. Set aside to seal. Store in cool place.

Note: It is important to keep relish, jars and lids scalding hot until you are finished to ensure that jars will seal.

Sauerkraut Relish

Evelyn Horne
Macon, GA
Christmas Sampler

Makes 2-3 pints relish

1½ cups sugar
½ cup vinegar
**16-oz. can sauerkraut,
slightly drained**
**½ cup chopped green
pepper**
½ cup chopped celery
½ cup chopped onion
4-oz. jar chopped pimento

1. In a small saucepan bring sugar and vinegar to a boil. Boil syrup for 1 minute. Cool.
2. Combine sauerkraut, green pepper, celery, onion and pimento. Pour syrup over kraut mixture.
3. Let stand in refrigerator for 24 hours before using.

No-Cook Cranberry Conserve

Barbara L. McGinnis
Ocean City, NJ
Rosy Log Cabin

Makes 1¼ cups relish

**8-oz. can whole berry
cranberry sauce**
**½ medium lemon, thinly
sliced**
1 small onion, chopped
**¼ cup coarsely chopped
walnuts**
2 Tbsp. raisins
1 tsp. Dijon mustard
¼ tsp. hot pepper sauce

1. In medium bowl combine cranberry sauce, lemon, onion, walnuts and raisins and stir until blended. Stir in mustard and hot pepper sauce.
2. Cover and let stand at room temperature for 30 minutes before serving.

Rhubarb Chutney

B. Helen Plauschinn
Pickering, ON
Mini-Tulip Quilt

Makes 2 pints chutney

**2 lbs. fresh rhubarb,
chopped**
2 cups chopped onion
1½ cups brown sugar
1 cup cider vinegar
2 tsp. cinnamon
1 tsp. ground ginger
½ tsp. ground cloves
2 tsp. salt

1. Combine all ingredients in large heavy saucepan. Cook until thickened, stirring often (about 30 minutes).
2. Pack into hot sterilized jars and cover with canning lids. Set aside to seal.

Cranberry Chutney

Sherry Carroll
Delta, PA
Sampler

Makes 3 cups chutney

16 ozs. fresh cranberries
**¾ cup brown sugar,
packed**
½ cup raisins
½ cup chopped celery
½ cup chopped apples

½ cup chopped pears
½ cup water
**¼ cup coarsely chopped
walnuts**
**2 Tbsp. minced candied
ginger**
2 Tbsp. lemon juice
¼ tsp. ground cloves
1 tsp. onion salt (optional)

1. In large kettle bring all ingredients to a boil, stirring constantly. Simmer, uncovered, for 15 minutes, stirring occasionally.
2. Store in refrigerator. Will keep several weeks.

Norm's Dill Pickles

Emilie Kimpel
Arcadia, MI
Bunny Patch

Makes 8 quarts pickles

1 quart vinegar
1 cup pickling salt
3 quarts water
8 cloves garlic
8 large fresh dill heads
8 hot peppers
Small cucumbers

1. Combine vinegar, salt and water in saucepan and bring to a boil.
2. Sterilize quart jars and put 1 clove garlic, 1 dill head, 1 hot pepper and enough small cucumbers in each jar to fill it. Pour boiling brine over pickles.

3. Cover each jar with sterilized canning lid. Set aside to seal. Store in cool place.

Note: Keep brine and lids scalding hot until all jars are covered.

Big Valley Church Pickles

Minnie A. Stoltzfus
Lancaster, PA
Log Cabin

Makes 2-3 quarts pickles

1½ cups pickling salt
1 gallon water
**2-3 quarts 2-inch firm
cucumbers**
5 cups water
1 cup white vinegar
7 saccharin pellets

1. Combine pickling salt and water in large bowl. Add cucumbers until they are just covered with water. Let soak overnight.
2. In the morning drain cucumbers.
3. Combine 5 cups water, vinegar, saccharin pellets and drained cucumbers. Heat, but do not boil.
4. Sterilize glass quart jars. Use spoon to pack hot pickles in jars.
5. Bring vinegar and water mixture to a boil and pour over hot pickles.

Cover with canning lids and set aside to seal. Store in cool place.

Note: Keep pickles, brine and lids hot until finished.

Lime Pickles

Kathleen Leach
Mooresville, IN
Round the World

Makes 8-10 pints pickles

8 lbs. cucumbers
2 cups pickling lime
2 gallons water
Chipped ice
8 cups sugar
2 Tbsp. salt
8 cups vinegar
1 Tbsp. turmeric
½ tsp. powdered alum
2 tsp. celery seed
2 Tbsp. allspice
1 Tbsp. mustard seed

1. Slice cucumbers into ¼-inch pieces. Mix cucumber slices and lime in 2 gallons water and store in cool place for 12-24 hours.
2. Drain and rinse cucumbers thoroughly. Cover with chipped ice and let stand another 12-24 hours. After 12-24 hours cover with fresh chipped ice to crisp cucumbers.
3. Combine sugar, salt, vinegar, turmeric, alum, celery seed, allspice and mus-tard seed in large kettle and bring to a boil. Cool quickly.
4. Drain cucumbers from ice water until as dry as possible.
5. Add cucumbers to cooled sugar solution and let set 12-24 hours.
6. Simmer in manageable amounts for 30 minutes, gently lifting cucumbers continually.
7. Sterilize glass pint jars. Pour pickles and solution into hot jars. Cover with sterilized canning lids and set aside to seal. When sealed, store in cool place.

Spicy Tomato Preserves

Joyce Swinney
Mooresville, IN
Tree of Life

1 cup water
4 lemons, thinly sliced
4 lbs. sugar
1 Tbsp. nutmeg
1 Tbsp. ground cloves
1 scant Tbsp. allspice
4 pieces fresh ginger,
  minced to 2 Tbsp.

2 lbs. red cherry tomatoes
2 lbs. yellow pear tomatoes

1. Combine water, lemons, sugar and spices and bring to a boil. Simmer for 15 minutes. (If syrup is too thin, boil down to reduce.)
2. Add tomatoes and gently boil until tomatoes are clear (about 20 minutes), stirring frequently.
3. Sterilize 8- or 16-oz. jars. Pour scalding hot mixture into hot sterile jars. Cover immediately with sterilized canning lids. Set aside to seal. When sealed, store in cool place.

In addition to quilting, I have also spent the past 42 years collecting cookbooks. I now own more than 900 cookbooks and pamphlets. The oldest book in my collection is a small volume called *Some Famous Old Recipes* published by the author in 1904.

—*Joan Lemmler, Albuquerque, NM*

Pickled Green Onions

Joyce Niemann
Fruitland Park, FL
Lap Sampler

Makes 4 cups relish

1½ cups sugar
¼ cup water
¾ cup white vinegar
¼ tsp. salt
Few drops green food
  coloring
Few drops yellow food
  coloring
4 cups sliced onions
½ tsp. mustard seed
½ tsp. celery seed

1. In a saucepan combine sugar, water, vinegar and salt and bring to a boil, stirring occasionally. Cool. Add a few drops of green and yellow coloring to syrup to make an attractive green color.
2. In a one-quart container combine onions, mustard seed and celery seed. Pour syrup over all. Cover container and let stand overnight. Add more onions to fill container.
3. Refrigerate for 2 or 3 days before serving.
4. Onions will keep in refrigerator for up to 3 weeks.

Grandmother's Pickled Beets

Thelma Swody
Stonington, CT
Sunnybrook Farm

Makes 2 cups beets

½ cup white vinegar
½ cup water
½ cup sugar
1 tsp. salt
⅛ tsp. freshly ground
  black pepper
1 large Spanish onion,
  thinly sliced
2 cups sliced, canned beets

1. In a 1½-quart saucepan combine vinegar, water, sugar, salt, pepper and sliced onion and bring to a boil. Simmer for 5 minutes.
2. Meanwhile, place the sliced beets (plus juice) in serving bowl. Pour the hot marinade over beets and let cool until room temperature. Cover the bowl with plastic wrap and refrigerate for at least 6 hours, stirring every few hours to keep the slices moist. Serve.

Red Beet Jelly

Cindy Wilkinson
Houston, TX
Drunkard's Path

Makes 4-6 pints jelly

1½ lbs. red beets
8 cups water
½ cup lemon juice
2 pkgs. powdered pectin
8 cups sugar
6-oz. pkg. raspberry gelatin

1. Peel beets and bring to a boil in 8 cups water. Cook until beets have softened.
2. Drain 6 cups juice from beets.
3. In large saucepan bring beet juice, lemon juice and pectin to a hard boil. Add sugar and gelatin and mix well. Bring to a boil again and boil for 6 minutes. Skim.
4. Pour into sterilized jelly glasses and seal.

Peach Jelly

Anna Oberholtzer
Lititz, PA
Dahlia

Makes 4-6 pints jelly

2 cups crushed pineapple
4 cups diced peaches
8 cups white sugar
6-oz. pkg. orange gelatin

1. In a saucepan combine pineapple, peaches and sugar and bring to a hard boil. Boil for 20 minutes.
2. Remove from heat and add gelatin. Stir well and pour into jars and freeze. (Allow room in each jar for expansion.)

State Fair Blueberry Jam

Joyce Swinney
Mooresville, IN
Double Wedding Ring

Makes 5 12-oz. jars jam

4½ cups fresh blueberries
⅓ cup fresh lime juice
½ cup water
1 Tbsp. grated lime rind
1 pkg. powdered pectin
4 cups sugar

1. In 8-quart pan combine all ingredients except sugar and mix well. Bring to full boil over high heat, stirring constantly.
2. Quickly add sugar. Stir constantly and bring to full rolling boil again. Boil hard for 1 minute, stirring constantly.
3. Remove from heat and skim quickly if needed.
4. Quickly ladle into sterilized jars and seal.

Luscious Lemon Curd

Cleda Cox
Estes Park, CO
The Eagle Quilt

Makes 1 pint curd

Grated rind of 1 large
   lemon
⅔ cup sugar
7-8 large egg yolks
½ cup fresh squeezed
   lemon juice
⅛ tsp. salt
8 Tbsp. butter, melted

1. In a saucepan combine lemon rind, sugar, egg yolks, lemon juice and salt. Stir in the hot melted butter, a little at a time.
2. Cook over low heat, stirring constantly with wide, flat utensil such as a gravy stirrer or a flat spatula until thickened and clear. Let cool, stirring occasionally.

3. Store in covered pint jar. Keeps well.
4. Serve on toast, biscuits, muffins or angel food cake.

Note: This burns very easily and must be carefully watched.

Mincemeat

Shan D. Lear
Middleton, MA
Nine Patch and Hearts

Makes about 18 pints meat

9 lbs. apples
1 orange
1 lemon
2 lbs. raisins
1 lb. suet
3 lbs. ground beef
3 lbs. brown sugar
½ cup molasses
⅓ cup salt
2 lbs. seedless raisins
¼ lb. citron
1 Tbsp. cinnamon
1 Tbsp. nutmeg
1 Tbsp. ground cloves
1 Tbsp. allspice
1 jar currant jelly

1. Grind whole apples, orange, lemon, raisins and suet in food processor or grinder.
2. Combine all ingredients in large kettle and bring to a boil. Simmer for 3-4 hours. Pour into sterilized jars and seal.

Strawberries to Freeze

Minnie A. Stoltzfus
Lancaster, PA
Log Cabin

Makes 10-12 pints jam

5 quarts strawberries
1 pkg. clear gel
1 cup light corn syrup
½ cup white sugar
(optional)

1. Slice or slightly crush strawberries. Add clear gel and let stand 15-20 minutes.
2. Add syrup and sugar and mix well.
3. Spoon into pint-sized containers and freeze.

Orange Ice

Carol Price
Los Lunas, NM
Double Wedding Ring

Makes many medicinal servings

1 cup sugar
2 cups water
1 tsp. unflavored gelatin
2 cups orange juice
4 tsp. lemon juice

1. In a saucepan bring sugar and water to a boil and boil for 5 minutes. Remove from heat, add gelatin and stir to dissolve.
2. Combine orange juice and lemon juice and stir into sugar mixture.
3. Freeze. Remove from freezer and beat thoroughly. Freeze again.

Note: This may be used as a sherbet or sorbet, but my family needs it as a medicine. It tastes so good when one has a sore throat, upset stomach, cold or flu.

Sweetened Condensed Milk

Thelma A. Lowther
St. Marys, WV
Tumbling Block & Ohio Star

Makes 1 cup milk

1 cup instant nonfat dry milk solids
⅔ cup sugar
⅓ cup boiling water
3 Tbsp. butter *or* margarine, melted

1. Combine all ingredients in blender. Process until smooth.
2. Store in refrigerator and use as needed.

Yummy Sundae Topping

Betty Krueger
Rogue River, OR
Crazy Patch

Makes 2½ cups topping

½ cup sliced, pitted dates
½ cup dark corn syrup
¼ cup brown sugar
¼ cup water
⅛ tsp. salt
½ tsp. vanilla
½ cup chopped pecans

1. Combine dates, syrup, sugar, water and salt in a saucepan. Bring to a boil and cook 2 minutes over medium heat, stirring constantly. Add vanilla and pecans.
2. Cool and serve over vanilla ice cream or frozen yogurt.

Hot Fudge Sauce

Emilie Kimpel
Arcadia, MI
Bunny Patch

Makes 1 cup sauce

¾ **cup sugar**
¼ **cup butter** *or* **margarine**
1½ **squares unsweetened**
   chocolate
2 **Tbsp. light corn syrup**
Dash salt
¼ **cup milk**
2 **tsp. vanilla**

1. In small saucepan combine sugar, butter, chocolate squares, corn syrup and salt. Mix well.

2. Cook over moderate heat, stirring constantly until sugar dissolves and chocolate melts. Add milk and bring to a boil, stirring constantly. Remove from heat immediately.

3. Stir in vanilla and serve warm over cake or ice cream.

Variation:

Melt 1 Tbsp. butter and 1 square unsweetened chocolate on low heat in a heavy saucepan. Add ⅓ cup boiling water, 1 cup sugar and 2 Tbsp. light corn syrup. Simmer for 5 minutes, stirring constantly. When thickened to syrup consistency, add 1 tsp. vanilla and dash salt. Serve with ice cream.

Sandra Church
New York, NY
Log Cabin

Index

About the Author

Louise Stoltzfus learned the arts of quilting and cooking from her mother, Miriam Stoltzfus. While she puts occasional stitches in one or another of the many quilts her mother always seems to have in frame, Stoltzfus regrettably seldom finds time for quilting.

With Phyllis Pellman Good she has co-authored two other cookbooks, *The Central Market Cookbook* and *The Best of Mennonite Fellowship Meals*.

Stoltzfus is an editor for Good Books and also serves as director of The People's Place Gallery in Intercourse, Pennsylvania. She lives in a restored rowhouse in Lancaster, Pennsylvania.